Lost Ha

McGill-Queen's Native and
Northern Series
Bruce G. Trigger, Editor

1 When the Whalers Were Up North
  Inuit Memories from the Eastern Arctic
  Dorothy Harley Eber

2 The Challenge of Arctic Shipping
  Science, Environmental Assessment, and
  Human Values
  *David L. VanderZwaag and Cynthia Lamson,
  Editors*

3 Lost Harvests
  Prairie Indian Reserve Farmers and
  Government Policy
  Sarah Carter

4 Native Liberty, Crown Sovereignty
  The Existing Aboriginal Right of Self-
  Government in Canada
  Bruce Clark

5 Unravelling the Franklin Mystery
  Inuit Testimony
  David C. Woodman

6 Otter Skins, Boston Ships, and China
  Goods
  The Maritime Fur Trade of the Northwest
  Coast, 1785–1841
  James R. Gibson

7 From Wooden Ploughs to Welfare
  The Story of the Western Reserves
  Helen Buckley

8 In Business for Ourselves
  Northern Entrepreneurs
  Wanda A. Wuttunee

9 For an Amerindian Autohistory
  An Essay on the Foundations of a Social
  Ethic
  Georges E. Sioui

Lost Harvests

Prairie Indian Reserve Farmers and Government Policy

SARAH CARTER

McGill-Queen's University Press
Montreal & Kingston • London • Buffalo

© McGill-Queen's University Press 1990
ISBN 0-7735-0755-8 (cloth)
ISBN 0-7735-0999-2 (paper)

Legal deposit fourth quarter 1990
Bibliothèque nationale du Québec

First paperback edition 1993

Printed in Canada on acid-free paper

This book has been published with the help of a grant from the Canadian Federation for the Humanities, using funds provided by the Social Sciences and Humanities Research Council of Canada.

Canadian Cataloguing in Publication Data

Carter, Sarah, 1954–
   Lost harvests
   (McGill-Queen's series in northern and native studies; 3)
   Includes bibliographical references.
   ISBN 0-7735-0755-8 (bound)
   ISBN 0-7735-0999-2 (pbk.)

   1. Indians of North America – Prairie Provinces – Agriculture – History. 2. Indians of North America – Prairie Provinces – Reservations – History. 3. Indians of North America – Canada – Government relations – 1860–1951. I. Title. II. Series.

E92.C35 1990   338.1'8712'08997   C90-090179-9

This book was typeset in 10/12 Palatino by Typo Litho composition inc.

For Walter and Mary

Contents

Illustrations   between pages 114 and 115

Figures   viii

Preface   ix

Introduction   3

1 Two Solitudes: Myth and Reality of the Plains Indian and Agriculture   15

2 The "Queen's Bounty": Government Response to Indian Agitation for Agricultural Assistance   50

3 The Home Farm Experiment   79

4 Assault upon the "Tribal" System: Government Policy after 1885   130

5 The Pioneer Experience: Prairie Reserve Agriculture   159

6 Prelude to Surrender: Severalty and "Peasant" Farming   193

7 Without a Leg to Stand On: Undermining Reserve Agriculture   237

Appendices   259

Notes   265

Bibliography   299

Index   317

Figures

1 Districts of Saskatchewan and Assiniboia, ca 1900   xi
2 Subdivision of the Piapot reserve   206
3 Acres under cultivation, selected Indian agencies, 1889–97   234
4 Acres under cultivation, selected Indian agencies, 1889–97   235

Preface

The standard explanation for the failure of agriculture on western Canadian reserves is that the Indians could not be convinced of the value or necessity of the enterprise. It was believed that the sustained labour required of them was alien to their culture and that the transformation of hunters into farmers was a process that historically took place over centuries. When I began to investigate the question of why agriculture failed to provide reserve residents a living, I thought I would add detail to this explanation but essentially retain it intact. Before I got very far into the sources, however, I found that little evidence existed to support this interpretation.

It was the Indians, not the government, that showed an early and sustained interest in establishing agriculture on the reserves. Although the government publicly proclaimed that its aim was to assist Indians to adopt agriculture, little was done to put this course into effect. In fact government policies acted to retard agriculture on the reserves. The Indians had to persuade government officials of the necessity and importance of agriculture. In treaty negotiations and later assemblies, they sought assurance that a living by agriculture would be provided to them, and they used every means at their disposal to persuade a reluctant government that they be allowed the means to farm. They proved anxious to farm and be independent of government assistance, despite discouraging results year after year. Not all Indians wished to farm but many did, and circumstances compelled some to consider this option at a time when there were few others. In the decade after 1885, government policies made it virtually impossible for reserve agriculture to succeed because the farmers were prevented from using the technology required for agricultural activity in the West. The promotion of reserve land surrender after the turn of the century further precluded the hope that agriculture could form the basis of a stable economy on reserves.

I would like to thank Jean Friesen under whose direction this study began. I also very much appreciated the advice of John Kendle and my advisers in the field of contact culture, Tim Anna and George Schultz. Special thanks are due to Arthur Ray for his comments and encouragement. Others who were kind enough to read all or sections of the manuscript and give their suggestions and criticisms include J.R. Miller, A. Blair Stonechild, and Bruce Trigger. The study benefited greatly from the careful editing of Audrey Hlady. Many librarians and archivists have been of tremendous assistance, but I would like to thank in particular the staff at the Manitoba Legislative Library, who tolerated a chaotic carrel for years. The staff of the Treaty and Aboriginal Rights Research Centre in Winnipeg have always been generous and kind. Louise Valentin typed the manuscript with great care and diligence and remained enthusiastic about the study through all the changes. David Elrick skilfully drew the maps. I was fortunate to receive a Social Sciences and Humanities Research Council of Canada Post Doctoral Fellowship that allowed me the time to develop this book. I would like to thank my parents, Roger and Mary Carter, for their support and longtime interest in prairie history. Above all, I am grateful to my husband, Walter Hildebrandt, for his sustained enthusiasm, encouragement, and valuable criticism.

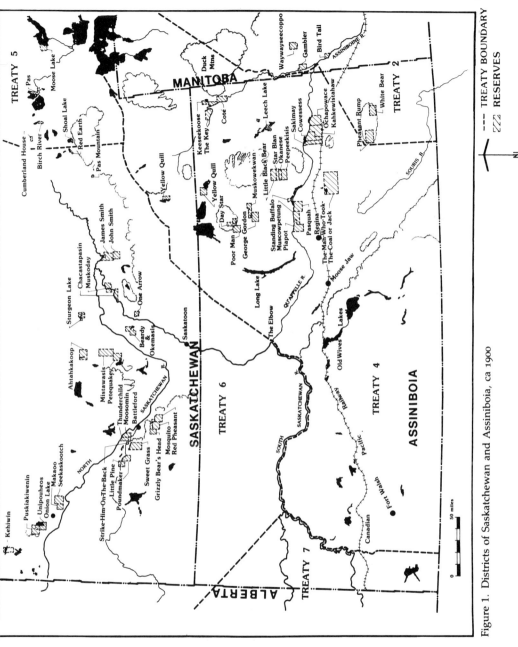

Figure 1. Districts of Saskatchewan and Assiniboia, ca 1900

Lost Harvests

Introduction

The Indian farmer has been accorded an insignificant role in Canadian prairie history. Although the Plains Indians were among the earliest and largest of groups to attempt farming west of the Red River Settlement, immigrants from Europe and the older provinces of Canada are routinely credited with the pioneering efforts to farm the prairies. Not only were the Indians excluded from histories of the sodbusters, but they were not even recognized as having the capability to farm. As one commentator wrote in 1924: "The Indian was not a natural farmer. He was a born hunter and warrior. Century upon century had ingrained in him the nomadic instinct; steady labor, so many hours a day, week in and week out, was as foreign to his nature as a dog kennel to a fox."[1]

That Plains Indian men, who were skilled hunters and warriors, held farming in disdain and dismissed it as woman's work is a firmly established axiom, often uncritically repeated. There is no evidence, at least among the Indians of southern Saskatchewan, that farming as an occupation was held in contempt. Indian representatives at treaty negotiations of the 1870s and subsequent councils did not express that attitude; indeed, they were concerned that they be allowed the means to farm, insisting that they were willing, and they later proved themselves able to farm. It has been Euro-Canadian observers, not the Indians themselves, who have claimed that Indians and agriculture are incompatible. Like privileged groups in other systems of dominance, Euro-Canadians have concluded that there are fundamental and profound differences between native and white that are irreconcilable and unalterable.[2] It is believed that Indians failed to adapt to agriculture because they lacked initiative and diligence, and reverted to "primitive" behaviour patterns ruled by superstition.

Although written over fifty years ago, G.F.G. Stanley's interpretation of why farming failed to provide a living for reserve residents remains the one most widely accepted. In *The Birth of Western Canada* (1936), Stanley argued that the Indians' fundamental problem was that by "character and upbringing [they] were unfitted to compete with the whites in the competitive individualism of white civilization, or to share with them the duties and responsibilities of citizenship."³ Indians were unable to adapt; they wished to preserve "traditional" values, which were incompatible with economic development. They were a people concerned only with immediate necessities; it was not in their nature to accumulate property and to look to the future. The Indians were content to live off relatives and then the government. They socialized, travelled, and shared too much. The cultural traditions the Indians cherished and refused to relinquish made them notoriously poor farmers, stockmen, and businessmen.

Stanley's approach reflected ideas about Indians that prevailed in his generation and beyond. The Plains Indians were depicted as a simple and primitive people whose fundamental nature was a "wild love of freedom and intolerance of restraint." During their "golden age" of freedom, they lived in "savage opulence," hunting the plentiful herds and warring among themselves.⁴ The years brought no change to their static existence until the arrival of the white man. Stanley's view was that because theirs was a fragile, weak, primitive culture, the Indians inevitably declined under the impact of a more complex civilization. The destruction of their self-reliance and independence began with the introduction of the white man's manufactures, to the extent that "one time luxuries became necessities, and the hapless Indian, forgetting the weapons and usages of his fathers, henceforth became dependent upon the white man for his homely needs, and even for life itself." With the rapid changes marked by the coming of the railroad, the influx of settlers, and the extinction of the buffalo, the Indians, "centuries behind in mental and economic development," could not readily adapt to meet the new conditions of life, which were strange and unfamiliar. In Stanley's words, "his savage self-reliance gave way to a childlike dependence, and he [was] overwhelmed with a feeling of helplessness."⁵

The administration of Indian affairs in Canada was, according to Stanley, marked by "strict honesty, justice and good faith."⁶ The government undertook to protect, care for, and guide the Indians during the difficult period of transition from "savagery to civilization." It pursued a deliberate course of placing Indians upon reserves, developing an interest in labour among them, and attaching them to agriculture in order to teach them the white man's means of support. As well, instruction in agriculture would prepare them for a "higher civilization" and encourage them "to assume the privileges and responsibilities of full citizenship."[7]

The Indians, Stanley believed, had no desire to settle down. "They were loath to abandon the thrilling life of the chase for the tedious existence of agriculture."[8] When the buffalo suddenly disappeared from the plains, the effect was disastrous, but only then did the Indians realize the necessity for some radical modification of their way of life. The lure of rations pried them loose from adherence to their nomadic culture, although some clung desperately to the past. Despite destitution, they congregated about Fort Walsh in the Cypress Hills of southwest Saskatchewan because they wished to be where their friends were and where their dead were buried. Considerations of international policy, and social and economic reasons, demanded that these Indians be removed; if they were to be profitably employed and instructed in agriculture, reserves would have to be found elsewhere. The Indians were "reluctant," "dilatory," "full of complaints," "excuses," and "impossible demands." But government officials and the North-West Mounted Police (NWMP) eventually succeeded in persuading them that their only hope for survival lay with agriculture on their reserves.

The government's agricultural policy, however, was not an unqualified success. The program was open to some criticism, but Stanley found that it was essentially the character of the Indians that militated against a rapid advance in agriculture; for "the character moulded by centuries could not be transformed in a few years." Indians had a restless disposition. Their aversion to uncongenial labour was proverbial. Unable to resist the temptation, wild Indians were prone to raid their own garden plots. The optimistic, sanguine expectations of officials were "not based upon an understanding of Indian character, or a thorough appreciation of the distance which the primitive Indian had to travel to reach the white man's scale of proficiency."[9] It was the Indians' characteristic mental attitude, not government policy or economic and environmental factors, that kept them in poverty.

Reserve agriculture has not been the subject of a thorough study, but when historians have touched on the issue, most have agreed with Stanley's interpretation.[10] In a recent study (1987) of the Blackfoot Confederacy from 1880 to 1920, the factors of geography, climate, a poorly executed policy, a lack of competent instructors, and a shortage of implements are all cited as reasons agriculture met with little success. But the author, H. Samek, also stresses "powerful cultural obstacles," the "cultural chasm," and the "persistence of basic irreconcilable differences between aboriginal and Western cultural values."[11] Warriors and hunters had no agricultural tradition, and teaching "plains tribes farming would involve the transformation of their entire worldview." Although officials devoted much energy and expense to the goal of turning Indians into farmers, they failed "to convince many native people to accept the cultural values necessary to support such a system."[12] These powerful cultural obstacles are not detailed except that the Indians' "most basic objection was against turning Mother Earth 'wrong side up.'"[13]

It is commonly suggested that agriculture violated concepts sacred to the religion of the Indians, which they were unable or unwilling to abandon.[14] Because they had a deep-seated respect for nature, they treated the earth well, leaving no great scars. Thus they could not bring themselves to lacerate Mother Earth's breast with the plough.[15] Evidence for this belief is attributed to Smoholla of the Nez Percé, who founded the dreamer religion and preached the rejection of white man's civilization in the late nineteenth century. "My young men shall never work. Men who work cannot dream; and wisdom comes to us in dreams. You ask me to plow the ground. Shall I take a knife and tear my mother's breast? Then when I die she will not take me to her bosom to rest. You ask me to dig for stone. Shall I dig under her skin for her bones? Then when I die I cannot enter her body to be born again. You ask me to cut grass and make hay and sell it and be rich like white men. But how dare I cut off my mother's hair?"[16]

Smoholla's statement has been widely used to explain the failure of Indian farming all over North America.[17] As concluded in a recent study of agriculture in the Oregon country, farming was "antithetical to the traditional native lifestyle" and was "also at odds with the Indians' spiritual doctrine, for they believed in the inviolable oneness of humanity and nature and in the supreme chieftaincy of the earth, their mother. Some Euro-american pursuits, including cultivation, violated this belief."[18] Again, Smoholla's words are used to support this claim.

Those who adhere to the view that Indians rejected farming because of their spiritual relationship with nature explain the success of precontact native agriculture in North America by stressing that the digging stick or hoe carefully caressed rather than violently tore at Mother Earth.[19] Many believe that non-natives, who did tear at the earth with the plough, a practice that appalled the Indians, might have learned from the Indians' sense of the sacredness of nature.

"Decades of soil erosion, brown rivers, and dust bowls that followed the plow seem to show that the Indians had good reason for feeling the way they did."[20]

Students from disciplines other than history have considered the issue of reserve agriculture. In *Tribe under Trust: A Study of the Blackfoot Reserve in Alberta* (1950), anthropologists L.M. Hanks and J.R. Hanks argued that the initial reaction of the Blackfoot to farming was that such activity was beneath their dignity. The efforts of instructors therefore met with stubborn resistance. "In fact, to grovel in the dirt when one was accustomed to riding over it on a fast buffalo horse seemed demeaning. Though the instructors tried to enlist the young men by threats and promises, many were set against it. This was the white man's way of doing things, and they were Indians. The whites had already done enough to disrupt the Indian way of life without insisting that all work like whites."[21]

The Hanks believed that most of the Blackfoot condemned agriculture because they did not want to forsake Indian ways and patterns. Only those unsuccessful from a Blackfoot perspective, those undistinguished in warfare or lacking in property, those with little to gain from following Indian patterns, adopted agriculture.[22] Many of the chiefs changed their minds about farming, however, when they saw there could be benefits in the way of immediate, tangible rewards for their efforts, such as axes, blankets, and beads.

According to the Hanks, the Blackfoot embraced agriculture only to the extent that it was consistent with or enhanced their own traditions and customs. They did not, for example, adopt the idea of working steadily to improve the standard of living in the future, nor did they wish to acquire the possessions with which a white man would equate success. The Blackfoot had a different concept of wealth; once they had acquired shelter and enough food and clothing to allow for a comfortable existence, there was no need for further exertion for their own behalf. Farming was incorporated as a means of becoming wealthy according to Blackfoot custom and tradition, that is, to be able to afford ostentatious give-aways and to display generosity on visits to neighbouring reserves. The goal of the Blackfoot farmer was to acquire a sacred bundle, a "supernatural assurance against vagaries of weather and fortune," which was a token of concrete achievement in Blackfoot society and had always been the Blackfoot way of indicating a change in status. What the Blackfoot wanted above all was to be allowed to "gather and sing their songs, to eventually join their deceased friends in the Sand Hills and live apart from white society." "All the grandeur for the Blackfoot," the Hanks wrote, "lay in the past."[23]

Academics from a variety of disciplines have also examined reserve agriculture and its lack of success. The authors of the 1966 report *A Survey of the Contemporary Indians of Canada*, edited by H.B. Hawthorn, studied the issue with regard to reserves such as Piapot and James Smith in Saskatchewan, and Oak River and Peguis in Manitoba. Although they were situated in the midst of fine farmland, they were among the most depressed and dependent of all Indian reserves. There was not enough land to support all band members, but even what land they had was not used at peak efficiency, and the farms were marginal or submarginal. On many reserves, farming had been abandoned entirely. The authors believed that while the Department of Indian Affairs had devoted much time and effort to the encouragement of farming, pouring in large amounts of capital and technical aid over many years, it could not be blamed for the failure of farming. That, the authors stated, probably lay in "attitudes of apathy or disinterest among Indians to farming as a way of life." Indian disinterest in farming combined with their small-scale, inefficient methods. Without the motivation, skill, and experience of the white farmers, they perpetuated unprogressive, obsolete methods of agriculture. "Encouragement of Indians to farm," it was concluded, "seems a particularly inappropriate policy in all but a few cases."[24]

The authors believed that the Indians were attuned to a set of values, ideas, and attitudes that precluded them from farming. As a "nonindustrial" people, "modern" concepts of economic status and prestige were meaningless to them.[25] Indians did not act as "economic men" as understood by non-native society, but functioned according to their own rules. They had no natural impulse to acquisitiveness and were content with a standard of living at a near-subsistence level. They had no concept of working harder or longer to accumulate money and goods. Close ties to family or kinship groups discouraged the acquisition of capital and stifled success at business, because a man's relatives claimed a share of any good fortune. Even rhythms of work were different in nonindustrial cultures. Indians were accustomed to working at an irregular pace; at certain times of the year activity was strenuous, but whole seasons were devoted to relaxation.

The findings of the Hawthorn report reflect the dualism theory devised in the 1950s and 1960s by social scientists to explain the origins and coexistence of development and underdevelopment in Africa and Latin America.[26] Dualism theory recognizes two distinct and largely independent sectors of the economy. The modern, industrial, or capitalist sector is "characterized by high productivity, is market-oriented, receptive to change, and pursues rational and maximizing aims." The other "traditional" sector is regarded as precapitalist, subsistence based, primitive, and small scale. This sector is stagnant, without innovation or change, and is affected by incentives totally different from those the capitalist economy responds to, such as price changes and wage raises. The primitive sector "displays little market awareness, shows a high preference for leisure, and tradition or custom dominates over rationality."[27] Instead of saving or making productive investments, those in the traditional sector fritter away savings and acquire prestige items.

Dualism theory is applied to studies of the labour market, as well as to agricultural economies. In explaining how Afro-Brazilians were marginalized in the labour market from the 1880s to the 1920s, sociologist Florestan Fernandes argued in 1965 that because of their slave heritage, blacks acquired a set of racial characteristics such as ignorance and apathy. They had few skills and rejected the modern, dynamic, capitalist sector, preferring undisciplined, irregular work. Fernandes claimed that Afro-Brazilians were precapitalist, even anticapitalist. This use of dualism theory has come under considerable criticism in recent years. The dominance of European workers in Brazil has been attributed not to the supposed racial characteristics of blacks, but to a state policy that flooded the labour market with immigrants, kept wages low, and weakened the labour movement.[28]

Applying dualism theory to the agricultural economy of Africa, researchers argued that the root cause of rural poverty was the failure of the traditional sector to adapt their tribal economy to novel conditions and to learn modern methods of farming.[29] Africans, it was stressed, were hostile to innovation and market relations, as they were inhibited by their traditional attitudes toward land, property, and family ties and adhered to supernatural beliefs. They were improvident and carefree, did not rationally dispose of their resources, and perpetuated unscientific agricultural methods. Despite the best efforts of missionaries, agricultural instructors, and administrators, the Africans resisted economic rationality. The problem lay with the nature of African society; because Africans could not adapt their traditional economy, they thus forfeited participation in the market economy.

These ideas proved attractive to segregationists in Africa.[30] They argued that ordinary economic incentives clearly did not apply to a "primitive" people. Raising wages could be dangerous among a people who did not respond to cash incentives and had a high preference for leisure, as labour could be withheld or production could decline. The theory supported the view that the primitive sector did not want integration, but wished to live apart to pursue a traditional way of life. It also upheld the view that Africans were content with a near-subsistence standard of living. The majority of legislators in the assembly of Southern Rhodesia in 1960, for example, believed that Africans would produce no more than what they required for subsistence because they had a high leisure preference, low income goals, and were innately lazy.[31] The attitudes and mental responses of Africans explained the disparities between the European and indigenous sectors of the economy, and the policies adopted by the assembly perpetuated these differences. A minority of legislators dissented, arguing that indigenous and European producers had the same aspirations and that Africans must be provided with the means to increase their production.

The dualism theory approach to African history has recently been criticized by historians of agriculture in Central and Southern Africa.[32] In *The Rise and Fall of the South African Peasantry* (1979), Colin Bundy argued that the prevailing explanation for the "failure" of African agriculture has overlooked or underestimated an initial period of early prosperity when many African farmers responded positively and successfully to economic changes and market conditions. A large proportion of Africans reacted rationally to the expanding market economy with its new pressures and opportunities. Some participated in the market economy to a limited extent, while others made considerable adjustments, and for them producing a cash crop for market became a principal concern. Bundy found that during this initial period of positive response, Africans enthusiastically embraced advanced methods of crop rotation and technological innovations. This stage, however, was short-lived. By the 1880s symptoms of rural decay and underdevelopment were evident.

Bundy argued that a variety of interventions and interests operated to curtail and distort the direction of economic change that had little to do with the supposed backwardness of the traditional sector. Groups who sought to inhibit or deflect peasant production translated their interests into political action. Laws were designed to check African farming and protect white farmers from "unfair" competition. By curtailing African farming, the flow of labour to white farms was stimulated. Communal systems were replaced by individual tenure, which set tight limits on agricultural productivity. African agriculture was not aided by the same massive program of subsidies, grants, rail facilities, and credit programs that were available to the white sector. The Africans' access to markets deteriorated. These factors reinforced and perpetuated disabilities owing to geography and natural setbacks of drought, flood, and fire. As a result, African agriculture retrogressed. Advanced methods of cultivation became impractical or redundant. Anthropologists and other twentieth-century observers of Africans on their reserves found the residents to be living what appeared to be thoroughly traditional lives, stubbornly persisting in conservative, obsolete methods of agriculture and totally unaffected by the modern, progressive sector. The cause of African rural poverty, they concluded, was the persistence of African "backwardness." Evidence of an earlier period of an initial positive response was not apparent to the eye but lay hidden in government, missionary, and other records.

In a recent study of American Indian farming, a similar pattern was detected. In *Indians, Bureaucrats and Land: The Dawes Act and the Decline of Indian Farming* (1981), Leonard A. Carlson found that before general allotment of Indian reservations was enacted in 1887, many residents proved willing and able to farm. Although not all Indians were farmers, participation in farming was widespread. But this initial stage was followed by stagnation and regression. Indian farming declined markedly after the 1887 Dawes Severalty Act. A stipulated acreage was individually allotted to each head of family, and the remaining reservation land was thrown open to non-Indian settlement. Much of the land allotted to the Indians also eventually ended up in the hands of non-Indians. This act, Carlson argued, was shaped by non-Indian economic interests. Indian farmers then fell further and further behind white farmers.

Very little has been written on agriculture as practised by Canadian Indians in the reserve period, but one study of reserve farming in Ontario, "Parry Island Farmers: A Period of Change in the Way of Life of the Algonkians of Southern Ontario" (1975), by E.S. Rogers and Flora Tobobondung suggests that the pattern of an early positive response, only then followed by a decline in farming, prevailed in Ontario as well. The Algonkians of southern Ontario rapidly adopted farming between 1820 and 1840, growing wheat, oats, peas, potatoes, Indian corn, and other vegetables. They often sold grain to Euro-Canadians. Somewhat later Indians to the north adopted farming. By 1875, and for several decades after, the Parry Island native farmers differed little from their Euro-Canadian farming neighbours, but in the early years of the twentieth century Indian farming began to decline markedly. A recent article on Ojibway agriculture in northwestern Ontario also attests to the rise and decline pattern of native farming. Tim E. Holzkamm and Leo G. Waisberg (1989) found that by the time of the signing of Treaty Three (1873) agriculture had become an important component of the Ojibway economy. This activity, however, had virtually ceased by the early twentieth century, owing to the construction of hydroelectric projects and to regressive policies of the Department of Indian Affairs.[33]

The prevailing view that the Indians of western Canada failed to adapt to agriculture because of their cultural traditions is in need of revision, and through several studies this process has begun. John Tobias argued in "Indian Reserves in Western Canada: Indian Homelands or Devices for Assimilation" (1977) that the Plains Cree were anxious to acquire the skills and tools that would allow them to farm but that eventually they gave up agriculture because of restrictive government regulations including the permit system, the subdivision of reserves, and the ban on the use of machinery. In "Canada's Subjugation of the Plains Cree, 1879–1885" (1983), Tobias similarly argued that the Cree did not reject an agricultural way of life and that much of the political activity of their leaders was based on concern about the lack of assistance to farm.

In "Agriculture and Agitation on the Oak River Dakota Reserve, 1875–1895" (1983), I found that there was an initial period of enthusiasm for agriculture at Oak River in southwestern Manitoba, which was accompanied by some success. However, a period of stagnation and decline followed. The reasons for the decline were not that the Indians' culture limited their capacity for farming, but that along with environmental setbacks, Indian farmers were subject to regulations that denied them the technological and financial opportunities to form a strong agricultural base.

In "An Opportunity Lost: The Initiative of the Reserve Agricultural Programme in the Prairie West" (1986), Noel Dyck also questioned the notion that the Plains Indians were incapable of adapting to the demands of a settled, agricultural way of life.[34] Dyck concluded that that because of a lack of commitment on the part of government officials, the opportunity to create self-supporting communities through the reserve agricultural program was lost. Dyck believes the events of 1885 sealed the fate of the agricultural program because of the coercive system of administration that was subsequently imposed.

These articles share similar approaches to and conclusions about reserve agriculture, but they do not deal with the issue in a comprehensive manner. This study suggests that many reserve residents initially responded positively to farming. Not all Indians wished to farm, but farming was not limited to just a few individuals. Nor did the Indians meet government efforts with suspicion, apathy, and resistance. The Indians in the period under study in this book consistently displayed greater resolution and determination to see farming succeed than did government administrators, quite in contrast with the well-established view that the government made constant, sincere, unflagging efforts to cajole and pressure the Indians into taking up an unfamiliar and unpopular way of life. In spite of their initial positive response, nothing like prosperity was ever achieved, and Indian farmers did not enter the grain-centred cash economy of their white neighbours that began to take hold after 1896. Factors having little to do with cultural distinctions combined to atrophy agricultural development on reserves. Those who stress that the fundamental problem was that Indians were culturally or temperamentally resistant to becoming farmers have ignored or downplayed economic, legal, social, and climatic factors. Reserve agriculturalists were subject to the same adversities and misfortunes as their white neighbours were, but they were also subject to government policies that tended to aggravate rather than ameliorate a situation that was dismal for all farmers.

Although the study of western Canadian and native history has flourished in the past decade, the notion that reserve residents rejected agriculture persists. Despite a now-widespread recognition that Plains Indians adjusted rapidly and coped creatively with altered circumstances in the period before European contact as well as during the fur trade, such adaptability seems to grind to a halt when historians describe the reserve era. To declare that Indians were not passive victims but active resisters of agricultural programs is to present in a slightly new form the old argument that Indian farming failed through their own disinterest and lack of ability. This interpretation still rests on the assumption that Indians and agriculture are incompatible and is a return to the belief that native cultures are static, dormant, and incapable of change. It does not alter the traditional paradigm of a government intent on imposing agriculture on a reluctant group of people. This study, however, presents evidence that the reluctance was on the part of the government. The age-old admiration for the "noble savage," for native people who remained aloof from western cultural influences, is also evident in an approach that stresses Indian resistance, whereas greater antipathy had traditionally been exhibited toward those who adapted rapidly to new requirements and opportunities.[35]

This study seeks not only to describe and analyse government policy but also to look at Indian strategies for coping with new conditions. There are no subordinate passive victims here. To begin with, Indians demanded that they be provided with the means to farm in return for their offer of an opportunity for peaceful expansion.[36] Early on there set in a tradition of protest against policies that denied them what was viewed as a promise made in the treaties – that they be able to develop agriculture on the reserves. That these early efforts at farming floundered cannot be reduced to simplistic assumptions about rejection of agriculture as a program designed to achieve assimilation. Describing the Indians of Upper Canada during the early decades of reserve life, historian John Milloy wrote that tribal councils were in favour of agriculture, resource development, and education but objected to new programs of the 1860s that aimed at assimilation and destruction of traditional culture. "Revitalization of their traditional culture within an agricultural context, they would have," Milloy wrote. "Assimilation, the total abandonment of their culture, they would not."[37] The same might be said of the Plains Indians during the early reserve period. While men welcomed the technology and training that allowed them to farm when hunting was no longer possible, they resisted those policies that, for example, prevented them from holding their religious ceremonies. Similarly women welcomed new skills such as making bread and butter to augment their store of traditional knowledge. When farming failed, however, and reserves developed into pockets of rural poverty in the West, it was all too easy for government to lay the blame on the shoulders of the Indians themselves for resisting change. It is unfortunate that this image persists in histories of western Canada.

CHAPTER ONE

Two Solitudes: Myth and Reality of the Plains Indian and Agriculture

In an address on the aims of the government in its dealings with the Indians, Hayter Reed, deputy superintendent general of Indian affairs from 1893 to 1897, stated that the permanent solution to the Indian problem involved "the laborious and often dangerous work of transforming bands of savages into peaceable agricultural labourers." Quoting from the book *Bible Teachings in Nature*, Reed emphasized the benefits of an agricultural life.

Corn precedes all civilization; with it is connected rest, peace and domestic happiness, of which the wandering savage knows nothing. In order to rear it nations must take possession of certain lands; and when their existence is thus firmly established, improvements in manner and customs speedily follow. They are no longer inclined for bloody wars, but fight only to defend the fields from which they derive their support. The cultivation of corn, while it furnishes man with a supply of food for the greater part of the year, imposes upon him certain labours and restraints, which have a most beneficial influence upon his character and habits.[1]

Reed's belief that agriculture was the great panacea for what were perceived to be the ills of Canada's Indians was a conviction shared by most Canadians who pondered the future of the Indians. That the Indians were not farmers was viewed as an essential weakness of their society. Canadians in the Victorian era believed Indian life was full of imperfection, but at the foundation of their objection was the certainty that a life of virtue was dependent upon an agrarian base and that vice resulted from a hunting, migratory base.

PERCEPTIONS OF INDIAN LIFE

The general perception of Indian culture reflected long-established, deeply embedded Western attitudes toward the wilderness and those who lived there, attitudes that were codified in the Scriptures.[2] Concepts of order and progress were framed by biblical injunction. "Be fruitful and multiply, and replenish the earth and subdue it: and have dominion over the fish of the sea; and over the fowl of the air, and over every living thing that moveth upon the earth."[3] Man's purpose on earth was to reclaim and resurrect the wilderness, to "break" the land, "bust" the sod, and impose on it a human will and purpose. Victorians, enormously proud of their railways, steamships, and factories, were confident that during their lifetime man was reaching the pinnacle of the vast crusade to subdue nature.[4] Reason and civilization were replacing the superstition and barbarism of the nomadic, predatory, precarious life of the past.

A source of anguish to late nineteenth-century observers of western Canada's native population was the Indians' apparent ignorance of man's obligation to subdue the earth. The Indians displayed no visible evidence of any degree of mastery over the environment; they appeared to be, not in control of, but at the mercy of natural forces. The most glaring evidence of the Indians' inability to master their environment was that they left no marks of their presence on the land. Living by hunting, fishing, and gathering, they were perceived as doing nothing to work and improve the land. The Indians of the plains were viewed as "thoughtlessly, carelessly living on the surface. Like the butterfly flitting from plant to plant, so these men roamed and camped and dreamed, not of mines and means which were above and beneath them on every hand."[5]

The buffalo hunting of the Plains Indians was perceived as an unhealthy enslavement to natural forces. Because their mobility, social cycle, and material comfort were dependent on the buffalo's pattern of concentration and dispersal, the Plains Indians were viewed as "the most dependent among men," as "without buffalo they would be helpless, yet the whole nation did not own one."[6] The buffalo and "tribal communism" prevented the ideas of private property and individualism from taking hold, two concepts regarded as essential to civilization.[7] "Owning the land in common, there was in it no wealth to any one of them" wrote one authority on Indian life.[8] Such a system, it was thought, restricted individual activity and ambition. As well, the Indians' propensity to share their possessions was an obstacle to self-reliance. Without private property, without any particular place to call home save for a "miserable wigwam," it was believed that the Indians had no focus for their hopes, interests, and ambitions. Lacking a fixed abode, they could have no notion of a proper family life; nineteenth-century literature on the Indian described a cruel and heartless domestic regime in which children, women, and the aged were mistreated.[9]

Most Canadians believed that private ownership of property and possessions would put an end to Indian warfare, which was viewed as an irrational, bloodthirsty sport, perpetuated endlessly because the Indians had little property to lose. It was felt that Indians kept their possessions to a minimum in order to make war effectively. They had to be prepared to fight and to run: "if they had much [property] it impeded progress, which with them meant fight, or it would be stolen and enrich the enemy."[10] One missionary lectured the Indians that private property would promote peace among the tribes. "You call this your country, but even now in the dead of winter you dare not sleep in quiet. 'No', said I, 'not until a stronger power friendly to you comes upon the scene will you really own a bit of land and live at peace with other men.'"[11]

According to informants of the late nineteenth century, Indian society lacked not only an idea of private land ownership, but also any concept of the need to possess a margin of surplus. They appeared to place themselves wholly at the whim of nature's caprices, refusing to consider their economic future. "Improvident" was the label most commonly ascribed to them. On an incessant quest for food, Indians were always subject to feast or famine. With no forethought, they would gorge until not a mouthful was left, rather than provide for judicious consumption.[12] Thus they continually exposed themselves to want and often faced long periods of starvation.[13] Also seen as a cause of poverty and starvation was the Indians' willingness to share the spoils of a hunt with neighbours. To the Victorian-Canadian observer, these practices were evidence of a listless, lethargic approach to life.

Indolence, the twin of improvidence, was seen as another unfortunate characteristic of the Indians. As an early missionary to the West commented, the Indians were without "acquired wants and appetites which rouse men to activity in civilized life, and stimulate them to persevering industry, while they keep the mind in perpetual exercise and ingenious invention."[14] The Indians' reluctance to work was viewed as a cause of their inability to bring the natural world within their control and ownership. It was believed that only with private property would the Indian be induced to adopt steady habits of work.

Hunting was not considered work in Victorian circles. It may have been a pleasurable pastime, but it did not involve the requisite systematic, habitual toil toward the creation of something of lasting value, such as a building, a farm, or a city. Hunting was rightfully a leisurely recreation for those who could afford it. Describing the Plains Indians, one authority explained that "in the first place, they had never worked. The Indian loves his gun, his bow and arrows; he rejoices in hunting, trapping, and fishing, occupations that are the sports of the aristocracy in the civilized countries from whence have come his rulers."[15] Other negative images of the Indian as hunter abounded. Indians were primitive, since hunting was assumed to require little skill, knowledge, or technology. Indians were reckless and improvident, since hunting was considered as living off the fat of the land. Indians were wanton, since not satisfied with the ordinary methods of destroying the buffalo, the Indians constructed pounds, which led to "indiscriminate slaughter."[16] Hunting as well promoted an unhealthy family life. The "proud lords" lounged at their ease about the camps, leaving any hard labour to the women. Nineteenth-century literature depicted the life of the Indian woman as little better than that of a beast of burden.[17] Once they had outlived their usefulness, they were casually slain or abandoned to perish.

AGRICULTURE, THE SOLUTION

Agriculture was seen as the solution to the at-best peculiar and at-worst deplorable characteristics and idiosyncrasies which the Indians tenaciously and perversely cherished. The Indian had to be taught to make his living from the soil. No other occupation could so assuredly dispossess the Indian of his nomadic habits and the uncertainties of the chase, and fix upon him the values of a permanent abode and the security of a margin of surplus. Agriculture would teach an appreciation of private property and impart a will to own and master nature. With one place to call home in which to centre hopes and ambitions, the Indian could enjoy the ennobling, refining influences and virtues of a happy family life, which included sobriety and respect for women and the elderly. Farming a piece of land would promote an independent spirit and foster competition, qualities which would erode the tribal unit. Agriculture would nurture habits of industry and diligence. Required to perform regular duties at certain times of the year, the Indian would grasp the necessity of habitual toil, systematic work, and attention to detail.

Indian women as well as men would acquire a new set of values and code of conduct through an agricultural, settled life. The Indian wife would be the mistress of her home and no longer a servile, degraded beast of burden. She would acquire discipline, modesty, and cleanliness, virtues impossible in a nomadic society, and she would pass these attributes on to her children. Indian women could learn the skills of farm wives, such as raising poultry, gardening, butter- and cheese-making, but they also would have time for the gentler arts, such as needlework, quilting, and knitting.

The Indian's farm was to be his place of probation, a training ground in the lessons of civilization and citizenship. No other trade or profession could provide this firm foundation; only perhaps with subsequent generations could loftier aspirations be contemplated. Agriculture was also seen as particularly suitable to the Indian character. Some thought Indians might suffer spiritually and physically in the confines of a shoemaker, tailor, carpenter, or blacksmith shop.[18] Farming offered a healthy, vigorous outdoor life more in keeping with their current way of life.

In the scientific community, agriculture was viewed as a key stage in man's evolutionary sequence of progress from savagism to barbarism to civilization.[19] Each step, from the invention of the bow and arrow to the domestication of animals and cultivation of maize to smelting iron ore and so on, was regarded as essential to the next and could not be transcended. The Indians of North America had to follow the logic of progressive development. Agriculture and private property would afford the Indians the opportunity to climb the remaining steps to civilization within the space of a few generations, greatly speeding up the process that had been so gradual in other cultures. One Canadian authority on the Indians explained that it was only when the Germanic barbarians became landowners that the way was paved for their civilization.

> When they were compelled by a change in their circumstances to adopt a sedentary life, and follow the pursuits of agriculture, there arose an inequality among the people from the fact that the chiefs became landed proprietors and employed those under them as laborers. The former equality, arising from their tribal relationship, gave place to an individuality which paved the way for the evolution of the Germans, Hungarians and other civilized nations of the nineteenth century.[20]

Agriculture as an occupation was not subservient to the world of business, industry, medicine, or law but was the worthiest of employments, not just for Indians, but for all who would choose to settle the prairie and help create a vast agrarian empire. Homesteaders were assured of this through a "country life ideology," which emerged as settlement proceeded, resurrecting ancient idealizations of the agrarian way of life.[21] This ideology was propagated through schools, newspapers, agrarian periodicals, railway promotional literature, agricultural exhibitions, women's institutes, homemakers clubs, and other farm organizations. Farmers were told that agriculture was the foundation of the wealth and prosperity of a nation, "the mainspring of national greatness and the moulder of national and personal character." Farming was promoted as a noble and sacred occupation, a natural and healthy way of life that elevated "morally and emotionally, if not intellectually."[22]

The country life ideology endowed the land with an almost mystical power to transform and elevate, even the lowest or weakest of men. As master of his own quarter section, the homesteader enjoyed individual freedom and personal accountability. This ideology was embedded in the homestead policy. Designed to accommodate single-family establishments, this policy deliberately made the Canadian prairies "the region of the small independent operator, the place where every man had his own small plot of land on which he could live according to the dictates of his own conscience and from which he could derive benefits commensurate with his own exertions."[23] The decision to base the settlement of the West on the family farm was not the result of vigorous scientific inquiry into the best means of bringing the rich prairie lands under cultivation; rather, it was the social and religious thought of the time that determined the pattern of western settlement.

To all those who shared in the powerful ideology of the developing order in western Canada, there was no question but that the Indian way of life had to stand aside. In their refusal to progress, improve, develop, and prosper, the Indians were ignoring God's gift. It was inconceivable that this prospective home for millions could forever continue to be the hunting ground of the Indians. This was a land for a hardy, thrifty race of men who would farm and build houses, roads, and railways. The fertile prairies were too valuable to be kept as mere buffalo preserves; the land cried out for "real occupation."[24] That the Indians were not perceived to be in "actual and constant use of their land" was a conventional nineteenth-century rationalization for their displacement, a view that appeared self-evident to non-native observers.[25] Citing the Swiss jurist Emmerich de Vattel's *Law of Nations*, an 1844–45 report on the affairs of the Indians in Canada argued that an "unsettled habitation" did not constitute a "true and legal possession" and that other nations were lawfully entitled to take possession and settle these lands. It was believed that the failure of a people to cultivate the soil meant that they were incapable of occupying the country and were thus in no particular need of most of the land. A crowded nation was justified in laying claim to land that "belongs to mankind in general, and was designed to furnish them with subsistence."[26]

That the Indians did not farm was ample justification for others to lay claim to their land, but a further rationalization was that since Indians could be taught to farm, they would gain much more than they would lose. The reward was the prospect of an ennobling enterprise through which they could achieve status, stability, self-respect, and dignity. An added advantage was that the Indians would not be in need of their extensive hunting grounds, as they would have the means to feed themselves.

It was assumed that Indians had the desire to control nature but that they lacked the necessary skill, knowledge, and technology. The Indians were viewed as amenable to training. With adequate incentive they would work and their latent energies blossom.[27] They required intervention to push them along this course, however. Left to themselves, the Indians would be quite content to remain as they always had been. Authorities on the Indians often remarked on their obstinate pride in their culture and their misguided view that theirs was the superior civilization.[28] It was believed that centuries of isolation, without opportunity to compare their customs, beliefs, and accomplishments with those of other cultures, had produced a "sublime ignorance," as well the unfortunate notions of superiority.[29] The Indians were perversely reluctant to countenance any change. "They believe the native culture is best suited for themselves, and having developed under it, and enjoyed it so long, they care not to give it up for an untried system."[30] Present contentment, however, was not a suitable goal for any race of men, especially when they were the inhabitants of a land with enormous resource potential.

> They never thought of nor speculated upon the magnificent array of mighty power within their sight and sound, and in the centre of which they were living all the time. They worried not because of stacks or stooks, nor yet "stocks". They lost neither appetite nor sleep because of marts or merchants. They heard not the clank and clink of multiple machinery, and much less the roar and rush of transcontinentals. None of these things moved them, for truly it had not entered into their life, nor come as yet into their thought.[31]

Officials, missionaries, and others concerned with the Indians generally assumed that their future was among the stacks and stooks. This assumption did not emerge from any commissions of inquiry into the future of the Indians of the West; it simply appeared as a natural evolution, so natural in fact that very little thought was devoted to the issue of the best way to encourage and patronize Indian agriculture. The idea that Indians should become farmers was warmly applauded by Canadians, but when the time came to put ideas into action, there was little willingness to provide what was necessary to begin and sustain such an enterprise.

GOVERNMENT POLICY TO THE 1870S

The goal of transforming the Indians of western Canada into farmers was not, however, one of the driving forces behind the move to bring the West into Confederation. This project was conceived by a predominantly commercial elite in central Canada who wished to see the West exploited as a means of ensuring the viability of their own region.[32] The economic blueprint for the West that was evident in the Confederation debates and that later became embedded in Sir John A. Macdonald's National Policy involved the construction of a transcontinental railway, the rapid settlement of the West, the creation of a grain-exporting economy, and the growth of a highly protected domestic market for finished goods from the East. The aboriginal occupants of the West were largely irrelevant to these plans, except to the extent that their land had to be surrendered and their peaceful acquiescence secured. It was clear that the region was to be an agricultural frontier, and those who took into account the future role of the Indians in this scheme offered farming as the recipe for a secure and decent life. Although there was recognition that the Indian situation in Manitoba and the North-West differed in many respects from that in the older provinces, government officials followed the general principles of Indian policy that had evolved there, originally inherited from the imperial government.[33]

The traditional means of placating the Indians of British North America was through treaties, which provided compensation in return for the extinguishment of Indian claims to the land. The Proclamation of 1763 laid the foundation for the treaty system.[34] Intended to minimize contact with the Indians, a provision of the proclamation established a boundary line, essentially creating a vast Indian country in which the Indians were regarded as the proprietors. A basic principle of British Indian policy, first articulated in this proclamation, was that only the Crown and not private citizens could acquire Indian land. Responsibility for Indian affairs was then a branch of the military and the major purpose of Indian policy was to secure the loyalty and contentment of these valuable military allies. Although a program of settlement and civilization was envisaged in the proclamation, steps toward this ideal were not taken by the military administrators. The imperial government distributed presents and rewarded wartime service to confirm the Indians' allegiances, and this policy was successful in maintaining the loyalty of the Indians during the American Revolution and the War of 1812.

The value of the Indians as military allies began to wane after 1815 as immigration increased and border hostilities declined. With their usefulness at an end, the policy of distributing presents to the Indians was brought into question, as was the need for the existence of an Indian department within the military.[35] Threatened with the elimination of his department in 1828, the superintendent of Indian affairs suggested a different function for it, advocating that "steps be taken to civilize and educate the Indians and that agricultural goods be substituted for annual presents."[36] Here was the genesis of a new policy toward the Indians that took shape in the 1830s and continued well into the twentieth century.

The ultimate goal of that policy was to bring about the cultural transformation of the Indian to eventually achieve their total assimilation into white society. As a distinct cultural group, Indians would disappear. The three basic means to this end were missionaries, schools, and agriculture. It was believed that this policy could succeed only if the Indians were collected into settlements where they could be instructed in religion and trained in agriculture. Theoretically, however, the need for special settlements or reserves or even a special Indian branch of the government would one day disappear if the policy of assimilation succeeded, since the Indian would be fully equipped to enter white society. With this program officially adopted in 1830, Indian affairs ceased to be a branch of the military and was brought under civil control. Here costs could be kept to a minimum, as the budget would be under the annual scrutiny of Parliament. Public money was not to be used, however; the program of civilizing the Indians was to be funded by the sale of the Indians' own land.

The philanthropic attitude toward the Indian was vigorously supported by a vocal humanitarian lobby in Britain that was critical of the Empire's treatment of its new subjects. It advocated the need to reclaim Canada's Indians from their state of barbarism, instruct them in the industrious, peaceful habits of the civilized, and protect them from unscrupulous interests while this process proceeded. These sentiments coincided with the concerns and goals of missionaries working among the Indians. Missionaries came to be increasingly relied upon as agents of assimilation, particularly since they financed themselves. The policy of settling Indians on reserves also fit in well with the demands of the settler economy that was taking shape in central Canada. To the pioneer heading into the wilderness intent on working and improving the land, the Indian was regarded as a nuisance and a barrier to progress.[37] As the family farm was to be the unit of settlement, the Indians were not required as a labour force. The sole economic benefit to be derived from the Indians was through the transfer of their land. Land surrenders, which became necessary as European settlement accelerated, were accomplished through treaties between the Crown and an assembly of the Indians involved. The earliest of these Upper Canadian treaties provided only once-for-all payment in goods, but later treaties included annuities.

The concept of the reserve as a training ground or laboratory for civilizing the Indian began to take shape in the 1830s with the adoption of the idea that Indians should settle in villages, be weaned from their nomadic life, and be taught to cultivate the land.[38] It was believed that these laboratories of transformation would best succeed if they were remote from the rest of civilization, as it was felt that native people adopted only the worst characteristics of the surrounding white society.[39] The program was launched with two experiments at Coldwater and Lake St Claire in Upper Canada. The plan was that the Indians would first clear land for a communal farm, which would supply them with rations while each family prepared its sixteen-acre plot for cultivation.[40] Labourers, farmers, and mechanics were hired to provide guidance by their example, and missionaries and teachers worked among them. Over the years other reserves were set aside, but by 1850 there was considerable disillusionment with the policy of settling Indians on remote reserves. The schemes were not considered a success, as few concrete achievements had resulted.[41] A re-evaluation of the reserve program led to the conclusion that reserves should not be isolated but surrounded by settlement. It was decided that smaller reserves for individual bands should be located next to non-Indian communities to serve as positive examples and thus lead to more rapid assimilation of the Indians.[42]

In the 1850s the goal of Christianizing, educating, and making farmers out of the Indians of Upper Canada still appeared to be in the distant future. Legislators believed that in the meantime, steps should be taken to protect the Indians during their period of incubation. Thus the Indian was given special status in legislation passed in 1857. The Gradual Civilization Act defined who an Indian was and stated that such a person could not enjoy the privileges and rights of other Canadians until he could prove that he was literate, free of debt, and of high moral standing.[43] As a reward for meeting these criteria, an Indian would be given fee simple title (absolute ownership) to up to fifty acres of reserve land, and after a probation period of one year he would receive the franchise. The curious paradox of Canada's Indian policy was codified in this act. Although the ultimate purpose of this policy was to eliminate all distinctions between Indians and other Canadians, it actually created such distinctions through exclusive laws. The act singled out Indians as a race apart, placed them on settlements remote from non-Indians, and provided them with a special administrative agency that would serve Indians only. This policy tended to preserve rather than destroy the corporate and distinct character of Indian society.

The Canadian government took over control of Indian affairs from the British authorities in 1860. Under British control, a number of departments shared responsibility for vital decisions, and the result was neglect and unsystematic administration.[44] In 1862 policy was centralized in one "clientele" department, despite concerns that it might duplicate services, increase costs, and foster the isolation of the Indian population. The new Indian Affairs office was first an agency within one of the branches of Crown Lands, and, after 1867, within its successor, the Department of the Interior. The bureaucracy in Ottawa, however, gave no thought to the Plains Indians until the 1870s when the Dominion acquired the North-West and some decisions had to be made.

PLAINS INDIAN LIFE TO THE 1870S

The Indians who peopled the mind of the Victorian Canadian bore scant resemblance to the actual residents of western Canada in the nineteenth century. The would-be farmers of the southern plains of present-day Saskatchewan were primarily Plains Cree, with smaller groups of Assiniboine, Saulteaux, and Dakota. Plains life, which relied upon the buffalo and the horse, was secure, even bountiful, until the mid-nineteenth century; it was a life in which the material wants of the people were adequately satisfied. They had sufficient shelter and clothing and plenty of high-protein lean meat. Plains dwellers had a rich artistic and ceremonial life, and they enjoyed sports, craftwork, and other pastimes. Acquainted with the European trader since the late seventeenth century, they had incorporated aspects of this relationship into their social life and economy, but they had not become dependent on European technology. Bows and arrows, for example, were favoured above firearms for the buffalo hunt.[45]

The residents of the plains had few material possessions, a fact that to the Euro-Canadian observer indicated a low standard of living. But the prosperity of an efficient hunting band required a high degree of mobility. Once the food resources in the vicinity of one camp were depleted, it was necessary to move elsewhere. Therefore it was economically undesirable to amass stocks of food, clothing, tools, and ornaments. This life was quite far removed from the primitive foraging for subsistence, the aimless roaming from camp to camp under the ceaseless spectre of starvation, described in most literature of the nineteenth century. The movements of the Plains Indians were not haphazard and irrational but were based on a thorough knowledge of the terrain and the habits of their game. Theirs was a successful economy, which involved a great measure of planning, foresight, preparation, and discussion of tactics, although plans could not be rigid or formal. The plains dwellers had to be flexible and sensitive to shifting conditions and considerations, such as the weather, prairie fire, or the strategies of their enemies. They were resourceful and inventive in adapting to their environment and developing highly efficient techniques and aids to capitalize on their opportunities.

In the 1870s the land occupied by the branch of the Plains Cree who are the focus of this study extended from the Assiniboine River at the Qu'Appelle west to the Cypress Hills and from the forty-ninth parallel to midway between the north and south branches of the Saskatchewan River.[46] The plains in this region are separated into two levels, or steppes, by the Missouri Coteau. Its east-facing escarpment, the great prairie ridge that served as an observation point for hunters, heralds the beginning of "La Grande Prairie" to the west. Geographical expeditions that studied this land in the 1850s and 1860s were little impressed with this slightly undulating, treeless plain, concluding that it was arid and barren, unsuitable for the sustenance of man. The natural vegetation was grass – spear grass and wheat grass. As British army lieutenant William Butler wrote, the prairie was an "ocean of grass."[47] The only exceptions were the valleys of the rivers and streams where belts of timber fringed their sides, and the outliers such as the Cypress Hills, Wood Mountain, the Touchwood Hills, and Moose Mountain, where wood and water was available. These wooded, elevated points were important landmarks and watchtowers of the Plains Indian because from these sites the surrounding territory could be scouted for the buffalo. The tender grasses that so little impressed the exploring expeditions were vital to people of the plains, as they nourished the buffalo, the foundation of their economy.

A knowledge of the habits of the buffalo and its environment was essential to Indian survival and prosperity. The buffalo followed a natural cycle of concentration and dispersal that was seasonal and sufficiently regular to be described as migratory.[48] In the autumn and winter the animals scattered in small herds to the coulees, river valleys, and aspen parklands to the north. In the shelter of the wooded areas, the snow remained soft enough for them to paw through to the grass beneath. The abundance of grass on the open plains in the summer months drew the herds south where they grazed in huge masses. In general the herds moved northward to the parkland belt in the winter and southward toward the grasslands in the spring. Buffalo movements were not capricious and unpredictable, and the hunters did not simply travel at random, hoping to come across a herd. There were departures from this regular pattern, but the causes of these variations and their effects upon buffalo movements were to a large degree predictable and were understood by the local inhabitants.[49] In an exceptionally mild winter, for example, when there was little snow, the buffalo might remain far out on the grassland. Extensive prairie fire could also affect the normal migration pattern of the animal.

The horse, acquired by the Cree in the mid-eighteenth century, was also central to Plains culture.[50] It allowed the Cree to get to the game easier, to carry increased loads, and to congregate in larger encampments. The horse became an important factor in military and trade strategy, and it had an influence on recreation and social life. The Cree had to adjust their daily and seasonal habits to the care and protection of these domesticated animals. Campsites, for example, had to be chosen with a view to adequate pasturage.[51]

Indian life on the prairie followed a pattern of concentration and dispersal that paralleled that of the buffalo. In the mid-nineteenth century, most of the Plains Cree gathered along the South Saskatchewan River in June or July when the grass was most lush on the open plains and the buffalo plentiful. Concentrated hunts were organized at these large encampments, policed by members of the Warrior Society, who kept order in the camp and ensured that the buffalo were not disturbed until preparations for the hunt were complete.[52] Individuals who broke rank endangered the whole camp, as the herds could stampede prematurely. Generally the summer hunt involved the Indians rapidly surrounding a herd and forming a corral.

The large supply of food in one vicinity, allowing the concentration of many people, as well as the acquisition of the horse, enabled the bands of Cree to begin to develop the cohesiveness of a tribal unit. For the "band" societies of the woodlands where game remained scattered, large populations could not be sustained in one area for any length of time, and the family hunting units were dispersed and generally more independent of each other. But the Cree of the plains were able to define themselves as a definite political unit, separate from their neighbours. At their summer encampments, which functioned as their "intermittent town,"[53] the bands of Cree reinforced their solidarity in language, customs, and ritual. It was a time for visiting friends, for trading, gambling, and competing in sports together. The sun dance, a central ceremony of the Cree during which they asked their spirit powers to bless mankind, was held almost annually and was a major integrating force. Unity was achieved as well through the governing councils where the chiefs of the bands met to discuss trade and military policies and strategies. Markets and training programs were also active for these few short weeks, which helped reinforce the connection of an individual band to the larger, complex society.

Large summer encampments on the plains lasted only a few weeks. Once the herds were no longer in the vicinity of the camp, the bands separated and began to move in the direction of their wintering territory. Plant food, a vital ingredient in the diet of the Plains Cree, was gathered during the summer. A large variety of roots, berries, seeds, and fruits were collected, the most important of which was the prairie turnip, also known as the white apple, or *pomme blanche*. The harvest season for this tuber lasted only for a matter of weeks so that the progress of its growth had to be carefully observed.[54] Women and children harvested the root with fire-hardened, slightly curved digging sticks of cherry or birch. Large quantities of the plant were peeled, dried in the sun, and pounded until reduced to a fine powder. Stored in buffalo-skin bags for winter use, this flour may well have contributed to the health of the buffalo hunters because of its vitamin C content. Berries, collected in wooded areas of the hills and valleys in midsummer, were also dried and stored for winter use in puddings and in pemmican.

In the autumn residents of the plains, like the buffalo, retreated to the parklands, or uplands. There buffalo were hunted by driving them into pounds. Drive lines, or fences, were built of timber and placed to converge at the point of the pound, or corral. The pound was usually constructed just over the edge of a hill or coulee. Its size depended on the number of animals the people in the band could handle once they had driven them into the pound.[55] The poundmaker, responsible for the construction of the pound, was also in charge of the drive. Various techniques were devised to manoeuvre the animals to the pound from distances of as much as fifty miles. Smoke in the direction of the herd and the movements of runners gradually coaxed them to the drive lines, which might have been several miles apart and three or four miles out from the pound. At this point the man called "he who brings them in" caught the attention of the herd by giving the distress call of the bison calf, and the animals would gradually move toward him within the wings of the pound. If the buffalo began to stampede to one side, hunters manning the flanks would rise up and frighten them off in the opposite direction. Within the pound the animals were killed with bows and arrows. Using guns risked frightening the animals, which might break down the corral and escape.

During the months of buffalo hunting by pounds, large stocks of pemmican, tallow, dried meat, and buffalo robes were laid in for trade in spring at the Hudson's Bay Company posts.[56] Some Cree bands also trapped wolves, fox, muskrat, marten, and ermine for trade. The deepest cold of winter was the most difficult time; game was scarce and scattered, and what there was had to be stalked on foot. Moose, elk, and deer were hunted by some Cree bands, and small animals such as rabbits were snared. After spring break-up the Cree caught river fish by building weirs that interrupted the downstream run.[57] Spring was also a time for hunting wild fowl and for collecting maple sap, which was made into sugar. As the weather became warmer, the bands once again began to converge on the plains.

Plains Cree bands were loosely organized, shifting units, easily joined and easily left.[58] Several families, normally related to the chief, formed the stable nucleus of a Cree band, but it was an open and fluid organization. Saulteaux, Assiniboine, and mixed-bloods were often found in Cree bands. Newcomers might be young men who married into the band or those who were attracted by the reputation of the leader as a poundmaker, medicine man, or warrior. A chief who was a noted poundmaker might have a large following during the winter but a much smaller one during the summer.

The band members acknowledged the leadership of a man who inspired confidence and compliance. He was perhaps an individual respected for his good judgment and courage, known for his accomplishments in battle, recognized as an experienced and industrious hunter, distinguished as an orator, or revered as a medicine man. The chief also had to possess wealth and liberality. Like the head of an extended family, he was expected to show concern for everyone in the camp. He freely gave his possessions to the needy, his wife distributed the choicest cuts of meat after a successful hunt to those short of food,[59] and his household took in sons of the less affluent and orphans and treated them as members of the family. On occasions for ceremonial gift-giving and at feasts the chief was expected to donate the largest share. The more lavish he was in his charity and gift-giving, the greater his reputation. Since the chief's kinsmen contributed to his expenditures, at the same time enhancing their own prestige, a chief with a large network of relatives within his band could afford to be very generous. When quarrels and disputes arose in camp, the chief again had to be unstinting. To ease tensions, he often had to bestow a gift upon the aggrieved person or replace from his own possessions an item an individual believed had been stolen.

The chief of a band did not have exclusive control or hereditary claim to the title. Controversial matters were often referred to a council of prominent men of the band. A band also might have several chiefs, although one would tacitly be recognized as outranking the others or at different times of the year the services and expertise of one might be at a greater premium.[60] A chief's son clearly had an edge when the question of succession arose, as he already possessed the necessary wealth and support of a kinship network. But succession was not necessarily hereditary. If the abilities of a chief's son did not inspire confidence, another outstanding man would by common consent gradually be accepted as leader.

The Worthy Young Men Society and the Warrior Society ranked next to the chief in prestige among the Crees.[61] To be a member of the Worthy Young Men, an individual had to have gained a reputation as a brave fighter, daring horse raider, or skilled hunter. Exploits were ranked according to the degree of danger to which he was exposed. Killing an enemy from an ambushed position, for example, did not carry the same prestige as shooting at the enemy while also under fire. When a Worthy Young Man had acquired sufficient wealth in horses, hides, and other material possessions, he would be asked to join the *okihcitaw*, which has arbitrarily been translated as "warriors." According to a Cree informant, the Cree word does not have the implication of violence present in the English word. Rather, *okihcitaw* means "a person that does honorable things, like looking after his elders, feeding the starving orphans, anything like that."[62] As men of prestige and distinction, the members of this society were expected to sacrifice their possessions freely for the good of the community, to provide help to widows and the elderly, and to feed visitors. As previously noted, the warriors also policed the summer hunt.

Competitiveness and the quest for individual status were not absent from Plains Cree society. Gradations in status and material wealth were recognized. At council meetings, for example, men with "small, poorly furnished tipis and little surplus food were seated near the door ... and were not given a blanket or robe to sit on. Their inferior rank was indicated in this way and their opinions were little heeded."[63] Material wealth in horses, guns, hides, tents, and dogs was individually owned, but the conspicuous distribution of these goods was the means of attaining prestige and security.

The Plains Cree were well acquainted with concepts of debt and credit, spending, buying, and selling. By the time of the treaties in the 1870s, they were also familiar with the standards of pounds, shillings, and pence.[64] An American fur trader, writing in the mid-nineteenth century, described the Cree as "good judges of the qualities of merchandise, [they] count with facility and show great shrewdness in their dealings. They practise economy in their domestic life, trade only useful articles, take good care of provisions and make the most they can of everything. The majority reckon up on the value of their hunt and consult their wants before they enter the store and cannot be enticed to buy articles they do not need."[65] An employee of the Hudson's Bay Company at Fort Qu'Appelle noted that the Indians were endowed with "extraordinary memories as to recall each item they had given and received during the year, in many cases for years, if not for life."[66]

Quite contrary to the belief that the Indians of the plains had maintained an undeviating way of life for centuries, the Cree were recent arrivals to the prairie West and their history was one of constant change and adaptation. Before European contact the Cree had occupied the eastern woodland country from north of Lake Superior to Hudson Bay.[67] West of the Cree, inhabiting a mixture of Canadian Shield country and a large portion of the plains of south-central Manitoba, were the Assiniboine, a Siouian-speaking people who at some point had separated from their close relatives, the Yankton Dakota. The Cree and Assiniboine lived together peacefully and, as allies in trade and military strategy, their histories were closely parallel.

In their woodland habitat the Cree frequented the shores of lakes in summer to fish, and ranged inland in winter to hunt moose and caribou. By the mid-seventeenth century, the Cree were in contact with the western flow of European goods and were important suppliers of furs to the Ottawa-French trading network.[68] When the

Hudson's Bay Company was established on the mouth of the Nelson River in 1670, the Cree were in a strategically advantageous position to control the trade on the Bay, which focused on York Factory. Because inland groups coming to trade had to pass through the land of the Cree and Assiniboine, the two allied groups began to take over the position of middlemen, obtaining a large, steady supply of arms and ammunition at York Factory.[69] Adept in the manufacture and use of the canoe, the Cree were readily able to exploit the network of waterways in their terrain to transport trade goods and raw materials. A period of territorial expansion followed. The Cree and Assiniboine extended their trading and hunting territory in a northwesterly direction, sometimes by force, further isolating other tribes from the European source.[70] In 1720 the Touchwood Hills of present-day southeastern Saskatchewan marked the southern limits of Assiniboine territory; the territory east and north of them was occupied by the Cree.[71] By the early eighteenth century, the Cree and Assiniboine had effectively formed a blockade; very few other groups travelled to York Factory, and those that did were usually accompanied by a Cree or Assiniboine.[72] Cree contacts at this time included the Blackfoot whom they supplied with firearms and with whom they formed an alliance against the enemies of the Blackfoot, the Snakes and Kootenays.[73]

The trade in furs involved a partnership that required the cooperation of Indian and European. Recent studies have stressed that the Indians did not play a servile role in this relationship, that the Indians were not passive objects of exploitation, but that Indian and European shared a mutually beneficial economic system.[74] The trading system that evolved was a compromise between Indian and European traditions.[75] The Indians were active participants in this partnership and dictated the terms of trade to a large extent. They manipulated competition, bargained shrewdly, and were demanding consumers. The Assiniboine and Cree middlemen determined the kind and quality of trade goods, directing the rate and nature of material culture change. There was no rapid and complete dependence on European technology. The Indians did not become critically dependent on firearms, for example; after the late seventeenth century, gun sales took a decidedly downward trend.[76]

Shortly after the mid-eighteenth century, the Assiniboine began to move south and west, and the westernmost Cree, on the fringes of the prairie, began to spend time on the grasslands hunting buffalo. Several explanations have been suggested for these migrations. One is that the Cree were forced to abandon the woodlands because the fur and game resources had been depleted. More recent evidence suggests that the Cree made a conscious choice to opt out of the pelt trade in favour of the buffalo hunt.[77] The introduction of the horse, likely first acquired between 1732 and 1754, was a crucial factor in Cree adaptation to Plains culture. The Saulteaux migrated to the land abandoned by the Cree where an adequate fur-animal population remained to continue a profitable trade in prime furs. With the establishment of posts in the interior after 1763, the demand for provisions increased. Taking advantage of this new economic opportunity to work as provisioners to the trading companies, many Cree bands chose to become fully involved in the buffalo hunt.[78]

Another important impetus for the southward migration of the Cree was the development of links with the continent-wide Indian network of trade that centred on the Mandan villages on the upper Missouri River in present-day North Dakota.[79] Described as the "grand mart of the plains," the Mandan trade empire extended north to Hudson Bay, south to the Spanish settlements, west to the Pacific Coast, and as least as far east as the Lake of the Woods.[80] As this new network was established, and as the buffalo increasingly satisfied all the requirements of the Cree and Assiniboine, they became less interested in European trade goods.[81] In 1794 an employee of the North West Company described the inhabitants of the plains as "so advantageously situated that they could live very happily independent of our assistance. They are surrounded with innumerable herds of various kinds of animals, whose skins defend them from the inclemency of the weather, and they have invented so many methods for the destruction of animals, that they stand in no need of ammunition to provide a sufficiency for these purposes."[82]

By the 1790s the western branch of the Cree had followed the Assiniboine in adopting Plains culture. The most easterly bands of Cree retained the Woodland culture and some on the border of the plains practised a mixture of both. The Cree showed themselves to be remarkably flexible in rapidly adjusting to the rewards and demands of three different environments – the forest, parklands, and plains. Through their contact with other Plains tribes, the Cree learned and adopted many of the characteristics, techniques, and traits of Plains culture. Yet even those branches of the Cree that moved furthest to the west retained aspects of their Woodland heritage, developing a unique strain of Plains culture. They maintained the burial practices of their Woodland relatives and the use of the ceremonial long lodge, continued to make birchbark containers and to use snowshoes.[83] Unlike the other Plains Indians, the Cree did not treat the horse and buffalo as venerated objects in their religious ceremonialism.

The nineteenth century in Cree history is generally depicted as a time of growing dependence on imported goods such as liquor and guns, the use of which led to senseless, random acts of violence. This pattern of behaviour combined with the decimation brought by disease from the Old World to lead to the collapse of their political and social system well before they entered the reserve period.[84] A recent interpretation suggests quite a different image of the Cree in the nineteenth century.[85] It is argued that during this period the Cree nation was consolidated. The Cree forged and retained a tribal identity and developed a distinguished diplomatic and military record. This identity was not dependent upon or undermined by relations with European traders. Acquisition of a supply of horses was the underlying purpose of most of their military and trade strategy, and horses were not a commodity controlled by European traders. Throughout this period the Cree continued to make decisions with reference to their own interests, maintaining systems of political and economic alliances in which the European trader was one of several but not a determining variable. Although life on the plains was then characterized by hostility – wars and small raiding parties – these conflicts were not the aimless indulgence in bloodthirsty "sport" that the Victorian observer perceived. Cree leaders assessed and analyzed their current economic and military problems, devised appropriate strategy and tactics, and mobilized the forces necessary to carry them out.

The horse was the instrument and symbol of prosperity on the plains and was thus the focus of military and trade strategies to the mid-nineteenth century. For the hunt, and to maintain a high degree of mobility, the well-being of a Plains band depended on a sufficient number of fast, responsive, well-trained mounts. Until the early nineteenth century, the Cree had two sources of horses. One was through their alliance with the Blackfoot, who obtained the animals through the Arapaho-Cheyenne horse market.[86] Another was through the Mandan with whom the Cree and Assiniboine were also allied. From the Cree and Assiniboine, the Mandan received military aid against their common enemy, the Dakota. To the northern hunters, corn, a crop grown by the semi-sedentary Mandan, was important in the formation of this accord – it was sought after as an ideal portable food supply.[87] The Mandan controlled the major horse mart of the eastern plains, but their horses were expensive and became more so to the Cree and Assiniboine after 1795 when they ceased to be the sole suppliers of European goods to the Mandan. A trend toward stealing Mandan horses in the early years of the nineteenth century marked the beginning of the end of the Cree-Assiniboine-Mandan alliance. By this time the Cree-Blackfoot alliance had also broken down and the commanding role of the Cree and Assiniboine in the European fur trade had been undermined with the establishment of inland posts.

From approximately 1810 to 1850, the Cree sought to construct new trade and military patterns to replace those that had collapsed. To satisfy the growing demand for horses, the Cree and Assiniboine began a concerted program of horse raiding from the Blackfoot, the Hudson's Bay Company, and Canadian traders. In Cree society, to acquire a horse in this manner was a prestigious act, whereas to purchase one carried no merit. As one observer explained, horse raiding was not perceived as "theft."

As late as the sixties and early seventies it was common to say:
"Bringing them in," and not "Stealing" horses.
The gossip between the lodges never spoke of "stealing horses" – he "brought them in," "they ran them in." "Did you see that bunch of horses? He just now brought them home."
No imputation of theft was thought of. It was a meritorial [sic] act. Such feats of cunning, and skill and acts of daring as were accomplished in running off another man's horses, were lauded and placed the actor away above par among his fellows ... repeatedly to return from the land of the enemy with bands of horses gave the hero prominence and respect among his fellows.[88]

The horse raiding was followed by a period of concerted Cree-Blackfoot warfare. The Cree's purpose remained the acquisition of horses. Until 1850 a loose alliance of Cree, Assiniboine, Crow, and Flathead surrounded the Blackfoot on three fronts.[89]

After 1850 the growing scarcity of buffalo added a new factor in plains warfare. The retreat of the buffalo is illustrated in the progressively westward extension of Hudson's Bay Company posts. By 1830 Brandon House, on the Assiniboine River above the mouth of the Souris, had become marginal to the buffalo hunting territory and was replaced by Fort Ellice, near the junction of the Assiniboine and Qu'Appelle rivers. Fort Ellice became the key buffalo hunting post until the 1850s when the company began to receive the largest supply of its pemmican from the Touchwood Hills, a site in turn replaced by Fort Qu'Appelle further south in the 1860s.[90] In the 1860s a system of "flying posts" became important sources of pemmican. These were small temporary winter encampments in wooded areas or outliers such as the Turtle or Moose mountains where the buffalo hunters wintered.

As the herds retreated farther and farther west, during the hunting season the Cree and Assiniboine were forced to approach Blackfoot country to the west of the Cree. Among the few solutions open to the hunters of southern Saskatchewan was to extend their borders westward through military activity. In the 1860s the Cree and Assiniboine of the Qu'Appelle and Swan River districts were the aggressors and invaders of Blackfoot country and advanced toward the Cypress Hills.[91] A state of war existed all along the Cree-Blackfoot border after 1869, heightened by the Cree campaign of revenge for the death of Maskepetoon (Broken Arm), who was killed while approaching a Blackfoot camp on a peace mission. In the fall of 1870 the Cree organized a massive thrust into Blackfoot territory. Big Bear, Piapot, Little Mountain, and Little Pine led from six hundred to eight hundred warriors. They anticipated victory, believing that the Blackfoot had been greatly incapacitated by the smallpox epidemic of 1869–70. In a battle at the junction of the Oldman and St Mary's rivers, the Cree were soundly defeated, losing between two hundred and three hundred men. This battle was the last major Indian military confrontation on the plains. In the autumn of 1871 the Cree and Blackfoot concluded a formal treaty which continued unbroken, and the Cree were allowed to hunt what buffalo remained in Blackfoot territory.[92]

Invasion of Blackfoot territory was not the sole expedient open to the Cree. They also approached the problem of the growing scarcity of buffalo by attempting to exclude intruders from the hunt. At a Cree council in the Qu'Appelle in 1859, all the speakers objected strongly to the fact that the Métis were hunting in the plains country in winter.[93] All "strangers," they stated, should be required to purchase dried meat, or pemmican, and should not be allowed to hunt for themselves. In the 1870s the Cree explored the alternative of approaching the Canadian government to exact a promise to limit the hunt to Indians. The Cree and Assiniboine who congregated in the Cypress Hills into the 1880s, led by Piapot, Big Bear, Little Pine, and Foremost Man, continued to demand exclusive hunting privileges.[94] At a Cree council in the Qu'Appelle in 1876, each chief and councillor separately made the same request to the Indian agent that something be done to prevent the extermination of the buffalo.[95] In all the agent's previous relations with the Indians, he had never seen such a course adopted. He believed it demonstrated their alarm at the decline in their means of subsistence and the grave importance they attached to the issue.

INDIANS AS AGRICULTURALISTS

By the 1870s it had become clear to the Indians of the plains that economic conditions were once again changing and yet another adjustment was required. Anxious about a food supply for themselves and their children, many were willing to explore the possibilities of agriculture. Such an avenue did not constitute a complete, radical departure from their heritage, customs, knowledge, technology, and disposition, as many Victorian observers believed. Explorers, frontiersmen, missionaries, and other visitors to North America often failed to give much notice to the importance and extent of Indian agriculture, or they dismissed it as a form of gardening. Indian agriculture long predated the arrival of Europeans on the continent. The American Indian excelled in the art of plant domestication, profoundly modifying and moulding wild species to meet human needs. Northern Europeans, who borrowed all their domesticated plants, did not appreciate the skill and time involved in the process and did not place a high premium on this accomplishment.[96] As one historian has suggested, Europeans intent on settlement may have felt compelled to view the way of life of the "savage" as incompatible with agriculture. "Their belief in the virtues of agrarian life and the savage state of the native population was paramount. Firm in the notion that they were the vanguard civilization, to acknowledge that Indians could be farmers too required admissions that few were willing to make. Hunting and savagery were synonymous in the frontier mind and no one doubted the savagery of the Indians."[97]

Before European contact, agricultural products accounted for about 75 per cent of the food consumed by North American Indians.[98] The most intensive cultivation was in Meso-America where a large population was sustained. Indian corn, or maize, was the most important of the crops in the New World, but beans and squash were almost as common and a large variety of grains, fruits, legumes, roots, stimulants, and fibres were also cultivated. Agricultural operations were conducted entirely with hand implements. The digging stick, the basic agricultural implement, was used most frequently for planting and for lifting and turning the soil. Grass, brush, and trees were cleared mostly by burning. The northern Missouri River tribes manufactured rakes from wood to handle brush when clearing land. Hoes with animal-bone blades were used on the prairies. Certain fundamental characteristics of Indian agriculture reflected the exclusive use of hand implements, in particular, the practice of mixed cropping and of caring for individual plants.[99] The "hill" methods of planting was widespread and weeding was thorough. In the areas most intensively farmed, men did most of the work, but where agricultural produce was a secondary source of subsistence, women did the most, although men helped to clear and harvest.[100]

The Cree were acquainted with cultivated plant food and techniques of agriculture through several of their contacts. They had been in touch indirectly with the trading empire of the Hurons of the Lake Simcoe and Georgian Bay area. That network extended for hundreds of miles into the interior. Huron trading partners included the Algonkian of Lake Nipissing, who travelled farther north to trade Huron corn and tobacco for the furs and dried meat of the Cree and more distant tribes.[101] To the south, the Mandan, Arikara, and Hidatsa Indians maintained a flourishing agricultural economy on the upper Missouri. The Cree had ample opportunity to view the techniques and technology of the corn, bean, squash, pumpkin, sunflower, and tobacco culture of the Mandan and Hidatsa, developed over seven centuries on the northern plains.[102]

Agriculture was a far more ancient and indigenous tradition on the plains than the horse culture, which has come to be regarded as typical of the Indians there. The Mandan and Hidatsa kept gardens, not on the dry, hard ground of the prairie, but on the bottomlands by rivers where the soil was softer and easier to work. After the long grass was cut and burned, the ground was broken with hoes and digging sticks. The blade of the hoe was made from the shoulder of the buffalo until this tool was replaced by the iron "scapula" hoe in the early nineteenth century. Clearing and breaking were laborious tasks that continued all summer. Fields were not owned in common but by each family; boundary marks were set at the corners. Techniques suited to the climate of the northern plains developed over the centuries. One of the nine corn varieties, Flint, required only sixty days to mature, withstood winds, and resisted hail and frost. Fields were planted three years in succession and were then allowed to lie fallow for two years. Corn was planted in hills that were wide apart, which brought higher yields in a climate with little rain. Each year enough seed corn was kept to last two years, as crops were poor some years and did not yield quality seed or were sometimes destroyed entirely by frost. The farmers knew when to seed corn by observing wild gooseberry bushes, the first plant to leaf in the spring; when they were almost in full leaf, it was time for seeding.

The agriculturalists of the upper Missouri are generally regarded as being the most northerly of Indian farmers. Recent archaeological research, however, has presented firm evidence of prehistoric agriculture in western Canada.[103] On the east bank of the Red River near the town of Lockport, Manitoba, gardening hoes made from the shoulder blades of bison, grinding stones for milling seeds into flour, and kernels of corn were excavated at levels dating to the fourteenth century AD. Bell-shaped underground pits for the storage of the harvest were also located. Pottery found within the storage pits was decorated in a style distinctive to the corn farmers of the Dakotas and Minnesota. It is believed that women from the southern farming cultures married into the northern bands and introduced agriculture to the Red River Valley.[104] This phase of agriculture was apparently short-lived. Around AD 1500, a cold trend shortened the growing season and this phase of cultivation ended.

There may have been other such villages in western Canada. Excavations in southwestern Manitoba of a site overlooking Gainsborough Creek suggest sedentary settlement, as evidence of earthen structures, hearths, and storage pits has been found.[105] A fortified earthlodge village at Blackfoot Crossing on the Bow River in Alberta, known as the Cluny site, has been dated to sometime between 1730 and 1750. The occupants, who stayed only briefly, planted corn along the river.[106] The earliest historical evidence of Indian cultivation is provided by Hudson's Bay Company trader Matthew Cocking. In western Saskatchewan in 1772 he found an Indian "Tobacco plantation. A small plot of ground about an hundred yards long and five wide."[107] It is believed that as better quality tobacco became available through European traders, the cultivation of this plant discontinued.

A phase of Indian agriculture in western Canada also took place after the European presence. Although it was to some extent influenced by the Europeans, it remained essentially Indian in character.[108] An early centre of Indian agricultural activity was at Netley Creek, just above Lake Winnipeg. Here a small group of Ottawa Indians, who had migrated from the Michilimackinac area in the late eighteenth century, cultivated corn and potatoes from at least 1805. In the early decades of the nineteenth century, Indian agricultural activity was noted at sites on the Red River, on the Assiniboine River between Brandon House and Portage la Prairie, and on the shores of Lake Manitoba. Indian agriculture also expanded into the lake country to the east, at Roseau River and Lake of the Woods. On sites on a number of islands and along the shore of Lake of the Woods, potatoes, corn, pumpkins, onions, and carrots were reported to be growing. Sites near large bodies of water were found to be advantageous because the moderating effects of the water extended the growing season.

It is believed that the Ottawas played a critical role in disseminating agriculture among the Saulteaux, who migrated to the Manitoba lowlands in the late eighteenth century.[109] According to John Tanner, an Indian "captive" in western Canada in the early nineteenth century, it was "Sha-gwaw-koo-sink, an Ottawa, a friend of mine and an old man, [who] first introduced the cultivation of corn among the Ojibeways [sic] of the Red River country."[110] When the Ottawas left Netley Creek in 1811 or 1812, the Saulteaux continued to grow corn and potatoes on the site. About 1819 D.W. Harmon, fur trader with the North West Company, noted that the "Saulteaux were becoming agriculturists."[111]

In nineteenth-century Manitoba before the treaties of the 1870s, Indian participation in gardening and farming was not uncommon. Even where the climate and soil quality were prohibitive, such as at Norway House and Grand Rapids, the Indians kept gardens.[112] At Fort Alexander on the Winnipeg River, the Indians cultivated wheat, potatoes, and corn.[113] At the Indian settlement of Fairford on Lake Winnipeg, a stopping place for Hudson's Bay Company brigades, quantities of produce were raised that helped support the fur trade.[114] The Indian settlers of St Peter's Parish on the Red River farmed to such a large extent that in 1875 it was reported that they had two thousand acres under cultivation.[115] Yellow Quill's band grew potatoes and corn along the valley of the Assiniboine at a place traditionally known as the Indian Gardens, which had been cultivated by themselves and their forefathers for a great number of years. Chief Nanawanan and members of the Roseau River band kept large gardens, which were cultivated long before treaty was made with them.[116] In the early 1870s the Dakota Indians planted gardens and small grain crops, such as oats and barley, along the Assiniboine.[117]

Indians also worked as hired hands on the farms of settlers in Manitoba. In 1871 W.M. Simpson, Indian commissioner, reported that "where labour is scarce, Indians give great assistance in gathering in the crops. At Portage la Prairie, both Chippewas and Sioux, were largely employed in the grain field, and in other parishes I saw many farmers whose employees were nearly all Indian."[118] In 1875 J.A.N. Provencher, Indian commissioner at Winnipeg, observed that the Indians of Manitoba had become "sufficiently familiar with the elements of industry and agriculture," and therefore the government was not obligated to provide instruction or aid in farming beyond the distribution of implements, tools, and cattle.[119]

Some Indian agriculture was encouraged by missionary activity. Archdeacon Cochran of the Church Missionary Society was instrumental in organizing the Indian agricultural settlement at St Peter's in the 1830s. In the late 1850s Cochran established a second Indian mission at Portage la Prairie and some 120 people took advantage of this opportunity.[120] Father G.A. Belcourt founded an agricultural settlement of Indians and Métis at Baie St Paul on the Assiniboine River in the early 1830s. Indian efforts at mission agriculture are generally depicted as meagre and in the long run unsuccessful.[121]

Until after 1870, however, few residents of the North-West farmed extensively. In the predominantly "mixed-blood" parish of St Andrew's, for example, a flexible economic strategy of small-scale agriculture combined with hunting, fishing, gathering, and wage labour was maintained.[122] This mixed economic base was well adapted to the North-West's limited markets, climate, and available technology. This was a more successful economy than that of the Selkirk settlers, based entirely upon agriculture, which proved fragile and easily undermined.

At the same time, for very few was the farm an exclusive object of industry and attention. When H.Y. Hind, a Toronto geology professor and leader of the Red River exploring expedition, visited Red River in the late 1850s, he commented that with the few exceptions farming operations were conducted in a slovenly manner.[123] Fields appeared altogether abandoned as weeds abounded. Valuable manure was piled in front of stables or was thrown in the river. In Hind's opinion the negligence and imprudence that characterized farm operations at Red River were mainly owing to the absence of a market. A Mr Gowler, for example, who farmed fifty acres on the Assiniboine a few miles from the forks of the Red and Assiniboine, could have put in crops on more land that he owned, but there was no market for any surplus produce. Acreages were kept small for other reasons as well. Implements were primitive and few at Red River. There a field of five acres was considered large. Until the introduction of barbed wire in the 1880s, the fencing of large fields was considered too expensive. Also, before 1869 no one farmed away from the rivers because the belief that water could be secured by digging wells was not popularly accepted.[124] Indian efforts at agriculture in the period before treaties in Manitoba would have compared favourably with the farming activities of most other residents.

Several generations of Indians west of Red River had the opportunity to observe and even participate in agricultural activity by the time of the treaties. The farms at fur posts served as models and sources of inspiration. At Fort Carlton on the North Saskatchewan River, abundant crops of barley and potatoes were raised, and wheat and hops met with some success.[125] Barley and potatoes were grown at Edmonton House and Fort Vermilion. Domestic cattle were also introduced at Hudson's Bay Company posts. A garden was kept at Brandon House from 1795.[126] At first the crops were limited to potatoes, turnips, and Indian corn, the latter fed to the horses. In the spring of 1804 the vegetable crop was more varied: onions, beans, peas, carrots, pumpkins, melons, cucumbers, and thyme were planted. Wheat, oats, and barley were cultivated in 1816. Later the Hudson's Bay Company kept gardens and grew small grain crops at Fort Ellice, Fort Pelly (north of present-day Yorkton), and Fort Qu'Appelle. Indians were hired to tend the crops, to hay, and to look after the horses and other stock.[127]

These farms were hardly "model" in the sense of being exemplary, but observers of these early experiments gained some knowledge of the difficulty of farming in the as-yet unchartered conditions of the North-West. Crops were often damaged by frost and scourged by squirrels, gophers, and dogs. Grasshopper plagues occurred almost annually, often totally destroying everything but the potato crop.[128] In the early years of the nineteenth century, the crops at Brandon House in particular suffered this fate. Like an approaching storm or prairie fire, grasshoppers appeared on the horizon, reducing fields to blackened ruins within the space of a few hours and robbing the trees of their leaves. From his experiences at Fort Qu'Appelle in the 1860s, Hudson's Bay Company employee Walter Traill despaired that "farming here is all a delusion." During one plague, he reported, grasshoppers lay three inches deep inside the stockade of the fort. Traill continued:

To prevent them from filling the Fort I had to keep half the men in double shifts carting them out in order to live. The ducks and prairie chickens ate grasshoppers until they were unfit for us to eat. Even the eggs tasted of them. The train dogs got fat and the cattle became poor for lack of grass. The whole valley looked like a burned-over prairie. They came in clouds like smoke and for twelve days the air was alive with them as high as one could see. They darkened the sun and lay an inch thick on the ground. The lakes and rivers stink with the dead ones.[129]

The grasshopper plagues of the nineteenth century may account for why the Plains Cree abandoned their early efforts at agriculture. From his post at Fort Union on the Missouri River from 1833 to 1856, fur trader Edwin T. Denig was acquainted with a band of Cree Indians, the Pis cha kaw a kis, or Magpies.[130] They were settled at what he called the "Tinder Mountains," and they "lived in log cabins covered with earth and raised considerable quantities of maize and potatoes."[131] The Tinder Mountains were likely the Touchwood Hills of present-day Saskatchewan, which were known to the Métis as Les Montagnes des Tondre, the latter word being a mispronunciation of the English *tinder*.[132] (Touchwood, a fungus which swells on trees, was used as a tinder, as it catches fire readily.) Denig was convinced from the agricultural successes of this settlement and those at Red River and Pembina that the soil of the territory claimed by the Cree was of excellent quality.[133] The agricultural settlement in the Touchwood Hills, however, dispersed. When Rev. Joseph Reader of the Church Missionary Society arrived there in 1875 he found only two or three families resident. He believed that a few years earlier a fair-sized settlement of Indians and mixed-bloods had lived in houses and cultivated the soil but that grasshoppers had compelled most of them to seek refuge elsewhere. Many of their houses had since been burnt by "ill-disposed persons," but the scattered former residents remained "willing and desirous to farm."[134]

According to Reader, a catechist named Charles Pratt had been responsible for this early agricultural settlement in the Touchwood Hills. Explorer Capt. John Palliser had met Pratt in 1857 at Pratt's house on the Qu'Appelle River, which was surrounded by "an excellent garden, in which he rears among other things hops and Indian corn." Palliser reported Pratt's conversation that the Cree were "beginning to apprehend scarcity of buffalo, and many are most anxious to try agriculture. He thinks that if they had agricultural implements, such as spades, hoes, and ploughs, they certainly would commence operations. This opinion I found pretty general among the people of the Hudson's Bay Company." James McKay, postmaster in charge of Fort Ellice, told Dr Hector, a member of this exploring expedition, that "the Indians here are very anxious to farm – & bother him every spring for implements & seed." The Stoney Indians further west also were, according to Hector, "very desirous of having tools and a few simple agricultural implements."[135]

A number of bands in parts of what became the Treaty Four district in southwestern Manitoba and southeastern Saskatchewan had been engaged in some form of agriculture or stock-raising prior to the treaty of 1874. These were predominantly Saulteaux bands, which included among their numbers mixed-bloods of Indian-French and Indian-English descent. In the early nineteenth century, the westernmost branches of the Saulteaux had followed the Cree west and south, but, unlike the Cree, most did not fully become plains dwellers. Although they rode out on long hunts into the grasslands, they were not solely dependent on the buffalo for subsistence. The movement west continued until at the time of the treaty their territory was on the western margin of the transitional zone between the plain and the parkland belt. The journals of Fort Ellice, the Hudson's Bay Company post at the junction of the Assiniboine and Qu'Appelle rivers, attest to this westward movement. In the 1820s the Saulteaux only occasionally went to Fort Ellice, but the number of visits gradually increased to the extent that for the last thirty years of the life of the post, until the early 1880s, the Saulteaux supplied most of the furs.[136] That Saulteaux also provided much of the casual labour at company posts in western Manitoba and eastern Saskatchewan also gives evidence of their westward migration.

Chief Pasquah's band of fifty families of Saulteaux and mixed-bloods raised crops of potatoes, turnips, and carrots, had a small herd of cattle, and houses at Leech Lake, just south of present-day Yorkton.[137] Little Bones' band, a predominantly mixed-blood band of Saulteaux, many of whom were employed regularly at Fort Ellice by contract or as casual labour, also had houses and gardens at Leech Lake.[138] In 1883 Little Bones showed a government surveyor a plough, purchased from a Métis at Fort Qu'Appelle and dated 1861, they had been using for thirteen or more years. They also had a byre "wherein they kept their cattle in olden times."[139] Seven Saulteaux families known as the Fort Ellice band had houses and cultivated land on the north side of the Qu'Appelle River at Round Lake.[140] Yellow Quill's Saulteaux band at Egg Lake, a small outpost of the Swan River district north of Quill Lake, had houses at Fishing Lake where they raised root crops and kept horned cattle and horses. Gabriel Coté, or Mimiy, the "Pigeon," chief of a band of Saulteaux and English mixed-bloods associated with Fort Pelly, had houses and cattle and farmed on a small scale near Swan River.[141] The bands of the Key and Kishikonse just to the north of the Coté band cultivated potatoes and other root crops and had herds of cattle and horses. In 1875 Kishikonse's band of thirty-six families had ninety-seven head of cattle and fifty-seven horses.[142]

The need to diversify their economy likely accounts for the tendency of these Saulteaux bands to turn to agriculture. The rapid decline of the buffalo in their region forced them to turn to other game animals and to explore other alternatives. Company journals from the Swan River district suggest that a serious shortage of food existed by mid-century as game resources were depleted. Before this time many of the bands had trapped furs in the autumn and early winter in the woodlands and hunted buffalo in mid-winter in the adjacent parklands.[143] As the herds scattered and withdrew south, the Saulteaux bands would have been forced to abandon their woodland-trapping region entirely in winter to travel to the buffalo ranges. They could not continue to both trap furs and rely on the buffalo as a source of food. Beset with serious food shortages, they either had to migrate permanently to pursue the buffalo or to obtain an alternative food supply. Most of the Saulteaux remained in their woodland-parkland environment, responding in part to seasonal and local food shortages through their gardens and cattle. Their crops, which were predominantly roots, formed an important winter food supply. Their initial source of seed and cattle was quite likely the Hudson's Bay Company posts. Their close association with this company, and their experience as farm labour there, undoubtedly encouraged and enhanced their agricultural efforts.

THE DOWNSTREAM PEOPLE

Plains Cree bands in the district covered by Treaty Four, concluded in 1874, are the focus of this study. They lived west of the Saulteaux of the parkland and included Saulteaux, Assiniboine, and mixed-bloods among their number. At the time of the treaty, these bands subsisted almost entirely on the buffalo. They settled on reserves in the Touchwood Hills, in the File Hills, along the Qu'Appelle River at the Crooked Lakes, and east of Fort Qu'Appelle. Collectively they were known as *mamihkiyiniwak*, the Downstream People, as opposed to the Cree to the north of the South Saskatchewan and the Qu'Appelle, known as the Upstream People.[144] The Downstream People consisted of four main groups. The *pusakawatciwiyiniwak*, or the Touchwood Hills People, hunted between Long Lake and the Touchwood Hills. The *katepwewcipi*, or the Calling River or Qu'Appelle People, hunted from the Crooked Lakes west to the Cypress Hills and north to the Big Sand Hills.[145] The most easterly of these bands wintered around the Qu'Appelle Lakes and in the File Hills. They tended to stay farther east in their hunt, along the Qu'Appelle River as far as the elbow of the Saskatchewan, although they attended large encampments in the Big Sand Hills. By the 1870s a western group of the Calling River People spent most of their time far out on the plains toward the Cypress Hills and along the south branch of the Saskatchewan. They wintered on the Coteau near Old Wives Lake and, in the early 1870s, along Swiftcurrent Creek and near the Cypress Hills. A mixed Cree-Assiniboine group, known as *nehiopwat*, the Young Dogs or Little Dogs, ventured the deepest into the far plains.[146] The Cree also referred to them as *paskwawiyiniwak*, or the Prairie People, indicating their remoteness from the parkland. Quite likely they were in the vanguard of the Cree migration into buffalo territory. Of all the Downstream People they appear to have participated the least in trade with the Hudson's Bay Company. The last group, the *wapucwayanak*, or Rabbit Skin People, hunted between the Qu'Appelle and Assiniboine rivers in wooded country. Rabbit Skin People belonged to the "brotherhood of the Rabbit" and observed exogamous rules across tribal lines, so that a Cree boy of the Bear gens could not marry a Saulteaux girl of the same gens.[147] Totem animals, which included Bear, Duck, Eagle, Crane, Thunderbird, and Rattlesnake, were inherited through the father, but children could not marry into their mother's totem either. The Rabbit Skin line of chiefs were members of the Rattlesnake totem.

Cawacatoose, also known as the Poor Man, the Lean Man, or Le Maigre, was chief of what is believed to have been the main portion of the Touchwood Hills People at treaty time. In 1876 the band consisted of thirty-nine Cree families.[148] The Hudson's Bay Company recognized Poor Man as the head chief of the Touchwood Hills People.[149] Poor Man was noted as a brave warrior who had gone to battle armed only with a lance made of a saskatoon shoot topped with an iron head. He had once stolen two women from the Blackfoot, an accomplishment for which he was highly regarded.[150] His brother Kanocees was also respected for his skill and courage. At a battle on the Belly River between the Blackfoot and Cree in 1871, Kanocees was credited with saving the defeated Cree from the same fate as the 135 who died, which included 20 from the Touchwood Hills.[151] This band settled on a reserve in the Big Touchwood Hills.

In the 1870s Kaneonuskatew, One That Walks on Four Claws, or George Gordon, was chief of the most mixed of the predominantly Cree bands. His band consisted of forty-seven families of Plains Cree, Swampy Cree, Saulteaux, Scottish mixed-blood, and Métis origin.[152] The chief was well regarded by the Hudson's Bay Company as, among other things, a first-rate guide, and was responsible for leading cart brigades from the plains back to company posts.[153] Gordon's father, Pipe Stem, had been chief before him, and his grandfather, Wing, also chief, was from the Crow tribe.[154] This band had settled in several houses and had farmed on a limited scale in the Little Touchwood Hills before the treaty.[155]

Twenty-five Plains Cree families formed a band under Kisecawchuck, or Day Star, who had come from the north. His father, who had traded at Fort Edmonton, was of the Savannah People, or Swampy Cree.[156] It is believed that the time of the treaty this band had only recently formed a distinct group apart from the main body of the Touchwood Hills People.[157] Moving westward in their hunt to the area of the South Saskatchewan, the band was closely associated with Ready Bow's band of the Qu'Appelle People. Day Star, Ready Bow, and Little Black Bear were reputed to have led 900 lodges of Cree and Saulteaux in successfully repelling a Blackfoot attack in 1866 at Red Ochre Hill, near Swift Current.[158] While only 15 Cree fell in this battle, 300 Blackfoot were killed. This band settled on a reserve in the Big Touchwood Hills.

Muscowequan, or Hard Quill, led a band of forty-six Saulteaux and mixed-blood families which eventually settled in the Touchwood Hills. Muscowequan's father, Kakenawup, was chief at the time of Treaty Four but died shortly afterward. Before the treaty some members of this band had maintained gardens along the Qu'Appelle Valley.[159]

The main portion of the Calling River People settled on reserves at the Crooked Lakes. At the time of the treaty, Kakeesheway, or Loud Voice, led fifty-five Plains Cree families.[160] His father, Short Legs, had been a chief before him.[161] These were the most easterly of the Calling River People, hunting along the Qu'Appelle River as far west as the elbow of the Saskatchewan. In 1876 Loud Voice, then about eighty years old, was described as having "always been the acknowledged chief of the Qu'Appelle Cree tribe and is yet the principal leader although now an old man. All the other Cree chiefs give way to his decision and in many instances demand council from him before acting."[162] As spokesman for the Cree at the treaty negotiations, Loud Voice must have been respected for his ability to deal with white people. He was recognized by the Hudson's Bay Company as the head chief of the Qu'Appelle Cree and regarded as a man "always for the causes of peace and good will."[163] Loud Voice was also a distinguished medicine man and was noted for his bravery and sound judgment in battle.[164] As his name denotes, the chief had a distinctive voice, which he used to full effect. According to a Hudson's Bay Company man, "you could hear him from a long distance, quite distinctly in the early mornings calling up his tribe from their slumbers, and the echo was often heard, when he raised his voice in measured tones, in the Qu'Appelle valley."[165] He died in 1884 and was succeeded as chief by his son Ochapowace, whose name was given to the reserve. Chief Chacachase's band, numbering 110 in the mid-1870s, was connected with the eastern division of the Qu'Appelle People and eventually settled with Loud Voice's on the reserve at Crooked Lakes.[166]

Kahkewistahaw, or He Who Flies Around, had a large following of some sixty-three families at the time of the treaty.[167] The band was primarily Rabbit Skin Cree with some Saulteaux members. The chief was a son of the celebrated Plains Cree leader Le Sonnant, who had signed the Selkirk Treaty in 1817, and an older brother of the Fox, a head chief of the Cree at mid-century and a distinguished hunter, scout, warrior, and linguist. This band hunted farther west than the rest of the Qu'Appelle People and approached the Cypress Hills in the 1870s. This chief and his followers did not rate highly with the Hudson's Bay Company, which indicates that they were likely not markedly affected by the trade.[168] Sakimay, a prominent

Saulteaux, followed Kahkewistahaw at the time of the treaty, and his group also settled at Crooked Lakes.

Chief Cowessess, or Little Child, was a Saulteaux who led a mixed band of Plains Cree and Saulteaux.[169] In the mid-1870s this band hunted on the plains as far west as the Cypress Hills. Louis O'Soup, a prominent Saulteaux spokesman, was a member of this band.

Chief Pasquah's band of fifty families came to occupy a reserve on the Qu'Appelle River about five miles west of Fort Qu'Appelle. Pasquah, or The Plain, was a son of the Fox, the Rabbit Skin Cree chief, although Pasquah's followers were predominantly Saulteaux.[170] Before the treaty this band had resided at Leech Lake where they had had houses, gardens, and cattle. Muscowpetung's predominantly Saulteaux band settled on a reserve west of Pasquah's.

The main body of Young Dogs, or mixed Cree and Assiniboine, followed Chief Piapot at the time of the treaty. Piapot's band was estimated to be over one thousand in the late 1870s.[171] It is believed that he had influence over the Assiniboine, the Qu'Appelle Cree, and the more southerly Upstream People when they were camped in the southern plains. This band hunted west to the Cypress Hills, north as far as the South Saskatchewan River, and south to the Missouri River, and wintered at Wood Mountain or in the eastern Cypress Hills. Piapot was regarded by the Hudson's Bay Company as ambitious and troublesome, but honourable.[172] The reserve for this band was later established west of Muscowpetung's.

Among the people who settled at the File Hills were the followers of Keeskee hew mus coo musqus, or Little Black Bear. This band consisted of Assiniboine, Saulteaux, Young Dogs, Dakota, and Calling River Cree. The band was split up at the time of the treaty, and some settled with the Assiniboine chief The Man Who Took the Coat on a reserve near Sintaluta.[173] Little Black Bear was a noted warrior, having been one of the Cree leaders at Red Ochre Hill in 1866.

Wahpemoosetoosis, or White Calf, led a band that had taken up residence at the File Hills when it was under the leadership of Ahchacoosacootacoopits, or Star Blanket.[174] This band was not large, numbering seventeen Cree families in the mid-1870s.[175] Associated with the Calling River People who followed Loud Voice, the band hunted from the File Hills region to Wood Mountain and the Cypress Hills. Twenty-eight Rabbit Skin Cree families followed Okanese, or Rose Berry, also a son of the Fox, and they eventually settled on a reserve at the File Hills. The band under Cau ah ha chapew, or Ready Bow, was reported to comprise twenty-six families at the time of the treaty.[176] Descendants of the band claim that they were originally Assiniboine but intermarried with the Cree to the extent that they attached themselves to the Qu'Appelle People, although they hunted with some of the Touchwood Hills People.[177] This chief's son Peepeekisis, or Little Hawk, succeeded to the band leadership, and the reserve at the File Hill bears his name.

In the 1870s many of these Indians of Treaty Four appeared willing to explore agriculture as an alternative to the hunt. They were keenly aware well before the food crisis that began in 1878–79 that the buffalo could no longer sustain them. Missionaries in the Touchwood Hills, for example, reported appalling conditions of poverty and near-starvation in the early and mid-1870s.[178]

Agriculture appeared to hold out the hope of a steady supply of food. Indians of the plains were acquainted with agriculture and its products, and some had begun to supplement the hunt with small crops and cattle even before the 1870s. In many ways their training made them better suited to farming than new arrivals to the West. Although the Plains Indians lacked formal education in agriculture, their highly specialized empirical knowledge of nature approached a science. They were aware of the vegetation in their environment, and they knew when and how to harvest it. They were much better informed on rainfall and frost patterns, on the availability of water, and on soil varieties than the settlers from the East and overseas who were to follow. Having horses, they knew about the care of domestic animals and about summer pasturage and winter forage requirements. Even the most experienced of Ontario farmers, who did not always succeed on the prairies, might well have benefited from the training Indians had to offer.

Yet the Indians needed assistance to farm. They required implements, seed, and oxen, as well as interim provisions while they settled and developed a piece of land. The Indians could also profit immensely from a practical program of instruction in agriculture. These were among the demands that Plains Indians brought to the bargaining table when the treaties were negotiated. Because Victorian Canadians saw farming as the key to the permanent solution to the "Indian problem," conditions appeared favourable to a meeting of mutual interests. The Canadian government, however, showed little determination to see agriculture established on the reserves. That the Indians might become agriculturalists provided justification for limiting the Indians' land base and isolating them on reserves. Once these goals were accomplished, the Indians were largely left on their own. The image of the Indian way of life as the antithesis of an agricultural way of life persisted and was often drawn upon as an explanation for the failure of farming to provide an adequate economic base for the Plains Indians.

CHAPTER TWO

The "Queen's Bounty": Government Response to Indian Agitation for Agricultural Assistance

The 1870s are generally described as a time during which prairie Indians, clinging desperately and stubbornly to the "old ways," preferred to roam the plains aimlessly in search of buffalo and only reluctantly settled on reserves after much cajoling by the government.[1] Once on their reserves, according to this interpretation, Indians proved indifferent, apathetic, even hostile toward government efforts to teach them to farm. But from the beginning it was the Indians that showed the greater willingness and inclination to farm and the government that displayed little serious intent to see agriculture established on the reserves.

INDIAN POLICY TO 1874

Indian affairs on the prairies were administered from Ottawa by the Indian branch of the Department of the Interior, which was created in 1873. The minister of the interior was also superintendent general of Indian affairs. The branch was elevated to the status of a department in 1880, but it remained under the direction of the minister of the interior, who continued as superintendent general. This officeholder, however, rarely devoted much attention to the affairs of Indians, as they represented an insignificant and powerless constituency. The most influential of the Ottawa bureaucrats was the deputy superintendent general.

Lawrence Vankoughnet was appointed to that position in 1874, and there he remained for nearly twenty years.[2] He was from a Loyalist family long acquainted with John A. Macdonald, whose son, Hugh John, married a Vankoughnet. Family and political connections led to Vankoughnet's appointment with the branch, for he knew nothing about Indians. The deputy superintendent general has been described as a conscientious, earnest, model Victorian civil servant, although his "personal inflexibility, his attitude of administration 'by the book' left too little room for common humanity."³ Vankoughnet centralized decision-making in his own hands, as did subsequent holders of the office. He showed little confidence in the ability or advice of men-on-the-spot in the "outside" service and allowed them few powers. His administration was not responsive to local needs, and because he insisted on reading everything himself and on saving money by seldom using the telegraph, it was slow and inefficient.

Indian policy for the North-West was never the result of long-term planning, of adopting and deliberatly carrying out a predetermined, settled course. In a study of the policy-making process in British colonial administration of the mid-nineteenth century, historian John Cell regarded policy while it was being implemented as something in flux, as a "perpetual adjustment between ends and means." Very often a firm direction was absent. Policy in the sense of a deliberate, consistent series of decisions was rare. "At any given moment there is not so much policy as policy formation, an unsettled and changing set of responses by government to the continual interaction among men, forces, ideas and institutions."⁴ Only with hindsight might these responses take on the appearance of a settled course purposefully carried out. Much the same might be said of Indian policy for the North-West. With hindsight it might appear, for example, that the government pursued the long-term goal of encouraging the Indians to take up agriculture. In the years immediately after the treaties, however, the government did not function to this end but proceeded in an ad hoc, tentative manner.

What did prescribe the responses of the government was a prevailing ideology, a set of shared attitudes and assumptions about Indians that might be called the "official mind" of the bureaucracy, often evident much more at the centre than at the periphery. The department's clients were seen as chronic complainers. Their grievances and demands were dismissed as being without substance or credence. Indians were viewed as "beggars," hoping always to defraud the government and make gains without having to work for them. They were regarded as gullible, susceptible to the influence of usually unnamed, nefarious "outsiders." Pragmatic convenience, expediency, economy, and the need to keep order dictated Indian policy.

The question of what policy should guide Canada in its relations with the Indians of the North-West appears not to have been a matter of wide discussion by the public or in the press. Some interested parties did place recommendations before government officials from time to time, and outside advice was occasionally sought by the government. Rarely, however, were these parties well acquainted with Indians or conditions in the North-West. The Indians themselves were not consulted. Foremost in the minds of those concerned with Indian affairs in the early 1870s was the establishment of law and order. Alarming reports of unchecked crime, anarchy, and disorder were received from residents and observers in western Canada. American traders who offered whisky to the Indians in exchange for buffalo hides or ponies were seen as the cause of the pandemonium. It was believed that the future of the region depended on the swift enforcement of the law.[5] The Minnesota uprising of 1862, an outbreak of violence against white settlers caused by Dakota dissatisfaction with their treaty, was vivid in the memories of commentators, and there was widespread anxiety that there was potential for a similar disaster in Canada's West. Promoters of the North-West Mounted Police, organized in 1873, were generally concerned less with the future of the Indians than with the security of the lives and property of prospective settlers.[6]

Some observers, however, sensed that a prevailing spirit of unease and discontent among the Indians of the North-West was caused, not by the liquor traffic, but by an anxiety about a future supply of food. By the early 1870s Ottawa officials had been repeatedly warned by missionaries, explorers, and government officials in the field that the buffalo was an endangered species and were being urged to adopt protective measures quickly. Recommendations were made to limit the hunt to Indians only, to prohibit the export of buffalo hides and pemmican, to prevent the slaughter of buffalo by pounds, and to regulate the hunt so that each hunter procured annually only what he required for himself and family.[7] Since it was recognized that these measures would only temporarily alleviate the problem, however, other schemes and options were proposed to government officials.

E.H. Meredith, deputy minister of the new Department of the Interior in 1873, was, among other things, responsible for drawing up memos on Indian affairs in the West. Like most of his generation of Ottawa civil servants, Meredith had never visited the West and had no knowledge of or acquaintance with Indian people.[8] Meredith sought the advice of Alfred Selwyn, director of the Geological Survey of Canada, on the question of the future of the western Indians. Selwyn, whose expertise was gained through one trip from Manitoba to the Rocky Mountains in 1873, suggested that a hardy race of domestic cattle be introduced in areas in which the buffalo were already absent. Because the Indians cared well for the horses they raised, there was every possibility, in Selwyn's view, that they could become a "contented pastoral people, the change being the natural gradation from the hunter to the agriculturist." Selwyn believed that to continue the policy of treaties involving annual payments was a mistake. On the basis of his experience, Indians squandered any money they had and so were reduced to being permanent paupers instead of learning to become industrious and self-reliant. Selwyn recommended that in place of a cash annuity, the Indians be given credit at stores to be drawn upon only in cases of dire necessity. He also suggested that an efficient border police could be raised among the Plains tribes to help stop illicit trading and enforce measures which might be adopted for the preservation of the buffalo.[9]

Meredith was impressed with Selwyn's ideas. His proposal for food provision in the North-West incorporated many of Selwyn's recommendations, including the one that cattle be introduced in an effort to make the Indians a pastoral people before they attempted agriculture. To prevent the Indian from becoming a "permanent state pauper," Meredith proposed that they work on the railways and survey crews and that they serve as guides and constables in the military and police.[10]

Charles N. Bell, a young man also with the Geological Survey, provided government officials with a number of suggestions about the Indians of the West. His central idea was that what game remained in the territory should be kept exclusively for the Indians so that they would not starve while they learned to farm. Anticipating that the Indians would object to settling on reserves, he proposed that the selection of final sites be delayed until they were reconciled to the idea. In the meantime each tribe could be confined to its own territory in "large temporary reservations," which encompassed its hunting grounds, until the game disappeared. Troops would have to be stationed at the borders of these reserves to hold the Indians "in check" and to prevent encroachment by settlers, hunters, and miners. Such encounters, Bell believed, could lead to warfare in which the Plains Indians would "fight it out to the last."[11]

Other policy suggestions for the Indians of the North-West came from John Christian Schultz, trader, surgeon, and prominent member of the "Canadian party" at Red River that agitated for union with Canada. In 1873 Schultz stated in the House of Commons that the annuities paid to the Indians of Treaties One and Two were inadequate in meeting even their most essential needs. Estimating that those Indians ceded an average of forty square miles a person in exchange for only three dollars a person, he urged that subsequent treaties be more liberal. Instead of a perpetual paltry annuity, the Indians should receive a larger sum annually for a stipulated period of perhaps, twenty-one years. Reserves should also be larger – 160 acres for each individual rather than for each family as provided in Treaties One and Two – and should be located far from centres of white population. Schultz recommended as well that a fund for the Indians be created from the sale of one section from each township of Dominion Lands, just as two sections in each were set apart as an endowment for education.[12]

THE WESTERN TREATIES

The government disregarded the advice not only of Schultz but also of those who advocated that the unique needs and characteristics of the people of the North-West be taken into consideration in devising policy. Instead, the government relied on the policies and approaches that had been pursued in the East, those that were conveniently at hand, in concluding seven numbered treaties in the West between 1871 and 1877. Like the treaties with the Indians of Lakes Huron and Superior negotiated by William B. Robinson in 1850, the western treaties arranged for the transfer of large tracts of land well in advance of settler pressure. Aboriginal title was recognized and its relinquishment accepted. In return the Indians received annuities, reserves, and assurances that they could continue to hunt and fish on the unsettled portions of the land they had ceded. Negotiations were entrusted to treaty commissioners who held large public meetings with Indians.

The Indians played an important role in determining both the timing and the nature of the western treaties. The Saulteaux of southern Manitoba and the North-West Angle of the Lake of the Woods effectively created the fear of violence against those who might venture into their territory before treaties were negotiated with them. This pressure influenced the timing of Treaties One, Two, and Three, which were concluded by 1873.[13] Plans were to extend this process westward eventually, but the government did not believe it had compelling reasons to do so in 1873, the cabinet having decided to proceed only as land was required for settlement.[14] The Indians of the North-West, however, urged that some form of agreement between them and the government be effected.

For several years Plains Indian spokesmen had expressed a sense of unease and anxiety about the intentions of the Canadian government. Among the rumours that had swept over the prairies were that the land had been sold without consultation and that troops stationed at Red River threatened hostility to Indians.[15] In 1871 a deputation of Cree chiefs expressed these concerns to William Joseph Christie of the Hudson's Bay Company at Fort Edmonton.[16] They were assured at that time that they would be liberally treated when the government applied for their land. Each succeeding year anxieties heightened, however, as no moves were made to proceed with treaties. The Cree were reported to be extremely restless in the spring of 1874. As government representatives had not yet appeared, they had "the idea that no treaty is to be made with them, but that settlers are slowly moving west, occupying their country, killing their game and burning the woods & prairies."[17]

Uneasiness increased with the presence of railway, telegraph, and survey crews. The Plains Indians were concerned about the survey of large tracts of land around Hudson's Bay Company posts in the winter of 1873, and disputes arose about the rightful ownership of these sites.[18] In the fall of 1873 the Saulteaux of Fort Ellice had notified Alexander Morris, lieutenant-governor of Manitoba and the North-West Territories, that they were disturbed by the presence of survey crews in their midst and that they had never been party to a treaty to extinguish their title.[19] The following spring Chief Poor Man of the Touchwood Hills sent his brother Kanocees to interview Morris and ascertain whether someone was coming to see them about their land.[20] By interfering with the survey, and preventing the construction of the telegraph, the Plains Indians made it clear that they would not allow settlement until their rights were fully recognized.

The Indians of the North-West were anxious to negotiate treaties as a means of ensuring their economic security in face of a very uncertain future. Early on they adopted the strategy and goal that any arrangement for their land had to involve assistance in developing an agricultural base. In 1871 the Cree chiefs of the northern plains conveyed this message to Adams Archibald, lieutenant-governor of Manitoba and the North-West Territories. Their spokesman, Sweet Grass, stated: "We heard our lands were sold and we did not like it; we don't want to sell our lands; it is our property, and no one has a right to sell them. Our country is getting ruined of fur-bearing animals, hitherto our sole support, and now we are poor and want help – we want you to pity us. We want cattle, tools, agricultural implements, and assistance in everything when we come to settle – our country is no longer able to support us."[21]

Once negotiations were under way, the Indians were responsible for the introduction of terms which provided for an alternate subsistence base. The government initially had intended to offer only reserves and annuities.[22] In Treaties One and Two the government's terms were rejected by the Indians, who demanded implements and farm animals. Because the treaty commissioner claimed he had no authority to give his assent to these requests, they were listed in a memorandum entitled "outside promises." It was not until 1875 that the government accepted these requests as formal obligations, after considerable agitation from the Indian leaders of Manitoba. The Saulteaux of Treaty Three also requested agricultural aid and twice refused treaties that offered only reserves and annuities. The provision of farm implements and domestic animals became a standard clause of subsequent treaties, but the Indians made every possible effort to ensure that the terms would adequately provide the necessities for a new way of life.

The Qu'Appelle Treaty, or Treaty Four, was negotiated in September 1874. The treaty commissioners were Lt.-Gov. Alexander Morris; David Laird, minister of the interior; and W.J. Christie, then retired as a chief factor of the Hudson's Bay Company. Loud Voice was the main spokesman for the Cree. It appears that many of the Cree were absent on the buffalo hunt; certainly Piapot's and Okanese's bands were not present.[23] The negotiations were marked by tension and disagreement between the Cree and Saulteaux. Discussion was dominated by the Saulteaux through their spokesman, the Gambler, who insisted that the status of the Hudson's Bay Company be settled before any of the treaty terms be considered. According to Morris, the Cree were willing to discuss the treaty from the beginning, but the Saulteaux held out and attempted to encourage the others to do so as well.[24] The Saulteaux objected to the survey of the Hudson's Bay Company reserve without their consultation. They claimed that the three million pounds paid by Canada to the company should rightfully be theirs. They did not want the company trading in their territory, except at the posts, and they asked that the debts owed by the Indians to the company be cleared as some compensation for the company's profits from the transfer of their land.

It was not until the sixth and final day of the conference that the terms of the treaty were considered. Questioning, bargaining, and discussion were very limited. In this instance the Plains Indians did not seek guarantees that they be provided with the necessities on which to base a new agricultural life. At the request of Kanocees, the terms of the North-West Angle Treaty, or Treaty Three, made with the Lake of the Woods Indians, were explained by Morris, who stated they could expect no more than what was granted there. They would in fact receive proportionately less, as they numbered about one-half of the Lake of the Woods Indians. In return for the release and surrender of their rights, titles, and privileges to the tract ceded, the Indians were to be assigned reserves after consultation with each band. These were to be of "sufficient area to allow one square mile for each family of five, or in that proportion for larger or smaller families."[25] The treaty stipulated that the government could sell, lease, or otherwise dispose of these reserves once the Indians' consent had been obtained, but that the Indians were not themselves entitled to sell or otherwise alienate any of their reserve land. To encourage the practice of agriculture among the Indians, certain articles were to be given "once for all":

to any band thereof who are now actually cultivating the soil, or who shall hereafter settle on these reserves and commence to break up the land, that is to say – two hoes, one spade, one scythe, and one axe for every family so actually cultivating; and enough seed, wheat, barley, oats and potatoes to plant such lands as they have broken up; also one plough and two harrows for every ten families so cultivating as aforesaid; and also to each Chief, for the use of his band as aforesaid, one yoke of oxen, one bull, four cows, a chest of ordinary carpenter's tools, five hand-saws, five augers, one cross-cut saw, the necessary files, and one grindstone.[26]

The terms providing for the encouragement of agriculture differed in some important respects from those negotiated by the Plains Cree at Treaty Six two years later. Treaty Six families received more hoes and spades, and every three families rather than every ten shared a plough and harrows. Treaty Six chiefs received more livestock, as well as horse harnesses and wagons. A handmill was to be given to each Treaty Six band that raised sufficient grain to warrant its use. Perhaps the most significant difference bearing on the encouragement of agriculture was the promise in Treaty Six that for the first three years after reserves were surveyed, bands actually cultivating would be granted provisions to the sum of one thousand dollars.[27] The Treaty Six Indians were persistent in bargaining for these interim provisions to allow them to begin farming. It appears likely they were aware of the limited progress made by the Treaty Four Indians, who did not have such provisions. The Indians of Treaty Six were also promised that in the event of pestilence or general famine, they would receive assistance, a clause not included in Treaty Four.

SELECTING RESERVES

During the first four seasons after Treaty Four was signed, new or expanded agricultural activity was minimal. Unfortunately these years were critical: the beginning of an agricultural base could have been established before the buffalo disappeared altogether from the plains. Yet farming was possible only for the small number of bands whose reserves had been surveyed during this period, for according to the government interpretation of the treaty, implements and cattle had been promised only to those bands settled and actually cultivating. Many bands wished to have their reserves surveyed immediately so that settlement might begin, a request that surprised government officials. Consultations between officials and Indian bands on the selection of reserve sites did not begin until the fall of 1875. The issue was not immediately raised after the treaty was signed, as was the case in Treaty Six.

W.J. Christie was assigned the task of conferring with the bands in choosing reserves "where they shall be deemed most convenient and advantageous to the Indians."[28] Christie, one of the Treaty Four commissioners, was the mixed-blood son of Gov. Alexander Christie of the Hudson's Bay Company.[29] He had been educated in Scotland and had had a distinguished career with the Hudson's Bay Company, having served as chief factor in charge of the Saskatchewan district before his retirement to Brockville, Ontario. Having been chief trader at Swan River in present-day western Manitoba in the 1850s, Christie was familiar with the residents of the Treaty Four region and was fluent in Cree and perhaps also in Saulteaux. Christie's assistant, M.G. Dickieson, a clerk in the Department of the Interior, was present at the "long interviews" held with the bands in the fall of 1875.[30] William Wagner of the Dominion Land Survey, who had experience surveying reserves in Manitoba, also attended these sessions.

Christie's instructions from David Laird, minister of the interior, were that the reserves should not be too numerous and that as far as possible he should group as many bands that spoke the same language as would consent to such an arrangement.[31] Laird provided Christie with a memorandum, with which he concurred, drawn up by the surveyor general, Col John Stoughton Dennis, on the question of reserve sites. In it Dennis suggested that a tract of land suitable for a reserve should include a mixture of water, timber, arable land, and land on which the Indians might continue to hunt: "The interests of the Indians should be considered so far as to give them all the necessary frontage upon a river or lake, to include an abundance of land for farming purposes for the Band [and] at the same time the tract should be made to run back and include a fair share also of land which may not be so desirable for farming but would be valuable for other purposes connected with the Band, such as hunting etc." With the possible exception of land for hunting, the features of ample water, timber, and arable land did not differ from those which an average homesteader of the time might have considered necessary for a successful venture. A further suggestion, however, did not reflect concern that reserve sites be located near markets to make them viable agricultural tracts. Dennis recommended that they "be selected in such manner as not to interfere with the possible requirements of future settlement, or of land for railway purposes." A map was included to show the approximate line of the Canadian Pacific Railway (CPR) in order that reserve lands would not be established "in the vicinity of the line."[32] The proposed route of the line ran through the heart of what was then considered to be the land with the greatest agricultural potential, the fertile belt. Clearly Dennis did not consider it necessary or important that the reserves be located within this belt or that Indian farmers have access to railway facilities for reaching distant markets.

The exploring expeditions in the late 1850s of Capt. John Palliser and H.Y. Hind were largely in agreement about the agricultural potential of the North-West. Through their work the terms *fertile belt* and *Palliser's Triangle* became standard in geographical descriptions of the land. The southern treeless prairie, deficient in wood, water, and vegetation, was regarded as arid and unfit for permanent habitation. The fertile belt, dramatically depicted in Hind's *Narrative*, published in 1860, extended from the Pembina River up the Red to the Forks and northwest along the Assiniboine, taking a southerly swoop to include the Touchwood Hills, continuing to the forks of the Saskatchewan, and following the North Saskatchewan to the Rocky Mountains.[33] Also included within the fertile belt were isolated outliers on the arid plains such as Moose Mountain, Pheasant Hill, and the File Hills. The good soil, ample timber, adequate precipitation, and rich pasturage of the fertile belt were believed capable of sustaining a vast population. The image of an arid south and a fertile parkland belt persisted into the 1880s. It was not until then that suitable dry-belt farming techniques, which helped cope with conditions peculiar to the western plains, began to develop. Rejecting Palliser and Hind's gloomy assessment of the southern plains, botanist John Macoun claimed that the "so-called arid country was one of unsurpassed fertility."[34] His evaluation of the potential of the grasslands lent support to a decision taken in 1881 to reroute the CPR directly westward from Winnipeg.[35] Many of the Treaty Four reserves, initially surveyed in the belief that they were remote from the proposed railway through the fertile belt, ended up in enviable proximity to the main line when the southern route was adopted.

In the mid-1870s, however, the image of a barren southern plain and a fertile parkland belt prevailed. This belief was reflected not only in the proposed route of the CPR but also in the progress of the subdivision survey for settlement, which proceeded in a northwesterly direction from Portage la Prairie in Manitoba. W.J. Christie's own opinions on the land most suitable for farming in the West were squarely in agreement with those of Palliser and Hind.[36] He praised highly the valley of the North Saskatchewan River from the forks to Edmonton, as well as the land north of Edmonton. He did not consider country to the south as well adapted for farming. Christie's criteria were essentially good soil, abundant timber, plenty of water, and lakes with whitefish.

The Indians' criteria in selecting their sites and their concept of a reserve in 1875 are more difficult to ascertain. In the recorded proceedings of Treaty Four, the issue was not discussed at any length. In contrast, the commissioners at the Treaty Six negotiations were met with pointed questions and concerns, including whether reserve residents would be free to select another site if the original did not please them and whether they would be free to take timber anywhere on the common if it became scarce on their reserve. At Qu'Appelle the assembly was simply told that reserves would be surveyed when people were ready to "plant the seed."[37] Nothing was said about the move to reserves being compulsory; they were told it might be a long time before the land would be settled, and they were assured that in the meantime they could continue to hunt and fish wherever they liked.

In 1875 the government indicated a readiness to survey reserves only for those bands that clearly manifested a desire to settle and farm immediately. Bands that selected sites in the mid-1870s in the Touchwood Hills and Qu'Appelle Valley were not interfered with. At that time the region seemed remote from the farms and towns expected to spring up along the fertile belt. The same cannot be said of bands farther east, whose site selections potentially interfered with the proposed railway line. Sites in the Cypress Hills were initially granted but later denied.

Following interviews with the bands in 1875, Christie divided the Indians into three groups. Nine bands within Treaty Four had begun to farm already "to a slight extent" and wished to have their reserves surveyed as soon as possible.[38] Among these were the bands of George Gordon and Poor Man, who chose the Touchwood Hills, a site long used as a winter encampment, near the Hudson's Bay Company post they were accustomed to trading with. Pasquah was also ready for the survey. He wanted his reserve at Leech Lake where his band had houses and gardens, but he later changed his mind. A second group of eight bands were not yet prepared to settle but described to Christie where they wished their reserves to be. Included in this group were the bands of Loud Voice, Star Blanket, Ready Bow, Day Star, Piapot, Little Black Bear, and Muscowequan. Christie defined a third group that did not as yet wish to select reserves and begin farming, which included the bands that followed Kahkewistahaw, Chacachase, Cowessess, and Okanese.

In August 1875 William Wagner was instructed to survey George Gordon's reserve at the Little Touchwood Hills, Poor Man's at the Big Touchwood Hills, Pasquah's at Leech Lake, as well as one at Crooked Lakes for seven families from the Fort Ellice band. Wagner's duties included much more than simply running the boundaries of reserves. In the case of Gordon's reserve, for example, Wagner was obliged to negotiate for a number of days before the band agreed to choose a site. He had to calculate the number of square miles the band was entitled to, and that year he also had the responsibility of distributing implements among some of the Treaty Four bands and of reporting whether adequate provision had been made for wintering stock. In fact the task of implementing some of the most immediate treaty terms fell to a surveyor.

Wagner began with a survey of Gordon's reserve on the west side of the Little Touchwood Hills where the band had several houses and about twenty acres under cultivation.[39] The surveyor calculated that the band was entitled to seven square miles more than the forty-one suggested by the Indian commissioner. He described the reserve as generally hilly, broken by lakes and ponds with "bad water" inhabited by muskrats. It was for the most part well wooded with prairie to the southeast, which was covered with willows and hazel. The soil was "good" and rated as class two, which meant moderate limitations might restrict the range of crops. Wagner noted that most of the land in the immediate vicinity of Touchwood was fertile, a prairie which was "part [of] or [a] continuation of the Fertile Belt." The site of the reserve itself, however, located "in the woods," confirmed Wagner's belief "that from this and the next generation no hope can be entertained that the 'red man' will entirely devote himself to agriculture – but gardening will be carried on," provided, he continued, that they were given instruction for two years.[40] In 1876 another official appeared to disagree with Wagner's assessment, describing Gordon's reserve as "well adapted for farming and grazing purposes. It is well wooded with poplar but no other kind of timber is to be found on it. What there is however answers very well for building and fencing. The soil is very good and easily worked and is well watered by several lakes which in summer time swarm with wild fowl affording an almost inexhaustible supply of food for the Indians."[41] Government officials were divided in their opinions of what constituted potential agricultural land.

In the fall of 1876, Angus McKay, Christie's replacement as government agent for Treaty Four, met with the chiefs and headmen of the Treaty Four bands at Fort Qu'Appelle where they were gathered to receive their annuities. McKay was well acquainted with Plains Indians. He was a prominent Red River Métis, born at Edmonton House.[42] He was fluent in Indian languages as well as in French and English. Four days were spent on the issue of reserves. Day Star and Ready Bow expressed a desire to begin farming and McKay believed that some members would begin work in the spring of 1877. Loud Voice also wished to go on his reserve. Two bands that had not pointed out localities the year before, those of Chacachase and Kahkewistahaw, indicated where they wished their reserves to be surveyed.

Wagner surveyed three more reserves in the Touchwood Hills in 1876: Poor Man's on the south side of the Big Touchwood Hills at a place called the old Fort; Day Star's on the west side of Poor Man's; and Ready Bow's on the south side of the Big Touchwood Hills, east of and adjoining Poor Man's. McKay reported that the three reserves were very similar. They consisted of very good farming country with numerous grass meadows and small lakes. The timber available was small in size but "fit for building purposes of the Indians." He believed the timber supply would improve greatly in a few years because it grew rapidly. The land was rolling, "with good soil in parts rather light but easily worked."[43] Yet within a few years all the reserves in the Touchwood Hills were found to contain far too little arable land for successful agriculture.

A small reserve was surveyed that same year for seven families of the Fort Ellice band, also known as the Mosquito, or Sakimay band,[44] at the head of Crooked Lakes where they had houses and land already under cultivation. McKay praised it as a site for a reserve mainly because of the large number of fish and wildfowl found there. He described the soil as light on top of the bluff but good in the river valley, although portions were covered with young poplar. It was well supplied with grass meadows, which promised a large supply of hay.

In 1876 Wagner also surveyed a reserve for Pasquah's band on the south side of the first, or upper, Qu'Appelle Lake, a few miles west of Fort Qu'Appelle. The main advantage of the location, according to McKay, was that the lake was well stocked with fish, on which, along with wildfowl, many families subsisted for much of the summer. The timber was very small and the soil in parts light, however, to make the reserve "rather a poor one," according to McKay, although there were numerous hay meadows. A number of families were living on the reserve in 1876 and beginning to farm.

THE FIRST FOUR YEARS AFTER TREATY

The bands that were cultivating at the time of the treaty or that expressed a desire to begin farming received little assistance or encouragement in their efforts. Government officials were reluctant and tentative about distributing those items promised in the treaty for this purpose. During the 1875 season no steps were taken to issue implements and seed, and two oxen and four cows were supplied only to Pasquah's band.[45] The bands prepared to farm expected their supply of implements, cattle, and seed immediately, whether or not their reserves had been surveyed.

In mid-July 1875 chiefs from the Qu'Appelle, one of whom was Poor Man, sent two messengers to Winnipeg to inform Lieutenant-Governor Morris that they wanted their cattle and implements delivered at once.[46] Morris anxiously wired the minister of the interior, David Laird, for instructions. Laird replied that the Qu'Appelle chiefs were "rather fast," since their reserves had not yet been selected,[47] but if W.J. Christie reported that fall that they were really farming, their application for cattle and implements would receive immediate attention. Government officials were determined to adhere strictly to the exact wording of the treaty, which stated that implements, cattle, and seed would be given to "any band ... now actually cultivating the soil, or who shall hereafter settle on these reserves and commence to break up the land." This wording was quite deliberate and was repeated in Treaty Six. Morris explained at those proceedings that goods were to be given only to those actually cultivating the soil, "for if given to all it would encourage idleness."[48] The surveyor who was to distribute these goods, however, simply did not believe that Indians could properly take care of farm implements and cattle. The concern of the Department of the Interior in July 1875 was that "the Government should not be put to the expense of sending implements and cattle that are not likely to be used for the purpose for which they are intended."[49] Morris informed Poor Man's messenger that according to the terms of the treaty, cattle and implements were to be distributed only when the Indians were on their reserves.⁵⁰ Since Poor Man's reserve was not surveyed until the following year, he could not receive his share. The messenger was also told that Christie would report on the numbers of Indians who had begun to cultivate the soil and that, as soon as possible, the promised implements would be supplied.

W.J. Christie, who had been present at the messengers' interview with Morris, recognized that the Indians were crippled in their efforts to begin farming. He recommended that implements and cattle be given not only to those actually cultivating the land, but also to those who "manifested a disposition to do so."⁵¹ In July 1875 he reported that the Indians themselves had stated that without implements they could not begin to break the land. Surveyor Wagner was authorized to distribute implements among some of the Touchwood Indians in the fall of 1875, but the order reached him too late. Wagner, however, stated that he would not have issued them even if the order had reached him in time because he was convinced that the Indians would only sell them. According to Wagner, "outsiders" at the Touchwood Hills were not buying goods from the Hudson's Bay Company store but were awaiting the distribution of tools and implements among the Indians. The surveyor was also authorized to deliver cattle to Poor Man's band if he determined that adequate provisions for wintering stock existed. Wagner decided that there did not. He was cynical about the ability of the Indians to care for cattle: he had been told that Pasquah had attempted to sell one of his oxen but, being unable to do so, "had commenced to eat a cow." The surveyor warned the officer in charge of the Hudson's Bay Company store at Fort Qu'Appelle that purchasing cattle given to Indians was considered a misdemeanour, but he was not optimistic that many would be left in the spring.⁵²

These distressing reports from Wagner alarmed the government into further caution and parsimony in distributing cattle and implements. The notion that Indians consumed the animals and grain issued them, and sold or abandoned their implements, although based on little evidence, governed further distribution. In April 1876 Angus McKay was authorized to distribute implements only to those he believed "would actually require and use them."⁵³ To discourage their sale, implements were to be marked clearly with the letters ID (Indian Department) by means of a branding iron. A small quantity of seed grain, potatoes, and garden seed was to be purchased for the Treaty Four Indians, but McKay was to see that these goods were used strictly for the purpose for which they were intended and not sold or consumed. A small quantity of provisions, not to exceed one hundred and fifty dollars, was also to be supplied to those engaged in planting. As well, McKay was instructed to learn the fate of the cattle given to Pasquah's band and to recommend whether cattle should be given to any other bands that would actually require them and take good care of them. Similar instructions governed the distribution of ammunition and twine; they were to go only to those Indians likely to make good use of them. Two sets of carpenter's tools McKay was issued were to be given only to those bands settled on reserves and likely to make use of them in building houses.

By the time instructions reached McKay in the spring of 1876, the season was too far advanced to purchase seed wheat.[54] McKay bought potato and turnip seed in Winnipeg, which proved to be of little use, as the potatoes were damaged en route and the season was too far advanced to plant either. McKay did not arrive at Fort Qu'Appelle until mid-July when most of the Indians were hunting buffalo in the vicinity of the Eyebrow Hills. Some members of what he called the Qu'Appelle band were present to accept their seed, and he distributed fifty bushels of seed potatoes among them. Pasquah's band received part of this amount and was also issued a tool chest, one plough, two harrows, twenty hoes, and other implements.[55] Gordon's band received a similar complement of seed and implements.[56] These bands were the only ones in Treaty Four to receive implements that year, despite the fact that at least three other bands had clearly expressed the desire to build houses and break land the following spring.

Agent McKay sympathized with the Indians' dilemma. While travelling among the Qu'Appelle and Touchwood Indians, he noted that "in one or two cases they had already commenced building houses and putting up hay for winter use, in anticipation of getting cattle from the government." Indians complained to McKay that they could not construct buildings because they had no animals to draw timber, and they could not break land until they were supplied with implements and animals. While attempts had been made to do both, little could be accomplished without draught animals. McKay himself did not believe that Indians were likely to consume their cattle. He reported that Pasquah's excuse for killing one of his cows was that "he had not been supplied with scythes and snaithes the summer before, and consequently he was unable to put up a sufficient supply of hay to feed them over the winter."[57]

During 1876, then, agriculture progressed not at all in the Qu'Appelle and Touchwood portions of Treaty Four. It was realized that if seed grain was to be of any use, it had to be sent to distribution points in the autumn. It was found that the department could purchase most of the seed required from the Hudson's Bay Company posts in the vicinity, which would save the cost of transporting goods from Winnipeg. Barley was purchased that fall at Portage la Prairie and stored for distribution in the spring. It also became evident that grave problems were involved in asking the Indians to congregate at certain points in the spring to receive their seed. When McKay arrived at Fort Ellice in mid-June 1876, he found the Indians there in a state of starvation.[58] They had understood from Christie that seed would be issued early in the spring, and because they were expecting the seed daily, they had not gone out to hunt. They would have suffered severely had the postmaster not supplied them with rations in return for making a road. The Indians at Fort Pelly were similarly angry at the delay in the delivery of their seed and implements.

Angus McKay's career as Indian agent for Treaty Four lasted only the season of 1876. Deputy Superintendent General Vankoughnet explained to Sir John A. Macdonald in 1879 that the Department of the Interior viewed McKay as a most "undesirable person," whose record "is not of such a nature as to justify it in placing much confidence in him." Interior Minister Laird had reported that McKay had incited the Indians to express dissatisfaction at the manner in which they were treated by the government, "founding his statement to them upon the fact, that certain farming implements and presents which were under the Treaty agreed to be given the Indians at a certain time were not forthcoming on the date they were expected by them." According to Vankoughnet, McKay knew very well that the delays were caused by great floods that year. Rather, he suspected that McKay had "intrigued" with his brother, the Honourable James McKay, freighter of supplies to the Indians, to delay the distribution of articles for several days after they had arrived and to bill the government for the large sum that it cost to feed the Indians while the goods were detained. McKay had to be sent where he could "do little or no harm."[59] Despite his frequent requests for a transfer to a more settled region in the West, McKay rounded out his career with Indian Affairs in northern Manitoba.

Allan MacDonald replaced McKay as Indian agent for Treaty Four. Born at Fort Langley in British Columbia and educated in Montreal, MacDonald was the son of chief factor Archibald McDonald of the Hudson's Bay Company. His mother was of part-Indian ancestry.[60] He had experience with agriculture, his father having farmed at Fort Langley and later at Fort Colvile, near present-day Colville, Washington, where MacDonald spent his childhood. He also helped his father to manage a farm near Montreal where his parents retired in 1848. MacDonald was a captain in one of the companies composing the expedition of Colonel Wolseley to Red River in 1870, and he was with the military escort that accompanied the treaty commissioners at the signing of Treaties Three and Four. Unlike Christie and McKay, who had journeyed into the agency for only a few months of the year, MacDonald made Swan River his home.

MacDonald was one of a small number of agents working within what was by 1877 called the North-West Superintendency, which included the area covered by Treaties Four, Six, and Seven, some 206,000 square miles, with an estimated population of 17,000 Indians.[61] David Laird, a recent resident of Battleford, in present-day Saskatchewan, combined the duties and responsibilities of lieutenant-governor and Indian superintendent for the North-West Superintendency after having served as minister of the interior until 1876.[62] M.G. Dickieson was appointed Laird's assistant, and he also held the position of Indian agent for Treaty Six. As Laird outlined their duties, the resident local agents were to pay annuities, distribute the "annual presents," instruct the Indians in farming, and encourage them to help themselves. It was also hoped they might exercise a "moral and industrial influence" over the bands.[63]

Agent MacDonald's report for 1877 suggests that the Qu'Appelle and Touchwood Indians had made little progress in agriculture that year. Before MacDonald's arrival at the agency, a man hired for a few days in the spring worked with Gordon's band and gave them a small quantity of provisions.[64] During his August annuity payments tour, MacDonald distributed some implements but was unable to assist with the farming operation because all the payment sites were some distance from the reserves.

Two bands in the Touchwood Hills began farming that spring. Poor Man's band was reported to have three acres under cultivation, but the crop was in a low-lying area and was damaged by the rains of the season.[65] MacDonald gave this band two hayforks, three whetstones, and a tool chest in 1877, the first implements they are reported to have received, although some may have been issued by the temporary agency man. MacDonald had no knowledge of what cattle and implements had been supplied to the Indians before his appointment, but those he issued to the three families from Day Star's band, who had also begun work on their reserve that spring, indicate that he adhered strictly to the formula outlined in the treaty. That band was given six hoes, two hayforks, three each of spades, scythes, snaithes, axes, and whetstones, but no ploughs or harrows. Although ploughs and harrows were on hand in storage at Qu'Appelle, they were not distributed, presumably because there were not as yet ten families cultivating as stipulated in the treaty.

After his first season with the Treaty Four Indians, MacDonald came to believe that the Indians had "far more difficulties to contend with in raising the first crop than is generally supposed."[66] A major problem was that there was not an adequate supply of food on hand on the reserves in spring when work was begun and families had to hunt or gather food off the reserves. He asked the department for permission to purchase provisions to be distributed to those engaged in ploughing and sowing. MacDonald also recommended that the Indians be paid annuities on their reserves, rather than asking them to travel to a payment site, in some cases over seventy miles away. He felt this might induce some families to establish themselves on the reserves and turn their full attention to agriculture.

David Laird also felt that the Indians of Treaty Four should be granted provisions at seed time. Noting that Treaty Six contained such a clause, he requested in December 1877 that one thousand dollars be set aside for that purpose for the next spring.[67] Laird asked for a further thousand dollars to hire competent persons to assist the Indians in putting in their crops in the spring. He believed the money would be usefully spent in teaching the Indians how to work their ploughs and other implements and the proper quantities and methods of sowing seeds. Originally from Prince Edward Island, Laird was not as yet familiar with conditions peculiar to farming in the West, but he was well acquainted with agriculture, as his father was reputed to have been one of the best farmers on PEI. Laird himself was also attempting to raise wheat and keep cattle at Battleford.[68]

For a number of years agents in the field had urged officials in Ottawa to provide the Indians with some instruction in agriculture. As farm instructors were not promised in the treaties, the government was not prepared to provide them. Agents were blithely expected to perform this duty, which soon proved impossible because of their other responsibilities over vast territories. In 1875 M.G. Dickieson informed Laird, at that time minister of the interior, that only with instruction in working the land and planting would the Indians be induced to settle and cultivate.[69] Otherwise, he remained pessimistic about their agricultural future.

Dickieson proposed that 640 acres of land on each reserve be set aside as a model or stock farm under the supervision of a skilful agriculturalist, who was also acquainted with the Indians' ways and their languages. The farmer would direct the Indians in cultivating their own plots, but Indians could also be employed building, fencing, and farming on the model farms. Dickieson suggested that one such farm be organized on an experimental basis at first. The surplus produce, he believed, could be sold to the North-West Mounted Police or to railway and telegraph crews. Laird disregarded this advice in 1875; it was not until he arrived in the West that he came to see the necessity of such instruction.

In a number of his reports, surveyor William Wagner also pointed out the pressing need for instruction in farming. Wagner was particularly concerned about the agricultural future of the Plains hunters of the Treaty Four district, who, he believed, were at a disadvantage compared with their Woodland neighbours to the east, who had at least observed farming and knew what to do with their implements. As for the Plains Indian, however, Wagner stated, "I am sure that of itself imagination will not be able to give him a clue how to set a plough share or cultivate seeds given to him." Wagner urged the government to provide those bands "whose interests for a bona fide settlement are proven" an agriculturalist fluent in their language to assist for at least six months, from seeding to harvest.[70]

As agents in the field became fully convinced that the Indians needed more assistance, particularly in the way of instruction in agriculture, before they could raise any quantity of produce, officials in Ottawa became less inclined to consider any increased expenditure. David Mills, Laird's successor as minister of the interior, was certain, despite the advice of his informants, that more than enough was being done to encourage agriculture. Mills' concerns were to keep costs down and to limit assistance; too much would encourage idleness and keep the Indians from making exertions to help themselves.[71] Mills approached his new job with the preconceived notions that implements and stock had been haphazardly and lavishly distributed, that storehouses were brimming with unrequired implements, that the issued tools were lying idle, and that the cattle were being consumed.

David Laird was unsuccessful in dislodging Mills' conviction that the government had been anything but generous in its treatment of the Indians. Laird was angry and discouraged to learn in the spring of 1878 that his request for funds to provide instructors and provisions was refused by Mills on the grounds that "there is no provision therefor in the estimates."[72] The winter of 1877–78 had been difficult for all residents of the North-West. Buffalo were scarce; the Indians were very poorly off and in some cases starving. Except for a few stray herds, the buffalo did not return after the fall and winter of 1879. A crop in the 1878 season appeared critical to government officials in the West: without a good crop, either starvation would result or the government would be forced to feed the Indians, certainly those of Treaty Six, who had been assured of assistance in the event of a famine. Laird and other agents in the field were certain that if the Indians were issued provisions in the spring, and given some instruction, potatoes and grain could be raised and therefore save the government the very large expense of feeding the Indians over the winter. In April 1878 Dickieson strongly urged Ottawa to approve Laird's recommendations, even though they were not provided for in the treaty. "As I think we are on the eve of an Indian outbreak which will be caused principally by starvation," he continued, "it does not do to scan the exact lines of a treaty too closely."[73]

The minister of the interior did not act on the recommendations of his representatives in the North-West. Laird's request for provisions for the Indians of Treaty Four at seed time was struck off the estimates, as Mills "did not think it well in the public interest to make an unauthorized expenditure, thus anticipating the action of Parliament." Mills also cut in half the amount Laird had proposed would be needed for the Indians of Treaty Six at seed time, claiming that the provisioning clause was to go into operation only when the Indians were located on their reserves, most of which had not yet been surveyed. Mills allowed Laird six hundred dollars to engage persons competent to instruct in agriculture. Laird's estimate of one thousand dollars was lowered because Mills regarded it as the duty of the local agents to direct and advise the Indians in their efforts at farming. "During the greater portion of the year the ordinary Indian Agents have very little to do," Mills wrote, "and the amount of compensation is very large in proportion to their work." The services of agents "not disposed or not competent to instruct and actively aid the Indians in putting in and taking care of their crops ought not in my opinion, to be retained," he continued.[74] Laird, incensed at the attitude of the minister, warned that the government had to chose one of three policies: "to help the Indians to farm and raise stock, to feed them, or to fight them."[75] As his suggestions were not being acted upon, Laird asked Mills for instructions. The situation appeared very simple to the minister, who replied that the Indians should be induced to raise the necessary means of subsistence themselves, which could be done only by getting them on their reserves and taking the requisite steps to instruct them in agriculture. "The Indians," Mills wrote, "should be constantly impressed with the necessity of their devoting themselves to agriculture at once to avoid famine."[76]

The crops of 1878 in the Treaty Four district saw no improvement over those of previous years. A grant for the purchase of provisions was approved too late to be of any use. Laird reported that the sole agent in Treaty Four could scarcely see to the distribution of seed grain and the payment of annuities.[77] That season only two ploughs, two harrows, four oxen, one bull, one cow, and a few hand tools were issued in all of Treaty Four.[78] This limited amount was in part explained by the number of implements and cattle issued in previous years, but also, Laird noted in his annual report, "it must be admitted that most of the Indians connected with that Treaty are very backward about engaging in agriculture."[79] Certainly there was a marked contrast between the progress of the Treaty Six Indians and that of the Treaty Four Indians, who had concluded their treaty two years earlier and should have been in the advance. In Treaty Six many bands had by 1878 made what officials lauded as "commendable efforts."[80] The bands of Red Pheasant, Ahtakakoop, and Mistawasis, all formerly Plains hunters, had from 20 to 40 acres under cultivation, and some, such as John Smith's band with 120 acres under crop, were remarkably successful.[81] In 1878 the Plains hunters of Treaty Four had little choice but to continue trying to make a living following the hunt. Department officials began to view the Indians of Treaty Four as wilfully rejecting the reserve system and an agricultural way of life, and inflexibly and stubbornly maintaining their traditions and customs, even in the face of the certain extinction of their means of subsistence.

Conditions were grim by 1878: distress, suffering, and death was the lot of the starving Indians. Applications for relief were made constantly to government officials, the North-West Mounted Police, and the Hudson's Bay Company. In March 1878 Charles Pratt reported that there was not a morsel of food in the Touchwood Hills, and all were starving.[82] By May the situation had not improved. There was no ammunition to hunt ducks, and other game was scarce. The same situation prevailed throughout the North-West. Thousands of destitute people congregated at posts, such as Carlton, Pitt, Battleford on the North Saskatchewan River, Walsh in the Cypress Hills, and Macleod in present-day southwestern Alberta. In June 1879 a group of desperate Indians broke into government stores at Fort Qu'Appelle, removing flour and other provisions left over from treaty payments.[83]

Early that winter in 1878 about seventy-five Indians were found starving on the plains fifty miles south of Fort Qu'Appelle.[84] They were unable to travel further, as the horses and dogs had been eaten. Several old people and children had died. The band camped near Fort Qu'Appelle that winter, which was severe. Toward spring they all contracted a fatal disease and died within three or four days. Because the ground was still frozen, the dead were simply placed in the snow, and when the Qu'Appelle overflowed its banks that spring and the valley flooded, the ice swept the bodies downstream.

Reports of starvation in the North-West were systematically denied by government officials and the western press. Battleford's *Saskatchewan Herald*, the first newspaper in the North-West, consistently denied reports of starving Indians in the eastern papers in order to set the minds of prospective settlers at ease.[85] Editor P.G. Laurie declared that in the winter of 1878–79 the Indians' source of food supply was no more restricted than in former years, but that the Indians had "not made the usual effort to help themselves" and had "contentedly resigned themselves to idleness, claiming to have the assurance that if they were hungry they would be fed."[86] The editor's usual reply to reports of starving Indians was the "Indians get more than many whites who live beside them."[87] Laurie pointed out that those unacquainted with Indians did not know that it was their custom to beg in formal speeches by making a "'poor mouth' over their condition, retelling all their grievances, real or imaginary, and dwelling on the hardships they suffer."[88] It was in fact newcomers like Laurie who were unacquainted with conditions in the North-West and underestimated the severity of the food crisis.

It was in the interest of the government to deny that there was starvation in the North-West; such reports could damage the reputation of the West, which the Department of the Interior promoted as a land of prosperity and plenty. Hungry Indians were presented as the authors of their own misfortune. They were regarded in much the same way as were the destitute farmers of the American Great Plains who suffered grasshopper plagues in 1873–78.[89] Although the farmers were victims of natural disaster, they were treated with suspicion and contempt by public officials, who blamed them for creating their own problems through idleness. Legislators of the day believed the remedy was to teach farmers to help themselves and to adopt habits of hard work, determination, and sobriety. It was thought that if they were offered relief, the state would be rewarding pauperism, encouraging dependence, and creating a permanent class of needy. Instead the farmers required advice, encouragement, and moral suasion. Similarly the starving Indians of the North-West did not have the means to improve their condition, and yet the legitimacy of their need was questioned. Relief was viewed as demoralizing and dangerous. Poverty was attributed to individual human conduct, not to its systemic causes.

Throughout this period the Plains Indians continued to manifest a desire to explore agriculture as an alternative to the hunt. They were clearly disappointed, however, at the government's indifferent approach toward assisting them. Dissatisfied with the Treaty Four terms, which, they believed, did not provide them with adequate means to create an agricultural subsistence base, they sought revisions, arguing after 1876 that they deserved to be on an equal footing with the Indians of Treaty Six.[90] They were also angry that the government was not faithful in honouring the treaty and delivering the farm equipment, seed, and cattle promised. Aware of the very limited progress of the bands who had endeavoured to settle on reserves and farm, chiefs had good reason to be sceptical about following their lead: it would be inviting starvation unless some assurance of support in their efforts could be attained. The Treaty Four Indians were in a more vulnerable position than those of Treaty Six, since they could not rely on the protection of a famine clause. There was little response, however, to the requests of the Treaty Four bands. Among many officials they gained a reputation for making outrageous demands, for being sullen and embittered, and for being unwilling to take steps to support themselves.

Although the Department of the Interior blithely claimed that the Indians had no complaints and that they were grateful for what was being done for them, there clearly existed an undercurrent of discontent from the time Treaty Four was concluded. When W.J. Christie returned to the scene of the treaty negotiations in 1875, he encountered an unexpectedly large number of Indians, about 468 lodges, or double the number present in 1874.[91] The Indians absent the year before believed that no treaty had been concluded and that the proceedings of 1874 were preliminary to the negotiation of a treaty that year. Christie had been warned before his arrival that this idea prevailed. His informant surmised that those Indians who had concluded the treaty on behalf of themselves and their compatriots did not have the courage on returning to the plains to tell the others that they had signed for all of them.[92] Christie was to secure the adhesion of those chiefs absent the previous year, but the terms were not open to negotiations; his duty was only to explain the terms.

The Indians gathered at Fort Qu'Appelle were prepared with a list of demands, as if in anticipation of negotiations. Their objectives reflected an anxiety about a future supply of food and a concern for learning the necessary skills and technology to farm successfully. They asked for someone to show them how to use their implements and tools, assistance in building their houses, a mowing machine for each reserve, a grist mill, a forge, and blacksmiths.[93] They wanted a store on each reserve, which could serve as a depot of provisions in years of starvation. They asked for a supply of medicine and requested that they not be called upon to fight in the event of war. The Treaty Six people were to put forward many of these same demands the following year.

For four days the Fort Qu'Appelle Indians refused to accept their annuities and to back away from their demands. Christie's position was that discussion was pointless. He warned the assembly that if they declined to accept the terms of the treaty, he would report to the government that they had broken the agreement. Officials saw the treaty as a "covenant" between the Indians and government; therefore it was impossible to comply with new demands.[94] The Indians asked that their requests be forwarded to those in authority, which Christie promised to do, and only then did they agree to sign the treaty. Christie included his account of these proceedings, not in his final report to Laird, but under separate cover, dealing with matters "which we thought you might not wish referred to in our general report."[95] Ironically an official publication describing the Qu'Appelle Treaty noted that a "gratifying feature" connected with the process was "the readiness, with which the Indians, who were absent, afterwards accepted the terms which had been settled for them, by those, who were able to attend."[96]

For several subsequent years, the time annuities were paid, or "treaty day," became an opportunity for the Indians to urge their demands collectively, which they customarily forwarded before they would accept payments. In 1876 a large number of the Qu'Appelle Indians had followed the diminishing herds of buffalo to the Cypress Hills where they were paid by Inspector J.M. Walsh of the North-West Mounted Police. Louis O'Soup, spokesman for the assembled bands, asked, among other things, for the cattle promised them, for a blacksmith, and for land to be broken for them on their reserves, since they were unable to do this themselves.[97] Walsh replied that their wishes could not be entertained but assured them they would have no trouble breaking their land because white men would be in the neighbourhood who would instruct them in the use of implements, which they could learn in a few days.[98]

Agent MacDonald was greeted by a much more tense and strained situation at Fort Qu'Appelle in the fall of 1877, where fourteen bands were assembled, or 2,290 Indians.[99] A few days before MacDonald's arrival, the Indians had demanded a share of the provisions ordered for annuity payments, which were on hand in storage at the Hudson's Bay Company post. They warned the man in charge, a Mr Mclean, that unless they were given supplies, they would help themselves to twenty bags of flour and twelve cattle. In a display of determination, 150 armed and mounted Indians paraded through the camp with the avowed intention of seizing supplies. A quantity of provisions was eventually issued, which eased the tension to some extent. The question of the amount of rations due the Indians was debated for some days after MacDonald's arrival. He agreed to increase the amount after receiving a message from Loud Voice, which stated that the agent was underestimating the numbers present; besides the treaty Indians, many more had a right to enter into the treaty, but even if some did not, all were hungry, and their women and children were calling for food.

Two days after the issue was settled, the chiefs with their bands assembled at noon near Loud Voice's lodge and advanced to accept annuities. MacDonald, accompanied by a policeman and an interpreter, met them within fifty yards of his tent and was introduced to each chief. In his account of their message, given by their spokesman O'Soup, MacDonald wrote: "At the time the treaty was made with them the Governor promised that all the Indians in the plains would be dealt with alike. They would like to know how it is that the Saskatchewan Indians have received more. By the Governors promise they consider they have not been dealt with in the same liberal manner as the others and they now ask that the same be extended to them."[100]

The resentment displayed by the Qu'Appelle Indians was not without some justification. Lieutenant-Governor Morris had clearly taken the position during the Treaty Four negotiations that the Queen wished to deal with all of her "red children" alike. They were told that the Queen's representatives did not have the power to grant more than what had been agreed to in Treaty Three.[101]

O'Soup further asked for a written promise that "they will consider their demand granted if the Agent goes to Qu'Appelle next year if it is not he need not come." It appears that the Indians were prepared to sever connections with the agents of the government if their demands were not met. MacDonald refused a written promise, assuring them his actual promise was good enough. He warned them that the agent was likely to show up whatever the outcome of their demands. The chiefs hesitated for some time to come forward and accept their annuities, but finally Loud Voice advanced to MacDonald's table. "With this many were relieved of an anxiety they had felt for nearly three days," MacDonald wrote, "as the Indians were exhorbitant in their demands and I had no power but myself."[102]

As with earlier appeals for increased assistance, no action was taken on the Qu'Appelle Indians' request that the more liberal terms granted the Saskatchewan Indians be extended to them. What appears to have had some impact on the policy-makers, however, was the lone deputation of Pasquah, who presented himself to Joseph Cauchon, lieutenant-governor of Manitoba, in the spring of 1878. His specific complaints were that although he and his men had broken thirty pieces of land for planting, they were not supplied with cattle to break and work the land, seed to sow it, or provisions to feed them while at work. Provisions were issued at seed time only once, with the result that they were compelled to eat their dogs. He claimed that although they had four ploughs, they had received only one yoke of oxen, one of which had promptly become lame and was useless. He also complained that they had been promised materials for houses when they were ready to build but could get none. The agent, he stated, was hard "like iron" in his dealings with them. Pasquah appeared to offer himself as an agent to his people of the government's good will declaring that if he would be given enough food and tobacco to hold a great feast, it would maintain peace. Besides the fatal scarcity of the means of life, the chief pinpointed other causes of apprehension and unease in his district: the frequent massing together of tribes that were hitherto apart if not actually hostile, the presence of the refugee Dakota in the Qu'Appelle, and recent arrests made by the North-West Mounted Police.[103]

Claiming that he had no jurisdiction in the matter, Cauchon dismissed Pasquah and told him to see Laird in Battleford. Pasquah received a small dole of provisions and nothing else as a result of his mission. An anonymous interpreter, who recorded Pasquah's message, seemed acquainted with the Indians of that region and sympathetic to their plight. He provided abundant commentary and observations on the chief's errand and was not hesitant to lecture Pasquah's hosts sternly on their want of tact and hospitality. He believed the treatment Pasquah received would produce a "bad effect" on his mind, and he warned that Pasquah and his people would see in it "an implied contempt for his nation, one ever steadfast in their friendship to the English people when they were but a handful in their midst, and indeed Sir, it is of old the wont of the great colonizing race to extend a velvet hand when weak and an iron one when strong." While bestowing tokens of friendship and good will upon Pasquah might not have been strictly provided for in the treaty, he suggested that such gifts were "readily embodied in the larger convenant of sound policy and good sense." The chief's request for presents was "slight and paltry" compared with the almost "ruinous concessions" that a "civilized people" might demand in an analogous situation. In asking for presents the Cree were "but following out their ideas of *expressed amity*," which involved the customary exchange of genuine covenants valued as pledges of good will. Pasquah's requests were not intended to increase his personal fortune, according to the translator. In fact the chiefs were "continually stripped of their effects in friendly alliance" and because of their deliberate generosity were frequently among the poorest in a band. Rather, Pasquah's mission was

to take you the representative of the Queen by the hand, and gather assurance of a continued spoken anew amity on your part, such acception [sic] as he can carry word back to his people and enlist their content and I would here say that it is almost to be regretted that the Governors of the Dominion in this newly acquired Indian territory are not permitted a just discretion in the way of such gifts, visible tokens of friendship to the Tribes as would recall often to them through their chiefs a well considered liberality.[104]

The interpreter also spoke in defence of Pasquah's claims that his band lacked animals, seed, and provisions, for of all the Indians in his district, this chief was "thoroughly alive to the future" and the necessity of farming, having had a large herd of animals of his own before the treaty. As a people "passionately fond of their offspring," the Cree would happily and easily adopt measures to provide their children with a secure supply of fish, potatoes, milk, and grain that could "*always* prevent hunger among their little ones in summer and can be secured against a similar pinch in winter." If they once acquired the means to provide this security, "they will not easily loose their hold upon such safety." At the moment, however, the Indians were divided in their attention to the chase, and not knowing about the possibilities in their favour, they were "at times profoundly depressed at thought of the future." The translator warned that the Cree were "subject at times to an irritation of feeling against the white race who while establishing themselves in every comfort in their broad domain, have directly or indirectly caused such havoc among their game and subsistence as would seem to leave no room for them to do other than suffer and die."[105]

Pasquah's audience with Cauchon in the spring of 1878 aptly summarized the legacy of the first four years of government administration in Treaty Four. Even those bands that had exhibited an enthusiasm for agriculture from the outset were able to display only the most meagre of results. Through a combination of neglect, parsimony, maladministration, and a lack of understanding, the Indians received little encouragement in their efforts to diversity at a time when it was clearly a most critical objective.

Indian policy for the West in the 1870s has been described as an enlightened one of "gradualism," which was suddenly proved to have been based on the wrong assumptions in 1878 and 1879 when the buffalo became "unexpectedly scarce."[106] This farsighted scheme envisaged that the Indians would gradually withdraw from the hunt and settle on reserves as farmers, but that the two livelihoods would for some time coexist, until the new became as familiar as the old. The gravity of the situation was simply not realized until the buffalo suddenly did not appear, according to this interpretation. The policy of gradualism, however, is little more than a retrospective justification for a period of indifference and neglect, when reports of the inevitable disappearance of the buffalo were disregarded.

The result of these early years of administration was an erosion in the spirit of amity and entente with which the venture might have been more successfully broached. The gulf of understanding between the Indians and department officials widened and deepened as both sides began to regard the other with fear, distrust, and aversion. The Indians had reason to feel that they had been deceived and led along a path that had ended in betrayal. Their irritation and anxiety were increased by hunger and an uncertain future. Department officials began to blame the Indians for their misfortunes and to view their spokesmen as troublemakers, incapable of telling the truth. They perceived the items promised to the Indians in their treaties as gratuities, or government charity, rather than as payments for the land that the Indians had ceded. Laird's reaction to Pasquah's mission, for example, was that the chief was a "great beggar," the "most untruthful chief whom I have met in the Superintendency," and he urged that not much importance be attached to his complaints.[107]

Pasquah's mission was not entirely futile. It sparked the beginning of a new policy for the encouragement of agriculture on reserves in the North-West, a policy which was hastened by alarming warnings of an outbreak among the Indians caused by starvation. As M.G. Dickieson wrote to Ottawa that same month: "When the Government has to spend $1,000.00 to perform what $10.00 would at present, they may wake up to the fact that they have been sleeping on a volcano."[108]

CHAPTER THREE

The Home Farm Experiment

A scheme which included instruction in farming to the Indians of the North-West was hastily contrived in the fall and winter of 1878–79. Information and advice were feverishly compiled. David Mills, minister of the interior, began this process in July 1878. Having in his possession the interpreter's record of Pasquah's interview with the lieutenant-governor of Manitoba, Mills interrogated his Indian superintendent, David Laird, on the issue of how the Indians might best be encouraged to farm.[1] In Laird's response of November of that year, directed to the new prime minister and minister of the interior, Sir John A. Macdonald,[2] was the genesis of a new policy toward Indian agriculture. In Laird's opinion the best plan was to have a permanent agricultural instructor resident with the bands. Where a number of reserves were grouped together, one instructor might take charge of three or four bands. For the first few years of farming, seed and provisions would have to be issued in the spring, a time the Indians were generally absolutely destitute.

Laird was sceptical about the viability of farming within the reserve system. The reserves, he believed, perpetuated tribal society, which frustrated the ambitions of individuals genuinely interested in farming, a point of view that was to gain wide acceptance among department officials. On reserves the industrious became the prey of the "indolent and thriftless" Laird thought. Farmers who made efforts to set aside produce for the use of their families, only to see it consumed by their starving brethren, lost heart and dropped to the level of the "precarious hand-to-mouth system of the band." In Laird's view, each Indian should be given in nontransferable scrip his own quantity of land, not in large blocks, but in any section open for settlement. Some might choose to live near fishing lakes, while others might opt to settle near centres of population where they could get work. If the Indians were settled among other residents of the West, Laird surmised, they could turn to their neighbours for the aid and example they might require.[3]

Macdonald also sought information from M.G. Dickieson on conditions in the North-West when the agent's alarming letter of November 1878 was brought to his attention.[4] Dickieson, concerned that officials in Ottawa had the faulty idea that the buffalo were still abundant on the plains, offered detailed evidence of their scarcity in his reply to Macdonald's request.[5] The Indians were starving, Dickieson claimed, even at the former principal wintering places of the buffalo. The widespread shortage of pemmican throughout the North-West was evidence of the rapidly diminishing herds. Hudson's Bay Company storehouses that had stocked thousands of bags in previous years were empty. Destitute Indians arrived almost daily at the Indian office in Battleford seeking assistance. In a review of the progress of farming in the North-West, Dickieson stated that while some bands had made commendable efforts, most Indians, certainly those in Treaty Four, were as yet dependent on the buffalo and would be destitute of food in a very short time. He urged that practical men be hired to instruct in farming and that the Indians be given some assistance in the way of provisions at planting time.

W.J. Christie was consulted on the issue of how the Indians might best be encouraged to farm. He was optimistic that what he called the Thickwood Cree, the Indians of Fort Pelly, the Souris, Fort Ellice, the Touchwood Hills, Fort Carlton, and the Victoria mission, who lived on the margin of the plains, would settle and cultivate. What remained of the buffalo herds could then be left to the true Plains Indians, among whom Christie included the Blackfoot, Blood, Sarcee, and the Cree of Forts Pitt and Qu'Appelle. In Christie's opinion the most feasible plan was to distribute cattle among these bands before the buffalo were completely extinct. Christie was certain that if the treaty provisions had been faithfully fulfilled, those Indians settled on reserves would possess what was required to cultivate the soil, although he stressed the need for instruction and supervision in breaking the ground and in the use of implements. He cautioned that the Indians always expected the faithful fulfilment of any promises made to them by white men.[6]

Christie recalled that at the treaty negotiations some of the Treaty Four bands, and nearly all of those in Treaty Six, expressed a willingness to settle on reserves. He recommended kind treatment and conciliatory measures beyond what was strictly stipulated in the treaty, as he believed the most forceful means of influencing the Indians to settle was to give every encouragement to those already on their reserves. Christie urged that the Indians be granted some of their repeated requests, especially for food when breaking the ground and planting for the first year or two, but also for farm instructors, blacksmiths, mowers, and others knowledgeable in building log houses. He recommended that depots of provisions be established at selected sites, noting that the Hudson's Bay Company had always assisted the Indians in times of need, often at great expense, but that this kind treatment allowed the company to maintain its position of influence.

THE NEW PLAN MATERIALIZES

The government's new program, which was to apply to both the North-West Territories and Manitoba, was first given official voice in the 1878 annual report by the deputy superintendent general of Indian affairs, Lawrence Vankoughnet.[7] The exact details of the policy were vague at this point. The Indians were to be furnished with instruction in farming or raising cattle, with the object of making them self-supporting. The priorities Vankoughnet outlined were to induce the Indians to abandon their nomadic ways by building houses and barns, to subdivide the reserves into lots assigned to each head of family, and to establish schools on reserves where there were sufficient residents to warrant one. At this time Vankoughnet had the idea that the schoolteachers would also instruct in farming and raising cattle. Inspecting officers would visit the reserves, mark the progress of the Indians, purchase cattle, seed, and implements for them, see that the instructors were attending to their duties, and organize annuity payments.

Specifics of the plan were hurriedly sketched in during the early months of 1879 with the creation of the position of Indian commissioner, which was central to the administration of the program. Edgar Dewdney, a civil engineer, Member of Parliament for Kootenay, a loyal Conservative, and a friend of Sir John A. Macdonald, was appointed commissioner in May 1879. In the prime minister's opinion, Dewdney was eminently suitable because he understood the Indians and their wants and was accustomed to frontier conditions.[8] As a surveyor, Dewdney was indeed acquainted with the life of the frontier, but he had had no experience with the Plains Indians and was probably chosen because of his political loyalty. That same year David Laird resigned as Indian superintendent. M.G. Dickieson served as acting Indian superintendent for a brief time, but as Dewdney's appointment rendered this position unnecessary, he was demoted to Indian agent. Dickieson left for Ottawa in 1879 to the more tranquil Department of Finance.[9]

Dewdney's responsibilities, as outlined in May 1879, included a variety of tasks of which the farming program was but one.[10] His more immediate priorities were to see to the distribution of relief to the destitute, to encourage the Indians congregated about Fort Walsh to settle on reserves, and to persuade the refugee Dakota under Sitting Bull to return across the border. The farming program itself was to be implemented through a squad of farm instructors, located at seventeen sites called farming agencies, initially selected by Laird. For the Treaty Four Indians, six were to be set up: one each at sites near Fort Ellice, near Fort Pelly, at Pasquah's reserve, in the Touchwood Hills, and two in the Cypress Hills. Nine farming agencies were to be established in Treaty Six and two in Treaty Seven. The agency farms came to be known as "home farms," a term that in Great Britain referred to the main farm on a large estate, which was usually worked by the landlord and which was situated near his residence. The other farms on the estate were let to tenants. Some were showpiece or "model" farms, while others were run purely as commercial propositions.[11]

The farming program also called for the establishment of two "supply farms," which were to be distinct from the home farms, in the Treaty Seven area, one near Fort Macleod and the other near Fort Calgary. Large quantities of produce were to be raised, but the farmers at these sites were not given the additional responsibility of instructing the Indians.

The program did not apply to the Indians of Treaties One, Two, Three, and Five. Although Vankoughnet had at first announced that the program was to extend to Manitoba, this plan must have been shelved in the early months of 1879. It was explained some years later that farm instructors were sent only to the Plains people, formerly dependent on the buffalo, whose means of subsistence had failed.[12] Clearly it was the food crisis in the North-West that generated the farm instruction program in 1879; it was not inspired by a benevolent concern that the Indians be aided in their transition to an agricultural way of life.

In July 1879 Thomas Page Wadsworth was appointed inspector of agencies.[13] Born in Weston, County of York, Ontario, in 1842, and of English descent, Wadsworth was a resident of Ontario at the time of his appointment, his first position with the public service. His duties were to supervise all operations in connection with the "practical farming schools," to purchase and distribute the food supplies, implements, and cattle required for them, and to help select the sites for these farms. He was to take note of what supplies were on hand and to confer with the agents about the condition and probable requirements of the Indians. As explained to Wadsworth, the object of the farm schools was twofold. The first was to "induce the Indians to come in and learn how to break [sic] up land, how to sow grain, to reap, save and thresh the latter, to put up houses, to take care of stock, to use and take care of farm implements, and generally to teach the Indians and Half Breeds, also, how they may become self subsisting without being dependent upon the chase for a living for themselves and their families."[14] The second was to raise enough produce to become depots of supplies for the Indians in case of famine. Provided with a map of the North-West Territories, Wadsworth was to leave immediately and, after the season's travel, take up residence at Battleford.

The new farming program was designed to solve, at one swoop, most of the problems that plagued administrators of Indian affairs in the North-West. It was hoped that the two objectives would solve both the short- and long-term question of subsistence for the Indians. Architects of the program sanguinely expected that the instructors could, after one year, raise enough grain and root crops to support themselves, their families, and employees. It was also hoped that within a short time they could raise a surplus to contribute toward the expense of feeding the Indians. To help solve the long-term problem of subsistence, the instructors were to impart their knowledge of farming to the Indians. As the program was initially conceived, the educational aspect was decidedly secondary to the mandate to raise food. A program designed primarily to teach the Indians to farm might have been planned quite differently. As it was, farm instructors were told to confine most of their operations to their home farms but to visit the Indians from time to time to instruct in breaking, seeding, harvesting, storing grain and root crops, and in building houses, barns, and root houses.[15] The educational aspect, as Dewdney understood it, was limited to what the Indians might learn by observing or by working on the home farm. In his opinion the government desired to "obtain as great a return of food for the distressed Indians at as cheap a rate as possible." Indians anxious to learn to farm would "soon pick up sufficient information to settle down and work a piece of ground for themselves."[16]

Home farms were also designed to function as depots of supplies of seed, implements, and provisions. During the first few years of treaty administration, it had been recognized that if these goods were to be on hand in the spring, they had to be transported in the fall and stored over the winter. The food crisis in the North-West, however, demanded the presence of supply depots on a year-round basis. Issuing relief was to become one of the primary functions of the farm instructors. Aid was not to be distributed gratuitously, however; it was to be used as a means of instilling a self-help mentality, which, it was believed, would eventually free the Indians from their poverty. In the minds of many officials, the Indians' want of food was due, not to the collapse of their economic system, but to personal failing, indolence, and extravagance. "Work for rations" would introduce the principle of toiling for one's livelihood. It was declared that the "system pursued in affording relief to the Indians is calculated to accustom them to habits of industry; and at the same time to teach them to depend on their own efforts for subsistence."[17] Massive aid was viewed as demoralizing and enfeebling; it would encourage idleness and pauperism. It was felt that the Indians would deliberately choose pauperism if they became comfortable with the idea that they would be abundantly supplied. Able-bodied Indians were to receive rations only when they had satisfied the farm instructor that they had performed some work of value either on the home farm or on the reserve. Thus it largely fell to the farm instructors to establish and administer the government's relief program.

THE FARM INSTRUCTORS

The instructors were burdened with responsibilities and duties of herculean dimensions that would have taxed the resources and patience of the most qualified, capable candidates. Unfortunately many of those assigned to the formidable task were ill suited and unprepared. The instructors were almost all from the eastern provinces, mostly Ontario. They were unfamiliar with conditions of life in the West and knew nothing of the Indians, their languages, customs, or recent history. They had to be provided with both guides and interpreters. Arriving in the midst of a famine, they tended to be shocked and repelled by the unsightly distress that surrounded them. While the instructors may have had extensive knowledge of farming, unique, unanticipated conditions prevailed in the North-West, which demanded modification of techniques suitable elsewhere. Red River farmers or former Hudson's Bay Company employees might have been more qualified for positions as farm instructors. A rationale forwarded for not choosing local people, familiar with the Indians and their territory, was that "strangers" were likely to carry out their duties better than local people, as they would not have their favourites and would treat all fairly and alike.[18]

It is clear, however, that the prime minister had his favourites and that patronage extended to the position of farm instructor. The instructors were chosen by Macdonald himself, from a list furnished by Vankoughnet, who claimed to have interviewed them all and to have made strict inquiries about their abilities as farmers.[19] The list was initially compiled by John Stoughton Dennis of the Department of the Interior, who sent letters to Members of Parliament asking them to submit names of candidates. In his letters Dennis explained that the object was to obtain young, practical farmers, who had some acquaintance with the construction of houses and outbuildings, such as were commonly used by farmers in the eastern provinces. They were to proceed to the North-West where they were to settle down among the Indians on their reserves for the purpose of teaching them how to farm and take care of stock. Dennis cautioned that the men would be isolated from white settlers by some hundreds of miles in several cases and must expect to have to suffer "more or less privation" for a salary of seven hundred and thirty dollars a year. For the first year they were to subsist on the supplies they had brought with them, but thereafter they were expected to live on the produce they had raised. The government would supply them with implements and stock and would defray their travelling expenses. Since the cost of sending men to the West was great, Dennis asked the Members to be very careful not to recommend anyone whom they doubted.[20]

It appears that even this initial process of compiling a list was not completed until the spring of 1879, whereupon instructors were hastily chosen and dispatched to the North-West. In the case of one instructor at least, Vankoughnet did not have the opportunity to conduct a personal interview. Thomas Farrow, Member of Parliament for North Huron, Ontario, had recommended a Mr James Patterson of St Helens, Quebec. Patterson's credentials included the fact that having arrived in Ontario when it was in its "primitive" state, he had experience with a new country. He was an excellent scholar, Farrow informed Dennis, and he could impart all the practical knowledge required for both farming and building.[21] Patterson left for the North-West with three others in late August 1879. F. White of the North-West Mounted Police encountered the party on their journey that fall and was dismayed to find that Patterson was an aged man and a cripple, who was walking with the aid of a crutch and stick. An embarrassed Vankoughnet informed the prime minister of the incident and explained that Patterson had not been required to visit Ottawa because the season was getting late when the last group of instructors was appointed. He admitted that "it cannot be supposed that a man so crippled as to require the aid of a stick and crutch can do farm work effectively," and he recommended that Patterson be recalled and an able-bodied person appointed in his stead.[22]

The farm instructors gained a reputation for being incompetent men, chosen from the government's "swarm of camp followers" and "carpetbaggers."[23] They were the object of much amusement, scorn, and, after 1885, indignant outrage, certainly among opponents of the Macdonald government. Whether these charges were an accurate assessment of the talents of the instructors, they and the Indian farmers were blamed for the limited success of a program that was hastily and poorly conceived and for which expectations were unrealistic. As Macdonald confessed in the House of Commons, there had not been time to theorize: men had to be sent at once to provide assistance. He hoped that when the problem could be considered at greater leisure, a more scientific mode of government for "our Indian wards" might be devised.[24]

In July 1879 a special train conveying one squad of farm instructors headed for the terminus of the railway, then at St Boniface, Manitoba. Some of the confusions and adversities that plagued the program from its inception may be illustrated by tracing the fortunes of one who was aboard, a Mr James Scott, appointed instructor to the Touchwood Hills bands. Scott's personnel file reveals nothing of his background except that he had "extensive knowledge of farming" and "general business experience."[25] He boarded the special train at Toronto on 21 June, leaving his wife and seven children behind in Brampton. In company with the instructors headed for Forts Pelly, Ellice, and Qu'Appelle, Scott left Winnipeg for the Touchwood Hills on 21 July. A guide was provided at Winnipeg to take them as far as Ellice, and there the Hudson's Bay Company officer was to hire guides to take them to their locations. They left Winnipeg "under protest," as they were very heavily loaded down "to please those in charge."[26] This was the instructors' first lesson in the fact that economy was to govern all their operations, even when good sense ruled otherwise. The instructors brought with them everything from farm implements and provisions to window sashes, doors, stovepipes, and teapots. Some supplies were sent on by boat to Ellice, but the men were still overburdened. They found it impossible to proceed farther than Portage la Prairie without acquiring two more carts. Here Thomas Heenan, the instructor destined for Qu'Appelle, was taken ill and returned home, leaving his outfit in the care of Scott. Scott arrived at Ellice on 10 August, only to learn that the balance of his supplies had not arrived as promised, and so he was obliged to purchase what was absolutely necessary for both his and the Qu'Appelle farm. He was also informed that Rev. Père Joseph Lestanc, his interpreter, had moved several hundred miles from the Qu'Appelle district. Scott arrived at the Hudson's Bay Company store in the Touchwood Hills on the evening of 20 August, his horses completely jaded and his carts badly damaged. His journey from Winnipeg had taken thirty days.

Accompanied by T.P. Wadsworth, Scott visited the reserves late in August and chose a site for the farm, which both described as excellent for agriculture.[27] It consisted of an optimistic 640 acres: 400 acres were intended for cropping, 80 for hay meadows, and the rest was mostly woodlands with a small lake. It was situated on the main trail between Winnipeg and Battleford, about a mile east of Poor Man's reserve and twelve miles from the Hudson's Bay Company post.

Wadsworth left Scott with a set of directives, which was distributed to all instructors. He was first to cut sufficient hay to winter his four oxen. He was then to erect a stable and a house for himself. These buildings were to be as small and as inexpensive as possible, and were later to be used as granaries. The rationale was that since it might be desirable to change the location of some of these farms before long, no more building than was absolutely necessary should be done.[28] Wadsworth advised that Indians be used for building, cutting and preparing fence rails, and pit sawing in exchange for flour, tea, and sometimes pork. Scott was to insist on work being done in exchange for the distribution of food, except to the infirm, in line with the government's work for rations policy. Next Scott was to look over his farm, decide how much land to sow, and determine the variety and amount of seed grain required. He was to visit each reserve and make similar plans for the Indians' farms. In deciding the kind and amount of seed required for the Indians, the instructor was to keep in mind the amount of acreage he could oversee and have properly planted for them. The inspector recommended that instructors resist the urge to overextend operations and emphasized quality over quantity. He asked them to plough the prairie twice, which, he admitted, was double the work and reduced the amount of land that could be sown, but the procedure would almost certainly result in a better crop. Scott was also to examine the tools each band had on hand. As the bulk of his provisions had not arrived, Wadsworth authorized Scott to purchase what he needed from the Hudson's Bay Company store.

Scott's farming operations did not begin until 10 September, mainly because of the late arrival of much of his equipment. His interpreter, who was also to be his general assistant, was over seventy years old and proved to be of little use as a labourer. Another of his assistants badly injured his foot while chopping wood and was unable to work for much of September. As winter was approaching, and housing timber was not available nearer than seven miles, Scott opted to build his granary and live in it until spring and haul timber for his house during the winter. He hired a mower and stacked forty tons of hay. As Scott's report for that fall made no mention of ploughing, it is likely that no land was prepared for a spring crop.

Some of the conflicts and tensions that were to beset the program soon became apparent. The question of who owned the produce raised on the instructor's farm became a contentious issue. Scott arrived with the impression that what he raised was his to dispose with as he pleased. He understood that his salary was for his services as instructor. On being greeted by the Touchwood bands, however, he found that "the Indians look on everything we have with us, and all we raise besides, as their property, and if we even cut the grass off their land for our stock, they can claim it, and in all probability will do so. Now if such is the case I am positive I did not understand it so and I am sure none of the other instructors did either, as we discussed it all over, on the train coming up."[29] Scott also found that the Indians would not tolerate his purchasing supplies, such as potatoes and barley, from the Hudson's Bay Company. They claimed the right to sell their produce to him and at Hudson's Bay Company prices.

Upon inspecting the reserves, Scott found that, for a variety of reasons, little progress in agriculture had been made. There was not enough arable land on some reserves. Scott discovered that the ploughs and harrows had been issued incomplete: "some wanting rods, some bolts or nuts and all of them without either clevis, doubletrees or wiffletrees."[30] In George Gordon's band the chief had been keeping the stock, implements, and tools for the use of his own and extended family, which was naturally resented by other members of the band. Scott submitted to agent Allan MacDonald a lengthy list of implements and livestock critical to the start of farm work in the spring. He tried to impress upon the agent the importance of having these on hand by the beginning of May because it was only through promises of help with the spring work on the reserves that Scott had persuaded anyone to work on the home farm.

During the winter Scott was beset with problems over the workers on the home farm. As he had as many as twenty-one labourers a day working for rations, Scott was low on provisions by January

1880. He was obliged to issue Indian Department pork, which, he reported "is both *musty* and *rusty* and totally unfit for use – although we are giving it out to the Indians, in the absence of anything better, but we *cannot use it ourselves*." That winter the workers cut timber for a barn, rails for fencing, and logs for homes. They complained to Scott that "if they could not get some clothing, they would be obliged to quit work, *which I knew to be the case*."[31] Without authorization, Scott purchased a few blankets and moose skins to help clothe the workers.

Farm instructor Scott became increasingly disillusioned with the job he remained at for two years. He rarely had adequate provisions to pay Indian labourers, even though they constantly applied for work. The harrows he received were "the worst specimens I ever saw and not worth the freight." In March 1881 Scott complained that he did not even have a horse: "I know no man living who can do justice to the Indians and be obliged to walk from the farm to the different Reserves." He had no stationery or stamps and resented having to request permission to purchase anything or take any action. Obliged to travel to Qu'Appelle to see a doctor about his own health, he wondered whether it was necessary for him to "write Mr Dewdney for permission?"[32] Scott did not even have the comfort of a family life, since he felt that the North-West was not the proper place to bring his wife and children.

The experiences of Scott were repeated, with variations, throughout the North-West Territories at the seventeen agency and two supply farms. As the plan was initially conceived in Ottawa, these farms were to be on the reserves, but as the program materialized, they became increasingly detached from the reserves and the Indians. Most of the farms were located off the reserves, and the instructors were urged to perform the bulk of the work "with our own labour," rather than Indian labour. Otherwise, Indian Commissioner Dewdney explained, the Indians would feel entitled to the improvements to the farm and to any crop raised.[33] Surplus produce, Scott and the other instructors were informed, did not belong to them, and it certainly did not belong to the Indians. It, as well as the stock and implements, was the property of the government and was to be stored in a central depot and held subject to the order of the Indian agent for the district.[34] Home farms were placed off the reserves for other reasons: to avoid jealousies among bands that did not have a farm on their reserves and to promote a sense of independence among the instructors. It was also learned through experience that disagreements over property were intensified when the home farms were located on the reserves. In the

Fort Pitt district, for example, Inspector Wadsworth and farm instructor P.J. Williams selected a site for the agency farm on Chief Sekaskootch's reserve while the chief and the band were away hunting.[35] When the chief returned, he would not permit Williams to occupy the farm or to make use of the hay he had cut and stacked unless he paid twenty dollars. Three days of negotiations followed, and in the end the department was required to take a lease on the land for five years, which gave the instructor the right to cut wood and hay.

From an administrative point of view, the home farm policy was disastrous. Difficulties with personnel arose early, and the program was characterized by resignations and dismissals. Frank L. Hunt, instructor to the Qu'Appelle Indians near Pasquah's reserve, had resigned by the spring of 1880. He had appeared eminently suitable to the task, with fifteen years' experience in farming and stock-raising and a "familiarity with frontier life and its requirements."[36] Unlike most other instructors, Hunt had some previous knowledge of and association with the Indians he was to work with: he spoke Cree and was married to Pasquah's sister, a daughter of the Fox. Hunt had been present at the Treaty Four negotiations and had published an article on the proceedings.[37] At the time of his appointment he was working as a journalist in Winnipeg. Hunt spent one bitterly cold winter at his new posting and found that his job consisted of administering relief to Indians in acute distress. He described the bands as genuinely in need: the people were suffering greatly and showing clear signs of starvation. The children, he wrote, were "*really* crying for food." His own supplies were totally drained, and he was obliged to purchase more from the Hudson's Bay Company store. Gravely concerned that the Indians would attempt to possess government property by force and worried that he would be the target of violence, he appealed for a strong military or police force to be near at hand. Hunt was uncomfortable about administering relief and had "grave doubts as to the outcome of this sort of aid."[38] Citing these reasons, as well as ill health, he resigned from his position.

Hunt was not the only instructor to leave in the spring of 1880. Mr Sherrin, instructor near the Battleford reserves, and Mr Read, his assistant, were both asked to resign.[39] Sherrin was found trading government provisions with the Indians for furs and cash and pocketing the proceeds. Read had informed on Sherrin, who countered with the claim that Read was unreliable, was a thief who stole from his own father, was lazy, and had never been on a farm in his life. Dewdney decided that the incident, claims, and counterclaims cast both in a poor light. Instructor Donnelly at Saddle Lake in present-day Alberta resigned that spring, informing Dewdney that he had hoped to bring his family out if the location suited him but found on arrival that he could not think of doing so.[40] R.W. Gowan, farm instructor to the Stonies at Morley in present-day Alberta, also asked for a replacement, remarking only that things were not satisfactory with the Indians and he could not carry out the instructions given him.[41] Although offered a position at a much reduced salary at Moose Mountain, Gowan's name disappeared from the list of farm instructors. H. Taylor, in charge of the government supply farm near Fort Macleod, tendered his resignation in May 1880. Although an investigation into the matter proved inconclusive, he and an accomplice were implicated in the slaughter of government cattle that winter, and it was claimed that they sold the meat to settlers.[42]

Dewdney was irritated at the situation in the spring of 1880, as a good number of the new home farms were without instructors. The outlook for a successful crop year already looked dim, the instructors having arrived too late the previous year to prepare much land for sowing. To salvage the season, Dewdney was determined that men on the spot be hired as replacements. Convinced that residents of the North-West would be much more suitable appointments, he was angry that the prime minister continued to insist the positions be filled by men on his patronage list. Macdonald's priority was not to meet the needs of the Indians but to keep his political allies content.

A dispute between Dewdney and the prime minister erupted over the appointment of Charles Daunais De Cadis of Terrebonne, Quebec, recommended to Macdonald by the Member for Terrebonne, Louis F. Masson.[43] Having been notified by Macdonald to appoint this man on the first vacancy, there being no French-Canadian instructors in the North-West, Vankoughnet decided that De Cadis would replace Sherrin at Battleford. Dewdney had already hired an instructor and an assistant from Winnipeg, however, and he objected to the appointment of more farmers from the eastern provinces. He believed that many of the farmers had made "a convenience of the Government" in accepting their positions, seeing "a good chance of getting their expenses paid to enable them to look at the country and see for themselves where would be the best locations to settle if the country suited them." Since transporting men from the East incurred large expenses, Dewdney urged that farmers vacating their posts within a certain time be required to give three or even six months' notice or be asked to pay the cost of their transport and other expenses. He believed it was imperative that steps be taken to hire only those acquainted with Indians: it was the exception to find a farm instructor formerly unacquainted with the Indians who was able to "hold his own" with them. "This is especially so when they are starving," Dewdney wrote, as the instructors "either give away too much and that means being too lavish with the Government supplies or they get disgusted with their position and take the first opportunity of getting out of it." Many of the farmers from the East had no idea what they had to contend with once they arrived on their farms. Dewdney argued that only those likely to be contented with their lot should be appointed. He had reason to believe that a number of the farmers felt they were above the position and were thinking of "their own advancement more than the work they have undertaken from the Government."[44]

Despite Dewdney's objections, De Cadis was appointed to Battleford, where he proved unsuccessful as both a farmer and an instructor. He took little interest in the Indians and was not on good terms with them.[45] After just over a year, De Cadis was transferred to the Edmonton district, where he was placed in charge of a soup kitchen. Macdonald, however, was eventually persuaded to hire men already resident in the North-West. They were paid at a much reduced rate, and the time and expense involved in transporting men from the East were saved. Those who were still offered appointments from Macdonald's patronage list were told they would have to pay their own transportation, which discouraged many.[46]

The farming program was the target of severe criticism in the House of Commons in the spring of 1880. David Mills, the main spokesman for the opposition, claimed that the instructors were entirely unsuitable to the task. These men were not farmers, he stated: Scott at Touchwood and Sherrin at Battleford had been engaged in "mercantile pursuits" before they went West, and Hunt at Qu'Appelle had been a newspaperman in Winnipeg.[47] (The prime minister replied that "perhaps it was an agricultural newspaper.") Joseph Royal, Conservative Member for Provencher, Manitoba, regretted that the farm instructors were not chosen from among the mixed-blood population. He believed that clever farmers might have been selected at a lesser cost, and with a greater chance of success, than the "indifferent Ontario farmers" sent out.[48] To the opposition, however, the instructors were not at the root of the problem; they objected to any increased expenditure on the Indians. Mills believed that the government's new policy acted "not to secure a survival of the fittest, but a survival of everybody, to put the industrious and enterprizing upon an equality with the careless and idle."[49] He urged the government to throw the Indians upon their own resources, stating that the Indians who left their reserves were more prosperous than those who remained. Edward Blake, Liberal Member for West Durham, Ontario, agreed that the Indians should not be allowed to look to the government for help, but, rather, a spirit of independence should be implanted.[50] Also alarmed at the increased expenditure, J.C. Schultz, Conservative Member for Lisgar, Manitoba, remarked that in his opinion it was impossible to convert the horse-riding, buffalo-hunting Indian of the plains into a farmer. He favoured a plan that would see the Indians transferred to the "great fishing regions" north of the proposed railway line, distant from the land which would be desired by the settlers. Here could be found all the conditions required for successful agriculture, as well as those that would allow the Indians to indulge their "love of the chase." Such a move would also result in much relief to government expenditure in winter.[51] Royal agreed with Schultz that it was "sheer folly to attempt to make farmers out of the roaming bands of the plains."[52]

The prime minister mustered some arguments in support of his government's new program. He believed it was absolutely necessary that the Indians be induced to settle and take up agricultural pursuits to maintain peace. As long as the pressure for food existed, "starvation, operating upon the savage minds" might result in the Indians' quarrelling among one another or attacking the whites.[53] It was in the interests of the orderly settlement of the West that the Indians be taught to farm properly, as their "slatternly and slovenly" mode of farming retarded "civilization and improvement" in the vicinity of a reserve.[54] Macdonald agreed with Schultz that it would be highly desirable if the Indians could be induced to move north, but, he noted, that unless they consented to such a move, it would involve pressure. Although he had no evidence that the Indians were complaining about their instructors, the prime minister also agreed with Royal that residents of the West might have been employed as instructors, because to teach the Indians to break the ground, scientific farmers were not required. Rather, the job called for "a rough man who knows himself how to handle the plough."[55] Macdonald assured the House that future vacancies would be filled by residents of the West, who understood the Indian character. To counter the claim that government help destroyed the Indians' independence, Macdonald stated that they were not learning to rely on the government for food, as "we are rigid, even stingy" in distributing rations. His government's position on the Indians of the North-West was that "we cannot allow them to starve and we cannot make them white men. All we can do is endeavour to induce them to abandon their nomadic habits, and settle down, and cultivate the soil." "The whole thing is an experiment however," Macdonald admitted, "and if it does not succeed, we can alter the mode of operations."[56]

DIFFICULTIES FACED BY THE INDIAN FARMER

With criticism of the program coming even from the government benches, Macdonald would have welcomed any evidence of the success of his government's measures. Unfortunately Dewdney was not able to provide any. The farming program did not distinguish itself during the 1880 season, and the results of subsequent years were dreary. Department officials in the East and Members of Parliament, confounded by the discrepancies between the outlay for the farm program and the limited returns, had little appreciation of the difficulties involved in raising crops in the North-West or of the many factors that could frustrate and retard the enterprise. In attributing blame for the limited success of the program, they preferred instead to belittle and deprecate the abilities of the Indian farmers.

Farming at this time in the Territories was a dubious, precarious undertaking for anyone, even an experienced Ontario farmer. It was not to be for a decade and more that suitable techniques for dryland farming were discovered through trial and error and the work of the experimental farms. Prairie farming demanded new methods of ploughing, seeding, cultivation, and summer-fallowing to preserve moisture. For many of these operations, implements in common use in the East were found to be unsuitable to the prairie soil. The brief growing season required new, early-maturing varieties of seed, as well as the most efficient, time-saving machinery.

The Indian farmers and their instructors were without any of this information and technology when they began farming in 1879. It appears that when the program was established, it was not recognized that conditions peculiar to western Canada might prevail. It was already clear from the experiences of farmers in Manitoba in the 1870s that because of the late springs, early frosts, uneven moisture, and unrelenting winds, Ontario methods could not simply be transplanted with success.[57] None of this evidence, however, was taken into account. The Indian farmers and their instructors were simply expected to produce, and quickly. Through their pioneering efforts to farm west of Manitoba on any scale, they were the first to encounter many of the limitations and requirements of prairie farming that were later to baffle and frustrate the "homesteaders."

The first requirement of prairie farming was to break the sod, a slow and laborious process. Any bush had to be cleared first and any stones hauled away. If the spring run-off was early, a farmer might be able to harrow enough acres during a first season to plant small amounts of grain and root crops. With late springs, however, no land could be broken in time for seeding because oxen and implements would bog down after the first furrow. As well, farmers breaking the prairie generally ploughed twice. First they turned the soil in shallow furrows and then "backset" at a deeper level, not sowing until the following spring.[58] As previously noted, Inspector Wadsworth recommended this method to his instructors, although he recognized that it decreased the amount of acreage that could be broken.[59] Ploughing once, he explained, would turn up only a small quantity of very thin sod, which would make it difficult to cover the seed. A second ploughing turned the loose subsoil to allow for a seedbed on top of the sod.

The efforts of the Indian farmers and their instructors were hampered by the kind of ploughs the department issued. By the late 1870s Manitoba farmers had learned that American ploughs, especially the John Deere with its chilled-steel mouldboard, were far superior for western conditions than the Ontario models.[60] The Indian Department, however, endeavoured to introduce Canadian-manufactured ploughs, which proved to be unsatisfactory. Ploughs made by George Wilkinson and Company, of Aurora, Ontario, for example, "worked for a short time, but the mould-board and point both proved soft in temper."[61] Other Canadian ploughs were entire failures and were discarded as useless. It was not until after 1882 that the department began to request specifically John Deere ploughs for the North-West in calls for tenders, after determining that no Canadian plough was satisfactory for prairie work.

Grave problems arose as well in asking the instructors to attend to both their own farms and those of the Indians. In the climate of the North-West, only a short time is available for the completion of the main tasks of farming. Seeding, for example, has to be completed early in the spring to lessen the danger of exposure to frost. The instructor could not both prepare and seed his own land and oversee the same activities on many different reserves. To save time improper techniques were sometimes used, such as scattering the seed on the sod and merely harrowing to cover the grain lightly.[62] Seeding was performed broadcast by hand on these early farms in the North-West, a method, although successful in Ontario, was unsuitable on the plains. Because broadcast seeding left the grain only lightly covered, it speedily became too dry to germinate, it could not take advantage of the moisture in the subsoil, and it was subject to the unrelenting prairie winds. It was not until the late 1880s that western farmers began to sow their seed in drills at a uniform depth.[63] The inefficiency of the broadcast method of sowing may in part account for the limited returns from these early farms.

Wheat was the major grain crop on these farms, followed by barley and oats, with root crops of potatoes, turnips, and carrots next. Officials in the North-West expressed doubts about whether the Indians should rely heavily on wheat. A number of problems were involved. Wheat had to be planted as soon as the snow was gone in the spring and fall ploughed, so that with the few oxen available, only a small acreage could be assured of success. Without grist mills, it was of very little use. Barley at least could be soaked, pounded, and boiled in soup. Wadsworth believed his instructors should encourage the Indians to grow mainly potatoes, a crop with which they had the greatest success.[64] Seed of any variety, however, was often in short supply or of poor quality. Acres sometimes lay idle because no seed was available, and more land might have been broken had there been seed to sow.[65] Bad roads and swollen streams often made it impossible to transport seed before the season was too far advanced for planting.[66] Although the Indians were encouraged to save their seed for the following spring, this was difficult when food supplies ran low in winter.

Oxen provided the motive power for these early farmers and for the homesteaders who followed them. They were cheaper than horses, did not require stabling except in winter, and did not have to be fed oats. They were difficult beasts to work with at the best of times, having a tendency to head to a slough for a drink whenever they pleased, even while hitched to the plough or harrows.[67] If bothered by mosquitoes or flies, they simply refused to work. Some of the oxen supplied by the Indian Department appear to have been particularly stubborn. Freight animals, which had never ploughed or worked in pairs, were sent to some reserves.[68] Some of the oxen were not broken and would not allow the farmers to drive or go near them. In 1878 a good many bands received wild Montana cattle, which were unaccustomed to work and unapproachable except on horseback.[69] The milk cows they were given were of the same description. Those distributed to the Carlton bands were "sorefooted, poor and wild," and most of them died over their first winter.[70] In the spring of 1878 it was reported that little ploughing could be accomplished in the Touchwood Hills: not one of the oxen would permit being hitched to the plough.[71] The Indians attempted to hitch the bull, which also was unsuccessful.

Yet oxen were essential and influenced the extent and quality of farming operations. From the beginning of the farming program, the scarcity of working cattle was recognized and lamented by officials and Indians alike. Not as much land could be broken or prepared for seeding each year as the farmers would have liked. The limited number of oxen also affected seeding. That operation had to be completed in a short time after spring run-off, so that the seed had time to ripen before the onset of frost. If seeding was delayed, the crops could be destroyed by frost.[72] The presence of the home farms further complicated the situation. In some instances oxen were available to the Indians only when the greater part of the work on the instructor's farm was completed.[73]

The treaty provisions for oxen, as well as for farm implements, were found to be totally inadequate. In 1881 Dewdney noted that the "want of more teams and implements is felt by the Indians from one end of the territory to another." He singled out Treaty Four as particularly wanting, since only one yoke of oxen was distributed to each band and one plough to every ten families. To earn a living from the soil a yoke of oxen was required by every farming family, Dewdney claimed. During this period the department began to loan a limited number of cattle above treaty obligations to some bands.[74] Despite the fact that reports of the Indians killing their cattle were extremely rare, even during the leanest of winters, and despite comments by some officials that the Indians paid great care and attention to their animals, most officials were convinced that the Indians would prefer to eat their cattle than use them as beasts of burden. The system of loaning cattle was instituted only to prevent their "killing and abduction."[75] Loaning cattle led to some problems: in some cases the Indians refused to be responsible for wintering the animals and wanted to hand them back to the department once the season was over.[76]

All available oxen and wagons were required for haying and harvesting. Since these operations had to be completed at about the same time during most seasons, the scarcity of teams and implements placed both in jeopardy. Hay for winter feed was generally cut in midsummer, but the exact time varied, depending on whether it was a dry or wet year. The wild grasses were cut with sickles or scythes and left for a time to cure on the field where they were turned and shaken up to admit light and air. The hay was then gathered, loaded onto carts and wagons, and stacked. Haying was accomplished on most reserves with hand implements, although during this early period a few of the bands acquired mechanical mowers and rakes. As with most farming operations in the North-West, speed and efficiency were at a premium, and periods of dry weather had to be used to the limit. The interval between the time the wild grass had grown to sufficient bulk and the time it became woody and of inferior quality was quite short. Just at the time the prairie grasses were ready for cutting, the barley might well have ripened. The wheat harvest too often curtailed haying activities. Because hay made after the crops were harvested was inferior,[77] mowers and rakes were the earliest and most numerous of the machinery that farmers acquired in Manitoba.[78] Indian Affairs officials in the North-West began to recognize that such machinery was vital to farming in that region. With reapers and mowers to help speed the harvest of hay and grain, much less was lost to frost.[79] The department did not provide them, but several bands, including those of Pasquah, Cowessess, and Sakimay, sold enough hay to purchase mowers and rakes in 1883.[80] Groups or bands, not individuals, together owned these implements.

The harvest was accomplished with the scythe and grain cradle. After reaping, the grain was raked by hand, bound into bundles, and set into shocks, or stooks. A mechanical reaper was noted on only one reserve during the early 1880s, and binders, which not only cut the grain but also tied it into bundles, were as yet unknown in the Territories. Threshing, the process of beating the kernels of grain out of the heads, was done with the flail or by animals, which trampled the grain on a smooth surface such as hard-packed ground. On some reserves the grain was threshed little by little as required throughout the winter: placed on ice, the grain was beaten with a flail.[81] The grain then had to be separated from the chaff with the help of the wind, not a very agreeable task in frigid temperatures. Shovels of grain were tossed into the air when the breeze was right, to carry away the lighter chaff, and the cleaned grain would fall into a pile. Two bands in Treaty Six together purchased a threshing machine in 1881, but it had broken down by 1883, and the Indians were once again threshing on ice with the flail.[82] There was also a threshing machine in the Treaty Seven district, but it was in poor repair from being continually moved over great distances.[83]

In this period most of the crop failures were attributed to frost, either because a scarcity of teams and implements at harvest time slowed the process or because the grain failed to ripen altogether before it was struck. In the earliest period of settlement, frosts on the great wheat plains could occur every month of the year, an event now very rare.[84] It is not known what variety of wheat was attempted on the reserve and instructor farms, but it was to be many years before experiments secured an early maturing variety of wheat for the North-West. In the late 1870s Red Fife was found to yield well in the Manitoba lowlands, but even it took too long to mature in less favourable seasons in the North-West.[85] To lessen the risk of frost, fall ploughing was encouraged on reserves in the North-West during this period. It was believed that fields that had been so ploughed could be sown ten days ahead of the rest in spring and that the grain would ripen two weeks earlier.[86] The shortage of working oxen, however, often prevented the completion of fall ploughing. Frost destroyed not only grain but often large portions of the potato crop. Drought caused crop failure some years. Hail totally destroyed crops in certain districts. Damage to crops was also caused by horses and cattle breaking into fields.

Even if a wheat crop overcame all the obstacles and was successfully harvested and threshed, it was of little use if it could not be ground into flour. In his request for a grist mill, which he claimed was promised to him, Poundmaker stated that his people were starving beside their big stacks of grain, since they could do nothing with their wheat.[87] In attempting to explain why the expenses for feeding the Indians did not diminish from year to year, Commissioner Dewdney pointed out that because there were no grist mills, the Indians could not subsist on their own produce, which, he claimed, they otherwise possessed in sufficient quantity. He was also loathe to encourage or allow the Indians to travel great distances to the location of grist mills because work would stop and nomadic habits reinforced. Officials in the field often commented during this period that Indian farmers could not realize the value of farming until they had access to mills, a lack of which caused them to be disheartened and discouraged with the enterprise. Inspector Wadsworth too believed that "they will attach more value to farming as soon as they can have the products of their labour turned into a substantial article of food."[88]

The Indians laboured under other disadvantages as well. With the disappearance of the buffalo, their main source for all their apparel also vanished. After his first visits among the Indians in the fall of 1879, Wadsworth predicted that their lack of clothing and footwear would be the greatest drawback to their work the next spring.[89] In 1880 Dewdney stated that the Plains Indians were in a "deplorable state" with respect to clothing.[90] To cover their feet they were cutting up old leather lodges, but these were also rapidly diminishing. Three, and sometimes four, families were being crowded into one lodge. Often hungry, weak, and ill, they could not work, no matter how willing. Illnesses were brought on by the sudden reduction of their diet to flour and salt pork. Some of the bacon they were issued was "rusty, old and thin and altogether unfit for food."[91] Although rations were distributed, it was done in a manner calculated to discourage the recipients from thinking that they could rely on them as a means of support, and they were often suspended for many days at a time. To keep from starving the Indians were compelled to leave their reserves to hunt, trap, fish, and gather roots and berries over a much wider territory. Once seeding was finished, and sometimes even before, many residents of the reserves were out on the plains, leaving behind only a few to tend the crops. They were generally encouraged to go by their agents and instructors, as it resulted in a saving to the department, despite the fact that farming operations were virtually suspended.[92]

Opportunities to obtain capital to purchase clothing and other necessities were very limited. Although the Indians did work – on reserve or home farms, on public trails and bridges in some districts[93] – they were paid in rations. They also cut large amounts of rails for fencing and cordwood, often when there was no demand for most of the wood. Dewdney reported that work for rations was very difficult to enforce, particularly on the Plains Cree reserves. The Cree, he said, were quite willing to work, but the number of tools and implements issued under treaty could not keep very many employed. Newcomers, who constantly augmented the populations of the reserves during this period, were also promised rations on their arrival, and officials at times found themselves rationing to the same extent both those who had performed work and those who had not. Some agents believed the Indians would see the advantage of their work only if they were paid in wages to enable them to purchase clothing and other necessities. The Indians did not always see the work they performed for rations as their course of study in the mysteries of self-help and industry. The Piegan, for example, refused to work on the agency farm unless they received wages.[94] They were willing to work for themselves for rations, but for extra work expected wages.

Even those bands with surplus crops to sell during this period had no markets, since their farming experiment had begun before the appearance of the railroad and the small towns that followed its route. They were similarly at a loss for meat, clothing, tea, and tobacco.[95] Some officials urged the Indian Affairs Department to purchase surplus grain from Indians; money which went to contractors could go to the Indians, and the grain could be bought at a much lower price. Yet grain was reported to have been purchased from the Indians on very few occasions. In 1882 the instructor for Little Black Bear's band at File Hills bought eight bushels of seed wheat from them and in exchange distributed tea, tobacco, and calico.[96] Instructors and agents were later informed, however, that they could not exchange provisions for the Indians' wheat.[97]

Department officials hoped that the solution to the Indians' lack of capital would come with increased settlement, which would offer greater opportunities for employment. There was little recognition or concern that outside employment would directly interfere with reserve agriculture. Dewdney suggested that the Indians be hired to get out ties and grade for the CPR on a section of perhaps ten or more miles of line, which could be set apart for the purpose. The department would furnish the tools and provisions, "the price of which could be deducted from the amount agreed to be paid to the Indians for the ties furnished; any balance due them could be paid in clothing or other necessaries, and, perhaps, a little cash, which would be a great inducement for them to enter into this arrangement."[98] The plan was mentioned to the Qu'Appelle Indians, and, according to Dewdney, they were willing, even anxious, to undertake the work.

In districts where settlement had begun, the Indians worked at breaking land, getting out rails, and fencing for the settlers for which they were paid a good wage.[99] As had already been found in Manitoba, however, it was difficult to persuade the Indians to work on their reserves for rations when they could obtain wage employment elsewhere. The debilitating scarcity of implements and teams was further exacerbated when they were taken off the reserves at key times of the year.

The reports of agents and instructors throughout the Territories during this period confirm that the Indians began their agricultural enterprise with considerable energy and curiosity.[100] Officials in the field attributed setbacks, not to the Indians' character and traditions, but to the economic and climatic conditions that made farming a dubious and uncertain undertaking. Only one particularly vocal and articulate agent, whose views were eventually to be of considerable influence, claimed that peculiar idiosyncracies of the Indians' culture prevented them from becoming successful farmers. Hayter Reed, appointed Indian agent at Battleford in May 1881, argued in his reports that because of the Indians' "inherent, restless disposition," they simply found reserve life monotonous, and, rather than making any exertions, preferred to trust to the "Supreme Being" to care for them in their trials.[101] Reed assigned the causes of the Indians' poor crops to their religious ceremonies, which diverted attention from their farms, and to their propensity to share their crops and "raid" their own fields. His views were to prevail above those of many others. Reed's explanations for the Indians' limited success at farming were more convenient than those that involved a complex of factors which included climate, geography, oxen, implements, seed, mills, and markets. They also absolved the government of much responsibility in the matter.

EVOLUTION AND END OF THE PROGRAM

The home farm program had a very brief life in its original form. By 1884 the department had officially retired the policy, which had already undergone much modification. The number of farm instructors had been increased from seventeen to twenty-three, but their farms were to consist of no more than fifteen or twenty acres each. As previously noted, new recruits were no longer brought from Ontario but were men of the country, hired for their ability to work with Indians as well as for their skills as farmers. They were paid less than the original instructors and some were hired for the growing season only.

The idea that the home farms were to perform an educational function was abandoned. It was recognized that the instructors, in trying to make successes of their farms, had very little time to teach the Indians. According to one agent, the instructors preferred to work for themselves rather than be subjected to the "constant monotony of teaching." Being some distance from the reserves, seldom employing Indian labour, and producing little surplus, the home farms in fact performed no function at all. Nor did the instructors spend much time at the reserve farms. To supervise seeding and harvesting on reserves that were sometimes fifty or sixty miles apart required large teams of assistants. The instructors seldom visited the reserves and lacked even basic knowledge about the bands under their supervision, such as the population of each and the kind of implements in their possession.[102] As a result, the new appointees, as well as the original instructors, had been asked as early as 1881 to spend all their time and energy on the Indian fields.[103] The home farms were either closed or continued to operate on a very limited scale. The smaller agency farms would not monopolize labour and machinery, which could be put to use on the reserves.

As the plan materialized, the government found itself responsible for the support of the instructors, their families, and employees, who ran the farms with such dismal returns that they contributed very little to the expenses. The department had created for itself an immense burden in the North-West in addition to the initial problem of finding a means of support for the Indians. In response to concern that the cost of these farms was excessive, it was announced in the spring of 1881 that instructors were to be charged twenty-five cents a day for their board and that each family member would be charged half that.[104] The amount of food they consumed, from the produce raised on their farms, was also to be charged against them. Many farmers voiced strong opposition to the circular letter that brought this news. John Tomkins, instructor at Duck Lake, in the Treaty Six district of present-day Saskatchewan, insisted that the farmers had clearly understood that they and their families were to be supported by the government.[105] On the strength of this understanding, some had brought their families with them from the outset. Although Tomkins had waited to bring his family out until suitable accommodation was made, he would never have done so, which involved taking his children away from school, had he known that such a regulation would be made. Tomkins argued that his wife, who did all the housework and cooking for the agency, paid for her own and the children's board by saving the wages of an extra man. He also intended that his wife would teach the Indian women to do housework and to make butter and other items.

Others were similarly vocal in their opposition. James Johnston, instructor for the Pelly agency, did not have his children with him, but he objected to paying board for himself.[106] He considered that his services resulted in a great saving to the department. He had stacked enough hay, for example, to winter seventy-five head and had saved the department the expense of letting a hay contract. James Scott at the Touchwood Hills replied to the circular letter by billing the department for the support of his family in Ontario from 1 April 1879 to 1 April 1880. He claimed that each instructor with his family was to be supplied with board for the first year, and as this arrangement had been carried out for those who brought their families along, it should also apply to his in Ontario. Although he understood that after the first year he was to raise enough on his farm to support himself and family, he charged that the government had not fulfilled its part of the bargain in "sending them out early enough to get their breaking done during the summer and they had been set back nearly a year in their farming operations." As well, Scott still maintained that any surplus he raised belonged to him. He believed he had sufficient produce on hand that spring to cover the cost of his board and to support his family. The Indian agent, he stated, could purchase from him the seed grain and potatoes required for the Indians at the same rate paid to others.[107] Scott resigned from his position on 1 September 1881.

Besides the administrative problems involved with the home farm program, the government had to contend with increasing criticism from residents of the North-West as well as from members of the House. In the North-West it was believed from the outset that the program was unfair because too much was being done to equip the Indians to farm, more than was available to the true "homesteaders." This idea was to gain ground in the 1880s. The *Saskatchewan Herald* reported on 28 April 1879 that the Indian farmer was given too much in the way of equipment and food, and was not being "impressed with the idea that if he does not work, and work well and faithfully, as the white farmer has to do, neither shall he eat." Indians were acquiring a false sense of their "rights" with the farming program, and were on the way to becoming "hopelessly pauperized." On 28 March 1881 the paper dismissed the program as "worse than useless," "conducive to the destruction of self-reliance, and calculated to give them a false impression of what the Government owed them."

In the House of Commons, criticism, already noted in 1880, continued unabated. Opposition critics detected many of the obvious weaknesses of the program, but they also expected immediate, miraculous results. Opposition MP David Mills believed that the home farm policy allowed the Indians to watch other men do their work, and in cases in which farms were remote from the reserves did not even afford this advantage. Mills could not understand why non-Indians were employed on these farms. He insisted that if anyone was to be employed, it should be Indians: "It is said by Dr Cook, in his lectures to the theological students of Belfast, that clergymen should be taught to preach as we teach dogs to swim, by throwing them into the water; and it appears to me that Indians must learn agriculture in very much the same way. They must be put at the work, and it is by what they do themselves that they learn to cultivate the soil." Mills also urged that the Indians be given a share of the crop raised for their wages to give them a special interest in producing as much as possible and thus save the public treasury large expenditure.[108]

In his first annual scrutiny of the accounts for the farm instructor program, Mills could find nothing to indicate that the instructors had succeeded in producing enough to sustain themselves, let alone provide for the Indians. The instructors, he argued, were better supplied with the implements of husbandry than most farmers in the older provinces, and therefore they ought to be able to show something for their efforts. Mills did not see why the instructors should be paid at all; furnishing them with the necessary implements was adequate. If the government continued to pay them, and take their crops from them, they would have no motive to do anything, a situation that would assure the smallest results for the largest outlay. "They will be precisely in the position of the African slaves in the Southern States who, not receiving the profit of their industry and whose wages not depending on the results, will do as little as possible," Mills declared.[109] In the spring of 1882 Mills estimated that the cost of maintaining the farms in the Territories had reached ninety thousand dollars, with no results to warrant this expenditure. He objected to the purchase of any more implements, stating that these obligations had been met, and that as far as he could learn, the Indians only consumed their oxen and sold their implements. Two years later Mills continued to insist that the program was a great failure.[110]

Other opposition members attacked the home farm policy on different grounds. One contended that the program had failed because the government had continued to feed the Indians in their idleness, at the same time as it supplied them with all the means for agriculture.[111] James Fleming, MP, found no fault with the policy, which, he believed, was calculated to promote the well-being of the Indians, but he argued that this policy had not been carried out. Faith had not been kept with the Indians, who had been led to believe by the negotiators of the treaties that happiness and prosperity would result. He presented evidence that some bands had not received their implements, cattle, and seed and that other promises had been broken and frauds practised. The natural result of this breach of faith was that the Indians could well "resort to some means to make themselves square."[112] In his opinion the Indians were displaying less self-reliance than formerly as a means of protest.

Claiming to take Fleming's argument one step further, Philipe Casgrain, MP, stated that the policy of the government went against the "natural law" relating to Indians, which was that the Indian race was becoming rapidly extinct. It was therefore an enormous waste of money to attempt to "civilize" the Indians, as this was a goal that could never be realized. Casgrain knew of only one Indian who had ever become thoroughly "civilized," and he had white blood in his veins. Agricultural experiments only displayed the "inaptitude [sic] of Indians to enter into civilized life." Even if houses were built for them and garden plots set aside, they preferred their wigwams and neglected their gardens. The Indians of the North-West were a "doomed race," according to Casgrain; it was only a question of how soon they would disappear.[113]

For some years Prime Minister Macdonald attempted to defend the farm instructor program in the House. In 1881 he argued that the program had met with sufficient success to justify the expense.

The Indians, he claimed, had followed the example of their instructors and "betaken themselves, in a rude way, to cultivating the soil – to scratching it I might say." They were learning to use their oxen as animals of labour rather than as items of their diet. He contended that the Indians must have paid instructors: "You cannot get men, from motives of philanthropy, to settle amongst a band of Indians which is away from his own kindred and lineage." With few exceptions, Macdonald argued, the instructors had proved themselves worthy of their salaries. He acknowledged that the allocation for the Indians of the North-West was large and warned it would continue to be so until the Indians learned to cultivate the soil.[114]

By 1884, however, Macdonald had admitted in the House that "the Indian farms were an experiment; and I do not think that, on the whole, they have been successful."[115] His government was not to be blamed for this failure; its only fault was in overestimating the abilities of the Indians. Great pains had been taken to hire men well trained in farming, although it had been found that it was less important to have first-rate farmers than men accustomed to dealing with the Indians. His government had kept faith with the Indians; the provisions of the treaties had been carried out, and "if there is any error, it is in an excessive supply being furnished to the Indians." Expressions of discontent on the part of the Indians could readily be dismissed, as they always grumbled, never professed to be satisfied, bullied their agents, and played tricks to get more than what they were entitled to. Their dissatisfaction was encouraged by those who were "living and getting fat upon inciting the Indians to discontent." The policy had failed because the Indians, "idlers by nature, and uncivilized," could never learn to farm in anything but a rude manner. "What you want is to get the Indians to plant a few turnips, and perhaps in a rough way which would shock a model school alumnus, and raise cattle and roots, and perhaps by-and-bye [sic] grain, rather than that they should receive the instructions of a first-class farmer." Macdonald concluded that the Indians were more likely to become carpenters, blacksmiths, or mechanics. They were not, in his opinion, suited to agriculture: they "have not the ox-like quality of the Anglo-Saxon; they will not put their neck to the yoke."[116]

An official memorandum drawn up by Deputy Superintendent General Vankoughnet in 1884 announced that home farms were to be closed at Bird Tail Creek, Fort Pelly, Crooked Lakes, Qu'Appelle, Indian Head, Duck Lake, and Prince Albert. Vankoughnet explained that the Indians in the vicinity of these farms had "sufficient opportunity to observe how farms should be conducted and as these farms cost a great deal to work them, and the Indians derived little or no benefit from the work expended on them, it was considered in the interests of the Indians and at the same time a saving to the Department were the Instructors to devote the whole of their time and attention to instructing the Indians to cultivate and raise produce on their own farms in the Reserves."[117]

The decision to end the home farm program was not as sudden as suggested in the memo, which was primarily intended to clarify confusion in Ottawa about the state of these farms.[118] The government had been quietly retreating from the program, closing some home farms entirely while reducing the size and staff of others. The explanations publicly advanced for these closures tended to emphasize the successes rather than the shortfalls and blemishes of the program. For example, Prime Minister Macdonald announced in 1882 that farms were to be closed in several localities because "the object for which they were established, namely: the practical exemplification to the Indians of the manner in which farms should be managed, has been attained."[119] It is unlikely that either Macdonald or Vankoughnet had full confidence in this claim. The farms were closed because they had failed to raise large quantities of food for the Indians, they had cost more to maintain than the value of the products raised, and they had proved an administrative nightmare.

At that time the government felt it could afford to drift out of the program because of increased settlement, which, it was vaguely hoped, would help solve some of the Indian Department's difficulties. Some of the services provided by the home farms, for example, the provision of seed, tools, and other hardware, could be taken over by the new settlements. With other forms of employment available, there was less need for all Indians to farm. It was reasoned that those who could not make a living cultivating could work for settlers, mill-owners, or lumberers or on the railroad. The closure of the home farms would also dispel the image that the government was in competition with the settlers and businesses it had encouraged to move to the West, there being considerable jealousy over the very limited markets. The immediate benefit of closing the farms would be the anticipated substantial saving to the government. It was hoped that in some cases a profit could be made from the sale of the improvements.

The final demise of the home farms coincided with the inauguration of a new scheme to bring the Indians to "civilization." Through the industrial school system, unveiled in 1883, efforts would be concentrated on a new generation of Indians. They would be taught useful trades and English, both of which would increase their employment opportunities. The older generation, it was reasoned, had been given every encouragement to make a transition to farming but had proved themselves incapable.

Late in 1883 the last vestiges of the home farm scheme were put to rest. That year Vankoughnet undertook an extensive tour of the North-West, and he became convinced that there was much needless expenditure.[120] A massive program of financial retrenchment was hastily implemented following his return to Ottawa. The dismissal of many clerks, assistants, and instructors throughout the Territories was ordered. Agents were to act as their own clerks and storekeepers and to curtail greatly their travelling expenses. Farm assistants were to be hired for the growing season only. They would be called instructors but were not to receive the higher wage of that position. Vankoughnet was concerned that authority no longer be divided between the agent and the instructor; instructors were clearly to be subordinate to the agent and were to report directly to him. The local authority and discretionary powers of the agent, instructors, and Indian commissioner were reduced. No deviations from the acknowledged rules, no matter the explanation, were to be tolerated. In particular there was to be a much stricter supervision of the distribution of rations: they were to be issued only in return for work and under no other circumstances. The custom of distributing goods when important officials visited reserves was put to an end. Vankoughnet considered it a "most irrational" tradition, which squandered supplies at the same time as it demoralized the Indians, since they would not work as long as the food lasted.[121]

THE PROGRAM IN THE TREATY FOUR DISTRICT

The policy of financial retrenchment was applied throughout the Territories in the fall of 1883. Treaty Four was a particular target of cutbacks despite the fact that the Indians of the Qu'Appelle and the Touchwood Hills district of Treaty Four were generally recognized as among the most poorly off of all the treaty Indians. Compared with the Indians of Treaty Six, especially those on the Carlton reserves, they had made very little progress in farming. Inspector Wadsworth believed the Indians were not to blame for this situation, for they appeared "tractable and willing." Rather, he felt that the instructors sent to this district had not proven to be "good men" as had those in Treaty Six, who had taken an interest in their work and had remained at it.[122] He urged in his reports that instead of slackening, extra efforts should be made in this district and in 1882 recommended that a man be sent to each of the reserves to camp and work constantly with the Indians.

Among other reasons for the lack of headway shown by the Indians of this district was that they had made virtually no start at farming by the time of the starvation crisis of 1879. It was only in the face of the great want and distress he encountered in the spring of 1879 that agent Allan MacDonald distributed implements to all who applied for them.[123] The comparative lack of agricultural progress in Treaty Four during this period can also be attributed to the fact that many bands had only recently settled their reserves. They were not stubbornly refusing to settle or take to the plough. Rather, observing the government's timid measures to help those already settled, chiefs were reluctant to confine their bands to reserves, as they believed it would invite starvation and death.

The Indians of the Qu'Appelle and Touchwood Hills district had the benefit of some association with the home farm program as it was originally conceived. The farm started by James Scott in the Touchwood Hills in the fall of 1879 remained in operation until 1883. It appears that there never was very much more under cultivation than the original thirty-five acres broken by Scott. During its last season the farm consisted of twelve acres of oats, as well as root crops.[124] By 1881 the farm was not operating to the satisfaction of farm inspector Wadsworth. Despite the fact that he had helped select the site for the farm, he complained that it was entirely too far away from the four Touchwood bands, and the Nut Lake and Fishing Lake Indians to the north, all under the charge of the same instructor. In its location the farm could serve only as a base of supplies. Because the Touchwood Hills were so far away from the agency buildings at Fort Qu'Appelle, however, a depot of supplies was required at the Hills. Wadsworth suggested that the instructor work a small home farm and distribute his men on the reserves from seeding to harvest, discharging this staff in winter. Even though this farm employed nine men for varying lengths of time as well as a full-time instructor in 1881, Wadsworth found little improvement in the bands. This farm received his most pointed criticism. "I would sooner suggest the abandonment of this 'home farm' altogether than to continue the system of the past two years, where the pretence of work upon the home farm has been a cloak for idleness."[125]

Visiting the farm in 1883, Hayter Reed, recently appointed acting assistant Indian commissioner, recommended that the farm be closed "owing to the limited number of Indians on the different Reserves adjacent thereto, and the slight advancement made as compared with the outlay."[126] In Reed's opinion, the instructor should reside on the reserve which had the largest population and which was most distant from the best hunting grounds. A home farm should not be established, so that the instructor could give all his attention to the bands. Assistants could be temporarily hired for the outlying bands. Reasoning that bands occupying good hunting territory were not likely to devote any attention to tilling the soil, Reed was prepared to almost totally ignore their efforts at farming. The home farm in the Touchwood Hills was closed in December 1883.

Although farming had progressed to some extent on reserves in the Touchwood Hills by 1884, two central problems continued to plague agriculture in the district. As much of the land in the Touchwood Hills was swampy and covered with timber, there was a shortage of arable land, and there were not enough oxen for the acres under cultivation. On most reserves well over half the families farmed to some extent, so that a lack of interest in agriculture was not an obstacle.

Most commentators saw Day Star's band members as the most promising farmers in the Touchwood Hills. The chief was particularly interested in agriculture; his garden was described as "a model of neatness and everything growing luxuriantly," and earned him a silver medal from the governor general in 1881 for being the most advanced Cree chief in farming in Treaty Four.[127] In the spring of 1882 this band was well enough off to sell seed potato and wheat to the agent, as it still had a large supply on hand.[128] The shortage of arable land on this reserve was to a small extent ameliorated in 1881 when the survey lines were rerun to take in prairie land in exchange for timberland to the north.[129] By 1883, however, the chief was once again requesting that the reserve be resurveyed to include more arable land.[130] On George Gordon's reserve, which was mostly woods and lakes, the boundaries were also changed to take in some open prairie land suitable for farming.[131] The residents had been farming as best they could in the hills, on knolls, and in small clearings in the timber. It was recognized as early as 1877 that the reserve contained too little arable land, and therefore many of the farms were located off the reserve.

For the Indians of the Qu'Appelle a home farm was established in the fall of 1879 near Pasquah's reserve. The farm, located about five miles from Fort Qu'Appelle near a beautiful stream with wooded ravines, suffered from a constant turnover in staff. Frank Hunt resigned as instructor after his first winter. He was replaced by G. Newlove, who arrived in the fall of 1880 and was in turn replaced by S. Hockley in 1882. In that year the farm had twenty-five acres of wheat, oats, barley, and corn under cultivation, but that was its final year of operation. In the 1882 annual report of the department, it was remarked that the farm had been closed, and in future all work was to be done on the reserves. No specific reasons were given.

Owing to a number of advantages, Pasquah's band was very advanced in farming compared with others in the district. Being the only reserve in the vicinity for most of the life of the home farm, it received all the instructors' attention and its members alone benefited from the educational aspect of the farm. Inspector Wadsworth remarked in 1881 that at Qu'Appelle the system of having one man responsible for each reserve had met with excellent results.[132] Pasquah's band had also made a good start at farming before the famine crisis of 1879. The availability of oxen may also account for the success of their farming; in 1884 the band members had twenty-eight. Three families each purchased a yoke of oxen in 1883, and the agent presented them with ploughs and harness as an encouragement to others.[133] This band also profited from proximity to Fort Qu'Appelle. In the winter many band members worked for settlers and provided timber to the police post there.

Muscowpetung's band began to settle near Pasquah's reserve only in 1881, and so derived little benefit from the home farm scheme. Surveyor John C. Nelson conferred with the chief in the fall of that year, and a reserve was selected to the west of and adjoining Pasquah's, south of the Qu'Appelle River.[134] The soil was good, like much of the land in the Qu'Appelle district, Nelson stated. The bottomlands along the river front consisted of rich soil and extensive hay grounds. The supply of wood was limited, however; poplar and a few small maples grew only in the gulches that extended back from the valley. Opposite, on the north side of the Qu'Appelle, some hay grounds were reserved for the use of the Indian Affairs Department. Agent MacDonald described this reserve as one of the best in the treaty area for agricultural purposes.[135]

The home farms in the Touchwood Hills and near Pasquah's reserve were the sole manifestations in this district of Treaty Four of the program that was originally conceived in 1879. Many Indians who eventually settled in the Qu'Appelle, however, received instruction from two home farms established in the Cypress Hills where several bands had initially chosen reserves. In 1879 farm instructor J.J. English from Omemee, Ontario, started a home farm for the proposed Assiniboine reserve, eighteen miles from Fort Walsh on Maple Creek. Another home farm set up that year was also on Maple Creek, thirty miles northeast of Fort Walsh. Cowessess selected a reserve at that site and some members of his band settled there, although the survey was never completed.[136] In 1881 Piapot chose a reserve about ten miles north of that Maple Creek farm.[137] The farm was supervised by John Setter, who, unlike most in the first contingent of farm instructors, was a man of the country. He was the son of a Hudson's Bay Company man and had been born at Red River.[138] Agent MacDonald reported that Setter had excellent crops after one year, even though there had been no rain and seeding had been completed late in the season. He noted that the Indians had displayed a "great deal of energy in trying to make a success of their first agricultural enterprize."[139] The following year there were 115 acres under cultivation of wheat, oats, turnips, and potatoes.[140] Some of the Indians were reported to be working at their farms remarkably well; they took considerable pride in their gardens and were annoyed that more seed was unavailable. A number planted wheat for themselves, and the agent recommended that a portable grist mill be supplied, as he believed that if the Indians could grind their grain, many more could be induced to break up land for the following year. The agent was confident that the Indians could be self-sustaining in another year.

Despite the fact that John Setter's home farm in the Cypress Hills proved to be one of the great successes of the program, it, as well as J.J. English's farm, was closed because of the decision in the winter of 1881–82 that all Indians in the Cypress Hills be moved north or east. The reason generally cited for this decision is that officials feared conflict between the American and Canadian Indians living in proximity. A more recent interpretation suggests that Canadian authorities were concerned about the danger posed by a concentration of the Cree on contiguous reserves in the Cypress Hills, which would effectively create an Indian territory and make control of the residents difficult.[141] To encourage removal from the Cypress Hills, rationing was discontinued, Fort Walsh was closed, and the home farms were shut down.[142]

Many of the Indians who had congregated in the Cypress Hills settled on reserves at the Round and Crooked Lakes during the early 1880s. This area was described as "a most beautiful part of the country, right on the Northern [sic] edge of the great plains, [with] fine poplar bluffs, some small lakes and the choicest of wheat land, an ideal location chosen by the Indians themselves. This had always been a great wintering place for the Indians, there being plenty of fish in the lakes."[143] Setter, transferred to this site in 1880, was told not to run a separate home farm. His men were to work with and among the Indians on their reserves.[144] Loud Voice's reserve, Ochapowace, formed the eastern boundary of the reserves in the area;

Round Lake was its northern boundary. Chacachase's band settled in 1883 and 1884 on the western end of Loud Voice's reserve. Residents of this reserve worked large fields as a community, except for four who farmed on their own, and each head of family kept a small garden.

Kahkewistahaw's band occupied a reserve just west of Loud Voice's, in the valley between the Round and Crooked Lakes. Members of this band were among the last to leave the Cypress Hills region. In 1882 thirty-three followers of Kahkewistahaw were found starving at Wood Mountain, and they arrived at Fort Qu'Appelle in June of that year.[145] Those who farmed in this band worked one large field in common, and a few had separate fields.

Adjoining Kahkewistahaw's reserve on the west was one that was first known as O'Soup's. Louis O'Soup, a headman of Cowessess' band, persuaded a faction to leave the Cypress Hills and return to Qu'Appelle, where a reserve was surveyed in 1880.[146] O'Soup apparently hoped he would be recognized as chief in Cowessess' absence. In 1882, however, O'Soup received Cowessess with friendship when he arrived with the remainder of his band that year. On this reserve a number of notable individual farmers were emerging by 1884. Among these was Nepahpahness, whose operations Inspector Wadsworth applauded in 1884. He had

purchased, for the support of his family, fourteen sacks of flour since the spring. His live stock consists of three cows, two oxen, one heifer, two steers, three calves, three horses, two foals. He has planted – furnishing his own seed – thirty-two bushels of wheat, five bushels of barley, thirty-four bushels of potatoes, and one acre of turnips, and has about ten bushels of grain left in his granary. He has a mower and rake and double waggon in his house, a good cook stove, chairs, table clock, milk pans and churns.[147]

Wadsworth described Nepahpahness' grain as the best he had seen that year. Nekahneequinep, O'Soup, Sasalue, Louison, Jacob Bear, Ahkingkahpempatoot, Nasaagan, Joseph Sprevier, Alex Gaddie, and Petewaywaykeesick all had farms of their own and cultivated an average of nine acres each, mostly in wheat, with the exception of Gaddie who had twenty-five acres in wheat, nine in barley, four in potatoes, and two in turnips.

The predominantly Saulteaux Indians of this reserve had a long history of association with the Hudson's Bay Company as hunters and employees, and some of those who were most prominent in this relationship were among the well-to-do farmers. Nepahpahness had been a steersman with the company and Jacob Bear, a bowsman.[148] Gaddie and O'Soup also had close connections with the company. This association was maintained well into the reserve period. At the request of Nepahpahness and a number of others, the company opened a store on the reserve in 1883. N.M.W.J. McKenzie was sent to run it, which operated out of Nepahpahness' house.[149] McKenzie was also a carpenter and his participation may have been behind the superior housing that observers noted on the Cowessess reserve. He helped Nepahpahness build a one-and-a half-storey home, which the owner in later years ran as a stopping place for settlers heading north from Broadview.

At the western boundary of the Crooked Lakes reserves was the Sakimay, or Mosquito, band. These Saulteaux fur hunters, long associated with the Fort Ellice band, had seldom ventured out on the plains and had wintered at Crooked Lakes for many years. As previously noted, their reserve was surveyed in 1876, the first to be done in the area. In the early 1880s the band divided into two factions. About half, the brothers and families of the late Sakimay, known as the Shesheep faction, settled on the north side of Crooked Lake, the site of the original reserve.[150] This faction accepted no aid from the government in the way of oxen or implements. Yellow Calf led the other faction and began breaking land about two and a half miles south of the original reserve. His faction accepted its share of implements and livestock.

Reserves for Little Black Bear, Okanese, Star Blanket, and Peepeekisis were surveyed in a gridlike fashion in the fall of 1880 at the File Hills, where surveyor Allan Patrick noted several small houses and some evidence of cultivation.[151] Patrick surveyed upon the principle that each band was to have, in proportion to the number of members, an equal quantity of wooded land and fertile soil. The western slope of the File Hills, he noted, would provide the residents with hay lands and water, while the eastern slope was well adapted for farming. The hills in the centre of this group of reserves were covered with good building timber. It was soon recognized, however, that from the point of view of agriculture, the File Hills was not a good choice. Surveyor Nelson visited the reserves in 1884 and found that well over half, those on the western slope, were characterized by swamps, ponds, and lakes, with poplar bluffs and clumps of willow.[152] In the centre of the reserves, at the height of the Hills, were heavy woods. Prairie land suitable for farming was found only along the eastern slope, and Little Black Bear's reserve had the most. Agent MacDonald lamented in 1883 that the three other reserves were so cut up by lakes and marshes that large fields could not be made.[153]

James Scott's home farm in the Touchwood Hills, 1881. From *The Graphic*, Western Canada Pictorial Index JTA021206759

Indians regarded as having "sound judgment" and influence with their people were taken east in 1886 to witness the unveiling of a monument to Joseph Brant, war chief and statesman. They visited Parliament and were entertained by General Middleton, who commanded troops sent west in 1885. *Standing, left to right*: Louis O'Soup, Peter Hourie; *seated*: Mistawasis, Kahkewistahaw, and Ahtakakoop. National Archives of Canada, C 19258

Breaking new land with a walking plough and oxen team, White Bear reserve, 1902–3. Saskatchewan Archives Board R-A1883.

Hayter Reed, deputy superintendent general of Indian affairs, 1894. McCord Museum of Canadian History, Notman Photographic Archives 106454-BII

Farmer at work haying. Western Canada Pictorial Index MAA005801765

Harvesting with a binder on the Assiniboine reserve near Sintaluta, 1901. Saskatchewan Archives Board R-A1881

Threshing at the Battleford Industrial School. Parks Canada, Environment Canada, Prairie Region

Threshing at Muskeg Lake, Saskatchewan, ca 1900–10. Photograph by L. Cochin, Saskatchewan Archives Board s-e6813

Hayter Reed and child in costume for a historical ball, Rideau Hall, Ottawa, 1896. Photograph by W.J. Topley, National Archives of Canada PA 139841

Louis O'Soup *(left)* and the Gambler. From Canada, *Sessional Papers*, no. 27 (1901), facing p. 160

Delivering grain to the flour mill at Indian Head, winter, 1905. Indian farmers were always accompanied on such trips by the agent, foreman, or clerk, who would oversee their sales and purchases. Saskatchewan Archives Board R-B10919

Working with a sulky plough and three-horse team. National Archives of Canada PA 48475

Alex Gaddie, Cowessess reserve farmer, 1910. Saskatchewan Archives Board R-A253(3)

Fred Dieter (*left*) and Joseph Ironquill, farmers at the File Hills Colony. Saskatchewan Archives Board R-A21(1)

In 1911 a delegation from Treaty Four met with officials from Indian Affairs in Ottawa. *Extreme left*, Louis O'Soup; *extreme right*, Alex Gaddie. Saskatchewan Archives Board R-B584

Threshing on the Swan Lake reserve, Manitoba, ca 1920. Women and children helped in the fields, especially at haying, harvest, and threshing time. Western Canada Pictorial Index UCA066520422

A home farm on the 1879 model was never in operation at the File Hills. An agency farm, adjacent to Okanese's reserve, never consisted of more than about eight acres of barley, wheat, and potatoes. From the beginning, instructors were urged to devote all their attention to the Indian farms.

INDIAN PROTESTS

Although farming was off to a start by 1884 on the Touchwood Hills, File Hills, Crooked Lakes, and Qu'Appelle reserves, it could scarcely be boasted that the home farm program for these reserves had been attended with such success that massive cutbacks were warranted. Very little of the money and effort expended on the program had been directed toward this district of Treaty Four. The Indian leaders on these reserves insisted that they were not given enough assistance in the way of implements and teams to make farming a success. Like other Indian spokesmen throughout the Territories in the early 1880s, they grasped every opportunity to implore the government to allow them the means to make a living by agriculture. Indian protest of this period reveals a recognition that even if the farm materials promised by the treaty commissioners had been faithfully delivered, which in some cases they were not, they were not adequate to help form an agricultural economy on the reserves. The Indians felt that at the treaty negotiations they had been promised and assured that they could make a living by agriculture, and they now suspected that they had been duped and misled by the sweet promises of the commissioners. This spirit of discontent reached its height in 1884 and 1885, but it had been simmering for some years. No plot on the part of Louis Riel was needed to foment Indian dissatisfaction and resentment. Virtually all the Indians' grievances, however, were ignored by department officials and other representatives of authority.

The visit of the governor general, the Marquis of Lorne, in the summer of 1881 was welcomed by Indians throughout the Territories as an opportunity to voice their concerns collectively. Clearly the visit had been anticipated for some time, and presentations were carefully prepared.[154] The Indians appeared to regard this man as particularly powerful, especially because of his marriage to a daughter of Queen Victoria. Among the spokesmen present at the meeting, held at Fort Qu'Appelle, were Loud Voice, O'Soup, Yellow Quill, Kanocees, and Day Star. The Indians assured the governor general that they were committed to farming; as their hunting ground was a solitary wilderness, they saw no option but to work the ground.

They stressed that they could not live by what was given to them in the treaty; they requested a new arrangement, translated as a "reformation" of the treaty. They declared that their women and children were starving, that they had eaten their horses and dogs, that they had no shoes, mittens, or clothing, and that they could not live on the rations issued to them. They asked for more oxen and implements to work the land properly and to allow them the means to keep themselves alive. They requested that one of their number be permitted to go to Ottawa to plead their case. They implored the governor general not to pass by quickly, as many officials did, but to carefully consider and help settle the matters that concerned them. His Excellency, however, dismissed most of their grievances, believing that the Indians preferred to smoke their pipes and make eloquent speeches than to work. "Hands were not given by Manitou to fill pipes only but to work," he lectured the assembly at Qu'Appelle. He added: "I am sure that red men to the East when they work do well and do not starve and I have noticed that the men who talk most and ask most do not work."[155]

The Indians of the Territories continued to use every channel of expression open to them to express their need for more implements and cattle. These requests sometimes appeared in the annual reports of the Indian agents. In 1883, for example, agent MacDonald reported that Kahkewistahaw, Loud Voice, Little Black Bear, Peepeekisis, and Muscowpetung were asking for work oxen, ploughs, and harrows.[156] In having their case heard, however, the Indians faced many obstacles. Interpreters did not always faithfully translate the meaning of the Indians' words, and agents often refused to hear their appeals, claiming that they had no power to do anything about them.[157] Chiefs and others often applied to visit Ottawa. In a private letter to Dewdney of January 1881, an exasperated agent MacDonald wondered, "What is to be done with O'Soup: I never meet him without his bringing up the subject of his visit to Ottawa."[158] The matter went all the way to Deputy Superintendent General Vankoughnet, who thought that when the railway was completed, it might be a good idea to have some chiefs visit the settled portions of the Dominion. O'Soup was eventually to visit the East more than once.

Indians throughout the Territories also made their complaints known in letters to officials. In a letter to Dewdney of August 1881, Red Pheasant, chief of an Eagle Hills Cree band, asked for more implements and for a blacksmith to repair their tools.[159] In his annual report of 1882, Dewdney quoted extensively from a letter received from Poundmaker to show that the Indians were not simply begging for more rations so that they might live in idleness, but that they were truly committed to making a living by agriculture. Poundmaker asked for the grist mill and the oxen promised him and for his ploughs and wrenches. Not only had his band always been short of implements, but the previous year his people did not have enough potato and seed wheat to sow all the land they had prepared. There was a great deal of distress on his reserve, as rations had been suspended for forty-one days. Since they could not work on empty stomachs, members of his band were compelled to rove and hunt. Poundmaker concluded that "it seems to me that we are as anxious to be independent as the Government are [sic] to get rid of the burden of supporting us."[160]

Owing to the dire poverty of their people that winter, Cree chiefs of the Edmonton district wrote a letter to the prime minister and minister of the interior in January 1883, which was also published in the Edmonton *Bulletin*, to seek redress directly from the government. They had been compelled to write because their interpreters, hired by the government, refused to translate their exact words to the agents. If attention was not paid to their case, they stated, they would assume the treaty was meaningless and that "the white man has doomed us to annihilation little by little." They had understood that the conditions of the treaty were inviolable and reciprocally binding, and that neither party could be guilty of a breach of faith without impunity. They considered that their treatment constituted a breach of faith, as they had not received one-half of what had been promised to them. They had not been given the number of oxen, ploughs, axes, hoes, and other implements promised, and on no occasion had they received more than half the seed they required to sow the land they had prepared. Once a proud and independent people, they were now reduced to being "mendicants at the door of every white man in the country, and were it not for the charity of white settlers who are not bound by treaty to help us we should all die on government fare." Their young women, they claimed, were reduced by starvation to prostitution, a thing unheard of among their people before. They asked that they be given the means to allow them to work for themselves, as provided for in the treaty. They now suspected that the treaty was a farce enacted to kill them all quickly, and warned that the motto of the Cree was If we must die by violence let us do it quickly.[161] Prime Minister Macdonald dismissed their claims and grievances, remarking that Indians were never satisfied. He believed that the letter was written by a man he would not name but described as "one of the curses of the North West, one of the white men despised by God and Men."[162]

In the Treaty Six district, disappointment over the state of agriculture on the reserves culminated in a council of chiefs at Carlton in August 1884 at which they voiced their complaints. They alleged that the cattle given them were an insult, for many were wild or so intractable that they could not be cared for. The cows were also wild, and since they could not be stabled, they had died of cold and exposure. They believed this was evidence of bad faith on the part of the government, since they had been promised well-broken beasts. The chiefs claimed that the wagons they were issued were of a poor quality. The assistance they were given in the way of relief was not enough to allow them to work effectively on their reserves. They greatly feared the approaching winter, as they had neither food nor clothing. During the treaty negotiations, they had been told they would be taught to live like the white man. The Indians now saw that their farmer neighbours had threshing mills, mowers, reapers, and rakes. They believed they were entitled to this sort of machinery and asked that their inferior implements and wild cattle be replaced. It was stressed that there was not enough of anything supplied to them to allow all to farm, although a living by agriculture had been promised to them, and many desiring to settle were forced to leave the reserves. They feared that the government, which had pretended to be friendly, was cheating them. Requests for the redress of their grievances had been made again and again without effect. They were glad that their young men had not resorted to violence but warned that the treatment they received at the hands of the government was almost too much for them to bear, after the "sweet promises" made in order to get their country from them. If their council produced no results by the summer of 1885, they would take measures to get what they desired.[163]

Assistant Commissioner Hayter Reed was sent to make inquiries into these complaints. Reed visited individually the chiefs who had attended the council and reported that each had refused to restate the grievances. The chiefs had clearly agreed not to negotiate with authorities as autonomous bands, which would have shattered their leverage. Reed, however, believed this silence meant that there were really no grounds for complaint.

On the specific grievances, Reed reported that all the chiefs present had received their full complement of cattle, and while he admitted that there was "not a little" in what they said about the cattle being somewhat wild and difficult to manage, he implied that for the most part this claim was manufactured as an excuse for them to kill the beasts or not provide for them. The Indians, he stated, had been given cattle above treaty stipulations on loan, but they were objecting to this system simply because they had to care for the animals. The wagons Reed inspected appeared adequate, but he noted that every article in the hands of Indians received rough usage and had to be more than ordinarily well made to withstand the wear and tear it would be subjected to. Indians, he believed, were inclined to claim that anything they had damaged or spoiled was bad to begin with and had to be replaced. In his opinion, all implements issued to the Indians, save in a few exceptional cases, were of good quality. While they might be short of some items, Reed explained that the practice was to issue tools and implements only if the agent thought these would be used to advantage. They were not given out in the numbers demanded by the Indians, as they would have been broken or lost long before the Indians knew how to handle them properly. If the Indians were given more cattle, Reed admitted, they might be able to employ more implements, but, in his opinion, the implements issued from time to time were sufficient for the number of cattle on the reserves. As for the request for mowers, reapers, threshing machines, and other labour-saving machinery, Reed felt that the "stipulations of the treaty I think in so far as plows, harrows, hoes, scythes, etc. go, will cover all their reasonable requirements until they become well enough advanced to look after themselves."[164]

Bad crops in the past year had alarmed the better-conducted Indians, Reed explained, but the "ill-disposed" had used this pretext to urge upon authorities a grant of aid in the way of food supplies. He had evidence that several members of one band, who were "more half-breed than Indian," had been in touch with Riel and were "ready to endorse any movement which they believe might get them supplies without having to work for them." Reed concluded that "there are Indian as well as white agitators and the hard times make one and all, good and bad, only too prone to give any assistance they can toward procuring more from the authorities without having to work for it."[165] Reed's views reflected those held by many department officials that Indians' complaints were simply not to be believed because they were lazy, did not properly care for the cattle and implements given to them, and were encouraged to complain by those who might profit from such agitation. This approach to Indian petitions, letters, and deputations allowed grievances to be dismissed without serious consideration.

The discord that prevailed among the Indians of Treaty Six by 1884 had its parallel among the Treaty Four Indians. Not only did the new policy of financial retrenchment severely cripple an underfunded program, but it was enacted in the midst of one of the most severe winters since 1879. In December 1883 most department employees on the reserves were bluntly informed that their services were no longer required. Farm instructor Setter at Crooked Lakes was told in the middle of the month that his services, as well as those of every employee of the department, were to be dispensed with from 31 December.[166] The pretext for Setter's dismissal was that he kept the books carelessly, issued supplies and rations lavishly, and had Indians loitering about his house doing nothing. In the Touchwood Hills, Peter Hourie, a Scottish mixed-blood from St Andrew's, Manitoba, who was to have a lengthy association with the Indian Affairs Department, was sent in December 1883 to take over the stock, stores, books, and inventory from the farm instructor, who was abruptly dismissed along with all other employees there. A labourer on these reserves protested that he had nowhere to put his family at that time of year on such short notice and was willing to stay for half his salary, but his request was denied.[167]

The appalling conditions that prevailed in the winter of 1883–84 are evident in Hourie's report on the state of the Touchwood Hills bands. Because much of that season's grain crop had been destroyed by frost, the Indians had long since exchanged their barley for food and had consumed all their root crops. Only a few had a little grain they were attempting to save for seed in the spring. Nor were the Indians able to hunt anything. The weather was bitterly cold, there were very few animals, and the snow was too deep for stalking game. Hourie wrote that "for my part I have never experienced such a depth at this time of year." The Indians were poorly clad and had no shoes. There was no hide even to make the nooses of rabbit snares. There was plenty of work to do, such as cutting fence rails, but, Hourie admitted, the Indians could not work without footwear and clothing. He found that the Indians were "very much downcast and afraid they are going to starve."[168]

It was in the midst of this bitter winter that the few employees left on the reserves were instructed to reduce rations. Hayter Reed, having been recently appointed assistant commissioner, was anxious to impress his superiors with the strict enforcement of the retrenchment policy. Reed was known as Iron Heart among the Indians of Battleford where he began his career with the department, and his reputation was soon to spread.[169] Convinced that rations had been distributed too freely, he decided they should be issued to the aged only.[170] The young and able-bodied were to be given limited amounts of powder, shot, and caps to provide for their families. Some bands, Reed decided, did not require rations at all. Yellow

Calf's band at the Crooked Lakes was one. Reed believed the band could live on fish and game, and since a mill was expected to begin operation in the district, the band would soon have its grain ground. In February 1884 members were informed that their rations were to be curtailed so that enough would remain for the spring work. The announcement came at a particularly difficult time of the year, February being the leanest of months for the Indians; it was even impossible to procure fish, as at that time they refused to take bait.

A protest against the policy erupted.[171] On 18 February Yellow Calf and about twenty-five armed men demanded an interview with their new farm instructor, Hilton Keith. They requested enough flour and bacon to last them several weeks and warned that if they did not receive any, they would help themselves to the stores. Keith insisted that his instructions did not allow him to distribute rations to young men. They then made a rush for the warehouse. According to Keith, while trying to defend the stores, he was knocked down, kicked, bruised, and struck at with a knife. The Indians "swarmed in like bees" and stole flour and bacon. They then assembled and barricaded themselves in a shanty where what officials described as a "war dance" was held over several days.[172]

Inspector Richard Burton Deane led a party of ten policemen to the shanty, but as he estimated that about sixty persons were present, he felt it was out of the question to begin making arrests. He sent for reinforcements, and Superintendent W.M. Herchmer, Deane, and twenty men again approached the shanty on 23 February. Bloodshed was only narrowly averted. The Indians were armed and clearly displayed a determination to fire if the police persisted in their attempt to enter the shack. Yellow Calf stated that he might just as well die than be starved by the government. His words echoed those of Louis O'Soup, who several days earlier had explained to Deane that an Indian's reasoning was that "if he were allowed to starve – he would die – and if were doomed to die he might as well die one way as another."[173]

The matter was eventually settled through negotiation. Hayter Reed persuaded Yellow Calf and three others to give themselves up for trial. O'Soup, spokesman for the Indians, justified their actions on the grounds that because they were starving and their request for rations had been refused, they had no choice but to help themselves to the stores. Since the treaty, the Indians had consistently maintained that what was in the storehouses on the reserves belonged to them and in helping themselves they were only taking what was theirs. If the provisions were intended for the band, they should have them and not starve. The stand was similar to that of bread rioters in Europe, who proclaimed that the hungry were entitled to take bread where they could find it.[174]

The Indians' view was fundamentally opposed to that held by Reed and other officials. They saw the stores as the property of the government, not of the Indians; they were to be distributed in a manner to encourage industry and initiative, and the recipients were to be grateful and deferential. Reed refused to admit that the incident had been caused by starvation. He attributed the outbreak to the Indians' dancing, which, he believed, worked them into a frenzy, and "fanned by the re-iterations of the prowess of their fathers and ancestors," the Indians cast all reflection to the wind.[175] Reed claimed he was lenient to the offenders only to restore public confidence. Charges were eventually dropped against Yellow Calf, and the other three who pleaded guilty were discharged. Protest against the cutback in rations also led to an incident of assault upon farm instructor Craig of the Little Pine reserve in Treaty Six in the spring of 1884.[176]

Much of the protest in this district of Treaty Four centred on the concerns of Piapot, who did not permanently settle on a reserve until 1884. Piapot was not refusing to reconcile himself to the new order by defying reserve life. He protested that the government was not keeping its promises to the Indians settled on the reserves; as they were not provided with the means to make a living they were dying of sickness and starvation. Piapot also consistently maintained his right to choose a reserve for his band, an issue that was central to much of his defiance of authorities.

As previously noted, in the summer of 1881 Piapot chose a reserve in the Cypress Hills, but, by the next spring, he and other Cree and Assiniboine associated with the Qu'Appelle were told they would receive rations only if they moved back to their former territory. In preparation for their return, agent Allan MacDonald chose a reserve site for Piapot's band near Indian Head. The reserve featured two large lakes, which, MacDonald believed, had fish; it also had plenty of wood for building and fuel, extensive tracts of marshland for hay, and some fine areas for agriculture.[177] MacDonald was convinced that Piapot could do no better than to choose this location.

On 23 June 1882 Piapot left the Cypress Hills with about 470 followers.[178] They were given seventeen days' rations and were to be supplied with more at Old Wives Lake. During their move east, they succumbed to an alarming amount of sickness and a number of deaths resulted. The agent described the illness as a kind of diarrhoea brought about by the change from fresh meat to bacon.

Upon the death of his grandaughter from this disorder, an old and blind man committed suicide by pushing a sharp stick down his throat. The deaths had a demoralizing effect upon the Indian camp, the agent reported.

On Piapot's arrival at Qu'Appelle at the end of July 1882, a meeting of some Treaty Four chiefs, white settlers, and Major J.M. Walsh was organized.[179] Speaking very forcibly at this gathering, Piapot declared that the rations his people were receiving were not enough, that his people were sickening because they were accustomed to a diet of fresh meat, that he had heard the people on the reserves were dying of starvation, and that he did not want his followers to die that way. He intended to choose his own reserve and did not want one chosen for him. Piapot claimed he had been promised land in the Touchwood Hills when he signed the treaty, but he now thought of choosing the Qu'Appelle flat. Other chiefs present at the meeting were apparently brought to attest to the good treatment they had received since settling on their reserves. A speech by Cowessess pleased officials, but Day Star made many complaints.

Unimpressed with the reserve chosen by the agent, Piapot returned to the Cypress Hills, claiming that promises made to the reserve Indians were not being kept. He and other Cree leaders insisted on being granted the reserves promised them in the Cypress Hills in 1880–81.[180] Once again rationing was curtailed there to enforce the policy of removal, and Piapot and his followers were compelled to return to Indian Head. They were loaded onto boxcars at Maple Creek, two of which slipped off the siding and rolled down an embankment.

Piapot was still not pleased with his reserve at Indian Head, however, and by September 1883 he had not yet informed officials whether he intended to stay.[181] That winter forty-two members of Piapot's band died. Dr O.C. Edwards, who visited the reserve in the spring of 1884, reported that the disease, now general on the reserves, was a form of scurvy, caused entirely by the exclusive use of salt foods.[182] He recommended fresh meat and vegetables as the only proper treatment for the disease. Deaths on the reserves were also attributed to scrofula and venereal disease. Like an ominous portent, a fire that swept through Piapot's reserve that spring burned the trees in which the dead were placed, and the bodies were scattered on the ground.

Piapot and his band moved off their reserve in mid-May 1884, his reason being the large number of deaths at that location.[183] The chief maintained his right to choose a reserve for himself; claiming that the sickness was due to a diet of bacon, he wanted a site where his people could obtain fish. He also wanted a meeting with Indian Commissioner Dewdney in the presence of Charles Pratt of Touchwood to discuss the issue of the items promised him in the treaty that he had not received. For a time the band camped on the adjoining Assiniboine reserve but soon began to head for Pasquah's reserve where, Piapot stated, there was plenty of fish and where he intended to hold a sun dance. Piapot had a good number of sympathizers at that point, including members of Yellow Calf's and Loud Voice's bands. Pasquah was also known to be angry at the authorities. The previous year he had stormed out of the agent's office when his request for ammunition and clothing for his people was denied on the grounds that he could not expect to be given what he was able to earn for himself.

Officials of the Indian Affairs Department interpreted Piapot's desire to change his reserve merely as an excuse to avoid work. Reed felt that although the sickness among them, and their wish to have a site with running water and fish, "may weigh with them," he was certain that the real reason was a desire to get away from work on the reserves and "enjoy themselves in a sundance." Ingratiating himself with the distant Vankoughnet, Reed explained that the Indians' tales of "woe" were seldom to be believed and that experience in working with Indians was required before the truth could be ascertained. Stories of Indian starvation and death that had reached Vankoughnet's ear from the letters of newly arrived settlers were exaggerations according to Reed. The settlers were afraid of Indians; the Indians knew this and took advantage of this fright by imposing their "sad stories" on them. Reed informed his superior that department officials were often presented with piteous stories, which were found on inquiry to be false. One chief claimed that he was starving and had not had anything to eat for some days, "and by chance I found a large bannock in the capot of his coat."[184] In another case he once found a large piece of bacon hidden behind the door of a cabin of an Indian who said he was starving. Reed admitted that the death rate was high but insisted that "the first seeds of their complaints were sown during the sojourning of the Indians in the Fort Walsh District, owing to immoral habits, and were it not for this fact the use of bacon would not have such a hurtful effect."[185]

Agent Allan MacDonald recommended that a strong force be organized to seize Piapot and his men on the first overt act. This chief, he stated, "must be made to feel his power in this country is nothing."[186] Reed endorsed the view that Piapot be taught to be "a little more subservient to the wishes of the Department."[187] MacDonald was to see that a member of Pasquah's band objected to the presence of Piapot so that he could be charged with trespassing. A force of fifty-four policemen armed with a cannon left Regina on 18 May and found Piapot's encampment on 21 May. A dangerous confrontation was avoided, however, when Piapot agreed to a meeting at Fort Qu'Appelle to discuss his grievances.

In 1884 Piapot was the victor. He won the right to select his own reserve and he succeeded in holding a sun dance in June of that year. Piapot indicated that he wanted his reserve immediately west of and adjoining Muscowpetung's, near Pasquah's on the Qu'Appelle River.[188] If he could not have that site, he would like one at the Red Sand Hills or Red Deer Lake, 150 miles northwest of Regina, as it had abundant fish, plenty of wood, and good hunting. Officials did not endorse this site: it would place Piapot too close to the Treaty Six bands. Offered a reserve at Last Mountain, the chief declined, insisting that he wanted land with running water where fish could be found. Department officials were reluctant to grant the land near Muscowpetung's, as it already belonged to a colonization company and several residents had taken up homestead. It was to prove an administrative headache, but Piapot's initial request was finally granted. Agent MacDonald agreed that the location on the Qu'Appelle was good, since it contained arable land, running water, hay meadows, and sufficient wood for building and fence rails.[189] A large portion was stony, however, and for this reason MacDonald felt the location would not interfere with white settlement as long as better land was available elsewhere. In July 1884 MacDonald traced on a map two townships of fifty-six square miles, with a frontage of six miles on the river, for Piapot and three of his headmen, who agreed to the site. The chief and thirty-seven lodges settled this site in August 1884.

In 1884 the Indians of this district of Treaty Four were reported to be in a depressed and unsettled state of mind. The severe winter, the sickness and death, the reduction in rations, the Yellow Calf incident, and the protest of Piapot all contributed to their uneasiness. In the spring it was rumoured that the Indians were determined to do no more work, which did not materialize. It was reported in fact that some bands had never worked harder. At the File Hills, for example, the Indians were "never so anxious to get their crops in as they are this spring."[190] It was to be a disastrous farming season, however. It was a late spring, and the ground could not be worked until the end of April. Many of the oxen did not winter well, and they were too thin and weak to work. Not enough seed wheat was sent to some reserves and in many cases it arrived late. To add to this, it was a year of drought and crops were destroyed by frost.

Despite their many grievances, very few of the Indians of the Qu'Appelle participated in the resistance of 1885. That year the Métis of Batoche and St Laurent, in present-day Saskatchewan, began to actively resist government indifference to their long-standing grievances. After a March skirmish between the North-West Mounted Police and the Métis at Duck Lake, Canadian troops were dispatched west under the command of Maj.-Gen. Frederick Middleton. The decisive battle that broke Métis resistance took place at Batoche on 9–12 May. Indian participation in the resistance was limited. On 2 April some members of Big Bear's band, despite the protests of the chief, killed and captured some people in the settlement of Frog Lake. The incident fed fears of a widespread Cree uprising, but this never materialized. Poundmaker's Cree were attacked on 2 May at Cut Knife Hill by Lt-Col William Otter's forces and were thus drawn into the events.[191] Some Dakota from White Cap's band, and Cree from One Arrow's band, participated at Batoche, but most Indians of the North-West honoured pledges made in the treaties not to take up arms.[192]

Nineteen residents of the Qu'Appelle reserves were reported to have gone north during the events of the spring of 1885, but it was not established whether any took an active role.[193] A Hudson's Bay Company employee on the Crooked Lakes reserves, N.M.W.J. McKenzie, was placed in charge of government supplies for the duration of the uprising, and he was instructed to keep the Indians on their reserves at all costs. McKenzie reported that the young men kept nightly councils and had devised a plan to plunder the Pheasant Plains, join the File Hills Indians in the capture of Fort Qu'Appelle, and await reinforcements from the Moose Mountain reserves.[194] According to McKenzie, the older men in council were successful in restraining them.

The Qu'Appelle chiefs, however, chose to take advantage of what they perceived as a position of strength with the threat of widespread turmoil in the North-West to renew pressure for their treaty rights. As department officials were often on the reserves in the spring of 1885, there was increased opportunity to make appeals. Instructed to assess the state of mind of the Indians, officials were not as quick to disregard or dismiss their councils. Requests, messages, and petitions were forwarded to department superiors and members of the government. The Indians were perhaps encouraged to believe that they enjoyed some strength in bargaining, since the department's desire to keep them "busy and contented" meant a generous supply of seed grain that spring and increased rations. McKenzie reported that he kept the Indians "gorged" on flour, bacon, and tea.

Early in April 1885, in the critical days between the battle at Duck Lake and the final confrontation at Batoche, agent MacDonald visited all the reserves under his supervision to secure expressions of "loyalty" and confirmation that the Indians intended to remain on their reserves and sow their crops.[195] The Indians made it clear that they regarded their "loyalty" as a promise they had made at the time of the treaty to obey and abide by the law and to maintain peace and good order. They hoped in turn that the promises made to them would be honoured. In a telegram to the prime minister, which they asked to be read in Parliament, Pasquah and Muscowpetung, through Charles Asham, a headman of one of these bands, expressed these ideas. They asked that the prime minister not "think anything disloyal of us, it hurts us, we depend upon promises made by Great Mother to us because of our keeping faith." They hoped that when the troubles ended, more help would be extended so that they would make a better living.[196]

Piapot and his headmen also sent messages to the prime minister in April 1885 to show they intended to keep peace. The chief stated that he was counselling his men to stay out of trouble and he had given up fighting eleven years ago. The treaty to him meant that he was "not to interfere with the white man and the white man [was] not to interfere with me." His headmen stated that they were prepared to heed the chief's advice to refrain from hostilities and attend to their work, but they were short of tools and could not all be kept at work.[197] O'Soup, spokesman for the Indians of the Crooked Lakes reserves, also used the opportunity to appeal for more implements and cattle, particularly on behalf of the "rising young men," many of whom were married with children and had nothing to begin farming with.[198] O'Soup stated that they were very proud of their farming operations that spring, but 1885 was the first year they had been supplied with enough seed. His people, he claimed, were anxious to make themselves independent of government assistance.

The "loyalty" of the Qu'Appelle Indians may well have been facilitated by their proximity to the Canadian Pacific Railway where they could witness the trainloads of troops that embarked at Troy Station, camped at Fort Qu'Appelle, and headed north along the trail that went by the File Hills and through the Touchwood Hills. Hundreds of teams and teamsters freighted supplies along this same route in the spring of 1885. Many of the local farmers deserted their fields and took up freighting – a more lucrative and certain occupation. Detachments of troops were stationed in some of the settlements, and in villages such as Broadview volunteer militias brandishing rifles marched through the streets. Scouts kept vigilant eyes on the nearby reserves. Rumours circulated that the Indians intended to raid the plains, kill settlers, destroy homes, and steal cattle.[199] The farmers met to devise plans to pool their farm implements to form barricades, and in Broadview engines were kept hitched to railway coaches to spirit away women and children at the first sign of uprising. An atmosphere of panic and apprehension prevailed.

What is often overlooked in accounts of these anxious months is that reserve residents were equally uneasy and apprehensive. The presence of troops was particularly unsettling. For a time the Touchwood Hills bands congregated on Gordon's reserve. According to Chief Gordon, they were alarmed at the presence of so many soldiers on the road.[200] Some teamsters in the transport service damaged and burned houses and flooring on Poor Man's reserve, which frightened the band into moving off the reserve. Day Star's band followed their example. The File Hills bands were similarly anxious about the actions and motives of the troops. On 26 April a detachment of infantry and twenty men from the Governor General's Body Guard marched to the File Hills to intercept carts that were reported to be heading north to supply the Métis. Upon hearing that soldiers were marching toward them, the File Hills Indians formed one large encampment close to the woods on the Okanese reserve. Agent MacDonald could not persuade them to leave this camp, and the people were convinced that the soldiers would take them away to prison. Early in May the File Hills Indians suddenly moved off their reserves. Instructor Nichol believed the move might have been the result of a rumour brought in by a runner, but he also reported that the news of the loss of men up north had excited the troops stationed nearby, "who would like nothing better than to fight at the first chance."[201] The File Hills Indians were implicated in the theft of some horses and other property of settlers in the district, but they were soon persuaded to return to their reserves where they were read a "proclamation" from Dewdney, requesting them to remain on their reserves.

At the end of May it was reported that the File Hills Indians had continued to act in a "disloyal" manner by killing twenty head of cattle on their reserves.[202] Enraged at this behaviour, agent MacDonald recommended that they be treated in the same manner as the "disloyal" bands to the north who had been involved in the rebellion. Dewdney concurred in MacDonald's view that the chiefs and headmen be deposed, that the guilty be severely punished, that all be ordered to surrender their arms, and that their annuities be withheld until the costs of their actions were recovered. For many years the File Hills bands were to feel the weight of this punishment for their actions in the spring of 1885, which had been largely generated by fear but were interpreted as rebellious.

The other Qu'Appelle bands were not subjected to the same punitive measures. Indeed a few individuals perceived as setting an example of loyalty to the others were rewarded with livestock or instalments paid on their machinery. But they too were to feel the weight of new repressive policies that the government felt justified in implementing because of the "rebellion" of a few. What immediately evaporated after the defeat at Batoche was the position of strength, real or illusory, that the Indians felt they had enjoyed earlier in the spring. N.M.W.J. McKenzie noted with some satisfaction that with the news that the "war" was over, "the bottom was completely knocked out of every Indian on the Reserve and I could lead them with a silk thread after that. I also did not fail to 'rub it in' good and plenty, to many of the know-alls and hot heads who were so brave a short time before. They were completely subdued and quite tractable ever after, there being no more trouble with any of them during my sojourn among them."[203] Much of this tractability was due to the coercive regulations that characterized the years after 1885.

CHAPTER FOUR

Assault upon the "Tribal" System: Government Policy after 1885

DETRACTORS AND DEFENDERS

The Indian policy of the Macdonald government was the object of much criticism after the events of 1885. Malcolm Cameron, Liberal Member of Parliament for Huron West, amassed much of the hostile criticism and launched a stinging indictment of Indian administration in the House of Commons in April 1886. Cameron's speech, printed in the parliamentary debates and widely circulated in pamphlet form, included what he claimed was a mass of "independent testimony," which proved that gross injustice had been done to the Indians.[1]

Cameron's first target was the officials sent west, from Commissioner Dewdney to the lowest employee, who, he alleged, were totally unfit to discharge their duties. They had been selected for political reasons, without regard to qualifications or character. Cameron produced the opinions of missionaries, members of the North-West Territories Council, who administered or governed along with the lieutenant-governor, and other prominent citizens, who testified that Indian Department officials were dishonest, unscrupulous, and tyrannical in their relations with the Indians. In some cases they were brutal, drunken, and immoral, and their behaviour had contributed to the outbreak of rebellion. The Member for Huron West claimed that faith with the Indians had been "shamefully, openly, persistently and systematically broken by this Government." As proof that the treaties had been violated and promises broken, Cameron cited evidence from the department's own annual reports that certain bands had not received their oxen, implements, seed, and other items. These same reports, as well as newspaper accounts and police reports, showed the extent of hunger and privation among the Indians. Cameron charged that the department deliberately pursued a policy of starvation to force the Indians into submission, a policy he described as cruel and atrocious and one that ought not to prevail in any civilized country. It was no surprise, Cameron declared, that the Indians were discontented as a result of their being "robbed, defrauded and swindled, frozen to death and starved to death."[2]

Alternative policies and approaches were suggested by non-native critics of Indian administration in the aftermath of 1885. E.R. Young, a former missionary in the North-West and a recognized authority on the Indians, believed that the reserve system was a failure and a great mistake. His solution lay in the formation of a large Indian province north and east of Lake Winnipeg. Young contended that since the uprising had destroyed the confidence of the white settlers, peace and contentment would never be attained if the reserves remained scattered through the settled territory. In their own northern province, the Indians would be "more advantageously placed, both for their own happiness and welfare and for the future progress and safety of the great prairie regions, which we hope to see yet filled with millions of people, who will till the soil and live happy and contented on its resources."[3]

Young was not alone in his call for the "removal" of Indians. An Edmonton candidate for a seat in Parliament in 1887 demanded that the Indians be removed and their land opened up to white farmers.[4] This extreme policy was denounced by others, however. John Maclean, a missionary to the Blood Indians and noted authority on the native people of the West, argued that a removal policy was not in accordance with principles of justice. The one true remedy to end discontent among the Indians, he believed, was the establishment of Indian district councils, composed of agents, farm instructors, missionaries, teachers, and chiefs recognized by the government. The councils might meet annually to hear Indian grievances and send delegates to an Indian territorial assembly. Delegates would report on the "progress and poverty" of the bands in their district and present resolutions on matters affecting their interest.[5]

The Macdonald government's response to mounting public criticism and suggestions for a new direction in Indian administration was to justify past policy firmly. Critics were dismissed as irresponsible, partisan faultfinders; their reports of Indian misery, disease, and starvation were, it was claimed, fabricated by people without the remotest acquaintance with Indians. It was insisted that Indians had been provided with far more than had ever been contemplated in the treaties. In the 1885 annual report of the Department of Indian

Affairs, Macdonald was at pains to point out that the Indians of the West were happy, contented, and well fed.[6] The few bands that had revolted had been aroused and deluded by half-breed supporters of Riel, according to Macdonald. Their actions were portrayed as mad and lunatic; no rational reasons or sound motivations could account for their behaviour.

In his report for the same year, Commissioner Dewdney similarly argued that to explain the participation of some bands in the rebellion, one had to look for reasons other than the administration of Indian Affairs. In Dewdney's mind the wisdom of past policy might be thrown into doubt if the Indians had revolted en masse, but this had not happened. A few had heeded Riel's message, but, according to Dewdney, those who had were "extremely susceptible to influence." Because of their nomadic tendencies, they welcomed any change, without reflection for the consequences. Most Indians were contented and had remained loyal. Dewdney believed that their contentment was due entirely to the success of the policy of distributing liberal rations when work was performed and of refusing food when unjustifiable laziness was shown. All criticism of the policy was dismissed as the sentimental, sensational reports of "would-be-philanthropists," which were "based upon statements of lazy Indians, who may perchance, have had their rations stopped, owing to a refusal to work."[7]

Macdonald met criticism in the House of Commons with similar arguments. Although under no obligation to furnish food to the Indians, his government had shown nothing but tenderness and benevolence in distributing rations, which were issued to the Indian "without letting him feel that he had enough for himself and his family without working." "Pseudo-philanthropists" were telling the Indians that they were suffering and that the government would not let them starve. Statements such as these were encouraging the Indians to think they could eat without working.[8]

Macdonald did not attempt to answer all of Cameron's charges against the Department of Indian Affairs, but he sent a copy of the speech to department officials in the North-West, who were to investigate the allegations. Macdonald promised that the "vindication" of the department that would result from this inquiry would be distributed as widely as copies of Cameron's speech had been. The inquest was scarcely independent and impartial; officials were asked to probe into accusations of their own wrongdoing. Macdonald even admitted in the House that there was no question about the outcome of the inquiry into Cameron's statements: "The evidence will show there never was a greater tissue of false statements."[9]

The findings of the department's investigation were published in a pamphlet, *The Facts respecting Indian Administration in the North-West*. Past policy was staunchly defended. Cameron's speech was dismissed as the blind, partisan harangue of a Liberal motivated, not by zeal for the public welfare, but by the interests of his party. Department officials were depicted as zealous in their care for the interests of the Indians, who were treated justly and generously. The pamphlet supported and reiterated what had become the department's official view of the Indians. It stated that because the Indians had no habits of thrift and perseverance, they tried to get all they could from the government for free and believed it was the white man's duty to maintain them in idleness and comfort. It claimed that the Indians had received far more than they had been entitled to under treaty, but that to complain was a chronic feature of their nature, which led them frequently to make absurd and unreasonable requests. The Indians were encouraged to complain "by men who had the interests of the Indians less in view than the political effect of Indian dissatisfaction and even Indian warfare."[10]

For each of Cameron's "mis-statements," a "correction" was provided. It was argued that Cameron's charges were without foundation or that his evidence was wrenched from its proper context. Cameron, it was claimed, had in many cases mistakenly taken at face value the absurd and unreasonable requests of the Indians, which did not constitute evidence with which to condemn the department. Any sickness or disease was due in large measure to the Indians' fondness for whisky, as well as to their "custom of wearing moccasins, and their mode of life generally [which] are very unfavorable to longevity and to health." Cameron was accused of deliberately misconstruing the facts to incite another Indian rebellion. His speech encouraged the Indians in their "exaggerated" notions of their rights and could well ignite again the "lurid blaze of savage warfare," endangering the lives of thousands of peaceful settlers. Women could once again be dragged into horrible captivity and priests massacred. The statements by Cameron, the "apologist for these savages and the traducer of their victims," were unpatriotic and dangerous.[11]

The *Facts* pamphlet embodied and expressed what had become a formula response to all criticisms of the department's operations. Critics were either partisan, ignorant of the true situation, or gullible for believing the chronic grumbling of "lazy" Indians. Spokesmen for the Indians were simply not to be believed, no matter their statement. "Outside agitators" were seen as the cause of dissatisfaction in many cases. Much criticism was deflected by placing the blame squarely on the Indians, with their assumed disinclination to work, propensity to beg, and their fondness for alcohol.

Every year when the department's annual reports were made public, controversy over Indian policy and administration was vigorously renewed for a time in the press. Critics of the department's program emphasized reports of Indian starvation, rumours of unrest, and revelations of appalling conditions, the result of the government's harsh measures.[12] Department officials were described as political hacks, guilty of cruel and callous behaviour. While some expressed great sympathy for the plight of the Indians, others claimed they were a lazy shiftless lot, who were being fed and protected by the government in idleness, the line of defence used in *Facts*.

Defenders of the department pointed out that a humane, benevolent program had created prosperous contentment on the reserves. While some Indians remained listless and refused to improve their situation, the government was not to be blamed. Taking into consideration the former habits of the Indians, the achievements of the department were all the more remarkable. Department employees were lauded as knowledgeable, experienced, honest, energetic, and economic. Critics of the program were accused of unpatriotically breeding discontent. Those who expressed pity for the Indians' plight were viewed as sentimental philanthropists, who knew nothing of actual conditions. Those who demanded that rations to the Indians be increased were simply encouraging Indians to resist efforts to make them work for a living. Favourable comparisons were drawn between Canadian and American Indian policy, and these became particularly self-congratulatory after 1890 when the battle of Wounded Knee, the murder of Sitting Bull, and the "Messiah craze" in the United States all appeared to point to the fact that, in contrast, the Indians of Canada had been treated with justice.[13]

The issue of the Indians' ability to farm was central to this debate. Newspapers that approved of government policy gave the annual reports a warm reception each year and applauded the Indians' progress at farming. Under headings such as "Raising Crops Not Scalps," gratifying proof of the success of the system was presented.[14] As evidence of the rapid strides made in the transition to a quiet, settled life, statistics were quoted of the acres under cultivation, the number of bushels and value of produce raised, the ploughs, threshing mills, and other machinery in use, and the numbers of cows, pigs, sheep, and oxen under Indian care. All were depicted as important milestones on the road to civilization. Instead of performing their ancient pagan dances, the Indians of the West were "dancing around their threshing machines and spending most of their time in getting their produce to market."[15] A rapid transformation had been achieved.

Accustomed to a roving life, it was no easy matter to transform him into a farmer. But the work has been manfully undertaken, and now, instead of meeting in the Indian the feathered, painted, and treacherous master of the prairies, we find in him the inoffensive settler; poor, yet progressing; rough in his habits, yet much like a white man in that he boasts the dress of civilized life, with, in a few instances, a beaver or plug hat for Sunday wear.[16]

Another paper boasted that "an Ontario farmer visiting an Indian reserve might well be excused for taking it for a white man's farm worked on an extensive scale; and not one of the reserves of the children of the soil."[17] The participation of the Indians in agricultural fairs was hailed as evidence of their remarkable progress. Beside the spear points, bows, and other remnants of their former life were exhibits of grain, vegetables, livestock, bread, butter, and knitting. The Indians were reported to be "as happy and proud of the admiration their handiwork elicited as so many children."[18]

Newspapers favourable to the department often published the observations of visitors to the reserves. In May 1889 Dr Henry Dodd of the NWMP reported to the Regina *Leader* on a recent visit to the Crooked Lakes reserves. Dodd believed these reserves served as brilliant examples of the humane and farsighted policy of the government. He had the highest praise for the officials on the reserves, whom he found to be remarkably intelligent, earnest, painstaking, judicious, and energetic. Farming operations were progressing splendidly to the extent that Dodd predicted these Indians would be chiefly self-sustaining in the immediate future.[19] A Mr Malcolm McMillan, while on a pleasure trip through the Territories in 1889, visited the Assiniboine reserve near Indian Head. He was surprised to find nicely laid out, fenced-off fields, in which the ploughing was exceptional, much better than the work of a great many white settlers. Cattle, pigs, sheep, and poultry compared favourably with any he had seen on his trip. All these positive details reflected great credit on the efficient and courteous Indian agent. McMillan anticipated that, at an early date, the Indians would be supporting themselves by farming.[20] An unidentified, longtime resident of the West sent the Ottawa *Citizen* news of the success of the Indian farmers in the Battleford district, many of whom, it was predicted, would be self-sustaining after the season of 1890. Praise was heaped on

Commissioner Hayter Reed for his work in speedily advancing the Indian.[21]

With equal regularity, a school of pessimistic thought on the issue of the capacity of the Indian to farm published its views. Disparagement of the Indians' efforts arose from a mixture of motives. Liberal papers that condemned government programs tended to have little praise for the Indian farmers. Among the pessimists were residents of the West, from either party, who regretted that the Indians were allowed to retain large tracts of valuable land which could be occupied "by better men."[22] Articles, such as one in the Manitoba *Free Press* in 1889, questioned whether it was particularly praiseworthy or remarkable that the Indians of a certain reserve in the district of Assiniboia had produced 2,600 bushels of wheat in 1888. It was pointed out that the reserve had 100 Indians, as well as three instructors to supervise the work, while on a neighbouring farm an Anglo-Saxon bachelor had raised half that amount entirely on his own. It was concluded that the two white instructors on the reserve should have been able to produce the entire amount on their own, which proved that "these Indians were not only perfectly worthless themselves, but they completely destroyed the usefulness of a white man sent to instruct them in ways of industry and thrift."[23]

An article in the Qu'Appelle *Vidette* of the same year also used the example of the Assiniboine reserve to arrive at the "legitimate conclusion" that the whole band was more than useless and that the usefulness of two white men was destroyed by contact with Indians. It was argued that the Indians' white neighbours, with inferior land, had in some cases produced double the amount of grain. Credit could not be given to the Indians for their cattle and sheep, since the animals, along with abundant supplies of food, had been given to them as gifts. The "dark side" of the picture was that the "Indians are being fed in idleness, unconditionally, so that there is no incentive to industry, as the man who works helps to maintain himself, and the man who does not is provided for by the Government." The Indians, it was argued, should receive not one cent from the government, as in British Columbia and Alaska, where they were a "happy, contented, and prosperous people."[24]

INVESTIGATING ISSUES ON INDIAN POLICY

The public debate over Indian policy and administration that gained momentum after 1885 did not move the Department of Indian Affairs to investigate seriously and thoroughly past approaches and conduct. Instead, efforts to present a sterling public image became more marked after 1885, evident in a more deliberate editing of annual reports before publication, in the tendency to steer visitors and officials toward certain showpiece reserves and away from others, and in the increased emphasis on Indian participation in fairs and exhibits where the successes of the department were advertised. Public facade rather than serious inquiry was the priority after 1885.

An attempt was made, however, to determine whether the Indians had received the oxen and implements they were entitled to. Cameron had condemned the government for not honouring its promises at all, or for issuing inferior, dilapidated tools and inadequate livestock. An 1885 investigation had revealed that the department could not say with certainty what had been distributed, as the records were in a chaotic state.[25] In another attempt in 1886, Hayter Reed adopted the tactic of clouding the issue by dwelling on the confusion surrounding exactly how many cattle and implements were to have been initially distributed. He claimed that it was impossible to arrive at an exact account of the distribution. Problems arose when a family left one reserve for another and took their implements, which had been issued to a certain number of families. In an effort to define entitlement within its narrowest possible limits, Reed presented Deputy Superintendent General Vankoughnet with the argument that the population of a band at the time of the signing of the treaty could not be used as a basis for the distribution of implements and cattle. Since that time band size had decreased because of withdrawal from treaty, the division of bands, or natural causes. Although the experience of Piapot's band was scarcely typical, Reed drew on that band as his example of population change. The band had numbered 941 in 1882, but three years later had dwindled to 386. Reed believed it would be "manifestly incorrect" for the band to receive as their due the implements and oxen for 941 people.[26] He felt it might be reasonable to take band populations in 1886 as the basis for distribution, but he suspected that the Indians would claim they were entitled to the treaty tools and implements for those who had died since the treaty, withdrawn from treaty, or settled elsewhere.

Reed upheld the department's practice of issuing items only as it was considered they were required. He dismissed the Indians' claim that they should have received what was promised them immediately on settling on the reserves because many tools would have been thrown aside. According to Reed, the formula most in accordance with the words of the treaty was to take as the basis for distribution the population of each band in the year when the "greater proportion of the families therein having settled upon a Reserve had commenced to farm." In any case he was convinced that there was no danger of the Indians' not receiving their full complement, since the implements issued to them through the generosity of the department more than met any obligations under treaty.[27]

Vankoughnet agreed that the Indians could not justly claim that all should have received their cattle and implements once settled on the reserve. Because of the Treaty Four stipulations on distribution, it was evident to Vankoughnet that "the intention was only to give the implements and cattle to Indians who were then, that is at the date of the Treaty cultivating lands or who should afterwards commence to cultivate land." As the items were to have been given "once for all," he could see no difficulty in determining what might still be owing. The fairest means was to calculate the number of tools and implements given to families who had been cultivating every year since the date of the treaties, and estimate whether they had received their full quota. In Vankoughnet's interpretation of the treaties, the items were not to have been given to particular families but were to have been distributed to be shared in the proportion stated in the treaty. Treaty Four, for example, stipulated that one plough was to be issued to a band for "every" ten families actually cultivating.[28]

The investigation revealed that the issue of whether the Indians had ever received their full complement of cattle and implements was confused. Department officials could not say with certainty what had been distributed; nor could they agree on what should have been distributed. Publicly, however, the department maintained the position that the Indians had received what they were entitled to and more and therefore there was no truth to Cameron's allegations.

It appears that little effort was made to inquire seriously into other matters raised by Cameron, except for one. Cameron had charged that government employees were involved with Indian women on the reserves. Many of them, he stated in the House, revelled in "the sensual enjoyments of a western harem, plentifully supplied with select cullings from the western prairie flowers."[29] He claimed that 45 per cent of one class of official in 1885 were under medical treatment for a "peculiar kind of disease" as a result of their scandalous behaviour. Immediate action was taken. Lengthy lists were drawn up of who was married and who was single.[30] The single were instructed to marry posthaste, or they would be replaced by married men.

In 1887 some effort to examine and assess Indian policy was made in the Select Committee of the Senate on the Existing Natural Food

Products of the North-West Territories. The central aim of the inquiry was to find a means of saving money by encouraging the Indians to subsist upon the resources of the country. Under the chairmanship of Senator John Christian Schultz, the committee framed a list of questions that was sent to individuals seen as authorities on the North-West, including Senators, Members of Parliament, missionaries, Hudson's Bay Company men, and farmers. No Indians were consulted. Some replied in writing, while others were interviewed by members of the committee. The point of much of the questioning was that if the Indians were left without government support, what might they subsist on? Presumably natural products had once supported these people; why could they not continue to do so? Much of the committee's time was spent discussing how products such as wild rice, fish, and rabbits might be conserved and propagated rapidly. The commissioners were very interested in the possibility of wild turnip as a main source of food. It was speculated that the Indians might eat birds, frogs, grasshoppers, and gophers. Whether the Indians should raise buffalo rather than cattle on the reserves was also discussed.

The issue of whether the Indians were capable of feeding themselves through farming was central to the investigation. Each witness was asked: "What grains, grasses, fruits, roots and vegetables will ... yield the greatest results from the indifferent tillage which is to be expected from such bands of Indians as are new to agricultural pursuits?" The commissioners received contradictory evidence and advice. The opinions of Professor Robert Bell and Amédée Forget are representative.

Bell, a geologist, geographer, and scientist, who had made several visits to the West, was sceptical about the Indians' suitability for agriculture. His views were typical of an observer who had little acquaintance with Indians. Bell stated that, until the present generation, the Indians had never seen white men cultivating the ground, and they could not believe such a thing was possible. According to Bell, Indians looked upon sheep, pigs, and cattle "as we would on creatures from Africa." He insisted that the Plains Indians were the least inclined to agriculture because having been formerly dependent on the buffalo, they were lazy; all the Plains Indian had to do was get on his horse and his "squaw" did all the work. These Indians stubbornly refused to believe that the buffalo had been exterminated, Bell testified. He believed the "bush" Indians were more industrious, as they had learned over the years to stalk game in a manner that required patience and perseverance and they had been obliged to paddle as well as manufacture their canoes, which familiarized them with work. The Indian of the plains, however, could not work. Professor Bell found that their hands were "soft like a woman's."

They think it is beneath their dignity to work. They have not been accustomed to it, and they say it has never been done by their forefathers. I have lectured them on the subject, but they have told me: "It is according to the traditions of your forefathers, but we have never done anything of the kind, and our fathers have never worked." For an Indian to interfere with the ways of the Great Spirit by growing plants, seems something that they cannot comprehend – they cannot do it – they will not grow potatoes.

Nor would the Indians make provision for the future. When he gave them some seed, they boiled it up and consumed it that very evening. He claimed they would not dig a pit or build a cellar to store roots. Even with winter coming, they would sell their last bushel of corn or potatoes to buy some trifle. (Such as a pocket handkerchief, one of the commissioners suggested.)[31]

Bell's estimation of the Indians as farmers was in marked contrast with that of Amédée Forget, then clerk of the North-West Council. Unlike Bell, Forget was a resident of the West and was familiar in particular with the Indians of the Battleford district where he had farmed from 1877 to 1880, just at the time the Indians were beginning to cultivate. He had also recently visited the reserves along the Qu'Appelle. Forget maintained that Indian farmers "have been as successful as their white neighbours." He found that "in all cases where an Indian started a garden he seemed to be giving more care to it than we did ourselves. At any time during the summer you could hardly detect one blade of grass growing between their vegetables. Their gardens were kept clean." Forget was firmly convinced that the Indians were disposed to work but that they, like all other farmers, had to contend with difficulties in cultivating the land. Because of crop failure, they had not been rewarded for their work. Forget had "not the slightest doubt if the crops had been good every year, today the Indians would be as good farmers as any others," and he believed that if the Indians' crops had been equal to their anticipations, they would be in a position to sustain themselves to a great extent. He noted, however, that bad crops had discouraged the Indian farmers and had had a worse effect on them than on white farmers. The apparent reluctance of Indians to work, Forget claimed, was due to crop failure more than to anything else, and he had observed that where crops succeeded, all worked without complaint. Unlike Bell, Forget drew few distinctions between Indian and white farming on the prairie.[32]

The committee made a number of recommendations based on its investigation. The first was to seed the reserves with wild rice, a cheap and healthful food product that required little care and attracted wild fowl. It was also recommended that spawns of sturgeon, white fish, and other varieties be distributed and that methods of preserving fish by drying, salting, smoking, freezing, or pounding into pemmican be encouraged. Fish was particularly suitable for rations until the Indians learned agriculture. It was decided that bison should not be reintroduced, as "the presence of these animals would disturb the present agricultural training of the Indians, and interfere with the farming and herding efforts of the whites."[33] The report did not include any commentary on the broader issues of Indian policy and administration. No conclusions were ventured on the topic of the Indians as farmers, despite the lengthy testimony on the subject. Except for an effort to sow wild rice, which was unsuccessful, none of the other recommendations were adopted.

The recommendations of the Senators were indignantly rejected in the West. Editor P.G. Laurie of the *Saskatchewan Herald* wrote on 21 January 1888 that they would perpetuate the Indians' "migratory, restless habits to set them to digging for wild roots, or rearing wild animals." It was easier "to cultivate a hundred bushels of potatoes or turnips than to dig a bag full of wild ones." The Indians of the Battleford agency were, according to Laurie, in "a position to raise more grain than they could consume or find a good market for." In fact the Indians of that agency were so advanced in their agriculture by that time that non-native residents were becoming angry about Indian competition for markets.

With the lack of serious inquiry into past policies, they became even more firmly entrenched after 1885, and some were undertaken with much greater vigour and commitment. The emphasis after 1885 was on efforts to dismantle the "tribal" system and promote individualism and on increased supervision, control, and restriction of the activities and movements of the Indians. Aspects of both policies had an important influence on the progress of agriculture on the reserves.

HAYTER REED – A NEW EMPHASIS TO INDIAN POLICY

Hayter Reed was the major architect of Indian policy in the North-West in the decade following the rebellion. Although his training and career interests were military, Reed quickly rose in the department from the position of Indian agent at Battleford in 1881 through the ranks of assistant Indian commissioner in 1884, commissioner in 1888, and deputy superintendent general of Indian affairs in 1893, replacing the aging Lawrence Vankoughnet. Reed had had little direct experience with, or knowledge of, Indians before his first posting with the department.

Reed was born in 1849 in L'Orignal, Prescott County, Ontario, and was educated at Upper Canada College and at the Model Grammar School in Toronto.[34] He was devoted to a military life from an early age. At sixteen he was a volunteer in the militia, and that same year he graduated from the Royal Military School with a first-class certificate. At eighteen Reed was drill instructor with the Kingston Rifle Battalion. In 1871 he was serving with the Provincial Battalion of Rifles when it was dispatched to Fort Garry as reinforcements during the Fenian scare. Reed was adjutant to the battalion and eventually garrison adjutant to the whole force in service in the North-West, and he remained with this garrison until it was disbanded in 1878. He retired from military service with the rank of major in 1881. Although Reed was called to the bar of Manitoba in 1872, it appears that he was never active as a lawyer.

Like many soldiers from Ontario posted in the West, Reed remained there after his unit was disbanded. In 1880, in the midst of the "Manitoba fever," the boom years that saw the influx of thousands of immigrants to some of the best land in the province, he worked out of Winnipeg with the Department of the Interior as chief land guide.[35] That job was to provide information to settlers on suitable sites and sometimes to accompany them to assist in the selection of land. In this position, as in his later work with Indian Affairs, Reed showed a high level of ambition, as well as a dedication to the larger purposes of the government he served. The practical, daily tasks of the man on the spot were not, in Reed's case, allowed to obscure the goal. As a land guide he provided his superiors in Ottawa with numerous suggestions on how the entire immigration system might be improved, how Canadians might be prevented from making the United States their home, and how erroneous perceptions of the West might be dispelled.

The chief land guide was dedicated to the idea that anyone, even someone with very little capital, could succeed as a farmer in the West if he were enterprising and willing to forgo the superfluous luxuries of "modern" life. In 1880 Reed assured prospective settlers that opportunities were excellent, even as far west as Prince Albert, Battleford, and Duck Lake. There they would find wholesome food, comfortable clothing, and substantial housing, which, Reed believed, was all they would require. Despite the absence of railway facilities, pioneers could still be guaranteed a market for their produce: the government's demands alone for the Indians, the police, surveyors, and other crews would absorb all of a farmer's surplus. The old proverb While the grass is growing the steed may starve would not apply to prudent men willing to work hard and take advantage of all contingencies. "So soon as the prairie grass grows, with a good ox and a Red River cart, a man can 'go anywhere and do anything', as the Iron Duke once said of the British Infantry, and enjoy the fruits of independence."[36]

In 1881 Reed left his job as land guide and became Indian agent at Battleford. In later years he claimed he was dispatched to this post "owing to the fact of the Indians having become unmanageable," which suggests that he was not necessarily interested in or inclined toward a career among the Indians. Rather, he was responding to a call like a soldier being asked to dispose of an unpleasant situation.[37] And unpleasant he did regard it: Reed once described the Battleford Indians as the "scum of the plains."[38] The skills of the new agent were those of the military man – of the drill instructor and the officer; he was a man accustomed to giving commands and having them obeyed without question. He had been trained in the virtues of rigid discipline and strict adherence to rules and regulations. Deviation from the rules and insubordinate behaviour were not tolerated. Questions about, or objections to, the system were not permitted. From the beginning of his career with the Indian Department, Reed insisted upon such military conduct. The agent would not tolerate, for example, the Indians' practice of presenting their concerns at the annual treaty payments, and threatened instead not to pay them at all.[39] Reed believed it was folly to imagine that the Indians should be consulted about, or have any say in determining, their own fate. "As well might the Christian or civilized parent allow his children to follow uncurbed the dictates of the blind promptings of their own unregenerate human nature and grow up the outcasts of society, as leave an ignorant savage to determine his own course for himself."[40] A firm hand was necessary in dealing with the Indians, Reed was convinced, and he refused to negotiate, compromise, or make concessions. An inflexible attitude would soon demonstrate to them that "extravagant" demands were pointless.

In an address given in the 1890s, Reed expressed the view that the Indians' poverty and distress had nothing to do with broken treaty promises, a lack of implements and oxen, or any other "imaginary" injustice. He saw the Indians' propensity to blame the government for their misfortunes as simply a campaign to avoid work while still being fed. Reed claimed that the Indians' problem was a moral one – the Indians were "parasites," living off the work of others – and the cure lay in the reform of their character and tribal society. Through the introduction of the concept of "work," and by not tolerating "idleness," this reform could be effected. The job of the Indian agent, Reed believed, was to compel obedience, and "when moral suasion failed the only means of coercion was to stop their rations and try and establish the apostle's law that if a man would not work he should not eat."[41] From his earliest appointment with the department, Reed took the success of the work for rations policy as his special mission. With the ultimate goal of the policy always kept firmly in mind, the misery and suffering that it created could be viewed as a necessary stage in a training program.

Reed soon earned a reputation as a severe and unyielding administrator. Iron Heart refused to issue provisions unless work was performed, no matter how pitiful the pleas.[42] A farm instructor on the Poundmaker reserve described Reed as an exacting taskmaster. He had "calculated to a nicety how much work a yoke of oxen and a plow were capable of performing in a given time and the Indian fell a good deal short of this. He had figured out how little food it was possible to get along with and the Indian was always hungry. The Indian was lazy, therefore he must have short rations."[43] As Indian agent Reed did not win the admiration of many of his subordinates. Another farm instructor in the Treaty Six district described him as "entirely lacking in sympathetic understanding of the Indians, of their difficulties, and to his management or mismanagement of Indian affairs the writer attributes much of the unrest existing amongst the different bands."[44]

Hayter Reed's talents, however, were appreciated by his superiors. It is not surprising that his approach to Indian affairs pleased officials in Regina and Ottawa. Since Reed saw the Indians as solely responsible for their state of affairs, the government was absolved of any accountability. This approach justified a harsh, strict policy, and it allowed Indian grievances to be readily dismissed. Reed was promoted to the position of acting assistant commissioner in 1883, and assistant commissioner the following year. Dewdney's new second-in-command was appointed just in time to help implement Vankoughnet's scheme of retrenchment, which, as noted previously, involved much more severe rationing. Reed was in complete sympathy with this rigid approach. As incidents of Indian protest mounted in 1883 and 1884, Reed continued to insist that there were no just grounds for complaint. Dissent and dissatisfaction were generally attributed to outside agitators. For Reed this usually meant the Métis. He harboured suspicion, even contempt, for the Métis throughout his career.

Like a commanding officer whose orders have been disobeyed, Reed was outraged at the participation of Indians in the events of 1885, which he regarded as insubordination that warranted severe punishment. Reed was satisfied at the prospect of having a large number of Indians publicly hanged. Eight Indians were in fact hanged on the barracks square of Battleford Post on 27 November 1885. The assistant commissioner wrote Dewdney, "I am desirous of having the Indians witness it – No sound threshing having been given them I think a sight of this sort would cause them to meditate for many a day."[45] Reed also advocated extremely repressive measures in a memorandum on the future management of the Indians, which became the core of a memo Vankoughnet presented to John A. Macdonald in August 1885. It revealed a wrathful, vengeful anger, and Dewdney found parts of it intemperate.[46] The memo nonetheless defined the basic lines along which Reed would guide Indian policy as he acquired power and influence in the late 1880s and 1890s. Certain measures that were presented in 1885 as punitive, temporary, and only for selected bands became permanent and universal.

The assistant commissioner's 1885 memo divided Indian bands into the "loyal" and the "disloyal," and a system of rewards and punishments was devised. The loyal bands were those that had remained on their reserves, sown their crops, obeyed their agents and instructors, and ignored the messages of runners. Individuals in those bands who were seen as influential in maintaining loyalty were rewarded with cows, oxen, sheep, or a payment toward a piece of machinery. In Reed's view the rewards would help cement the bonds of unity between the loyal Indians and the authorities.[47]

Reed insisted that the participation of certain bands in the 1885 uprising constituted a violation of the treaties, which meant that for these bands the agreement was negated. In the case of the disloyal bands, he recommended that the tribal system be abolished and that the chiefs and councillors be deposed and deprived of their treaty medals. By the "careful repression" of the leaders, "a further obstacle will be thrown in the way of future united rebellious movements."[48] Instructors and agents would direct their orders to individuals and would not be hampered by consultations with the chiefs. As a means of controlling the movement of Indians involved in the rebellion, Reed also recommended that those travelling off their reserves should be required by the police and the municipal authorities to produce a pass from an official of the department declaring their business in the locality.

UNDERMINING THE "TRIBAL" SYSTEM

The recommendations contained in Reed's 1885 memo, that the tribal system be abolished and that the Indians' movements and activities be more rigidly supervised, became entrenched aspects of Indian policy, and not only for the "rebel" bands. These were not new ideas, and Reed was not solely responsible for them, but they were the policies he fully endorsed and attempted to enforce. Appointed Indian commissioner in 1888, Reed was in a position to articulate his views and compel obedience to them. His professed goal was to amalgamate the Indians with the white population.[49] As he explained in a speech dating from the 1890s, "It can surely never be seriously contended that it is for the interest of the commonwealth to continue a day longer than is necessary a foreign element in its midst, for even should such element be controlled as not to constitute a source of [illegible] danger, it must assuredly for negative reasons, be one of weakness to the State. Unity of interests, unity of sentiments are required to give strength to the whole."[50]

Because the banding together of Indians on reserves militated against their conversion into citizens, Reed's ultimate aim was to see the reserves broken up. He believed, however, that the Indians of the present generation were not prepared to merge with the white population. Therefore, in the meantime, "it seems better to keep them together, for the purpose of training them for mergence with the whites, than to disperse them unprotected among communities where they could not hold their own, and would speedily be downtrodden and debauched." The Indians on reserves had to be gradually trained for enfranchisement and for the privileges and responsibilities of citizenship. They had to be led step by step to provide for themselves through their own industry and to be inculcated with a spirit of "self-reliance and independence." Reed boasted that under his administration the "policy of destroying the tribal or communist system is assailed in every possible way, and every effort made to implant a spirit of individual responsibility instead."[51]

Reed believed that the most effective means of undermining the tribal system was through the subdivision of reserves into separate farms. In his view large fields worked in common fostered the tribal system and did not encourage pride and industry, since the individual farmer did not feel it worth his while to improve greatly land that other members of the band also claimed as their own.[52] With a certificate of ownership, the enterprising Indian would make permanent improvements. Reed was also convinced that private property created law-abiding citizens. Property would render the Indians averse to seeing the existing order of things disturbed, for "among them as among white communities, the lawless and revolutionary element is to be found among those who have nothing to lose but may perhaps gain by upsetting law and order."[53]

Subdividing in severalty was not a new idea in Canadian Indian policy. Nor was Reed the first official to promote the scheme for the Indians of western Canada. Dewdney had heartily endorsed the idea as a means of striking at the heart of the tribal system by fostering self-reliance and a spirit of emulation of white society. He argued that the Indians should have initially been given individual farms so they would have learned a sense of personal proprietorship and responsibility.[54] During Dewdney's term as commissioner, agents were asked to impress the advantages of this system upon the Indians, and the program was implemented on three reserves in Manitoba. Under Hayter Reed the survey of reserves in severalty was much more extensive and the program began in earnest.

At the outset of his career as commissioner, Reed was convinced that another means of fostering an independent, proprietary spirit among the Indians was to allow the industrious to purchase some property, in the way of wagons and implements, from the proceeds of produce they were allowed to dispose of. Their rations, however, could not suddenly and completely be withdrawn once they met with some success to avoid leaving them wondering whether their exertions had been worth the effort.[55] If the industrious were compelled to devote all their earnings to the purchase of food, while those who produced half the crop received the balance from the government, there would be no incentive to work. The diligent had to be allowed to invest a fair share of their earnings. Reed's policy was to continue to assist the enterprising Indian for a time so that he could purchase wagons, harness, and implements, and so that "he develops into the stage of being a property holder, and soon begins to look down upon those whose laziness compels them to seek assistance from the government. Meanwhile what he had purchased secures him the means of assured independence while he has been acquiring the spirit to make it safe to discontinue helping him and his position awakens a spirit of emulation in his less industrious brother."[56]

Reed further believed that as the farming Indians gained a sense of pride in their prosperity, they would be less inclined to share their produce with their "impecunious neighbors," as in the days when communist ideas prevailed.[57] By this means, it was hoped that the more reluctant Indians would be pressured to similarly devote themselves to agriculture. For most of the 1880s the Indians' purchase of mowers, horse rakes, threshing machines, and other machinery was heralded in the annual reports as evidence of a new spirit of individualism, of prosperity and overall progress. Such purchases were also used as evidence that the Indians were not squandering their earnings as many were convinced they were prone to do.

Another means of encouraging individualism, responsibility, and a sense of pride in property was the cattle on loan system, which Reed endorsed. Known as the Birtle system, it was first introduced in Birtle, Manitoba, by agent Lawrence Herchmer in 1886. Through this system Indians acquired, under certain restrictions, proprietary rights to cattle. A trustworthy individual was loaned a cow and was to raise a heifer, either of which had to be returned to the agent. The animal the Indian kept became his property, although the agent's permission was required to sell or transfer ownership. The agent was then to lend the returned animal to another Indian of the band who had no cattle. The philosophy behind the program was that the Indians would have greater incentive to care for their cattle if they were given an interest in them. On some reserves agents had reported that it was difficult to get the Indians to provide and care for their cattle because the herds were the common property of the band and no individual felt responsibility for them.[58]

Before the introduction of the Birtle system, any cattle given to the Indians above those stipulated in the treaty were on loan only, apparently to prevent abduction or slaughter. As noted previously, some Indian farmers had protested that since the cattle were not theirs, they would not winter them, which was costly, but would instead hand them back once the work season was over.[59] The problem was that the Indians received little benefit from keeping cattle, a situation Inspector Alex McGibbon recognized in the Touchwood Hills in 1886. The Indians there received the benefit of the work performed by their oxen but nothing more. Their cattle could not be sold or slaughtered without the consent of the agent. The department did not buy cattle from the Indians for their rations but instead imported bacon. There was nothing to encourage the Indians to raise and keep cattle. McGibbon wrote that "at present [the Indian] has to feed cattle and look after them but he cannot see what it is for ... if he knew he would get something in hand for his labor it would make a great difference."[60]

The Birtle system became the source of much confusion. Its central purpose of fostering a sense of individual ownership was largely defeated because the department would still not allow an Indian to dispose of any beast without the consent of the agent, which was rarely given. At the same time the Indians were to be made to understand that the animal's progeny was theirs alone. It is not surprising that agents complained that they had difficulty in making the Indians understand that while the cattle was theirs, they had to have an agent's permission to sell, slaughter, or barter.[61]

To undermine the tribal system, the policy of destroying the traditional system of leadership was also pursued. The chiefs of bands perceived to be disloyal in 1885 were deposed, and Reed hoped that as the other chiefs and headmen died off, these offices might be allowed to lapse. Reed did not try to hide the fact that he welcomed the death of "notorious" chiefs such as Pasquah and Peepeekisis. The influence of the older chiefs was not beneficial, he explained, because they were naturally conservative. Even if they did feel they should help their people become industrious, they were often compelled "in order to retain their influence over the lazy and intractable, to become, against their better judgement, the mouth-piece for the ventilation of imaginary grievances and the presentation of utterly unreasonable demands."[62] Reed wished to abolish the offices of chief and headmen altogether "as one of the strongest aids towards the destruction of communism, and the creation of individuality."[63] Individuals were to seek the advice and leadership of their agents and instructors directly. Government officials were to deal with individuals or families, not with bands. Agents were instructed to visit Indians in their own homes and not allow the Indians to assemble in council. Chiefs and councillors were not to be regarded as spokesmen for a band unless they fully endorsed the policy the department was implementing.[64]

RESTRICTING THE INDIANS' MOVEMENTS AND ACTIVITIES

To carry out the second prong of Reed's policy recommendations, the much more rigid supervision of the movements and activities of the Indians, the number of department employees in the West was greatly increased after 1885. In the region now known as Saskatchewan, the number of Indian agencies expanded from two to ten. Allan MacDonald, for example, previously the sole agent for Treaty Four, was moved to the Crooked Lakes, and three others were appointed to the reserves formerly under his supervision. Resident farm instructors were placed on most reserves.

The increased resident supervisory staff facilitated the implementation of the pass system after 1885. A pass system was first adopted as a temporary measure during the crisis of 1885 to control and monitor the movements of the Indians, essentially to keep them from joining the "rebels." On 6 May 1885 Maj.-Gen. Frederick Middleton wrote to Dewdney whether it would be "advisable to issue proclamation warning breeds and Indians to return to their Reserves and that all found away will be treated as rebels. I suppose such a proclamation could be disseminated without difficulty." Dewdney replied that while he had "no power to issue proclamation as you suggest," he had, however, circulated a "notice" advising Indians to stay on their reserves or face arrest on suspicion of being "hostiles."[65]

This notice was distributed throughout the agencies.[66] It stated that the large bodies of troops in the North-West might attack Indians found off their reserves, as the commanders would be unable to tell whether they were hostile or friendly. Indians were warned that because the troops were arresting and punishing all runners from Riel, who were spreading "lies and false reports," it would be necessary to "arrest all Indians, or any suspicious persons whom they may see" unless the Indian had special written permission from an authorized person. Good and loyal Indians were to remain quietly on their reserves. A reward of fifty dollars was offered to any loyal Indian who might provide information leading to the arrest and conviction of runners from Riel or hostile bands of Indians.

By June 1885, with the final confrontation at Batoche over for some weeks, Dewdney was prepared to relax the restrictions on the movements of the Indians.[67] He viewed the pass system as a temporary measure, adopted because of the exigencies of the time. As the system had no validity in law, Dewdney believed it was futile to continue to attempt to confine the Indians to their reserves. Neither the Indian Act nor any other federal legislation empowered the department to institute such a system.

The possibility of implementing a pass system had been raised on occasion before 1885 but had been rejected because it ran directly counter to promises made to the Indians. Treaty Six, for example, stated that the Indians had the "right to pursue their avocations of hunting and fishing throughout the tract surrendered."[68] Although in the early 1880s Lawrence Vankoughnet had been in favour of a pass system, Prime Minister Macdonald and Commissioner A.G. Irvine of the North-West Mounted Police rejected the proposal. Irvine believed that any attempt to confine the Indians to their reserves would be "tantamount to a breach of confidence with the Indians," since they had been assured that they were at liberty to travel and that residence on a reserve was not compulsory. Irvine, present at the Treaty Seven negotiations at Blackfoot Crossing in 1877, recalled that "this concession largely contributed to the satisfactory conclusion of the treaty with the Blackfoot."[69] In the years before 1885 the Vagrancy Act was on occasion applied to Indians as a means of inducing them to return to and stay on their reserves. In 1883 Irvine reported that he explained the terms of the Vagrancy Act to some people congregated at Maple Creek and warned them that they would be arrested if they did not promptly return to their reserves.[70]

Hayter Reed did not share his superior's reluctance to continue the pass system. In August 1885 Reed informed Dewdney that he was not allowing Indians of the Battleford district to leave their reserves without passes. On their daily patrols, the NWMP sent back any people found off the reserves without passes. Reed was aware that "this is hardly supportable by any legal enactment," but he argued that "we must do many things which can only be supported by common sense and by what may be for the general good."[71] In his 1885 memo on the future management of the Indians, Reed recommended that the pass system be implemented throughout the West.[72] Although he recognized that the treaties gave the Indians permission to go wherever they pleased, Reed believed that towns and villages, which were owned by municipalities, might be regarded as properties from which the Indians, by treaty, were prohibited from entering. The treaties had stipulated that Indians could not encroach on the property of white settlers. Dewdney by this time concurred with Reed's views on the necessity of a pass system for all Indians, as did Vankoughnet and John A. Macdonald.[73] Macdonald believed that if the pass system could be introduced "safely," it was "in the highest degree desirable." He clearly recognized that the system rested on no legal foundation and cautioned that "in case of resistance on the grounds of Treaty rights [it] should not be insisted upon."[74]

Books of passes were sent to the Indian agencies in 1886.[75] When an Indian applied to the agent for a pass, first he had to produce a letter of recommendation from his farm instructor.[76] Indians who had acted in an "unsatisfactory" manner during the crisis of 1885 carried passes that noted this fact for the information of the police or other officials to whom they might be presented.[77] As the system evolved, Indians were required to carry passes for all activities that took them from their reserves, including hunting, trapping, fishing, picking berries, collecting seneca root, shopping in the towns, or visiting another reserve. Indians visiting their children in industrial schools also required passes.[78] They were issued only to parents who promised not to interfere with their children or try to bring them home. As the presence of adults was seen as a disruptive, degenerating influence, this system effectively limited the number of visitors, the period of time they were allowed to remain, and the frequency of visits.

The pass system was effectively enforced, especially in the years immediately following the 1885 resistance. It became routine work of the NWMP to intercept or arrest Indians without passes and turn them back to their reserves. In 1886, for example, in the Battleford district it was reported that "no Indians were seen off their reserves without a pass, except a few vagrants who came to Battleford, and were sent out again."[79] Indians found without passes in Battleford were arrested under the provisions of the Vagrancy Act.[80] Indian agents reported to the police when parties left the reserves in order that they might be intercepted. In 1887, for example, several families from Piapot's band were tracked by ten members of the force. The "deserters" were discovered in a wooded ravine and escorted back to the reserve.[81] In 1889 some Indians in the Duck Lake district left their reserve without permission to attend a sun dance. The police intercepted them and turned them back.[82] The borders of reserves were patrolled by police. Col S.B. Steele described how police frequently came in contact with Indians while on night duty patrol along the borders of reserves in the Macleod district. They were "obliged to make their arrests at the pistol's point. Conflicts occasionally occurred, but such episodes had to be made light of and kept as quiet as possible lest the settlers be alarmed and rumours of a disturbing nature be circulated throughout the country. The Indian War of 1885 had made the people very nervous, and the slightest rumour caused many to see Indian risings every spring when the grass was good." It was not in the interests of the Indians that reserves were patrolled but rather to ease a "general unsettled feeling prevalent ... among the settlers ... which feeling was almost as intense as during the time of the rebellion."[83]

It was difficult for the Indians to ignore or protest the pass system, as agents threatened to withdraw the recalcitrant from the rations list.[84] They could register protest by being as stubborn as possible about returning to their reserves. Policeman John G. Donkin wrote that "it is tedious and unpleasant work doing guard over travelling redskins, who are worse than Government mules for obstinacy. They will only move when they choose, and will only proceed a certain distance at their own pace. They throw all sorts of obstacles in the way of progress, and you are not allowed to use force, except on rare occasions."[85] In the districts of Assiniboia and Saskatchewan the pass system appears to have effectively confined people to their reserves. More varying success was reported by police from the Alberta district especially in spring and just after treaty payments. The Bloods were the most difficult to contain. Superintendent Richard Burton Deane reported in 1888 that Indians absent from the Blood reserve "come with all sorts of plausible pretexts for being off their reserve without a pass. Some do not appear to think a pass necessary at all. One Indian produced a pass which was exactly a year old, and therewith was quite content."[86] Hayter Reed instructed Indian agents that even when they felt it was impossible to prevent large numbers of Indians from leaving a reserve, it was nonetheless expedient to issue passes, rather than refuse them, so that agents could keep track of who was going where and for how long. If control could not be achieved, it was important to maintain the appearance of control. Reed warned the Indian agents that "the greatest caution has to be exercised, for were they to offer resistance and conflict ensue, they have the law on their side. Under these circumstances Agents must often against their own wishes issue Passes to Indians who they know will leave in any case, and so preserve an appearance at least of control and a knowledge of their movements."[87]

Reed believed it was important that the agents conceal from the Indians the fact that the pass system had no validity in law. It appears, however, that the Indians were well aware of this. In 1888 Deane wrote that in the Lethbridge district some Indians "seem to be aware that in point of law they have as much right to roam about the country as white men, and that confinement to a reserve was not one of the provisions of their treaty. It thus behoves the police to be very careful in handling them, to avoid being compelled to take back water, in case of an Indian's asserting his right to freedom of action, and maintaining it."[88] Similarly Steele reported in 1891 that his men in the Fort Macleod district were doing their best to turn back Indians without passes but that "a difficulty arises in the fact that few of our men can speak sufficient Blackfoot to make themselves understood and the Indians when it suits their purpose can be very obtuse: they are aware too that we have no legal right to turn them back."[89] Government officials compounded the confusion surrounding the pass system by not publicly admitting its existence. A letter by Dewdney, published in the Calgary *Herald* in 1890, stated that the government could not insist that the Indians stay on their reserves and that, under treaty, "they are allowed to move about as freely as white men, provided they behave themselves."[90]

Officials of the NWMP were never comfortable with the absence of any legal foundation for the pass system. The lack of a legal basis in this case undermined the validity of all NWMP operations: they were trying to demonstrate to the Indians that the police enforced a rational system of laws that operated to the benefit of all. In 1892 Commissioner L. Herchmer was advised by circuit court judges that the system was illegal and that the police would surely lose if their right to enforce it was challenged in the courts. The legal opinion of government law officers was sought, and they proved to be "unequivocally opposed to continuation of the practice."[91] In 1893 a circular letter was issued directing all police officers to refrain from ordering Indians without passes back to their reserves.

Hayter Reed would have none of these weak-kneed, legalistic concerns. He urged the police to continue enforcing the pass system on the grounds that the "moral responsibilities of the Indian Department transcended treaty obligations."[92] Reed's views triumphed. By at least 1896 the police had reversed their position. In that year Commissioner Herchmer issued a circular letter instructing police who encountered any Indian without a pass to "use all possible pressure to persuade him to return to his reserve."[93] Yet the police continued to vacillate. In 1904 they once again informed the Department of Indian Affairs that they would not order Indians back to their reserves.[94]

The imposition of a pass system in the spring of 1885 is perhaps understandable as a temporary measure during the resistance. Although its essential purpose was to control and confine what was perceived as a potentially hostile population, it also functioned to protect the Indians during the months of crisis. The bitter fighting had dimensions of a racial confrontation. According to one side's interpretation, all whites were loyal citizens and all with darker complexions were under suspicion. Their fears fed by tales of atrocity at Duck Lake and Frog Lake, the settlers and the troops distrusted all Indians and Métis. In this tense atmosphere it was perhaps in the interests of the safety of the Indians that they be confined to their reserves.

A more perplexing question is why the pass system was continued after 1885. It should have been allowed to lapse, as Dewdney suggested, as early as June 1885. Architects of the policy professed that it was in the best interests of the Indians. Authorities on the Indians had long testified that contact with white people was physically, mentally, and spiritually injurious to the Indians.[95] In the white settlements natives always found "the lower stratum of society ready to teach the willing learner lessons of immorality; and degradation is sure to follow any close relationship with white people in the early stages of their training."[96] In particular it was hoped that the pass system would prevent Indian women of "abandoned character" from loitering about the settlements. It was also a means of severely limiting the Indians' access to alcohol. It was believed that the pass system would enhance the agricultural program on the reserves, as the Indian farmers could be prevented from leaving their crops at critical times of the season. The rural life offered the Indians a noble and healthy occupation that was morally elevating. Urban life, by contrast, was a corrupt environment that led to physical and moral degeneracy.

The pass system was authorized and sanctioned by the idea that, as "probationary" citizens, the Indians had to be kept separate from the rest of society. But it is clear that the system also served the interests of the resident and potential white settlers. To begin with, it was used to allay any anxiety that the Indians were a military threat. In 1885 Indians made up almost half the population of the North-West, and they outnumbered the white population in the districts of Saskatchewan and Alberta.[97] Wild and frightening rumours of Indian unrest and uprising continued to circulate for some years after 1885. To restore confidence in law and order, and to ensure that peace would prevail, the Indians were confined to their reserves. Prospective settlers had also to be assured that they had nothing to fear from Indians if they homesteaded on an isolated patch of Canadian prairie. Eastern Canadian, American, and European newspapers had published exaggerated, sensational accounts of blazing homesteads and scalped settlers.[98]

Assurances of peace and order were necessary to keep alive Macdonald's vision of a densely populated West. The Indians and Métis had dealt a crippling blow to immigration to the prairies: in 1885 it was at a virtual standstill. Part of the government's National Policy, which envisaged large numbers of settlers in the West to develop its agricultural potential and create a staple for export, was in danger of dying. More than any other measure, the pass system ensured that the Indians could no longer threaten the dream of a prosperous, peaceful West. The settlers' interests, not the Indians', were paramount. As historian John Jennings has observed, "The human rights of the Indians, as well as the treaty promises, were sacrificed in deference to the success of the National Policy."[99]

In the early years of the pass system, correspondence of the Indian Affairs Department reflected concern that the Indians potentially constituted a military threat. Hayter Reed was determined to prevent united rebellious movements in the future.[100] A primary function of the pass system was to keep Indians from communicating with each other, to limit opportunities to scheme and intrigue. Should any strange Indians arrive on a reserve, agents were to carefully inquire into their business and to inform promptly the office of the commissioner of Indian affairs in Regina of such arrivals.[101] As memories of the 1885 crisis faded, however, the Indians came to be viewed as more of a source of irritation and annoyance than as a military threat. The pass system was maintained as the best method of expunging this vexatious nuisance. By the settlers it was viewed as a means of preventing the Indians from loafing about the towns for whatever immoral purposes, killing settlers' cattle, and hoarding all the game and fish of a district.

Once the pass system was in place, public pressure was applied to maintain it. Citizens' groups approached the department about strengthening the system. With the Sarcee reserve in close proximity, citizens of Calgary were particularly vocal and strident in demanding that the system be enforced. For example, in 1890 the Calgary Gun Club requested that Indian agents issue no passes to Indians from the beginning of nesting season until 1 September as a means of ending the Indians' "war of extermination" against immature birds.[102] When in 1893 the police temporarily stopped enforcing the pass system, a storm of angry criticism followed. Newspapers loudly protested that their towns were being overrun by Indians.[103] A Calgary paper argued that the government could legitimately curtail the Indians' right to free movement guaranteed under treaty because it had itself gone beyond the terms of the treaty by issuing rations to the Indians.[104] There is evidence that the pass system was still in use in the areas covered by Treaties Four, Six, and Seven as late as the mid-1930s.[105]

Not only did the department control Indian movement after 1885, it also came to have control over the financial transactions of the Indians. Through the permit system, the Indians' ability to sell their products and purchase goods was strictly monitored. A series of amendments to the Indian Act prevented the Indians from selling their possessions, and products of the reserves, and discouraged anyone from purchasing the same.[106] Under section 80 of the Indian Act of 1880, Indians were forbidden from trading or bartering the "presents" which they received under the terms of their treaties, without the assent of the superintendent general or his agent.[107] Amendments to the Indian Act in 1881 and 1882 stipulated that the Governor-in-Council could from time to time prohibit or regulate the sale, barter, exchange, or gift by an Indian or Indian band of any grain, root crop, or other produce grown on any reserve in western Canada. This regulation did not cover furs and game, and Indians did not require permission from the agent to sell these.

Subsequent amendments concerned penalties to the possessors of presents, roots, grain, and other crops sold to them by Indians.[108] The department was anxious to curtail purchases of "useless articles at excessive prices," and there was concern about the accumulation of debt. To trade or barter with Indians in Manitoba or the North-West Territories, a special licence from the department was required after 1891. Before a merchant was allowed to trade on a reserve, he was obliged to submit a list of his goods, and he was forbidden to sell what were regarded as trinkets or useless articles.[109]

The rationale behind restricting the sale of the Indians' products and regulating their purchases was, as John A. Macdonald explained, that if "the Indians had the power of unrestricted sale, they would dispose of their products to the first trader or whiskey dealer who came along, and the consequence would be that the Indians would be pensioners on the Government during the next winter."[110] Not only were the Indians viewed as utterly helpless in managing their own business transactions, but it was believed that they should not be permitted to sell anything as long as they accepted government rations and did not raise enough to feed their own families. The permit system was seen as a means of teaching the Indians to husband their resources and of protecting them from unscrupulous merchants selling at excessive prices. Regulations restricting the sale of the products of the reserve took into consideration that these resources were held in common by the band, and they acted to check the possibility that one or just a few members might acquire more than a fair share.[111]

Although the Indian Act empowered agents to make such regulations before the mid-1880s, it was not until then that the permit system was rigidly enforced in the West. The police had on occasion, however, arrested white settlers for purchasing produce from Indians. In cases tried at Fort Macleod in the early 1880s, for example, individuals were fined one hundred dollars for buying potatoes from Indians.[112] But it was only by the mid-1880s that Indian crops were sizable enough to warrant strict attention. In 1884 Dewdney anticipated that on some reserves in the North-West large quantities of grain would be raised. He was concerned that "as very few of our Indians are capable of looking after their crops when the grain has been threshed out, I think it is a matter of great importance that some well defined plan be adopted for the purpose of securing to the government, a return for the assistance given the Indians to help them to raise food and also to secure for the Indians a proper return of their own crop."[113] Dewdney argued at this time that some of the larger reserves would require a new kind of farm instructor, one who was also a business manager, who would handle financial transactions for the Indians and keep a separate account with each family.

Control of Indian transactions through the permit system, as well as control of their movements, placed restraints above and beyond those they shared with other farmers in the West. The restrictions had an enormous impact on the agricultural activity of the Indians just when they were beginning to overcome some of the obstacles that had sabotaged their efforts in the past.

CHAPTER FIVE

The Pioneer Experience: Prairie Reserve Agriculture

NEIGHBOURING HOMESTEADERS

Indian residents of the Qu'Appelle region were not joined by significant numbers of newcomers until 1882. Until that time settlers had largely ignored the Qu'Appelle in favour of the Saskatchewan country to the north. They had believed the land was more fertile and wooded there and had anticipated that the transcontinental railway would be built through that region. The Canadian Pacific Railway, however, was built across the southern plains and created a land rush in the Qu'Appelle in 1882 and 1883. The number of homestead entries plummeted in 1884 and 1885, and immigration was at almost a complete standstill in 1886.[1] In that year the population of the Qu'Appelle region, broadly understood as extending from Virden, Manitoba, to Moose Jaw, Saskatchewan, numbered 23,500.[2] Settlers from Ontario and Britain composed about half the population; a diversity of ethnic groups, including Germans, Hungarians, and Icelanders, made up the other half.

Settlement at this time was clustered along the CPR; few homesteaders had ventured more than thirty miles north of the line or twenty miles south. Farming in the more distant areas was not seen as feasible until branch line construction was completed. Transportation was the essential prerequisite of agriculture, as it permitted the development of an exportable cash crop and the import of essential farm implements, household goods, and food. Because of this vital transportation facility, immigration agencies, the Department of the Interior, and the railway itself promoted settlement in the Qu'Appelle. And settlers came – not because of the agricultural potential of the area, but because of the railway. At this time it was uncertain whether agriculture was possible in this region of variable rainfall and early frosts, and suitable techniques for farming the dry land had yet to be devised.

The single family homestead was the principal economic unit in the development of the Qu'Appelle district. Homesteads of 160 acres were available for a ten dollar registration fee. Within three years a homesteader could receive title to his land if he met a residence requirement, had constructed a habitable dwelling, and had a certain number of acres in crop. Farm-making costs varied considerably, but few homesteaders made a large initial investment. It has been estimated that the costs for the average settler to set up a homestead in his first year fell in the range of $590 to $1,193.[3] This estimate takes into consideration the cost of constructing a house, stable, granaries, fencing, and a well. The settler also had to purchase some provisions and to begin cultivation a breaking plough, a stubble plough, a mower and rake, a team of oxen, and a wagon.

Farming operations were primitive for the first few years of limited equipment and small acreages. Seeding by hand was a common practice as was harvesting with scythe and cradle, hand-binding, and threshing with a flail.[4] In most cases this early pioneering stage, characterized by crude cultivation methods, did not last more than a few years. The farmers of the Qu'Appelle began early on to specialize in grain, particularly wheat. Even in the mid-1880s farms were more specialized here than just to the east in Manitoba where there were more cattle and mixed farming.[5] The larger acreages of the specialized wheat farmer, and the necessity for speed because of early frosts, demanded the use of machinery such as the mechanical drill seeder, the self-binding reaper, and the steam thresher.

Although the single-family homestead was the most common farming enterprise, other types were found in the Qu'Appelle district in the 1880s.[6] A number of community experiments were set up, as well as ethnic, religious, working-class, and aristocratic colonies. Hungarians settled at Esterhazy, Icelanders at Thingvalla, and Russian Jews at Wapella. A New Sweden and a New Finland were also established in the district. There were English colonies such as the East London Artisan's Colony near Moosomin, the Scottish crofter colony south of Wapella, and the Primitive Methodists of the Pheasant Plains. Aristocratic Englishmen settled at Cannington Manor, and a community of French counts and noblemen took up residence near Whitewood. The Major William R. Bell Farm at Indian Head, founded in 1882, was the largest company farm in the West, comprising over 57,000 acres and employing 300 men in the summer.[7]

The settlers who joined the Indians in attempting to farm this district in the 1880s provided no real model of successful husbandry. The 1880s were characterized by failure rather than by success and have been described as a "nightmare to pioneers."[8] Among this generation of settlers, references to the "drought years" meant not the 1930s but the 1880s.[9] Many of the colonies found farming a severe struggle and did not survive the decade.[10] The Bell Farm was bankrupt by 1889. Homesteaders deserted the district in large numbers after 1883. In 1886 homestead cancellations greatly outstripped entries.[11] In a case study of three townships in the Abernethy district of the Qu'Appelle in the 1880s, historian Lyle Dick found that most settlers did not persist and that 59 per cent of all entries were cancelled. Dick argues that the Darwinian model, based on the survival of the fittest, is not in itself sufficient to explain why some farmers succeeded and others did not, although he identifies as a "deeply ingrained theme" in prairie folklore the idea that "hard work, determination and perseverance were the basis of the settler's success."[12] Dick contends that the question is much more complex and cannot be accounted for solely in terms of adaptability and individual enterprise. Certain districts revealed much higher incidents of failure than others. Much of it can be accounted for by a lack of rail service. Settlers most distant from the railway, such as those in the Balcarres district near the File Hills, registered the highest cancellation rates.

The adverse climatic conditions of the 1880s also account for the high failure rate. In 1886 drought nearly totally devastated crops after three successive years of crop failures: there was drought in 1883, drought and frost in 1884, and frost in 1885. In 1889 drought and early frost were again experienced, and in 1890 the crop was widely injured by frost. The farmers' techniques, used in their homelands where moisture was abundant, often aggravated the situation in the early years before methods suitable to semi-arid regions were developed. Many who broadcast their seed, for example, met with failure because the seed did not germinate.[13] Drought also created a problem for wintering stock in the Qu'Appelle district. When hay and water were scarce, some stock-raisers had to drive their cattle northward into the Saskatchewan country. Other hazards, including hail, prairie fire, and grasshopper and gopher infestation, made farming a precarious undertaking. Blizzards were a threat to livestock in winter.

A major difference between the Indian farmer and his neighbours in the 1880s was that while the newcomers had the option to leave and try their luck elsewhere, the reserve residents had little choice but to persevere. Clause 70 of the 1876 Indian Act excluded Indians from taking homesteads in Manitoba and the North-West, thereby preventing the Indian farmer from seeking better railway, market, or soil advantages.[14] This issue was brought to the attention of Indian Affairs officials in 1886 when Joseph Tanner, a member of the Gambler's Saulteaux band, attempted to take out a homestead near Maple Creek, at a spot where he and his family had resided for some time and had made improvements. Tanner, described by Commissioner Dewdney as a "well-to-do Indian earning his livelihood as a whiteman," ran the mail for the police between Maple Creek barracks and points in the United States.[15] He was not allowed to take out a homestead, as he refused to become enfranchised, give up his annuity and his Indian status. Tanner's wife applied for homestead entry but was informed that a farmer's wife was not the sole head of a family and could not obtain entry. Indian farmers then had no choice but to stay on their reserves; a new life on a different plot of land was not an option for them.

IMPROVING CONDITIONS FOR THE INDIAN FARMER

In the late 1880s, however, relations between the Indian farmers and their instructors were characterized by a high degree of cooperation. Indian farmers were anxious to see agriculture succeed. On the whole the instructors of this period appear to have been competent men who were also genuinely anxious to accomplish this goal. Despite the grim climatic conditions of these years, significant strides were taken from 1885 to 1890 toward alleviating many of the problems that had handicapped and impeded Indian farming in the past, although this resulted in few immediate rewards and created new difficulties. For the most part, local department officials played a constructive role in facilitating favourable conditions, although their superiors were often slow to respond and always claimed to be financially constrained.

The resident supervisory staff on the Treaty Four reserves was greatly increased after 1885. As noted previously, Allan MacDonald became the agent for the Crooked Lakes reserves. His staff consisted of three farm instructors, a clerk, interpreter, cook, and labourer. J.B. Lash was appointed agent for Muscowpetung. A former policeman, Lash had first worked in the Department of Indian Affairs and was serving as agent at Carlton in 1885 when he was taken prisoner by Riel. His clerk and interpreter was Henry Halpin, a former Hudson's Bay Company clerk at Frog Lake, who had been taken captive by Big Bear's band but had testified in defence of the chief at his trial when he was found guilty of treason.[16] There were three farm instructors at this agency, two interpreters, a farm assistant, storeman, and the wives of two of the instructors were hired as cooks. Hilton Keith was the agent for the Touchwood Hills. Keith had been instructor at Crooked Lakes at the time of the Yellow Calf incident. At File Hills, P.J. Williams was appointed agent. He was one of the original Ontario farm instructors brought west in 1879. For the most part the instructors were young married farmers from Ontario, the Maritimes, and Scotland. The interpreters were generally described simply as half-breeds.

In the years after 1885, reserve farmers began to acquire some of the machinery necessary to facilitate their operations. Mowers and rakes were the most common purchases. Some reserves were fortunate in their abundant hay supplies, and a number of bands sold hay on contract to other reserves, to settlers, and to the North-West Mounted Police. Selling hay was one of the very few opportunities for outside employment available to reserve residents. In 1886 there was a heavy yield of hay on the Muscowpetung agency and 200 tons were sold to the police in Regina.[17] With the proceeds, the Indians purchased a mowing machine and a horse rake, seven double wagons, and four double sleighs, items that could sustain and bolster this industry. Yellow Calf and his party sold 150 tons of hay in 1886 and purchased two mowing machines and horse rakes.[18] Little Bones' band, which had joined Sakimay's, also had a mowing machine, and the Chacachase party had a mower and were cutting hay for sale.

Agents and farm instructors felt that access to mowers and rakes was essential for all bands, not only those that sold hay. In 1884, for example, agent MacDonald had strongly recommended that the Touchwood bands be granted their request for this machinery because they could not get sufficient hay out with scythes and would not have their haying finished before harvest with the slow hand method.[19] The File Hills farm instructor similarly argued that as stock was increasing, the bands required mowers and rakes to provide enough hay.[20] Hay was particularly difficult to obtain with scythes in dry years, when the danger of not being able to procure enough was at its highest. Agent MacDonald reported in 1890 that on the Crooked Lakes reserves it would have been impossible to cut the amount of hay required to winter the cattle without mowing machines; because it was a dry year, two or three acres in some cases had to be gone over before a ton of hay was secured.[21] Some agents claimed that the Indians under their charge did not have enough strength because of illness to put up adequate hay with scythes.[22]

Reapers and self-binders were also acquired during this period. As one Treaty Four agent explained, the self-binder lessened the danger of being caught by frost during a protracted harvest, and it also reduced the waste experienced in binding with short straw, both advantages encouraging the farmers to cultivate a larger area.[23] The File Hills agent reported in 1888 that, without a reaper, it would be impossible to harvest the Indians' 130 acres of wheat in time to save the crop from frost.[24] Local agents and instructors argued that these implements were a necessity and were totally in favour of their acquisition. Distant officials were more reluctant to recognize these implements as necessary and were certainly not prepared to purchase them for the farmers.

The department's policy on the acquisition of mowers, self-binders, and other machinery was that if individuals could afford to buy them from their own earnings, they should be allowed, even encouraged, to do so. The goal was to get the "industrious" to invest in useful articles, so that they could gain a sense of pride in their property and be seen to stand above the more "lethargic" band members. The department itself provided these items only rarely, and requests of agents and instructors were regularly turned down. Generally the machinery was purchased by the band, or at least a number of farmers together, contrary to the goal of official policy. Individuals could seldom afford these items. The money came from the proceeds of crops or from pooled annuities. Machinery was rarely paid for outright but in instalments over a number of years. In 1888 Kahkewistahaw's band, for example, made its first payment of fifty-five dollars to Massey Harris for a self-binder from the proceeds of the sale of wheat.[25]

Bands were in debt to local merchants not only for machinery but for vital items such as binding twine. The Indian agents oversaw and kept account of these transactions. In 1887 members of one Crooked Lakes band entrusted their agent to purchase four self-binders for them, which they were to pay for out of that season's crop. In 1889 Little Black Bear's band bought a self-binder, which the agent acquired from a settler in the vicinity, and that same year the Touchwood bands purchased a self-binder. Bank loans, available to all settlers who had proof of title, were not open to Indian farmers, as they could not put up their property against a loan.

In 1885 MacDonald arranged with the Massey Manufacturing Company to act as agent for implement sales within the Crooked Lakes.[26] He received a commission of 10 per cent of sales, which he invested in further equipment or supplies, such as binding twine, or used to pay for repairs on the Indians' machines. MacDonald was originally given authorization for this arrangement by Hayter Reed, and it continued for six years.

Indian farming in Treaty Four continued to suffer from a scarcity of threshing machines, although this was to some extent ameliorated during the years 1885–90. Agents and instructors appear to have discouraged the Indians from threshing their grain with cattle and ponies, and instead waited for the use of a community's threshing machine. But reserve residents were often among the last to have the use of one. For example, in October 1889 a farmer living near the Piapot reserve noted that when threshing was completed on his farm, the last to be done in the district, six Indians arrived with their oxen on the last night to take the machine to the reserve.[27] Often a machine was not available until December or January. In 1887 the Crooked Lakes reserves did not acquire the use of a threshing machine until March.[28] Until this process was completed, the crop was of no use to the farmers, either in flour or in cash proceeds. Threshing in winter created a number of difficulties. It took longer so that costs increased, and it also resulted in loss of grain. On reserves it involved "camping out" both for the men and for the horses, as there were no stables or houses near the stacks. When temperatures were thirty degrees below, as in January, threshing was almost impossible. The sheaves were simply frozen mounds of snow, and when they were heaved up, ice and snow covered the men.[29] The engine would often refuse to start in the bitter cold. Sheaf racks were mounted on sleigh runners in the winter, and because of the short days, lamps had to be lit to allow the pitchers to see where to throw the sheaves.

By the late 1880s distant department officials were recognizing the need, long felt by those on the spot, to have readier access to threshing machinery. The acquisition of a small steam thresher for two bands in the Carlton agency was approved in 1888.[30] The engine was also to be used for a grist mill. Each farmer contributed one dollar toward the purchase of the engine. A similar arrangement was approved for the Battleford agency the following year. In 1888 agent MacDonald of the Crooked Lakes purchased a steam engine and a separator from the Bell Farm.[31] The want of threshing machinery was still keenly felt, however, on the File Hills, Muscowpetung, and Touchwood reserves. Where threshing machines were available, the Indians soon became proficient at operating them, dispelling the concern of some officials that they lacked the ability to operate them properly. In 1889 Inspector Wadsworth visited a band engaged in threshing and noted that "these men have become expert in working a thresher; the farmer was there directing and going about the machine with an oil can, but the driving, feeding and other expert duties connected with working the machine, as well as the laborers' part, were being satisfactorily performed by the Indians."[32]

As well as pressing for more machinery, agents and instructors had for years lamented the fact that grist mills were seldom located near reserves. It was generally felt that the Indians' cultivation of wheat was to no purpose if it could not be ground, and it was believed that some bands could be entirely self-supporting if they had access to milling facilities.[33] Officials also felt the Indians could not fully appreciate the value of farm work until grist mills were established in the neighbourhood, as it was only then that they could actually see and consume the results of their labour. Upon obtaining a grist mill, one agent wrote that it had "effected greater practical results among the Indians than a thousand sermons preached to them on the benefits derived from labour; the prospect of raising their own bread supply has given an impulse to the efforts of all, and has made the hitherto idle ones obedient and industrious."[34]

In the mid-1880s the Department of Indian Affairs began a program of granting bonuses to individuals who would establish mills in the North-West. At Moose Mountain in 1885, for example, Captain Pierce and Robert Bird constructed a saw and grist mill with the "patent roller process" for flouring. The two thousand dollar bonus from the department secured for the Indians of the district precedence in grinding their grain for ten years. Rates of toll were to be one-quarter less than those paid by ordinary customers for the first two years and one-eighth less for the remaining eight years.[35] This appears to have been the first of such bonuses, and the system was extended in the ensuing years. The mills did custom work for farmers, with the miller securing an income by collecting grain as his customary fee. The larger merchant mills were less concerned with custom work than with the purchasing and marketing of grain. The miller graded the flour; first-class wheat might be graded "Strong Bakers," while coarse flour, gristed perhaps from badly frozen wheat, would be considered xxx.

Indian farmers of the Crooked Lakes agency took their grain first to a mill at Indian Head, then to one at Whitewood, and eventually to a department-subsidized mill at Wolseley. Muscowpetung agency farmers took theirs to a mill in Fort Qu'Appelle, and likely the File Hills Indians did the same. The nearest mills to Touchwood Hills residents were fifty-five and sixty-five miles away, vast distances to haul grain during a severe winter. The agents and instructors, as part of the effort to promote a sense of individual pride in the Indian farmer, had each present the miller with his own amount of flour, so that he could actually see and appreciate the return, despite the fact that in some cases it was nearly all returned to the agency warehouse, mixed, and issued as rations.[36]

The business of milling was open to much abuse in the North-West. Millers' tolls were not regulated by law, and it was found that the Indians, like the other farmers, lost a good deal to satisfy the "greed" of the miller.[37] Inspector Wadsworth complained that both the yield and the quality of flour from these mills were unsatisfactory, even at the subsidized mills, where the spirit of the contract was not always carried out. The charge of grinding was more than the Indians could pay. At the Wolseley-subsidized mill, Wadsworth found in 1890 that the Crooked Lakes farmers were returned only thirty-three pounds of flour to the bushel of No. 1 hard wheat, which was ten or twelve pounds less than it would yield with good milling.[38] He estimated that in the same year the Muscowpetung Indians lost 33 per cent of their crop in their transaction at the Fort Qu'Appelle mill. In some cases the miller reckoned the market value of the wheat, then deducted his toll, and paid the balance in flour and bacon at retail prices. Wadsworth found this to be a most unfair way of doing business, "for if the Indian sold his wheat for cash he could invest the whole money in flour and not have to pay for grinding that he never receives." He described the quality of much of the flour as poor and unwholesome: the File Hills Indians were eating bannock the colour of mahogany, and he "grieved" for the Indian farmers who had to eat these as the fruit of a hard summer's toil.[39] The agent admitted, however, that in this case he had mixed the Strong Bakers grade with the xxx.

Some owners of subsidized mills found it frustrating to grind for the Indians. Hillyard Mitchell at Duck Lake announced that he would do no more gristing for the Indians, for if he continued to do so, he would lose money.[40] Their grain, which they brought in small amounts of little more than half a bag, was "as a rule, dirty and full of smut, and they expect me to take these drib drabs and grind them for them."[41] Complaining that the mill was a source of trouble ever since it was erected, he stated in 1891 that he would be pleased to open negotiations with the government to take it off his hands.

In other quarters there was considerable lobbying and scrambling to obtain the government bonus toward the construction of a mill. In February 1890 a Mr Thorburn of Broadview travelled to Ottawa to ask Dewdney for a bonus toward a mill in his town.[42] In that year, however, the program of granting bonuses was ended. It was decided that it would be better to establish mills on the agencies, as the "excessive toll which is taken in the Territories is avoided, the Indians get the full benefit of their industry, are saved the loss of time consumed in going to the mills and hanging about them waiting for their grists, and a feeling of pride and independence is engendered."[43] Officials believed that trips to the mill allowed the Indians to loiter about town; a mill on the agency would further confine the Indians to their reserves. The agents and instructors could also see that all the grain was properly used by the Indians. They could grind for each family what it needed for a specific time, which would provide a lesson in economy.

With the government's bonus program ended, a mill was established on the Crooked Lakes agency in 1890. Deputy Superintendent General Vankoughnet remained reluctant about this move and wondered "whether in view of the uncertainty of growing wheat in the District, the department would be wise in incurring any great expense in affording facilities to the Indians for grinding grain."[44] Commissioner Reed, however, disagreed, as he believed the prospects for growing grain were "hopeful," and he felt the mill would encourage the Indians in their efforts.[45] On a recent visit of Governor General Stanley, the Indians had asked for a mill, and Reed wished to see this request complied with. The Crooked Lakes residents constructed the mill themselves. They cut and drew the logs, freighted materials and machinery, and built the mill and engine house. Indian farmers, however, still had to pay for the use of the mill to "cover the cost of working expenses."[46] They were charged in wheat bran or cordwood at the rate of eight cents a bushel. The toll for off-reserve customers was twelve and one-half cents a bushel.

After 1885 the department displayed greater concern to supply the services of blacksmiths, which bolstered the agricultural operations of the Indians. Blacksmith shops were built on some agencies, and skilled blacksmiths either visited or took in work from the reserves. In the past much time had been lost in sending repair work to the nearest town's blacksmith. During the critical brief periods of seeding in spring and harvesting in fall, breakdowns of implements and wagons were frequent and could cripple operations. Although wooden parts were sometimes replaced by the farmer, the breakage of metal parts was much more serious. Blacksmiths were also required to point, or sharpen, ploughshares. Allan MacDonald reported in the spring of 1889 that his agency's blacksmith, John Pollock, was kept constantly employed repairing ploughs and wagons and pointing shares.[47] Very little time was lost, as the farmer had to wait only a few minutes for the work to be done.

In 1885 a shortage of work oxen remained an acute problem on most reserves in this district of Treaty Four.[48] By 1890 most bands had much larger herds, which included work oxen, cows, steers, heifers, bulls, and calves. Much of this increase must have been due to the system of cattle on loan. In 1889 the File Hills agent reported, for example, that there were 281 head on all the reserves, four-fifths of which the Indians "owned" under the loan system.[49] In the tabular statements for most years, cattle were listed as under departmental control, which meant that the animals were branded ID and could not be sold, bartered, or slaughtered without the consent of the agent. Yet the livestock were held or owned by individuals, not in common by the band. In Kahkewistahaw's band, for example, the 110 head under departmental control were held by twenty-one Indians.[50] Some had work oxen only, others had cows only, while some had a variety. These individuals were likely involved in the cattle on loan program. As previously noted, owners of cattle thus acquired were to regard the beasts as their own, but the agent still retained final control in that the animals could not be disposed of without his consent. The advantage to the owner, besides the use of the work oxen and cows, was that from time to time he was permitted to sell or slaughter. Officials remained convinced that the Indians could not be trusted to dispose of their cattle in a prudent, wise manner. The judgment and discretion of the agent were seen as essential. The system eroded the practice of holding cattle in common, except perhaps for bulls, but it did not give the owners a full degree of proprietorship.

Indians could and did obtain private cattle that were not under departmental control. These were acquired by purchase, by an increase of private stock, by gift for "loyalty," by exchange for horses, or by "dickering" through some sort of barter. On the Ochapowace reserve, for example, there were in 1890 twenty-eight private cattle along with the eighty-four head under government control.[51] By the mid-1890s Inspector Wadsworth regarded it as a matter of alarm that private herds of livestock were on the increase in the North-West. Stock which the Indians could use, trade, sell, and kill as they chose, without reference to the agent, would be a "hard matter to control and contend against." The inspector noted that the private stock "not only receives the best care, but it *increases more rapidly* than that 'under government control.' I think if it is not regulated now, it will become a monster hard to contend against."[52]

The complexities of the issue were highlighted at branding time when the Indians were intent on establishing their private ownership. One agent complained that it was a "brain twister" to establish the proprietorship of private cattle: "to trace some of these through the twistings and turnings to their present owner is more difficult than pleasant."[53] The agent found that, at the "palaver" before branding, "it would take a man like Tallyrand [sic] to dodge some of their questions," although it usually ended with the cattle under the agent's control. It appears that department officials insisted on branding all cattle ID, but the Indians made some private mark of their own on their animals, usually a slit or hole in the ear.[54] In the mid-1890s permission was granted to Indians in "good circumstances" with a number of cattle to acquire brands of their own, but these were to be used in conjunction with the ID brand.

Despite all of the confusions of the cattle on loan system, and the thorny question of the private ownership of cattle, the problem of a scarcity of working oxen on the reserves was to some extent ameliorated during these years. Shortages, however, still existed at certain times of the year. In the spring of 1890, just at harrowing time, for example, the File Hills agent had to send most of the teams to three destinations for seed potatoes, seed rye, and feed oats.[55] The teams were gone for five days, and because of bad roads, the oxen were in poor condition on their return and were unfit to work for two or three days.

In the period 1885 to 1890, all settlers in the Qu'Appelle region were in the process of learning to cope with the environment. It was a time of experimentation, discovery, and adaptation of dryland farming techniques. The drought of 1886 pointed out the hazards of growing grain in the district and suggested that tillage operations would have to be carried out more carefully and changes in techniques would have to be made. Indian farmers participated in these innovations.

Farmers in the Treaty Four area were among the first in the North-West to experiment with summer-fallowing. The practice was widely adopted on reserves in Treaty Four as a means of conserving and replenishing soil fertility and of overcoming some of the problems of inadequate rainfall.[56] Credit for the discovery of the technique has been variously assigned to Angus McKay, an Indian Head farmer; W.R. Motherwell, an Abernethy farmer; and the Bell Farm at Indian Head.[57] In any case it was discovered in 1886 in the district of Assiniboia that during the drought of that year certain fields, those that had been ploughed but not planted the previous year, yielded considerably better than the others. A good number of fields were in this state because in the spring of 1885 farmers who had been engaged in the transport of troops and supplies to the north did not return in time to seed. The higher yield on land that had lain fallow throughout the previous summer pointed to the conclusion that, in areas of little rainfall, it might prove feasible to plant crops only every second year. In that way the crop could use the moisture from two seasons.[58] It was also found that fewer weeds grew on land that had been summer-fallowed.

Fall ploughing of the stubble fields was also recommended as a method of ensuring better yield. Both summer-fallowing and fall ploughing were found to improve yields on farms specializing in wheat. There was simply not enough time in the spring alone to prepare an adequate seedbed over large acreages. In the short run, however, until new fields were broken and ready, the adoption of summer-fallowing meant that less land was seeded, since fields were used only every second year. Summer-fallowing did not mean that fields were simply abandoned for a year; they were cultivated, harrowed in one direction, and several weeks later harrowed in the opposite direction, usually in June after the rest of the land had been seeded.

While the general adoption of the practice of summer-fallowing in the North-West was slow, it appears to have been widely in use on reserves as early as 1886. Agent MacDonald reported that on the Crooked Lakes reserves a good deal of the old land was being summer-fallowed, and by 1890 he noted that the Indians had land under crop for no more than two years in a row and then it was summer-fallowed.[59] On all the agencies wheat was no longer sown on "dirty" or "foul" land that was weedy. Instead it was left fallow. Breaking and fencing of new land continued, but, in the interim, the seeded acreage of the Indian farms did not increase during this period. Officials placed a great deal of confidence in the possibilities of the new farming techniques. In his annual report of 1887, Dewdney proclaimed that the disappointments of the past were due to imperfect systems of cultivation. He estimated that the area under cultivation on reserves was about one-tenth less than that in the previous year but explained, "This reduction of area is to be attributed to the teaching of experience which has convinced the best farmers in these Territories that success can only be hoped for from the more careful cultivation of a smaller acreage and the retention of a proportion of the land unseeded in order to allow of its being summerfallowed."[60]

As noted previously, fall ploughing was encouraged since the early days of reserve agriculture. It allowed earlier sowing in spring, although in later years the method came under much criticism.[61] At the time no one knew with certainty which techniques were most appropriate for the environment, and therefore controversy over methods arose. Passing through the Touchwood Hills in 1886, Inspector McGibbon noted that a problem on the reserves, and one common among white settlers as well, was that because fall ploughing only skimmed the ground, in a dry season the roots did not get the nourishment they needed.[62] Hilton Keith, the Touchwood Hills agent, attempted to regulate the depth of the furrow according to the moisture of the soil.[63] There was some deep ploughing as well as shallow on the reserves. Keith explained that many practical farmers in the district believed that deep ploughing did not produce good returns. During years of extreme drought, when the ground was dry and hard, the land could not be worked and little fall ploughing was done on the reserve farms. This situation was widely reported in 1886 and 1889.

In the years of almost total crop failure, the success of one or two fields served as a source of encouragement and inspiration. In 1889, for example, crops were disastrous throughout the Qu'Appelle Valley, but on the Cowessess reserve several fields yielded remarkably well.[64] This success convinced MacDonald that wheat, oats, and barley, with proper cultivation, could be grown in the district. He believed the methods used on these fields could serve to guide future operations.

Besides the interest in new farming techniques, experiments with various kinds of seed grain were also conducted during this period. In prairie agricultural circles, the debate over the use of hard or soft wheats continued throughout the 1880s.[65] Some farmers were convinced of the superiority of hard Red Fife, which, because of its hard kernel and flour strength, commanded a high price. Red Fife, however, required a fairly lengthy growing season. It germinated slowly and had to be sown very early, often before the frost was fully out of the ground when the soil could not be properly worked. As it was often sown after just the surface of the land was worked, the young plants were in a poor condition to withstand a dry season. Its long maturation time also made it subject to frost. Soft White Fife could be sown later, when the soil was better worked, which produced more vigorous, healthy plants. It generally ripened before the frost and was less prone to rust or smut than Red. With the evolution of a system of farming that permitted earlier seeding and harvesting, however, Red Fife became by the 1890s the dominant variety of wheat grown on the Canadian prairies. It was still too often caught by early frost, however, and experimentation with other varieties continued throughout the prairies.

Reserve farmers experimented with both Red and White Fife,[66] as well as other varieties. Agents and farm instructors communicated with William Saunders of the Central Experimental Farm in Ottawa, established in 1886. In 1889 Saunders supplied the Crooked Lakes reserves with eight bushels of "Russian" seed wheat, which the farmers experimented with, planting half on new land backset and the rest on deeply ploughed stubble.[67] Quite likely this was a sample of Ladoga, which Saunders brought from Russia in 1887 and which was tested extensively by farmers.[68] It ripened in advance of Red Fife but yielded much less. It was found, however, not to be a marketable wheat. In milling and baking tests of 1892, Ladoga produced a bread which was yellow in colour and coarse in texture. News of its shortcomings spread quickly through the agricultural press and grain buyers became prejudiced against it. In 1892 the Department of Indian Affairs considered acquiring this unmarketable grain from settlers left with supplies of it, since it could be obtained at a greatly reduced price.[69] Dewdney claimed he could not understand why the buyers were not interested in Ladoga; he felt that it surely made good flour.

Between 1885 and 1890 complaints about the late arrival of seed in the spring, and the lack of sufficient quantities for the acreage prepared, declined considerably. For the most part Indian farmers saved enough seed from their crop of the previous year, and seed was issued only to those just beginning to farm.[70] During some years, however, the seed was not worth saving for the spring, for example, when it was touched with frost.

In the adverse climatic conditions of these years, seed grain relief was provided to the Indians that required it, as well as to the other settlers in the North-West. Seed grain relief to new settlers was widespread before 1896. In 1886, for example, the government set aside $46,884 to supply seed to settlers in Saskatchewan.[71] As frost had destroyed much of the crop of 1885, the government had to supply, besides seed, foods, fuel, and other provisions to impoverished settlers.[72] The North-West Mounted Police identified the needy and distributed relief in winters of extreme want, sometimes having to establish temporary posts for that purpose.[73] In some years Indian farmers were able to retain seed for the spring when other settlers in the district had to be supplied by the government.[74]

Reserve residents experimented not only with seed grain, but with varieties of bushes for their gardens, such as currant, gooseberry, and raspberry, sent from the Central Experimental Farm.[75] Vegetables grown included potatoes, turnips, carrots, onions, beets, peas, beans, squash, pumpkins, and Indian corn.[76] Time and effort were also spent in tending ornamental gardens and in making their surroundings more pleasant. In 1886 it was reported that some of the

Crooked Lakes residents showed "considerable taste" in laying out the grounds around their houses.[77] In one case an attractive tree-lined avenue formed an entrance to a house and garden. Inspector McGibbon reported in 1889 that on the Pasquah reserve "some of the Indians have very tastefully laid out gardens, neatly fenced with flower beds and gravel walks, and borders of cobble stones. Currant bushes and many other plants, useful as well as ornamental, could be seen, the whole displaying considerable taste."[78] Agent MacDonald carried out his own experiments with trees, fruit bushes, and plants such as strawberries and rhubarb in his agency garden. In 1888 he planted Indian corn procured from the Gros Ventre. He believed his garden was instructive: "there is hardly an Indian visits the office without examining the garden before leaving."[79]

On some reserves individual farmers were more prosperous than their neighbours. As indicated previously, this situation was particularly noticeable on the Cowessess reserve where several outstanding farmers had emerged by 1884. In the late 1880s Louis O'Soup, Alex Gaddie, Nepahpahness, and Andrew Delorme were among the successful. A visitor to the reserve in the late 1880s was especially impressed with O'Soup's farm. "His two large log houses, joined together by a smaller, which served as a vestibule to both, were clean, tidy and well furnished." O'Soup had a splendid field of wheat of thirty to forty acres. The observer thought that O'Soup's house and farm "instead of being like those of an Indian, suggested the thought that they might belong to someone white enough to be called O'Brien or O'Grady."[80]

In the years 1885 to 1890 Indian farmers continued to participate in the agricultural fairs held annually throughout the Territories. The Indian women displayed samples of their preserves, bread, butter, knitting, sewing, and weaving, while the men exhibited livestock and farm and garden produce. The Indians generally participated in their own separate category, with individuals competing for prizes for the best produce or livestock. The judge for the competition was very often a department official from one of the reserves.[81] The department contributed a sum to the territorial agricultural societies toward the payment of prizes to Indian exhibitors.[82] It was widely believed that if the Indians were to compete in the general categories, against all other contenders, they would find the fairs a disheartening, discouraging experience. When the Indians did compete with the white settlers, however, they appear to have taken their fair share of prizes. At the Broadview fair in 1888, for example, Louis O'Soup took first prize for the best milk cow and for the best pair of three-year-old steers, and he won a special prize for the fattest steer.[83] That same year an Indian farmer from Pasquah's band took the second prize for wheat against all competitors. At the Prince Albert fair to the north, farmers from the Okemasis and Beardy reserves took first prize for wheat against all contenders. At the Regina Agricultural Fair of 1890, the first prize for White Fife in the general class was won by an Indian.[84]

The Department of Indian Affairs actively promoted Indian participation in the fairs and exhibitions of this period. They were viewed as a means of stimulating a healthy spirit of competition.[85] It was hoped that rivalry at the fairs might to some extent replace former pastimes such as gambling, horse stealing, and tribal warfare. Indian participation in the fairs was also seen as a means of displaying the worthy work of the department. Concrete evidence of Indian "progress" and "advancement" was exhibited for all to see. Newspapers favourable to the government applauded the Indians' exhibits and praised the department's efforts. At the fair in Regina were found "a thousand evidences of what the Indian Department is doing for the wards of the nation."[86] The Indian exhibits were complimented at great length in hopes of silencing the East's "cynics and slanderers" of government efforts. On 25 October 1887, for example, the Regina *Leader* reported from Qu'Appelle:

If any one wants any proof of the wisdom of the policy and the energy which is shown by the Indian Department he need only have attended the Agricultural Shows to be made certain that they are working out a grand result. The Indian exhibits have been simply grand and to see the interest taken in the competition by the Natives themselves, must be a great inducement to the Commissioner to not only foster, but increase the opportunities for exhibits by Indians. A bloodthirsty brave could not have exhibited greater joy when waving aloft a dripping scalp and recounting the engagements in which he had secured it, than at these shows did the now peaceful chief who would lead you gently to his exhibit and show with the greatest glee that he had obtained the scarlet ticket or first prize. All honor to the Lieutenant-Governor and his Indian agents for showing up this spirit of peaceful emulation amongst the different tribes.

Aside from their propaganda value, the agricultural fairs exposed the Indian farmers and their instructors to the latest innovations in farm improvement. The primary function of these annual gatherings was to disseminate new ideas. Fairs were showcases for farm knowledge. Countless demonstrations and displays dealt with a variety of topics: tillage methods, agricultural machinery, seed grain varieties, dairy farming, cheese-making, and stock-breeding. Practical agriculturalists exchanged opinions at these gatherings, drawing on their own experiences. Fairs were the prime media of farm improvement in the 1880s. Farmers could obtain both elementary, fundamental information to make their farm operations more successful and the latest in technological and scientific information. But for the white farmers as well as the Indians, rivalry engendered by competition was seen as the key to farm improvement, as it would teach the losers important lessons. "Moved by criticism of their exhibits, the also-rans and the ignorant would, in theory, discard their shoddy workmanship and inefficient ways, their inferior crops and defective seeds, their second-rate machinery and scraggly stock. Soon they would become paragons for others to follow."[87]

CONTRIBUTIONS OF INDIAN WOMEN

The exhibits at the agricultural fairs indicate that, like all farm women, Indian women were partners in the farm enterprise. The division of labour on prairie reserves was much the same as might be found on neighbouring farms. Men performed the tasks associated with field agriculture and the care of stock. They also freighted, lumbered, constructed dwellings and outbuildings, and hunted larger game and fur-bearers.

Indian women made essential economic contributions, both by drawing on their traditional talents and by learning new skills. They produced food for home consumption and to a limited extent marketed goods they manufactured or processed. In the unstable environment of the plains, women's work was crucial to "risk reduction," as they were largely responsible for diversifying the economic base of the farm. According to Cree informant Joe Dion, the economic contribution of particularly the elderly women in the mid-1880s was vital. When resources as well as spirits were low on the Onion Lake reserve, on the North Saskatchewan in the Treaty Six district, "much of the inspiration for the Crees came from the old ladies, for they set to work with a will that impressed everybody." The elderly women were "an example of industry and thrift" and "they could always be depended upon, especially in times of stress." "Everything that the elderly ladies gathered and stored away during the summer months was for the enjoyment and benefit of others," Dion wrote. "Theirs was the satisfaction of making their loved ones happy. Their cheerfulness could not help but be infectious, thus everyone was soon striving to do his share and the Crees were able to look on the bright side of things."[88]

Foraging activities continued, although they were more localized than in pre-reserve days. The plant food gathered varied according to terrain. The river and creek valleys provided a variety of wild fruit every spring, including saskatoons, raspberries, strawberries, black currants, and chokecherries. The fruit was dried or sold fresh by the pail. Kinnikinnick, a tobacco substitute, was gathered. Wild rhubarb was a favourite in soups. In the early spring sap was gathered from maple and birch trees, boiled down, and, according to Dion, "carefully stored away as a treat and soother for grandmother's pets later on." Roots such as wild turnip were collected, peeled, and dried. There was a market for seneca root, an ingredient in patent medicines, and for wild hops. Women cleaned and smoked fish that came up the creeks in spring and also caught fish through holes in the ice in winter. They snared small animals and birds such as prairie chicken. During moulting season wild fowl were killed in great numbers and women assisted in this. Much of the game was dried, smoked, and stored for the winter. In the fall the more northerly Cree women gathered muskeg tea and quantities of moss, which they dried to make moss bags for babies. Excursions organized by the women, whether for picking berries, hunting rabbits, collecting maple sugar, or raiding the creeks were like "happy picnics," according to Dion. Such a trip, however, was "usually a well organized affair, every detail being prearranged, hence there was never a hitch in the work once the location was reached."[89]

On the reserves women hauled most of the water for household use and collected firewood, which they carried on their backs. They manufactured and repaired clothing. In winter they wove mats, baskets, and straw hats from rushes and willows gathered in the summer. A market was found for their tanning skills, as neighbours brought hides onto the reserves and paid for this process. Considerable labour was expended on grinding grain into meal in the years before access to grist mills.

Indian women proved eager to receive instruction and readily adapted to new skills and technology. They did much of the work in the vegetable gardens. Women and children also worked in the grainfields, especially during peak seasons such as haying and harvesting. As these operations usually coincided, women helped so that the men lost no time with the hay.[90] In 1887 a neighbouring farmer visited the Assiniboine reserve and observed the harvest of "the best wheat I had seen this season. It was cut with a reaping machine and there were about 20 men and women, all Indians, going behind it and binding it into sheaves, and after them were papooses or children gleaning or gathering up the stalks and heads that had been left, and binding these up into small sheaves."⁹¹ Some Indian women were active in all aspects of the farm enterprise. In 1889–90, for example, it was reported that widow Sears of Day Star's reserve had built an addition to her house, summer-fallowed five acres, and purchased with her private means a new mower and horse rake.⁹²

Many new skills such as milking, butter-making, bread-making, and knitting were taught, and Indian women responded positively to the activities. Instruction was not always systematic in the early reserve years, consisting of what could be learned from the agent, farm instructor, teacher, missionary, or wives of these men. By the late 1880s the wives of many farm instructors acquired the title instructress. They held regular classes in "housewifery" and made visits to the Indians' homes. The women welcomed the new skills and were at times overly anxious to learn. Mrs Slater, an instructress in the Touchwood Hills, reported in 1891 that "early in the spring the women commenced to make butter with so much enthusiasm and success that it was found they were starving the calves, so halt had to be called and the calves were turned out with the cows."⁹³ In the industrial schools Indian girls were taught the arts of housekeeping, including mending, soap-making, gardening, milking, and caring for poultry.

Journalist Eleanor Brass, from the File Hills, wrote that a farm instructor, E.C. Stewart, first taught the "miracle of butter" to the women there in the 1880s. Stewart, who was fluent in Cree, arranged milking classes and lectured on the food value of milk products. Every morning and evening in springtime he would call out *toohtoos-ah-poo*! (milk time) several times until it was heard all over the camp, and he became known by that name. According to Brass, "the women would come out of their tents and teepees with pails to get their lessons in milking cows. With much laughing and joking among themselves, they became quite adept at mastering this new task." The lesson in butter-making that followed "delighted" the women.⁹⁴ Theresa Gowanlock, wife of a Treaty Six farm instructor, found that the women were easily taught and quick to learn. "I would do each special thing for them from cleaning, scrubbing, washing, cooking to sewing, fancy work etc. and they would rival each other in learning to follow me."⁹⁵

The milk, butter, and cream produced in the early reserve years were mainly for home consumption – most families kept only one cow – but some women sold cream and butter. As new skills were acquired, such as the raising of poultry, surplus goods were marketed. Women learned to bypass the permit system by raising things for which a permit to sell was not required.[96]

Upon learning to knit and crochet, reserve women made comforters, socks, mittens, and other garments. On reserves where sheep were kept, women were taught to card and spin yarn and weave it into cloth. With a chronic shortage of raw materials, however, it was difficult to apply what they had learned. There were no buttons, for example, for the dresses the women made, unless an instructress purchased them herself.[97] During a visit to the File Hills in 1891, Inspector Wadsworth remarked that "although I was informed that many of the women can knit I failed to see one of them engaged in that useful occupation, and the agent informed me that he had not any yarn to issue to them this year."[98] Instructress Gooderham reported from the Touchwood Hills that "her greatest drawback in accomplishing much is their extreme poverty, their lack of almost every article of domestic comfort in their houses, and no material to work upon."[99]

Indian women were to apply their lessons in housewifery in dwellings that with few exceptions were described as "huts" or "shacks." These were low, one-storey, one-room log structures with mud roofs and mud fireplaces. Many had flooring by the late 1880s, but few had amenities such as glass windows, bunks or bedsteads, cooking stoves, box stoves, chairs, dishes, and coal-oil lamps. The open fireplace, made of upright posts covered with a thick coating of clay mixed with water, provided both heat and light. The chimney, always open, served as ventilator. The sleeping places were seldom more than a bundle of rags on the floor. One instructress remarked that it was "hard to be a neat and tidy housewife in a 7 by 9 log hut, without a floor, where the whole family live [sic], cook, eat, sleep and use as a nursery."[100]

Inspectors continually lamented about the state of housing on the reserves. On some there was the problem of a lack of suitable timber for housing, but it was also reported with regret that Indians spent their surplus money on farming equipment and livestock rather than on the materials necessary to improve their domestic surroundings.[101] Although farmers everywhere were notorious for purchasing implements before attending to their homes and families, department officials saw this tendency as peculiar to Indians.[102] The barns, stables, byres, and corrals were generally found to be clean and comfortable, which prompted Wadsworth to remark often that the animals appeared to be better off than their owners. The tidy barns and stables proved plainly to the inspector that "the men attend to their part of the business better than the women do to domestic matters." Many department officials shared Wadsworth's view that "the present generation of Indian women are almost impracticable [sic]. As the men advance in civilization and attention to work, the women's backward condition becomes more apparent." Although he believed better housing was necessary to "excite their pride of home and self-respect," he was also convinced that Indian women wilfully refused to apply their lessons in housewifery.[103] Indian women were often blamed for the squalid living conditions and poor health of reserve residents; their abilities as housewives and mothers were disparaged as were their moral standards.[104] The systemic causes of poverty were ignored and overlooked.

There is little doubt that dirt was a prominent feature of these homes as it was in all early prairie farmhouses. Cows and poultry wandered about the yard close to the house. If it rained, mud in the yard could be ankle deep, and the roofs dripped liquid mud. Water for washing and drinking was not always readily available, especially in dry seasons when sources dried up and prairie residents had to wait for rain. Under such conditions baths were a luxury, as one well-to-do British woman discovered during a visit to the prairies. "Time was when I thought – with my class – that 'poor people' could at least keep themselves and the houses clean, for water was cheap. I know better now."[105] Personal cleanliness was particularly difficult for reserve residents, who, as one instructress remarked, "have only the clothes they are wearing daily, and many are but scantily clad."[106] Few reports of agents and inspectors failed to mention that the Indians lacked adequate clothing and footwear.

As Cree author Edward Ahenakew has written, the accusation that the Indian woman was a poor housekeeper was a "hasty judgement."

In the first place, what house has she to keep? Only an extraordinary being could manage to keep her family, herself, and her habitation clean, when that dwelling is a one-room shanty of falling logs, mud-chinked, that has to serve as a bedroom, dining room, play-room and sitting room all in one. She might scrub every day, and sweep all the time, but it would still be impossible to keep that one room neat and clean. It discourages her, and she abandons the effort that had been hopeless from the beginning. It is these shanties that have killed all natural regard for cleanliness, the regard that any right-minded Indian woman had in the teepee life of long ago. Even I can remember how the women would cut fresh grass each morning to spread over the ground inside the teepee, and the encampments were moved frequently.[107]

THE DROUGHT YEARS

Although serious effort was made from 1885 to 1890 to overcome some of the difficulties of farming in the Treaty Four district, the period can scarcely be described as one of agricultural success. In 1885 the Indians' promising crops were severely damaged by a general frost in August. In 1886 drought occurred throughout the North-West. With few exceptions, crops on all four agencies, File Hills, Muscowpetung, Touchwood Hills, and Crooked Lakes, were a total failure. The crops looked well until the end of June, but they stunted and dried up in the extraordinarily hot, dry weather of July.[108] By August it was clear that the grain was scarcely worth cutting. The harvest was remarkably poor; the File Hills agent estimated that if every bushel of grain on all four reserves was put together, it would not amount to 100 bushels.[109] The instructor on the Muscowpetung reserve reported that the harvest there could be put into two little sacks.[110] Barley and oats were a complete failure as was the vegetable and root crop. The Qu'Appelle River was dry, and because the land could not be worked, no fall ploughing was done.

Agents and instructors reported that the Indian farmers were acutely disappointed and dispirited at the meagre results of their efforts, and the officials seemed to share their despair. On the Day Star reserve, for example, the farmers were very disheartened because they had never had a grain crop after all their years of effort.[111] For several years frost had totally destroyed the crop and then drought produced similar dismal results. Inspector McGibbon reported from the Muscowpetung agency that year that "it is to be regretted that the labor bestowed has not met with more success, not so much for the loss as for the effect it has on the Indians."[112] Agent Williams at the File Hills was ready to give up on farming in 1886. It had consistently been a failure and he saw no signs of improvement.[113]

Severe drought also occurred in 1887. The crops looked well until June but then hot dry winds in July and August severely damaged the crop. Some fields suffered that year from gopher infestation, particularly on Pasquah's reserve. This was followed by wet weather in September, which interfered with the harvest. The 1888 season brought some relief from the drought. That spring a late thaw, cold, and snow delayed the commencement of operations until mid-April so that seeding was late, but moisture may have been preserved into the warmer months. The return of grain and roots on most agencies that fall was satisfactory. The File Hills agent reported that the Indian farmers were very gratified, this being the first year that they had enough to grist or sell.[114] Hail did a good deal of damage to crops on the Crooked Lakes reserves in July 1888, however, particularly on Kahkewistahaw's reserve.[115] The chief was reported to be very downcast; his wheat had looked promising but the damage was complete. The hail cut the ears off the wheat as if by a scythe. All but two farmers on the reserve totally lost their crops.

The drought returned with a vengeance in 1889. That year on the Crooked Lakes reserves every care had been taken to see that the land was well ploughed, properly seeded, and harrowed.[116] Anticipating a wet season, the Indians had seeded a larger than usual area in wheat, although not as much seed per acre had been sown. Agent MacDonald boasted in May that he had never seen the land in better shape. Hot dry winds soon appeared, however, and by June it was clear that many farmers would not even get back their seed. Crops were almost a total failure except for one or two fields on the uplands. When the threshing was finished, they had one thousand bushels instead of the eleven thousand expected in June. Agent MacDonald noted that not only the Indians but he and the instructors, were discouraged. They were not, however, defeated. He reported at the end of July that the Indians were turning the land over for another trial the next year, as "they say we must get wet years soon."[117]

The same dismal story prevailed throughout the district. The grain crops were a total failure, and the roots fared little better. Aside from the drought, frost was reported in some areas two or three times in July. When threshed and fanned, the File Hills harvest consisted of 135 bushels, much of which was "frozen at that."[118] The potatoes were no larger than marbles, and the Indians did not even realize the seed. The agent described the farmers of the reserves as "all disheartened at seeing no prospects of any return for their work done in the spring, in the way of crops."[119]

The 1890 season was more favourable. Spring was late and seeding delayed, but by July the growth of grain was extraordinary because of ample rainfall. In midsummer agent MacDonald anticipated that if the crops escaped hail and frost, the Indians would for the first time be well paid for their work and would be encouraged to go more extensively into farming.[120] Hail hit other farms in the vicinity but avoided the reserves. Crops were splendid on the reserves along the valley and ready to be harvested early, but then wet, cold weather set in. Because of long, continuous rains, the grain remained in stooks for several weeks and it shrank considerably. Some frost also touched the grain in August. Damage was particularly severe in the File Hills. Just as the harvest began there in September, heavy snow and high winds broke down all the uncut grain, which had to be salvaged with scythes and sickles.[121] For the most part, however, the 1890 crop was a vast improvement over that of other years.

Like other settlers in the Qu'Appelle district, reserve residents experienced problems wintering their cattle in the years from 1885 to 1890. In springs when the cattle emerged too weak to work properly, farming operations were greatly affected. An adequate supply of hay was often difficult to procure. It was scarce during excessively dry seasons; abundant sloughs one year might be completely barren the next. On some reserves during years when hay grounds were poor, arrangements were often made to allow Indians to cut hay on another reserve. Some bands had to obtain hay land off the reserve. Pasquah's band had a hay camp in the Touchwood Hills, eight miles east of Gordon's reserve.[122] The band members wintered their stock there, building stables and houses for the families who stayed. Some of the File Hills bands often had difficulty obtaining enough hay on the agency to winter all of their stock. In 1889 thirty-four head were sent to the Pelly agency to winter at the Coté reserve.[123] Little Black Bear's band wintered stock at the Beaver Hills, about thirty-five miles from the File Hills, where houses and stables were built. Hauling supplies from the agency over the hills in midwinter involved great hardship. The agent complained in February 1890 that it took three yoke of oxen four days to freight six bags of flour and two quarters of beef to the Beaver Hills.[124]

The predominantly dry weather of these years also created a serious hazard, particularly between 1885 and 1896. The grasslands were extremely susceptible to prairie fire, and many haystacks, as well as houses, stables, fences, and timber, were consumed. Dropping a lighted match or emptying a pipe could begin a fire, but sparks from the locomotives of the CPR were responsible for many, as it was only in later years that the railway was required to maintain fireguards on either side of the track by ploughing furrows. It was the Indians of the North-West who had pioneered the practice of burning the grass to form fireguards around the boundaries of their land in springtime, just after the snow had melted.[125] In the period before reserves, Indians protected valuable stands of trees by burning off the surrounding grass cover, just before the snow melted in the timber, reducing the risk of lightning igniting the grass and spreading into the adjacent timber.

It was only when settlement in western Canada became sufficiently dense to control fires that they ceased to be a major hazard.

In the 1880s, however, autumn was an anxious time. As one Qu'Appelle pioneer described it:

The prairie grass is, after the summer heat, dry as tinder, and, once started, the devastating fire will burn in thin lines of flame, spreading in all directions, for weeks at a time if no rain comes. It increases in volume as it grows, and with increasing heat creates its own wind. Sometimes, having decided that it is far enough away, and the wind in the wrong direction for it to come upon us, we went to bed, to be awakened an hour later to find it right upon us, a sudden change of wind having brought it down with a rush ... Twice we lost our winter supply of hay through these awful fires, and the year before we left, three horses were burnt so badly that the only humane course was to shoot them.[126]

Haystacks were particularly vulnerable. Ironically burning fireguards around them was one of the major causes of fires.[127] Fires also reduced the grazing capacity of large areas.

The drought of 1889 in particular was accompanied by disastrous prairie fires. The Muscowpetung agency lost 572 tons of hay to fire.[128] A fire started that summer at the Beaver Hills hay camp destroyed at least 100 tons of hay. In December the agent for the File Hills stated that this same fire was still burning, "as incredulous as my statement may seem."[129] In June 1889 surveyor Nelson, who was in the File Hills, reported temperatures of 104 degrees Fahrenheit in the shade, with fires raging in the woods, hay swamps, and surrounding prairie. The surface soil was burned in many places to a depth of six or eight inches. Nelson speculated that "bush and prairie fire probably cause more damage than frost and drought."[130]

Prairie fire swept through Okanese's and Star Blanket's reserves in July 1889 and destroyed buildings. The residents were forced to run with their children, tents, and belongings to the edge of a lake. As the fire occurred in the midst of haying season, haying could not be attended to.[131] After the harvest, little fall ploughing was done because most residents had houses, stables, and fencing to construct. If fencing was weak or damaged, cattle could break into the stacks, resulting in the loss of much hay. Prairie fires thus hampered the ability of reserve farmers to carry out the whole cycle of farming operations.

THE PRESSURE OF COMPETITION

Because of the scarcity of hay during some seasons, the Indian farmers found themselves in competition with other settlers for hay land.

Areas where the Indians customarily cut hay off the reserves became the subject of disputes. For years the Indians of Muscowpetung agency cut hay on a tract of land on the north side of the Qu'Appelle River. Reserve residents came to rely more and more on this tract as hay became scarce elsewhere. Local department officials believed that this land, although not strictly part of any reserve, was for the exclusive use of the Indians and for the department's horses and cattle. Confusion over who actually owned the rights to this land emerged in the late 1880s when settlers began to encroach, having acquired permits to cut hay there from the Dominion Lands agent in Regina.

In August 1888 J.B. Lash of the Muscowpetung agency confronted a number of settlers at the site. He warned them that they were trespassing, told them that their permits were cancelled, and stated that he would seize the hay already cut.[132] Refusing to recognize his authority, the settlers would not return the permits until they had cut the full quantity of hay their permits allowed. It turned out that the odd-numbered sections of this hay land were owned by the CPR, who refused to relinquish the land because it was "required by a number of settlers for their hay."[133] The secretary of the CPR informed Deputy Superintendent General Vankoughnet that the Indians did not really require the hay for their own use, since in the past they had sold large quantities of hay. Agent Lash vehemently defended the right of the Indians to sell hay, arguing that by doing so, they relieved the government to the extent of their earnings and made a step toward becoming "independent and useful members of the Commonwealth." The agent's chief ground of objection to the withdrawal of hay land was in fact the existence of this industry. "These Indians have with no small difficulty been brought to throw themselves heartily into the business of making and selling hay and to deprive them of those lands which they have cut there unquestioned so long that they regard them as their own, can hardly fail to have a discouraging effect."[134] The dispute over the rights to this tract of land continued for many years. In such disputes, despite the best efforts of agents in defending the interests of reserve residents, those of the other settlers usually emerged as paramount.

In 1886 settlers in the neighbourhood of Moosomin and Broadview began a campaign to have the Crooked Lakes Indians surrender their land that bordered the CPR. They informed the minister of the interior that "it would be desirable in the public interest and in the interest of the Indians themselves that they should be moved back six miles from the railway." The land was valued especially for its abundant hay. The citizens told the minister that the Indians would be "quite willing" to have their reserve narrowed if they were compensated.[135] Agent MacDonald strenuously disagreed, stating that such an act would be looked upon with suspicion by the Indians and that "no doubt a report would spread throughout the country that the Indians are being plundered."[136] MacDonald noted that hay land north of Sakimay's reserve might fairly be exchanged for the land in question, but homesteaders had already settled on the tract north of Sakimay. The agent felt that if the proposition was carried out, the Indians would be giving up more valuable land than they would be receiving. These arguments persuaded Vankoughnet in 1886 that a move to surrender these lands was neither prudent nor expedient.[137] When pressure was renewed in 1891, MacDonald voiced the same objections. "If these lands are surrendered by the Indians, no reasonable money value can recompense them, as their hay lands would be completely gone, and this would necessitate no further increase of stock, which would of course be fatal to their further quick advancement and would be deplorable, and the only alternative I can see is to give them hay lands of equal quantity and value immediately adjacent to the Reserves interested, which I do not think is possible now."[138] The surrender of 53,985 acres of land along the CPR was eventually obtained in 1907.

Similar pressure was exerted throughout the North-West, and very often it began with the settlers' desire for hay lands reserved for the use of Indians. In 1889, for example, non-native residents of Battleford and district objected to any increase in hay land for the Indians in a petition to the minister of the interior. They claimed that "the locking up of the best hay lands would be detrimental to the district at large." It was further claimed that the Indians had adequate hay lands and "to tie up more hay land than is really required is to throttle an important agricultural industry in its infancy."[139] Settlers who had taken up homesteads at Jackfish and Round Hill lakes with a view to ranching objected to the reservation of hay lands there for Indians, so that "pioneer settlers may be allowed to enjoy the benefit of their enterprise and expenditure."[140] In the summer and fall of 1889 hay was particularly scarce because of drought, frost, and fires that burned large stretches of hay land. It was also in short supply because for weeks at a time the Indians and white settlers had been busy fighting fires and could not attend to haying. In September P.J. Williams, the Battleford Indian agent, urged Commissioner Reed to take steps to set aside at once hay lands that had come to the notice of the settlers, as "nearly everyone who has stock is after these lands."[141] If the land were not secured, there was no alternative but to decrease stock on the reserve.

E. Brokowski of the Dominion Lands office, however, did not believe such a large additional area was required, particularly in view of the "evident dissatisfaction of white settlers" for whom cattle had become a main source of revenue because of crop failure.[142] The Department of Indian Affairs agreed to abandon claim to 2,080 acres of hay land, and Hayter Reed informed settlers that as he was "desirous to consider the feelings of the settlers as far as possible," he was endeavouring to dispense with a further 1,600 acres.[143] This did not satisfy the petitioners, however, who claimed that this particular hay land was not the land in dispute. They accused him of playing a "contemptible trick" and of deceiving the settlers.[144]

Stock-raisers at places with limited markets, like Battleford, had good reason to hope that Indians would not become too successful at raising cattle themselves, as the beef supplied to the Indian Department was an important market for their product. In 1888 the editor of Battleford's paper denounced any plan to "set the Indians up as cattle breeders, encouraging them to supply the beef that is now put in by white contractors with the Department."[145]

By the late 1880s farmers in parts of the North-West were complaining loudly about "unfair" competition from Indians. In his annual report for 1888, Commissioner Reed noted that "serious complaint has been made by some settlers of the effect of this competition upon them."[146] As noted previously, it was widely believed that government assistance gave the Indian farmers an unfair advantage. They were provided with equipment, livestock, as well as rations, and did not have to worry about the price at which their products were sold. On 7 November 1884 the Fort Macleod *Gazette* noted that the potato crop on the Indian reserves was "immense" that season, and that some Indians "have made a pretty good thing selling them to citizens. Some of the farmers justly complain of this, as the Indians, being fed and taken care of by the Government, sell their potatoes for next to nothing." An observer at Battleford in 1889 wrote, "'Tis true the Indian who is fed and supplied with farm implements, seed e.c. [sic] by the Government has the advantage in these respects of his less fortunate white brother."[147] On 2 August 1895 the *Gazette* lamented that Indians were earning money by "putting up hay with implements supplied by the government; by hauling supplies with wagons obtained from the same source ... in all of which occupations they compete with hard-working white men." The solution, according to the *Gazette*, was to spend no more money on agricultural implements and to abandon efforts to teach the Indians the "ways of the white man," as the accomplishment of this goal was "hopeless."

Residents of Battleford and district were particularly strident in their objections to Indian competition in the grain, hay, and wood markets. In 1888 they petitioned their Member of Parliament and complained that the "Indians are raising so much grain and farm produce that they are taking away the market from the white settlers."[148] During his visit to Battleford in October of that year, Hayter Reed reported that he was "assailed" by such complaints. He met with a deputation of farmers and one of townspeople and informed both that his department "would do whatever it reasonably could to prevent the Indians from entering into competition with the settlers during the present hard time."[149] Having served as an Indian agent there, Reed had friends in the district, and as a land guide he had urged settlers to consider points as far west as Battleford, assuring them that local markets for their produce existed.[150] Reed presented competition as not in the best interests of the Indians, who were taken advantage of. They were so anxious to find markets that they parted with their products for a "trifling consideration."[151]

Reed arranged with the Battleford citizens to divide up the limited markets in the district. Trade in cordwood was left to the Métis, which was their mainstay over the winter. The Indians were allowed to supply wood to the agency and for one more year to the industrial school. The sale of grain in the district was left exclusively to the white settlers. Their principal market was the NWMP barracks. Reed claimed that the Indians consumed most of their grain anyway but any surplus in flour might be purchased by the department. A notice in the *Saskatchewan Herald* on 12 January 1889 warned all persons against purchasing wood, hay, grain, or other produce from Indians without first obtaining written permission from the Indian agent. New policies that Reed introduced later that year further limited the Indian farmers' opportunity to raise and sell a surplus.

The government did offer to buy surplus oats from one reserve in the Battleford district in 1889, but not, however, at market prices. The Indians were offered twenty cents a bushel, although the market price approached twenty-seven or thirty cents. Reed explained that Indians were not given market value because the department provided them with all the necessaries to raise their grain.[152] This was a dubious statement, since Indian farmers purchased most of their own equipment. The Indians protested and threatened to sell their products to other buyers. Clearly they were not willing to part with their surplus for a "trifling consideration" as Reed had claimed. Because of his agreement with the citizens of Battleford, however, Reed could not allow the Indians to market their grain. He therefore authorized the agent to pay the market rate for "oats which we do not wish them to put upon the market."[153]

As the disputes over hay land and markets illustrate, the 1880s saw increasingly strained relations between Indian and white farmers, a situation that was aggravated by the lean times. Local department employees generally came to the defence of the Indians' interests, while more distant officials appeared more willing to placate the settlers, who were more politically powerful, at the expense of the Indians. The recent arrivals believed that everything should be done to encourage their enterprise, as they were the "actual" settlers, the true discoverers and developers of the country's resources. It was believed that the government had bought the land from the Indians, and it was now the government's "right and duty to look after the interests of the settlers, both present and future, for whom the land was bought, and out of whose earnings it is expected ultimately to be paid for."[154]

Throughout the North-West there occurred numerous incidents of encroachment on Indian land, principally for timber and hay. Some were more serious than others. In 1889 a disagreement over hay on the Little Bones reserve at Leech Lake became very tense. Settlers had been given permits to cut hay on the reserve, but the chief was convinced that they were cutting more than allowed. He raised the matter with a Mr Arthur Moore, who later claimed that, in the heat of the conversation, Little Bones threw his right hand behind his back as if to draw a knife.[155] Agent MacDonald and three constables were called to the scene and the matter was settled without violence. MacDonald believed Little Bones' denial that he had never attempted to draw his knife, and he warned Moore not to come to hasty conclusions with Indians without a proper interpreter.

During the late 1880s settlers continually trespassed on the Crooked Lakes reserves, removing logs and rails for fencing. In 1887 the body of a trespasser was discovered on the Kahkewistahaw reserve. He had nearly completed cutting a load of rails, which were piled near the body.[156] Nearby settlers were convinced that the murder had been perpetrated by the Indians, as the chief of that reserve had on several occasions displayed annoyance at the theft of logs or rails. To see that justice was done, the police and a party of citizens began crisscrossing the reserves, hunting out the "murderers." These actions did little to soothe a tense situation. Agent MacDonald was certain he could trace the crime to two individuals and clear the Indians.[157]

Reserve residents often found themselves blamed for incidents that enraged the settlers. In the fall of 1886 a Touchwood Hills farmer lost through fire 500 bushels of potatoes, stacks of oats, 40 tons of hay, and all his stables and granaries. He presented the Department of Indian Affairs with the bill, claiming that he had observed three

Indians ride by his stable that day in search of a stray bull. One of the Indians had been smoking. This settler was angry, not only at the Indians, but also at the weather, the country, and the whole business of farming. He had lost his first three crops to frost and his next to fire. Appealing to the prime minister himself, the Touchwood farmer stated that he would have to leave the country unless the department made good his loss. In an incoherent postscript he informed Macdonald that "I have had to batch it and live alone ever since I left Scotland, over eight years ago all through the loss I sustained by this fire which is the most miserable life under the sun."[158] The department refused to compensate the settler. The Indians in question claimed that they were many miles away when the fire had begun.

CONTINUING DIFFICULTIES

Besides their disputes with white settlers, a number of other problems plagued the Indians during the years 1885 to 1890. A lack of adequate clothing and footwear continued to make it difficult to do much work.[159] Secondhand clothing was periodically sent by church societies in the East, for which the agents generally appeared grateful. Inspector McGibbon objected, however, on the grounds that the department was trying to teach the young to be tidy and industrious, a goal that could not be accomplished with old, secondhand clothing.[160] Convinced that old clothing belonged to dead people, some Indians were prejudiced against wearing it. The health of the Indians also continued to be poor. They suffered from influenza, consumption and scrofula and were often reported to be too weak to work.[161]

Opportunities to earn money varied according to the reserve, but remained difficult for some from 1885 to 1890. The Muscowpetung and Crooked Lakes agencies enjoyed some decided advantages over the File Hills and Touchwood Hills. Land on the former reserves was better suited to agriculture and closer to the railway and to settlements where their products could be marketed. Greater access to milling and threshing facilities also existed. On the Muscowpetung agency the Indians cut dry wood, which they sold to the grist mill at Fort Qu'Appelle, and they sold hay in years of heavy yield. They also began to freight their own supplies of bacon and flour from the railway. It appears that it was up to the discretion of the local agent to decide which band needed, and was in a position to fill, a contract. One agent explained that he kept the cordwood market reserved for Indians who did not have flour of their own.

They borrowed oxen during the winter from the farming Indians who had flour.[162]

The Crooked Lakes Indians also earned money from the sale of hay and wood and from freighting. Some burned lime to sell to settlers at Grenfell. Others dressed hides, attended to cattle for settlers, collected seneca root, and sent cream to the Broadview creamery. Some worked on larger farms in the district, such as the chickory fields of the Count de Raffignon at Pipestone Creek. The Indians of the Crooked Lakes and Muscowpetung agencies had some cash and therefore were in a better position to acquire the wagons and machinery that could benefit their farming, freighting, and other small industries.

The residents of the Touchwood Hills and File Hills reserves were in a more difficult position. The problem was particularly acute in the Touchwood agency. Inspectors, agents, and instructors continually lamented that these people had absolutely no opportunity to earn money, since they were situated sixty to eighty miles from any settlements. The Touchwood Hills Indians were not permitted to do their own freighting of supplies. An added disadvantage in this district was that merchants charged exorbitantly high prices for all items because of the distance from the railway. The same situation prevailed in the File Hills, although chances to earn money were slightly better. In the late 1880s, for example, the File Hills residents were awarded a contract to provide cordwood to the Qu'Appelle Industrial School.

Local officials associated with the Touchwood and File Hills agencies urged the department to buy cattle from the Indians instead of importing bacon for rations. Indians would be able to earn some money and the cattle industry would be encouraged. The File Hills agent believed it could be a means of dispelling the despondency that existed.[163] This suggestion, however, was not approved. Nor would the department authorize local agents to allow the Indians to exchange their wheat, potatoes, hay, or other items for provisions such as tea or bacon.

Reserve residents had few options but agriculture. The hunt for fur-bearers, badgers, fox, ermine, lynx, wolves, and otter, continued only to a slight extent in the Qu'Appelle district during the 1880s. Hudson's Bay Company clerks reported that part of the problem was a growing scarcity of animals, but it was also regretted that hunters were paying more attention to farming.[164] In 1889 it was noted that there were still some good hunters on the Crooked Lakes reserves but "the hunting grounds are some distance away, and if they have any crop very few of them leave their Reserve."[165] Former hunters paid their debts to the Hudson's Bay Company in livestock rather than in furs. By 1891 Fort Qu'Appelle was no longer regarded as a fur-trading district.

Despite drought, frost, prairie fire, and hail, Indian farmers in the Qu'Appelle region made advances in the 1880s. Many problems that had hampered Indian farming in the past had to some extent been ameliorated, such as shortages of oxen and the scarcity of threshing and gristing facilities. Indian farmers were beginning to acquire the means and methods of expanding and promoting their enterprise. They were learning the techniques of dry-land farming, and they were acquiring the machinery their agents and instructors agreed was essential given the conditions of prairie farming. They were moving in the direction of commercial farming with specialization in wheat culture, although not always in conformity with the individualistic model of the independent homesteader. Bands pooled their resources for the purchase of implements and on many reserves tilled the fields in common. Local department officials found this system to be preferable to the cultivation of small, individual tracts of land. Inspector McGibbon felt it was better to have four or six men working a good-sized field than to have small patches here and there. Agents and instructors found that larger fields were easier to supervise than small separate fields.[166]

Indian farmers had survived the grim 1880s and were willing and had few options but to continue trying, unlike at least half the homesteaders who had become discouraged and left. Local white farmers remember the year 1890 as "the turn of the tide; after that all went well."[167] Although disappointing years lay ahead for the Qu'Appelle farmers, they were nothing like the string of misfortunes that had plagued them in the 1880s. All did not go well for Indian farmers in the 1890s, however. They did not make the leap to large-scale commercial farming, despite earlier indications that they were moving in this direction.

CHAPTER SIX

Prelude to Surrender: Severalty and "Peasant" Farming

As Indian farmers acquired skills and technology and reserve agriculture took hold, they began to pose a threat as competitors. Policies pursued by the Department of Indian Affairs beginning in the late 1880s were devised to divide Indian and white farmers into non-competing groups. The system was geared to protect and maintain the incomes of white farmers, to keep them content and, if possible, prosperous, in order to attract more immigrants. In the process reserve agriculture suffered. From 1889 to 1897 it was subjected to unprecedented administrative involvement by way of allotment in severalty and the "peasant" farming policy, both of which set extreme limits on Indian agricultural productivity. As the policies functioned to curtail the expansion of Indian farming, Indians did not appear to non-natives to be "productively" using their reserve land to full capacity. This perception paved the way for the alienation of much reserve land in the years after 1896.

GOALS OF THE SEVERALTY POLICY

In his annual report of 1888, Indian Commissioner Hayter Reed announced that reserves in the North-West were to be subdivided into separate farms.[1] He believed individual tenure was the best means of undermining the tribal system, as it would implant a spirit of individualism and self-reliance, thus creating self-supporting farmers. Reed shared his commitment to severalty with several generations of Indian policy-makers in Canada, before and after Confederation, and Great Britain. Although a general allotment policy was new to reserves in the North-West, the concept had long been endorsed and was a central feature of legislation dealing with Indians. The 1857 Gradual Civilization Act, passed by the Assembly of the United Canadas, was based upon the assumption that "civilization" could only be achieved if a bond were established between an Indian and his property, similar to that established between a white settler and his personal domain.[2] The act stipulated that if a board of examiners found an Indian applicant to be literate in either French or English, free of debt, and of good moral character, he would be awarded a plot of reserve land, which would be removed from band control. After a one-year probation period, the applicant was enfranchised and accorded the rights and privileges of other citizens. As a result, tribal ties would be cut. The goal of the act was full assimilation into colonial society and the abandonment of traditional, native culture. The independent, self-governing communities that had evolved on reserves were to disappear as individuals were enfranchised and reserves eroded.[3] Throughout Canadian history, severalty has been linked with the dissolution of reserves and the weakening of the band unit. The intent of the 1857 act and subsequent acts was that Indians would disappear as a distinct cultural group. The reserves too would disappear as individuals were enfranchised and took with them their share of the land.[4]

Canadian Indians consistently objected to allotment in severalty. Tribal councils across the colony immediately recognized the intent of the 1857 act, which would remove tribal control over reserves for the sake of enfranchisement. They wished to maintain tribal integrity through consolidation and firmly rejected the concept of individual tenure and subdivision of reserve land, which they saw as an attempt to "break them to pieces." Reserve residents refused to cooperate.[5] They launched a campaign to repeal the act, and only a handful of Indians ever applied for enfranchisement. The general Indian position that emerged across the colony in the 1860s was that they remained in favour of reserve resource development and education and endorsed activities designed to achieve self-sufficiency on the basis of an agricultural economy. They would not, however, participate in a system that promoted assimilation.

Despite opposition from tribal councils, the 1869 Enfranchisement Act implemented new coercive strategies to encourage individual landholding and enfranchisement. Officials attributed the failure of the 1857 act to the conservative, stubborn intransigence of Indian leaders and to traditional native government: obstacles on the road to "civilization." The act of 1869 instituted federal control of on-reserve governmental systems and did not recognize native self-government.[6] After 1869 the government had the financial and political control to make enfranchisement a reality.

The 1876 Indian Act permitted the government to further encourage and direct the subdivision of reserves by empowering the superintendent general to have reserves surveyed into individual lots. Band members could then be assigned lots by the band council. Individuals acquiring lots received "location tickets" as a form of title, but first they had to prove that they were literate, free of debt, and of good moral character, as under the earlier legislation. Upon receiving his location ticket, the applicant entered a three-year probationary period. If he proved himself "sober and industrious" and demonstrated that he would use the land as a Euro-Canadian might, he was enfranchised and given full title to the land.[7] Because the granting of fee simple title could potentially open up the reserves to white occupancy, most bands in the older provinces continued to oppose enfranchisement and refused to allot reserve land to individual band members. Without an allotment, a location ticket could not be issued; without a location ticket, enfranchisement was impossible. The ability of band councils to thwart the goal of enfranchisement was curtailed in 1879, however, when power to allot reserve land was taken from the band and given to the superintendent general.[8] Indians of the older provinces continued to resist the subdivision of their reserves by refusing to accept location tickets.[9]

Clause 94 of the 1876 Indian Act excluded the Indians of Manitoba and the North-West Territories from the eight clauses that pertained to enfranchisement. Their exclusion was repeated in clause 107 of the 1880 Indian Act.[10] Legislators felt that the western Indians were not "civilized" enough to take advantage of the enfranchisement clauses.[11] They were to remain exempt until the superintendent general considered them to be sufficiently advanced. The goal of reserve subdivision, however, was not shelved and forgotten for long. The earliest officials associated with Indian affairs in the North-West were committed to the idea of individual tenure. In his annual report for 1878, Deputy Superintendent General Vankoughnet wrote that reserves in Manitoba and the North-West should be subdivided into lots, with each head of family receiving a location ticket.[12] Indian Superintendent David Laird stated in 1878 that the great aim of the government should be to give each Indian his individual property as soon as possible, although he thought lots should not necessarily be on reserve land, but on any tract of land open for settlement.[13]

In 1886 Prime Minister John A. Macdonald instructed Commissioner Dewdney to allot to each Indian on every western reserve the land he would likely require for cultivation. While Dewdney was commissioner, portions of three reserves in Manitoba were subdivided into eighty-acre lots.[14] Department officials were clearly planning to implement a general severalty policy as early as February

1887. In that month A.W. Ponton, a brother-in-law of Hayter Reed, was named assistant surveyor to J. Nelson. In a letter regarding the appointment, Dewdney reminded Vankoughnet that "in pursuance of the policy which has been recognized as the only true one for the development of a sense of individual responsibility, as opposed to the system of communism among the Indians viz: the sub-division of reserves, it will be necessary to have a large amount of field work done."[15]

Under Hayter Reed's term as commissioner, as noted previously, the subdivision of reserves in the North-West proceeded rapidly. Reed announced his determination to implement the policy in October 1888 after completing a tour of reserves in the Saskatchewan district. Passing through the Battleford region, Reed was pleased to note signs of individualism, of the Indians taking up separate farms. He believed this resulted in nice, clean houses and other signs of "progress." He informed Vankoughnet that "I have come to the conclusion that the time has arrived when the Reserves should be divided up, and parcelled into separate farms. The Indians would I think, in the main be pleased to have this done, and I need hardly remind you of the advantage likely to result from such assault upon the communist system, which is apt to prevail."[16] Vankoughnet approved of Reed's policy; he felt it would contribute "materially and rapidly" to the Indians' advancement. He recommended that "where indications are manifest of a disposition on the part of Indians to take up separate holdings on the Reserves that the latter should at once be subdivided by survey."[17]

The severalty policy was presented to the public by officials as the instrument which would strike most effectively at the heart of the "tribal" or "communistic" system and implant instead a spirit of individual responsibility. A sense of possessory rights was proclaimed to be "essential to the formation of those self-interested motives which attach individuals to localities and render them unwilling to leave them for any light cause."[18] With a sense of proprietary rights, the allottee would be inspired to improve his holding. He would have to expend labour on cultivating, building, and fencing, which would result in superior cultivation, improved housing, and better fencing, all of which would have the effect of binding the owner to the locality. It was believed that ownership would implant in the Indians a "wholesome spirit of emulation," impossible under a system of community of ownership.[19] Dewdney insisted in 1890 that it was only "by inculcating such ideas and fomenting such motives in him will the Indian be reclaimed from his condition of savagery and led to adopt a mode of life which will render him both self-supporting and self-respecting."[20] Reed believed that teaching the Indians to hold and farm their land in severalty was the central means of preparing the Indians for enfranchisement.[21] Amalgamation with the white population was the goal, but first the Indians had to be inculcated with a spirit of self-reliance and independence.

Indians who objected to the subdivision of reserves were described as "lacking in intelligence" because they could not recognize the advantages to their people, or they were portrayed as the "idle-good-for-nothing," who rejected anything welcomed by the "better class" of more industrious Indians.[22] Indians, according to Reed, often imagined "sinister motives."[23] Based on experiences in the older provinces, department officials believed that objections to severalty arose mainly from self-interested motives. "It is probable," Dewdney wrote, "that men of influence in these bands, who have acquired possession of more land than they think they would be allowed to retain were a fair distribution of the land in the reserve to be made, use that influence with their unsuspecting kinsmen to cause them to object to the severalty principle being applied to them." Department officials dismissed all Indian objections to severalty on the grounds that once the superior advantages of the system were impressed upon them, apprehensions would rapidly dissipate. Indians who showed a preference for separate lots were lauded as those with the most advanced ideas.[24]

Public opinion appeared to endorse heartily the department's policy. Battleford's *Saskatchewan Herald* was the first to extol the virtues of individual land tenure for Indians. On 20 August 1887 it expressed admiration for the American policy of allotment of reserve land and noted:

In this country, too, the same system is being introduced, and under it the Indian will find himself better off than before. He will enjoy the fruits of his own labour. Whatever he grows will be for himself. He will no longer fret because he sees what he fancies his share of the common field given to another. And he will realize that the more he works the more he will have, and that if he does not work he must go hungry. Thrown thus on himself and left to work his farm without the aid of expensive machinery, he will content himself with raising just what he needs himself, and thus, while meeting the Government's intention of becoming self-sustaining, they at the same time would come into competition with the white settler only to the extent of their own labour, and thus remove all grounds for the complaint being made in some quarters against Government aided Indians entering into competition with the white settlers.

Respected spokesmen such as Father Lacombe, missionary to the Treaty Seven Indians, agreed that farming Indians could be made more industrious if they were permitted to take up land in severalty.[25] On 20 June 1889 the Ottawa *Journal* hailed the subdivision of the western reserves as a "step forward," for "as soon as the Indians are willing to throw up tribal connections and treaty money, they retain these lands as personal property, and become citizens." On 13 March 1890 the Moosomin *Courier* considered severalty to be a very fine stroke of "national policy" for the red man; "Chief Bull frog and his band" had already been introduced to the modern system of farming but they now needed individual ownership, as "self-interest is a wonderful stimulant." The *Courier* proclaimed that "superior houses, better fences, larger fields, and more extensively cultivated areas" already attested to the success of the policy, although it is unlikely that reserve residents were at this date conforming to the allotment survey. These words were taken almost directly from Dewdney's annual report of 1889 in which he had outlined the happy results likely to attend distribution in severalty.[26] According to the same article in the *Courier*, opposition to severalty among bands in the East was due to the nefarious influence of "the scoundrels who failed to cause a rising of our Indians in '85 – the political emissaries of a consumptive Party and their tools, the squawmen."

A letter published in the 13 November 1890 issue of the Ottawa *Citizen* from "Nichie" of Battleford gave a glowing appraisal of the severalty policy in terminology that bore striking similarities to that in department publications. The author observed that Indians with allotments made worthy efforts to improve and better their condition. He felt this system annulled tribal influence, "the bane of Indian progress," and instead engendered a healthy spirit of rivalry among individuals and bands. Under the system of all things held in common, the industrious worker had to share whatever was harvested with the idle, discontented, and worthless, which was discouraging to progress. The author perceived that the desire to occupy separate holdings was spreading, particularly among the young men, and he predicted that the time was not far distant when the Indians would no longer be consumers of government "grub" but producers, relieving the government larder.

The plan to subdivide reserves in western Canada coincided with a general allotment policy in the United States, which was codified in the Dawes Act of 1887. Allotment enjoyed a high degree of public support across the border. The policy of concentration and isolation upon reservations had failed to resolve the Indian "problem."[27] Private property was seen as the key to transforming the Indians into civilized agriculturalists. Pride of ownership would generate individual initiative and teach the Indians self-support. Private property would break up the tribal relationship; the yoke of authoritarian chiefs would be broken, and "progressive" Indians could accumulate wealth and property. An end to isolation would greatly further the progress of Indian farming, which was seen as tardy. They would reap the benefit of close association with enlightened white farmers and be open to progressive influences. Assimilation, through allotment in severalty, seemed to offer a permanent solution. Isolation was condemned as an obstacle to national unity and as a means of keeping alive racial distinctions.[28] Reservations seemed to have no place in a country that championed the concept of equal rights for all.

Many Americans involved in the movement for Indian reform in the 1880s had taken part in the antislavery movement. The reformers argued that the privileges of liberal democracy and civil rights should be extended to all. Severalty was seen as a final step toward treating Indians like all other Americans.[29] Individual ownership was seen as a right basic to the American heritage. Severalty was also seen as a means of protecting Indian lands from unscrupulous land grabbers, since it provided each owner with a valid title.[30] The American government had proved itself perpetually unable to restrain settlers from encroaching on and appropriating Indian land. Reformers were convinced that Indian title would be recognized as valid only when land was actually owned in fee simple. To humanitarian reformers, the 1887 Dawes Act was a major triumph.

The beauty of the American general allotment policy was, as historian Brian Dippie has written, that it appealed "simultaneously to humanitarian instincts and overt self-interest."[31] The Dawes Act appeared to guard Indian interests at the same time as it reflected the economic interests of non-Indians. It was obvious from the outset that allotment meant that much reserve land would be open for settlement. By granting land to individual Indians, "surplus" lands could be defined and made accessible. After a stipulated acreage went to each Indian family, the remaining land could be thrown open to white settlement and sizable portions of reservations could be sold. Many who supported the measure were simply interested in securing Indian land at a time farmland was becoming increasingly scarce.[32] "Left unsaid," Dippie has observed, "was the fact that past experience showed that the great preponderance of land actually allotted to the Indians would also wind up in white hands, thereby completing the sweep of the reservations."[33]

The Dawes Act empowered the president to allot in severalty part or all of any reservation. One hundred and sixty acre allotments were to go to each head of family, eighty acres to orphans, and forty acres to children under eighteen.[34] Individuals were allowed to choose their own lots, but if they failed to do so after four years, one would be chosen for them. The allotments were inalienable: they could not be sold for twenty-five years, and the president held the title in trust. If an individual proved himself sufficiently industrious after that time, he received title in fee simple. "Surplus" lands were to be disposed of by the government to "actual settlers." Proceeds from the sale of these lands were to be held in trust and could be appropriated by Congress for the purposes of Indian "civilization" and education.

Allotment proved not to be the grand panacea that its supporters had hoped. It appeared so simple – the land was to be parcelled out and the surplus sold – but the Dawes Act proved to be complicated to administer. Intricate legal problems arose over the questions of heirship and leasing. Government bureaucracy's role in Indian affairs increased rather than disappeared as had been assumed. The act had not provided for any future increase in the Indian population. Rather, it had been based on the assumption that the Indians were decreasing, even vanishing, or that Indians in the traditional sense would disappear as they were absorbed into the rest of the population. The twenty-five-year trust period was shortened in 1906 when discretionary powers to do so were granted to the secretary of the interior. The rate at which patents to the allotted land were granted was in this way accelerated. Sixty per cent of the Indians who had received their patents were dispossessed of their land in the first three years after restrictions were eased.[35] By 1920 more than two-thirds of those who had received clear title had been partially or totally dispossessed. Indian land in 1887 had consisted of 138 million acres. Sixty million acres were declared surplus and sold to whites. Of the allotted land, 27 million acres, or two-thirds, was sold.[36]

The western Canadian version of allotment in severalty bore resemblances to the American model, but there were also distinct differences. The rhetoric was precisely the same: allotment in severalty would create stable, sedentary farmers and would prove to be the shortest path to Indian enfranchisement. The ultimate goal of the disappearance of reserves altogether was also the same. Officials of the day never imagined that reserves would become permanent features of the landscape, and they worked to hasten their dissolution. As with the American plan, the allotment of western reserves would clearly demarcate the used and "unused" portions of reserves. Land that was "surplus," that is, available for surrender and sale, could be ascertained. As in the United States, few in Canada believed the Indians would ever need the land or that they should be in possession of unused land it appeared they had no need of. It is likely that Canadian policy-makers were influenced by the popularity of allotment in severalty across the border. Hayter Reed, a major promoter of the scheme, visited and consulted with American officials in 1888 and 1889 when optimism about the Dawes Act was high.[37] Canadian officials were aware of the potential profitability of severalty, however, well before that date.

John A. Macdonald expressed enthusiasm for severalty in 1886, not as a means of promoting private ownership, individual initiative, and self-support, but as a means of defining surplus land on reserves, which might be sold.[38] He reasoned that the funds so raised could help his government escape the financial burden of assisting the Indians. In this way a source of capital could also be established and used for the benefit of the bands, for example, in furnishing articles beyond those stipulated in the treaties.

Macdonald believed the process could be accomplished simply and swiftly. Dewdney was instructed to allot to each Indian on every reserve the land he would likely require for cultivation so that the amount of surplus land available for surrender and sale could be ascertained. Although favourable to the idea, Dewdney did not believe it could be hastily implemented. He claimed that he was attempting to locate families on separate plots of land but warned that "the process would necessarily be a long one." The time reserve land could be declared surplus was far away, he added.[39]

One impediment to the swift surrender of Indian land, which was a major departure from the American model, was that in western Canada reserve land considered surplus by non-Indians could not simply be thrown open for settlement. The sale of reserve land required the consent of the Indian band. Treaty Four, for example, stated that reserve land "may be sold, leased or otherwise disposed of by the said Government for the use and benefit of the said Indians, with the consent of the Indians entitled thereto first had and obtained."[40]

Reed worked diligently to facilitate the process of surrender and sale. As deputy superintendent general, he sought a means of evading the surrender provisions of the Indian Act in cases where reserves had been "abandoned" or where membership in the band had been greatly reduced.[41] Acting on a dubious interpretation of the legal opinion of the deputy minister of justice, and using an 1895 amendment to the Indian Act, his department began to arrange formal transfers for bands who had abandoned their reserves. Reed's objective was to deplete the membership of a band, leaving no one with a legal interest in the reserve. He believed this abandoned land could then be sold without formal surrender or compensation to the Indians.

Reed was interested in promoting reserve land surrender not simply to satisfy the cupidity of white settlers interested in prime agricultural land. He was intent on eliminating reserves regardless of the quality of the land. In 1889 Reed began to formulate a plan to dissolve the File Hills agency altogether. In a private note to Vankoughnet, Reed concluded that because the Indians there were a troublesome lot, the best course of treatment would be to break up the agency and distribute the bands throughout the Crooked Lakes, Muscowpetung, Touchwood, and Pelly agencies. Dispersed, the File Hills residents would, he believed, be discouraged from their "fractious" behaviour. The considerable cost of maintaining a separate agency would also be saved, Reed noted. He felt the abandoned reserves might be kept as hay land or "in some way disposed of, to allow compensating the Indians whose reservations might be called upon to receive additional occupants."[42] In subsequent correspondence, Reed presented further arguments for abandoning the File Hills, including "the disadvantages of the district for the cultivation of grain, the dearth of game, and the absence of a market for the industries of the Indians, and of opportunity for them to get freighting or other work, by means of which to contribute toward their own support."[43] Both Vankoughnet and Dewdney approved of Reed's scheme. Vankoughnet noted that the dispersal of Big Bear's band had been attended with good results and hoped that similar action with respect to the File Hills would be as successful.[44] Big Bear's band was never allocated a reserve, and his former followers were scattered after 1885.

SUBDIVIDING THE RESERVES

Reserve subdivision provided another means of facilitating surrender. Reserves in western Canada were subdivided according to the plan of ranges, townships, and sections of adjacent Dominion lands, but each section was further subdivided into sixteen lots of forty acres each, or one-quarter quarter sections.[45] The official reasons given for choosing the forty-acre lot as the standard were that it afforded "compact settlement" and it enabled each Indian to select a certain quantity of the choicest farmland on a reserve. If the subdivisions were larger, an individual might take in land unfit for cultivation or occupied by other Indians. Besides allowing the Indian farmer to select land most suitable for agriculture, Reed declared, the forty-acre lot did not compel him to take land he did not want.[46]

The plots were also kept small, Reed explained, because should a survey line cross existing improvements, two adjacent forty-acre lots could be selected to include them. Again, if the subdivisions were larger, the farmer might have to take in land that was not required. Reed stated, however, that in no case would an Indian be allowed to take up more land than the number of members in his family entitled him to. An 1890 amendment to section 16 of the Indian Act stipulated that an Indian would be granted no more than 160 acres, or four of the forty-acre plots.[47]

The subdivision surveys were to cover parts of the reserves already cultivated, or likely soon to be cultivated, and were to include "a certain area of the most desirable farm land."[48] Surveyor Nelson described his understanding of the policy. "As many of the Indian reserves are of large extent, and the area likely to be brought under cultivation, in comparison, small, it was decided that the subdivision surveys should cover only such portions of the respective reserves as may reasonably be expected to be required for settlement within the next few years."[49] Accordingly, surveyors subdivided the portions of reserves that were cultivated and what they believed to be a sufficient surplus to allow for any possible expansion in the next ten years.[50] Lands valued for hay, wood, or other natural products were to remain common property.

Indians desiring or induced to locate on the forty-acre lots were to be issued "certificates of occupancy" by the Indian commissioner upon the recommendation of the agent. Reed described the certificate as a "preliminary title towards the more complete tenure inferred by the issue of the location ticket." This temporary, intermediate system, he believed, would "pave the way for the more cumbersome and expensive [system] provided by law, which could not yet well be inaugurated in the present state of advancement of the Indians."[51] Under the 1876 Indian Act, Indians had to be literate, free of debt, and of "good moral character" to receive location tickets. As it was assumed that few Indians in the West could meet these stipulations, the certificate of occupancy was devised as an interim measure. In 1890 section 16 of the Indian Act was amended to provide that prior to the location of an Indian under this section, the Indian commissioner for Manitoba and the North-West might issue a certificate of occupancy for land which the Indian, with the approval of the commissioner, might select. The certificate might be cancelled at any time by the commissioner and simply vested in the holder lawful possession against all others.[52]

Reed and other department officials were particularly insistent that the subdivision surveys conform with the Dominion Land Survey. This was a departure from the method of subdividing reserves in the older provinces. Reed was convinced that unless the legal descriptions of the land conformed with the Dominion Land Survey, it would surely lead to much trouble when the Indians "begin to hand down their property to those who would come after them."[53] Vankoughnet agreed with Reed: "This [conformity with the Dominion Land Survey] will prove to be the most satisfactory course for every reason, inasmuch as if the Indians are allowed to take up farms without the same being defined by proper lines of survey, the matter of ultimately subdividing the Reserves will prove to be a most embarrassing one, as it has been found in the case of Reserves thus irregularly partitioned off in the older Provinces."[54]

The right of the Department of Indian Affairs to describe subdivisions of reserves as "legal," or in conformity with the Dominion Land Survey, was questioned by the inspector of surveys of the Department of the Interior in 1891. It was pointed out that reserves were not Dominion lands, and it was suggested that the townships might be described by some distinguishing name, such as that of the agency or chief. Reed strenuously defended the plan to conform with the survey. He explained that it would be much more convenient for the future disposition of land; he foresaw "the time when, as is now being done with the Pass-pass-chase Reserve, some Indian lands will be disposed of, or exchanged."[55] (The Passpasschase reserve south of Edmonton was the first in the North-West to be surrendered.) Reed argued that to designate the townships by some other distinguishing name would have the effect of "keeping alive that distinction between the two races, to reduce which, to the narrowest possible limits, is the object of the Department's policy, in dealing with the Indians." The objection of the inspector of surveys was withdrawn, and the subdivision of reserve land proceeded in accordance with the theoretic sections and legal subdivisions of the Dominion Land Survey. The inspector reminded Vankoughnet, however, that "the term 'legal subdivision' as applied to Indian lands has no meaning susceptible of a precise definition. The Dominion Lands Act defines what a 'legal subdivision' is as relating to Dominion Lands but there is no such provision in the Indian Act."[56]

To subdivide reserves in conformity with the Dominion Land Survey was expensive and time consuming. More road allowances had to be surveyed because of the small size of the allotments. The subdivision surveys included a two-mile long road running north and south through the centre of every two sections in addition to those surrounding the sections themselves. Reed believed an additional one-mile east-west road between every two sections should be run as well to "permit of ready communication between the different subdivisions of the Sections."[57] Reed clearly felt that extra road allowances were necessary if the blocks were to be reduced to forty-acre lots. Other officials of the department disagreed, both with Reed's suggestion of an additional road allowance and with the north-south roads already being surveyed.[58] They argued that the maintenance of these roads, either in money or in statute labour, would be burdensome and that these road allowances were simply a waste of land. They would require miles of extra fencing, which would drain the pocket of the farmer. It was pointed out that the road allowance system in the North-West had proved to be sufficient for the needs of the settlers and was also within their ability to keep in ordinary repair. Reed's request for an additional road was turned down but the north-south road was retained.

Subdivision surveys of reserves in the North-West began in the summer of 1889 on the Muscowpetung and Crooked Lakes agencies. Portions of the reserves of Piapot, Muscowpetung, Pasquah, Kahkewistahaw, Sakimay, and O'Soup were subdivided that year, and that of Cowessess the next. Many reserves in the Treaty Six district were also subdivided between 1889 and 1892. Agencies such as the Touchwood Hills and File Hills were not subdivided, although their boundaries were defined and made consistent with the Dominion Land Survey. In the Treaty Four district, subdivision proceeded only on those reserves that were close to the railway and were attractive for agricultural purposes. The forty-acre lots were located on the northern half of these reserves near the river, on land that was cut by deep ravines in places and was regarded by few as the best for agriculture (see figure 2). In most cases the southern portion that remained undivided had the superior farmland and hay grounds. The residents of reserves whose land was not highly valued were evidently not seen to be in need of the lessons private property was to impart. Reed stated that "considerable discrimination" had to be made in selecting the reserves for subdivision. One consideration was the degree of serious objection that might be anticipated from a band. Bands not "sufficiently advanced in civilization and intelligence" might, Reed admitted, not understand the necessity for this work. Suspicions about the department's purpose might be aroused, which could lead to "trouble of a serious nature."[59]

INDIAN PROTESTS TO SUBDIVISION

The subdivision surveys were protested by reserve residents, who were neither consulted nor informed before the crews arrived to

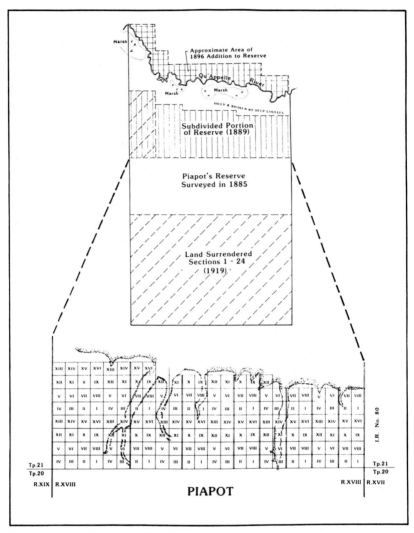

Figure 2. Subdivision of the Piapot reserve
Sources: National Archives, National Map Collection (NMC) 23720, Treaty no. 4, NWT, Subdivision survey of part of Indian reserve no. 75, Chief Piapot (1889); NMC 23719, Treaty no. 4, Indian reserve no. 75, Chief Piapot (1885); NMC 10735, Plan of surrendered portion of Piapot Indian reserve no. 75 and 75A (1919).

begin work. Trouble began on the Piapot reserve in July 1889. Before the survey began, Hayter Reed and surveyor Nelson held a council with Piapot and his headmen, to explain "the purpose of the survey, and the manner in which it would be performed."[60] The survey began the same day. The surveyor's policy was to employ residents of the reserve being subdivided at the rate of seventy-five cents a day, which would have acted as an inducement to cooperation.

The survey of Piapot's reserve proceeded without incident until 1 July when the Indians quit work and went to Regina for the annual races and sports. When they returned, they refused to resume work. The Indians asked for higher wages, but surveyor Nelson felt that the demand was not the only cause of their refusal to continue. Nelson met with Piapot who had been told by O'Soup at Regina that it was very wrong for Piapot to permit surveyors to cut up his land into little squares. He would surely come to grief, O'Soup had said, "as it was the intention of the Government to restrain him and his people within the lines that the surveyors were running inside the reserve." O'Soup had claimed that he would not allow the surveyors to plant stakes on his reserve. According to Nelson, Piapot was greatly disturbed after talking to O'Soup "and feared that he or any of his people who might assist in making the subdivision *might be poisoned (Muskegee)*."[61] The surveyor informed Piapot that he would be compelled to hire white men to complete the survey, and the services of a few men from the nearby Scottish settlement were secured for a few days. Eventually the Indians agreed to begin work again.

Officials saw O'Soup as a mischievous, obnoxious influence. Blame for the Indians' reluctance to comply with the survey was placed on his shoulders. Hayter Reed instructed agent Allan MacDonald to tell O'Soup that if it were true that he spoke in the way alleged, "I am much surprised that a man of his intelligence would do so" and thwart department efforts to advance the real interests of the Indians. Reed did not suppose that O'Soup really believed the department had any "sinister motives," but if he did harbour these notions, MacDonald was to persuade him otherwise and point out the advantages of the system, which would improve and elevate the Indian.[62]

In his interview with agent MacDonald, O'Soup cleared himself of any undue interference. He showed that he understood the "intention" of the department in subdividing the reserves and left the impression that an error or misunderstanding had occurred in Piapot's account of their meeting on 2 July. O'Soup testified that Piapot had said that the surveyors had taken him by surprise in surveying the reserve like a checkerboard and he could get no satisfactory answers about why it was being done. O'Soup placed himself in an exceedingly good light, stating that he was the first to go to the Crooked Lakes, choose a reserve, and request that it be surveyed. He claimed that he had tried to persuade Piapot that the survey was to the advantage of the Indians. O'Soup's account of his words to Piapot, as recorded by MacDonald, was as follows:

Look at the White man how he has his land surveyed to him. What quantity of land do you see that he receives. The Government wishes us to take an example by them, and wants our lands (that is the improvements) surveyed to us, and that we have to live on them for three years, and at the end of that time we get a paper to show that it is our individual property that no one else can take it from us, and that when the time comes for election for a member to represent us at Ottawa, we will have a right to vote the same as a Whiteman. This is what I understood the Government is going to do.[63]

O'Soup stated, however, that at Crooked Lakes the Indians were startled about the surveys because, like Piapot, they did not understand the government's intentions. He was going to leave it to his headmen to decide whether they wanted the survey. O'Soup claimed he was informing other Indians that they ought to be glad that the government took such an interest in them.

Survey work continued in the summer of 1889 on the Pasquah and Muscowpetung reserves. In September a council was held with the Crooked Lakes Indians to discuss the subdivision of their reserves, which was, according to surveyor Nelson, "a subject on which the Indians are desirous of hearing full explanations."[64] Agent MacDonald explained the purpose of the survey and showed the plans, but at the end of the meeting the headmen were unwilling to express an opinion. Chief Kahkewistahaw, however, agreed to cooperate and said he would take on his own shoulders the responsibility of having his reserve subdivided. While surveying this reserve, Nelson reported that Yellow Calf of the Sakimay reserve visited on several occasions to obtain information on the survey and requested that his be surveyed next. It was subdivided as were portions of the Cowessess reserve. Chief Ochapowace objected to the subdivision survey and no such work was done on his reserve. Opposition was grounded on the idea that the survey was a preliminary step toward depriving the Indians of their land.[65]

In 1890 at Moose Mountain members of White Bear's band also objected to the survey, although a portion of the land was subdivided. In his annual report of that year, Reed dismissed any protest but warned that great caution had to be exercised in the subdivision of reserves "to avoid rousing the suspicions of the Indians, who often imagine sinister motives in a manner and to an extent which those unacquainted with them could hardly credit."[66] Reed described the Indians who cooperated as the more industrious and intelligent members of their bands.

Indian objection to the subdivision survey continued after the survey work was complete. In the years to 1896 it was reported that individuals were occasionally taking up residence on their forty-acre lots, but there appears to have been no general movement to do so. Agents were to make every effort to induce the Indians to locate on the lots, but there was little they could actually do to enforce the policy. Officials reported publicly that the scheme was progressing and succeeding. Dewdney gave a glowing account in his annual report for 1891, but it is clear from his private correspondence that he had no idea to what extent Indians had taken up their locations. What information he had was not encouraging. He reminded Reed that it had cost the government a great deal to afford this "privilege" to the Indians, and he urged that every effort be made to induce them to take advantage of it.[67] Again, he was concerned that the Indians be properly located to avoid the disputes that had arisen in the older provinces.

It appears that after the early 1890s the concerted program of subdividing parts of reserves into forty-acre lots ended. After the change of government in 1896, subdivisions were generally surveyed only after land was surrendered for the purposes of sale. Officials saw no need to subdivide reserves where surrenders were refused.[68] The rationale for the earlier subdivisions, that they were in the agricultural interests of the Indians, was dropped. The subdivision surveys of the early 1890s, however, did allow department officials to effectively restrict Indian settlement on reserves to the subdivided portions only. Indians were not allowed to locate on unsubdivided land, were forced to concentrate, and could not disperse. In 1904, for example, a resident of the Cowessess reserve hoped to stop the imminent surrender of the southern strip of his reserve by locating in the extreme southwest corner. He was refused permission because this land had not been subdivided and location tickets could not be issued for unsubdivided land.[69]

RATIONALE FOR THE PEASANT FARMING POLICY

In 1889 Hayter Reed announced that one of the most potent reasons for insisting that Indians farm their land in severalty was the new "approved system of farming adopted."[70] This new system was implemented on prairie reserves for the next eight years. Indian farmers were to emulate "peasants of various countries" who kept their operations small and their implements rudimentary.[71] In Reed's opinion, a single acre of wheat, a portion of a second acre of root crops and vegetables, and a cow or two could sufficiently provide for an Indian farmer and his family. He argued that it was better for Indians to cultivate a small acreage properly than to attempt to extend the area under cultivation. This restricted acreage eliminated any need for labour-saving machinery. Peasants of other countries, Reed contended, farmed successfully with no better implements than the hoe, rake, cradle, sickle, and flail, and he believed that Indians had to be taught to handle these simple tools. They were to broadcast seed by hand, harvest with scythes, bind by hand with straw, thresh with flails, and grind their grain with hand mills. In some districts Indians were discouraged from growing wheat altogether in favour of root crops. They were to keep cows for household purposes rather than raise large herds. As part of the program, Indians were required to manufacture at home from materials readily available many items they needed, such as harrows, hayforks, hayracks, carts, and ox yokes. Each Indian family was to form a self-contained, self-sufficient unit, untouched by the fluctuations of the general market economy.

The central rationale advanced in support of the peasant farming policy was that it was "the manner best calculated to render [the Indians] self-supporting when left to their own resources."[72] In his correspondence and public pronouncements, Reed repeated many times that he believed the time was not far distant when the Indians would have to depend entirely upon their own resources. "Our policy," he stated, "is to make each family cultivate such quantity of land as they can manage with such implements as they can alone hope to possess for long enough after being thrown upon their own resources."[73] If the reserves were subdivided, the surplus land sold, and the Indians resident on their forty-acre lots enfranchised, the Indians would indeed be left to their own resources. There would be no bands, no reserves, and no Department of Indian Affairs.

Since the Indians were to aim, not at breaking up large quantities of land, but at cultivating a restricted amount that could be worked solely with the family's own resources, labour-saving implements, Reed argued, were "likely to be beyond acquisition by the majority of Indians for some time."[74] Reed was not pleased that Indians tended to purchase implements together, an action that reinforced the band unit. He wanted to see the Indians become self-sufficient as individuals, not as bands. On their own, however, they were unlikely to afford machinery. Although Reed conceded that there were individual Indians who were independent of government assistance and could not be restrained from purchasing machinery from their own earnings, he felt such cases were rare. If Indians received any assistance at all in the way of seed grain, rations, or other goods, then they were not self-sufficient and should not be making payments on machinery. Well-to-do farmers could instead pay for the labour of other Indians.[75] Indian women, Reed hoped, could work in the fields, particularly at harvest time. Agents and inspectors were to cancel the sales of machinery to Indians even though it was purchased by the Indians, not by the department. At Duck Lake in 1891, six or seven Indians together purchased a self-binder with the approval of the farm instructor.[76] The implement dealer had to acquire the consent of the agent, who was ordered by Inspector McGibbon to object to the sale. No sale or delivery took place.

According to Reed, the Indians should cultivate root crops rather than grain, which further eliminated the need for machinery.[77] Root crops, not cereal, taught Indian farmers to be diligent and attentive, Reed stated. "I've always advocated growing as many root crops as possible but Indians have to be humoured a good deal in such matters; and as soon as they begin to make some little progress they become fired with an ambition to grow larger quantities of wheat and other cereals [rather than] roots which require working and weeding at the very time they like to be off hunting while the former only require to have cattle kept away by means of a good fence."[78]

The need to go into debt to buy machinery was another justification for halting its use. Farmers who had to obtain credit were not regarded as self-sufficient. It was wiser, Reed felt, to wait and see whether the climatic conditions of the country warranted the purchase of labour-saving machinery. Machinery, he argued, would not bring prosperity; it had instead been the means of ruining large numbers of white settlers who purchased on credit.[79] Reed shared with other department officials the view that Indians were prone to run into debt and were unable or disinclined to discharge their liabilities.[80] By the early 1890s the department was alarmed that it might be thought liable for Indian debts. Because the Indian Act excluded Indians from taxes, liens, mortgages, or other charges, and from loss of possessions through debt, their commercial affairs were not open to the claims of creditors.[81] In 1891 a circular letter was sent to all agents to notify parties who traded with the Indians that the department would not be responsible for debts incurred by Indians "whether the same were by virtue of orders from agents, chiefs, Indian councils, or otherwise."[82] Merchants were warned personally and by advertisement that the department would not be responsible for any such accounts. Legislation was considered which would prohibit, under severe penalty, the giving of credit to Indians. Indian debt and credit were effectively controlled, however, through the permit system under which only transactions authorized by a department agent could take place between a merchant or buyer and an Indian.

Another argument Reed forwarded against the use of labour-saving machinery by Indians was that rudimentary implements afforded useful employment for all. The possession of machinery, Reed believed, allowed the Indians to do nothing but "sit by and smoke their pipes while work is being done for them without exertion on their part," a situation he believed they preferred.[83] In his view the use of such implements was justified only when manual labour was scarce, which was not the case on Indian reserves. Indian agents were to encourage women and children to assist in planting the grain, cultivating, and keeping down the weeds.

The same reasons were advanced for the necessity of home manufactures. Gainful employment during spare time prevented the "mischief which emanates from idleness" and trained the Indians for the time they would be totally thrown upon their own resources.[84] Indian men and women were first encouraged and then required to make an endless list of items in common use on a farm. Women's manufactures included mitts, socks, willow baskets, mats, and straw hats. Men were expected to make axe and fork handles, ox collars and harness, wooden harrows, bobsleighs, and Red River carts. Models of the items to be manufactured were provided. Indians were to get by with as little as possible in the way of metal goods, as in days of old.[85] Reed suggested that shaganappi (animal, traditionally buffalo, sinew) be used for purposes such as the tugs of ox collars. Instead of buckles, strings could be made from shaganappi for ox-cart harness, as they were for Red River cart harness. Indians were to learn to provide simple and efficient substitutes for items such as nails and hinges. Reed believed that much, if not all, of the carpentry work of the Indians could be accomplished with birch pins and wooden augers instead of nails and screws.[86] Compliance with this policy was readily enforced: requests for the purchase of these items were simply stroked off the estimates, and agents were not to allow Indians to spend their own earnings on items such as nails and hinges.

Reed drew on aspects of an evolutionary argument to support his peasant farming policy. In the late nineteenth century, those who took an evolutionary view of the North American Indian and other "primitive" people believed that immutable laws of social evolution were in operation.[87] It was thought that man developed progressively through prescribed stages from savagery through barbarism to civilization. Theses stages could not be skipped, nor could a race or culture be expected to progress at an accelerated rate. The Indians were perceived to be many stages removed from nineteenth-century civilization, and while they could take the next step forward, they could not miss the steps in between.

So too Reed argued that Indians should not make an "unnatural" leap from barbarism to a nineteenth-century environment, including all its appliances.[88] The Indian was "prone to desire to imitate the white man's nineteenth century civilization somewhat too hastily and too early,"[89] Reed noted. In the first of his annual reports outlining the peasant policy, he repeated: "The fact is often overlooked, that these Indians who, a few years ago, were roaming savages, have been suddenly brought into contact with a civilization which has been the growth of centuries. An ambition has thus been created to emulate in a day what white men have become fitted for through the slow progress of generations."[90] While labour-saving machinery was necessary and suitable for white farmers, then, Indians had first to experience farming with crude and simple implements. To do otherwise defied immutable laws of evolution. In Reed's view, Indians had not reached the stage at which they were in a position to compete with white settlers;[91] therefore they should not be equipped with the machinery that would allow them to compete.

Enlarging on an image of the Indians' "savage" past, Reed began in 1889 to emphasize in his public statements that Indians had a "naturally brutal disposition" toward their domestic animals, that there was a "disregard of animal life inherent in recently reclaimed savages," and that they had to be taught to be merciful to their beasts.[92] His opinion was in marked contrast with the observations of agents and inspectors who often noted that Indians were more concerned for the welfare of their animals than for themselves. Reed's message was that the Indians could be taught the proper care of their animals if every family kept one cow, but they were not yet prepared for an "unnatural" leap to large herds. And if Indians were not allowed to use mowers, they would be able to procure enough hay only to sustain a small number of cattle.

THE IDEAL: THE SELF-SUFFICIENT FARMER

The Indian farmer could maintain, Reed believed, a self-contained economic unit isolated from the fluctuations of the market economy. The ideal self-sufficient farmer was one who built with his own hands the shelter and furnishings required for himself and family.[93] The farmer's family ate food that was the result of their own labours.

They produced their own meat, cheese, butter, and bread and dried or otherwise preserved and stored garden products. They caught wild ducks, geese, prairie chicken, and rabbits and gathered berries. The family manufactured at home the nonagricultural goods required, including clothing, soap, axe handles, and sleigh runners. Self-sufficient farmers neither bought nor sold. They took no part in the exchange economy or such a negligible and insignificant part as to be unworthy of evaluation. The self-sufficient farmer did not produce for a market. Although he might acquire a surplus, it was not his primary objective; it was, rather, a "security blanket" or a "fortuitous result."[94] As such a range of goods were produced to satisfy the needs of his family, the self-sufficient farmer was not a specialist. Only a minimum of effort could be devoted to any single item.

Inspiration for the peasant policy may have been derived from a variety of sources. In the late nineteenth century, British and North American reformers, academics, politicians, and writers were interested in the possibilities of small allotments and imbued the peasant proprietor with a new respectability. Like Hayter Reed, none were themselves professional farmers or growers. Among others, John Stuart Mill opposed the concentration of landed property in the hands of a few great estate owners and favoured the creation of a class of peasant proprietors. Such a step, it was believed, would raise agricultural productivity, lower prices, and reduce urban unemployment. Peasant proprietorship would have social as well as economic benefits, since the owner would take permanent interest in the soil. He would be "thrifty, sober, honest and independent." With a stake in the country, former day labourers would be less inclined to "wanton aggressions" or "mischief" and instead would be interested in preserving tranquility and order.[95] These were exactly the qualities Reed attributed to his peasant proprietors. Reed's plan bears some resemblance to Joseph Chamberlain's 1885 election cry, "Three Acres and a Cow."[96] Chamberlain's loosely sketched agrarian reform policy involved the compulsory purchase of land by local authorities in order to repopulate the country with independent English yeomen. His visit to Canada in 1887 may have generated interest in his ideas on land reform.

In the 1880s these ideas had wide public support in England and the United States. In England an Allotments and Small Holdings Association was formed. Its honorary secretary, Frederic Impey, published in 1885 *Three Acres and a Cow: Successful Small Holdings and Peasant Proprietors*. Individuals and charitable organizations promoted small allotments as a means of reforming and controlling the behaviour of the working classes, veterans, immigrants, and criminals. In 1890 the Salvation Army's founder, William Booth, advocated settlement of the poor on three-to-five-acre allotments with a cottage and a cow in his book *In Darkest England and the Way Out*. A host of popular works bearing titles such as *Ten Acres Enough* and *Driven Back to Eden* described how a few acres in the country could sustain a family.[97]

It is often assumed that the start-up period in prairie agriculture was a time of subsistence, or self-sufficiency. Certainly it is true that pioneer farmers used to derive more of their consumer goods from their farms than subsequent generations did, but the self-sufficiency of the farm unit was never absolute. Pioneer farmers, economist Vernon Fowke has argued, were at no time self-sufficient but were "from the beginning tied in with the price system and the urban economy on a national and international basis."[98] If Canadian agriculture had approached self-sufficiency, it would not have required the governmental assistance it has received for over three hundred years. Agriculture, Fowke stated, has been consistently and deliberately moulded by public moneys in Canada because it has been used as a basis for economic and political power.[99] From the time of Confederation, western immigration and agricultural settlement were seen as essential to the well-being of the entire economy. To inject vitality into the Canadian economy and to enrich the East, commercial, not subsistence, farmers were required on the new investment frontier: farmers who would ship their products to distant markets and buy their implements, provisions, and clothing from eastern manufacturers.

From the outset the farmer in western Canada was intent on commercial rather than subsistence farming. Producing a surplus for market was equal in importance to producing for the family's needs. The surplus was not simply fortuitous but the result of the farmer's plans to earn the greatest returns, and he was prepared to shift farming practices according to the demands of the market. Farms became specialized, dependent units, integrated into the market economy. Western farmers' concerns and their problems of freight rates, orderly marketing, branch lines, and elevator facilities, evident from the earliest days, were all consistent with the needs of commercial farming.

Even in the start-up years, the homesteader was dependent on other segments of the exchange economy at the local level. The farmer had to purchase his transportation and outfit himself with the necessary provisions and farm implements. The equipment of the pioneer farmer, Fowke has argued, should not be dismissed as negligible, as these purchases contributed to the creation of profitable investment opportunities.[100] Although the farmer may not have produced a marketable staple for some years, some items, such as hay and wood, were sold locally. Exchanges might have been made through barter rather than with money, but they nonetheless constituted commercial transactions. Many homesteaders earned money away from the farm for a good number of years. Some worked as hired hands for a larger operator, while others had a second skill or trade and found employment in the towns. Farmers joined survey crews and railway construction gangs or worked as freighters. Some went to far-off mining and logging camps. Farm women sold or bartered items such as butter and eggs. Homesteaders were in need of cash and could rarely acquire enough to finance their operations. They could not borrow against their land until title was acquired, which took three years or longer. The farmer needed credit to secure his provisions, implements, and other supplies. It became standard practice to have credit advanced at the beginning of the crop season for seed, tools, and consumable goods with payment made at harvest time.

Towns that mushroomed along the Canadian Pacific Railway at Moosomin, Whitewood, Broadview, Qu'Appelle, Indian Head, and Sintaluta distributed great quantities of supplies. These trading centres could not have been sustained if the settlers had been self-sufficient. Older communities such as Fort Qu'Appelle, and older concerns such as the Hudson's Bay Company, began to cater to the needs of settlers. The towns of Kenlis, Chickney, Saltoun, and Pheasant Forks served settlers who lived some distance from the track. Staple groceries most commonly purchased included tea, sugar, salt, rice, oatmeal, and dried fruit.[101] Merchants accepted farm produce in exchange, especially butter and eggs, as well as wood, game, furs, and seneca root.

On pioneer farms of the prairie West, a short semisubsistence stage was followed by a rapid shift to highly specialized farming. The adoption of large-scale, single-crop farming and the introduction of the techniques and technology of dry farming likely encouraged the commercial aspect. Even the difficulties of the 1880s did not imply a need for self-sufficient farms. Like other western farmers, Indian farmers tended more toward commercial than subsistence farming, focusing on wheat culture, acquiring machinery to accommodate large acreages, and adopting techniques such as summer-fallowing. In their need to acquire cash, make purchases, and sell products, Indian farmers were just as linked to the larger economy as white settlers were. Yet the peasant farming policy required Indian farmers to step aside and function in isolation from the rest of western Canadian society. This attitude was unrealistic. Subsistence farming remained at best a questionable model for the arid Canadian plains. Western farmers were independent neither of the markets nor of each other. Settlement of the prairies required mutual assistance and cooperation among neighbours and relatives. Working bees, pooled purchasing, and beef rings were characteristic of the pioneer years. Indians were denounced, however, when they undertook such cooperative action. Indian farmers were expected to conform to the nostalgic ideal of the independent, self-sufficient yeoman.

That ideal continued to have general public appeal, however, whereas the concept of agriculture as a market- and profit-focused business was not universally accepted.[102] Commercial agriculture required new ideas, attitudes, and knowledge. What and how much should be produced were determined by external market conditions rather than by the family's needs and desires. Under market conditions the farmer made a business decision and had to take into consideration the nature of the soil, characteristics of commodities, access to markets, and world prices. Commercial farming involved a rational approach to technology. Potential profit rather than immediate need led the farmer to purchase expensive implements on credit; payment would in part come from the increased productivity made possible by the new implements. The efficient, profitable management of the farm enterprise thus required new attitudes toward technology, credit, and debt, for immigrant settlers and Indians alike. Hayter Reed felt, however, that Indians were incapable of understanding these concepts and could not operate farms as business enterprises. His belief in their inability thus precluded commercial farming.

In continuing to uphold the ideal of the self-contained family farm, Reed was not alone. The notion that self-sufficient farming was a superior way of life remained a cherished ideal, even though it may never have existed in reality. It has been observed that, in the United States, that ideal was never more than "a nice dream of a golden age when individuals supposedly were self-dependent and possessed all of the virtues that accompany such a position. In a sense it is the Robinson Crusoe story applied to that sturdy figure, the Colonial or frontier farmer. It is isolationism applied to the individual, since it is based on the idea that once upon a time individuals could function completely upon their own."[103] The concept of the independent, self-sufficient homestead was reflected in attitudes that persisted, even among some farmers, and Reed appeared to share in these. Many harboured a suspicion of new technology or change in farming practice and were alarmed at debt and credit, which were viewed as extravagant speculation.[104] The notion that the self-sufficient family farm possessed an immunity to financial crises persisted as did a disapproval of purchasing what could be produced at home. The farmer who accomplished all by the sweat of his brow was deemed to be the most worthy.

IMPLEMENTING THE POLICY

A circular letter dated 1 November 1889 first introduced the peasant policy to Indian agents.[105] Reed informed them that he was "very anxious to have every nerve strained in the desired direction, and to do so, employees must work early and late." Superintendent General Dewdney, he warned the agents, "insists so strongly upon the necessity of carrying out the prescribed policy, that it is clear, that upon the success in doing so, or the efforts made to have it fully tested, will depend on the advancement, or even the retention of farmers in their present position."[106] Reed was correct to anticipate objections to the policy. Farm instructors, agents, and Indian farmers all protested the system.

Despite the protests, Reed rigidly enforced the policy. As commissioner, he kept a vigilant eye on every kettle and lamp ordered, and later as deputy superintendent general, he maintained close surveillance. Agents were not allowed to spend a "single copper" without the authority of the commissioner.[107] Reed's replacement as commissioner, Amédée Forget, had very limited powers of expenditure; even the most minute expense had to be sanctioned by Reed. Forget could under no circumstances authorize the purchase, hire, or use of machinery. When Forget requested greater powers of expenditure in 1894 to be able to respond to requests requiring immediate action during critical seasons, Reed replied:

I would say that I am only too desirous that you take upon your shoulders this part of the work, and thus relieve me of it. The fear I have had – to be candid – is that my policy might not be strictly carried out, and I foresee that if it is slackened in the slightest, it will lead us not only to a largely increased expenditure but upset what I have in view, and this is, causing our Indians to work upward by learning how to cut and sow their grain in the most crude manner possible, and not beginning at the large end of the norm, with self-binders and reapers.[108]

During haying and harvest time the full weight of the policy was felt. Agents and instructors were to see that the Indian farmers accomplished these tasks without the aid of any machinery. Even if bands had purchased reapers and self-binders before the policy was adopted, the farmers were to use hand implements. Farmers with large holdings were to purchase the labour of others rather than revert to the use of machinery, or they were to restrict their acreages to what they could handle with hand implements. "The general principle," Reed explained in 1893, "is not to allow them machinery to save them work which they should, with hands available on Reserves, do by help of such implements as are alone likely for long enough, to be within their reach."[109]

Department officials in the field protested the peasant farming policy from its inception. They were dismayed by a policy that appeared to rob the Indians of any potential source of revenue. Their main objection was that the use of hand implements, particularly at harvest time, which coincided with haying, involved much loss in yield, as both had to be secured with haste. The Edmonton agent wrote in 1896: "Personally, I do not see how any band of Indians in this district can ever raise sufficient grain or cattle to become self-supporting as long as they have to work with sickles and scythes only, as the seasons are so very short, haying and harvesting coming together. Perhaps in the south where the seasons are longer the system would work successfully, but up here no whiteman attempts to do so."[110]

Agents throughout the North-West, however – even those much farther south than Edmonton – agreed that the seasons were simply too short for the use of hand implements. The Carlton agent advised that because the climate brooked no delay with regard to securing grain, conditions in the North-West could not be equated with those in the early days of farming in the eastern provinces when hand implements were used.[111] If not harvested as quickly as possible, grain could be lost to frost, hail, dry hot winds, or an excess of moisture. Agent W.S. Grant of the Assiniboine reserve protested that "the seasons in this country are too short to harvest any quantity of grain, without much waste, with only old fashioned, and hand-implements to do the work with." In his view it was not possible to harvest the 240 acres of grain on his reserve with hand implements without a great loss in yield. The grain had to be cut as soon as it was ready, since the harvest weather was generally hot, windy, and very dry, and the grain could overripen. Grant estimated that the amount of grain lost in his agency would be of sufficient quantity in two years to pay for a binder. Loss occurred, not only through the grain being too ripe, but in the gathering and binding by hand as well. Grant informed Reed that the prairie straw used to tie grain was dry and brittle and would break, which caused considerable loss. While the farmers on his reserve used long slough grass to bind grain, collecting it took up so much time that the grain was in danger of overripening.[112] Agents also complained that the cradles broke constantly during harvest, which caused delays for repairs.

The policy of employing labour to help take off a crop seldom proved to be feasible. Workers had their own fields to harvest. One agent reported that farmers who did hire others spent more in paying their labourers than their crop was worth.[113] He tried to get neighbours to exchange work in one another's fields, but those available to help usually had no crops and required pay for their labour.

Inspector Alex McGibbon was also critical of the peasant farming policy. In 1891 he informed Reed that it was contrary to common sense to ban universally the use of machinery. Exceptions had to be made and flexibility shown. McGibbon gave the example of the Onion Lake band, which had 500 acres under crop, much of which would be lost if the department insisted it be cut with cradles. Then, there was the case of a farmer with about fifteen acres "of as pretty wheat as could be seen anywhere." The man was in frail health, however, and could not secure the help of others, who had their own fields to look after. McGibbon observed the man cradling and his wife binding but was certain that "the waste on that field alone would be nearly half the crop."[114] McGibbon's reports sometimes contained more understated criticism. In 1890 he drew attention to a mower owned by farmers on the Moosomin reserve. The implement had been in their care for four years, was in perfect order, and had not required a cent in repairs. "This is a proof," the inspector wrote, "that some of the Indians take good care and know how to handle such implements."[115]

Agents and instructors reported difficulty enforcing compliance with the peasant policy. It was almost impossible to get the Indians to cut with cradles or sickles, especially those who already had labour-saving implements.[116] Agents provided Reed with numerous examples of farmers who started the work and gave up, refusing to return, and of others who would not even attempt it.[117] It was reported that the Indians became discouraged and lost all interest in their crops – and these were not "lazy" Indians.[118] Agent J.J. Campbell of Moose Mountain cited the case of an Indian farmer whom he considered to be the most progressive in the agency. The farmer began to cradle his grain but quit, declaring that he would let his grain stand and never plough another acre. By no means averse to hard work, the man chose to tackle instead the straw pile of a threshing machine, a job "not usually considered pleasant."[119] Agent Grant described the reaction of "Black Mane," who had fifteen acres of very good wheat: "When told that he would have to cut and bind it by hand, [he] gave up his oxen, and left both his wheat and *reserve*. I gave his wheat to his brother. I have been told that he is now at Wolf Point, in the States. This will show how hard it is to compel an Indian to harvest his grain by hand."[120] It was also the case that some Indian farmers were not strong enough, because of age or sickness, to harvest their grain by hand. In August 1890 the Pelly agent reported that "the Indians here, from scrofulitic [sic] effects have not enough strength to mow [hay] with a scythe and put up any quantity."[121] If they had only two or three head, they could manage to put up enough hay, but any more was beyond their ability with scythes and rakes.

The Indians were discouraged when they saw white farmers using machinery. Agent Grant reported that the Indians on his reserve used binders when they stooked for white settlers and not surprisingly were discouraged when asked to cut and bind their own crops by hand.[122] Indian farmers were also keenly aware of the methods used on reserves throughout the North-West. In 1891 McGibbon stated that "the Indians know all that is going on at the various agencies." The Carlton agency Indians knew precisely how many binders the Crooked Lakes Indians had and how many seeders were in another agency. Chief Mistawasis of the Treaty Six district demanded to know in 1891 why the Battleford Indians and John Smith's band had reapers when his farmers were not allowed them.[123] McGibbon curtly informed him that they had been purchased before the policy had been adopted, that such sales were now being cancelled, and that he and his men should be out in the fields cutting and stacking grain rather than wasting valuable time talking.

Restrictions on the use of machinery were not the only aspects of the peasant policy that agents disliked. The home manufactures program, which called for the use of Indian-made implements, also proved unrealistic. Homemade wooden forks, for example, were not strong enough for loading hay, grain, or manure. Iron forks were required and even those frequently broke or wore out and had to be replaced. In some districts, moreover, appropriate materials such as hides and lumber were not available to manufacture ox-plough harness, wagon tongues, or neck yokes. Poorly made or faulty neck yokes could break while cattle were going down a hill, and they could be injured, if not killed. Other items struck from agents' estimates included lanterns and tea kettles. Agents protested that Indians could not look after their cattle at night without lanterns and that not having proper kettles resulted in the waste of much time.[124]

At headquarters in Ottawa it proved difficult to even acquire some of the old-fashioned implements destined for the Indian farmers of the North-West. Duncan Campbell Scott, chief clerk in the 1890s and later deputy superintendent general, amused a 1916 audience with the story of one of his predecessors who thought Indians "should carry on their farming operations by pioneer methods; that is, they should reap their grain with the sickle and cut their hay with the scythe; that even the hinges should be made of willow wisps as in the old days, and their grain ground in hand mills." Scott had great difficulty finding hand mills, "although we inquired all through the Dominion." A Montreal hardware merchant had no such implement but replied to the department's letter of inquiry: "Kindly refer to Matthew, 24th chapter, 41st verse: 'Two women shall be grinding at the mill; the one shall be taken and the other left.' If you will find the one that was left, and apply to her, she will probably give you some information as to where to find the hand mills."[125]

Hayter Reed was not the slightest bit sympathetic to or moved by the objections and complaints of his agents and inspectors. His response was to dismiss their claims. Reed was aware of a "lack of sympathy" among agents and employees, but he was convinced that they were inclined to be too lenient with the Indians. "Naturally," he wrote to McGibbon, "Indians and their overseers prefer to take the method easiest for themselves, and it is only after a hard and long continued fight, that I am beginning to get the policy carried into effect."[126] Officials in the field, Reed believed, desired to make things as easy as possible for the Indians and consequently for themselves.[127] Indians "naturally" preferred to have machinery do their work for them.

Refusing to give in to the "whims of Farmers and Indians," Reed advised that losing some of the crop or growing less grain was preferable to the use of machinery.[128] He did not believe, however, that any grain need be lost by harvesting with hand implements. Loss in yield was due entirely to the "half-heartedness" of employees, but with greater firmness they could manage to save their crop. If grain was being lost, the solution was for the farmers to confine their acreage to what they could handle. Reed informed one official that "any loss suffered in the course of enforcing the policy will prove in the long run true economy."[129] Supplementary hay, Reed naively assumed, could be acquired after harvesting, and he saw no conflict between the two operations.

Farm instructors were told not to meddle in the issue of machinery but simply to obey orders. Agents explained to all employees working in the fields with the Indians that "it was their duty to set aside completely any opinions they might hold regarding the feasibility, etc., of carrying out this policy, and to act and speak always as if they had full confidence in the wisdom of getting the Indians to cut their grain by hand, and in the possibility of succeeding in doing so."[130] Inspectors were instructed neither to convene nor be present at meetings with Indian farmers, as this would give an "exaggerated importance" to their requests for machinery.[131] Instead, they were to defend vigorously the department's policy and severely discourage labour-saving machinery. Political opposition to the peasant policy was also dismissed by Reed. "It may distress one in opposition to the Government to see what he does not understand the reasons of, but I fancy if we were to pamper up Indians in idleness while we supply machinery to do their work, the opposition would soon give tongue to the distress occasioned by such a course."[132]

Department employees risked dismissal if they refused to comply with the peasant farming policy. Agent Finlayson of the Touchwood Hills agency was fired because he would not "make his Indians provide hay and harvest their crop without the use of labour saving implements as the department is opposed to for Indian use."[133] Despite this powerful lever of enforcement, Reed's policy showed signs of crumbling by 1896. That year many disgruntled and angry agents defied orders and used machinery. At his Regina office, Commissioner Forget was harangued by officials requesting permission to use machinery. It was of vital importance that the crop be cut as soon as it was ready because of severe hailstorms that season. Seventy thousand acres of crop had been destroyed in western Manitoba in one storm, and many settlers had been hailed out near Regina. Forget granted permission to several agents to borrow or hire binders from settlers. He informed Reed that authority was granted only on the understanding that the agent "make a bona fide effort to secure the whole crop, or as much of it as possible, by hand appliances and it is understood that only upon all such efforts failing to secure the crop with sufficient rapidity either on account of the state of the weather or the inadequacy of the workers, is the authority to employ machinery to be made use of."[134]

During the harvest of 1896 some agents openly defied the peasant policy or complied only halfheartedly. Agent MacDonald of Crooked Lakes stated that no efforts were made that season by himself or his staff to make the Indians harvest their grain without the aid of labour-saving machinery. Earlier attempts to do so had failed; the Indians became discouraged and would not work. MacDonald could not simply ask farmers such as Gaddie, O'Soup, and Nepahpahness to do away with their machinery, as they had large acreages under crop and all the necessary implements. Although he claimed to have done his honest best to carry out the department's policy, the Indians were "so far advanced" with such large acres of grain that he could make no headway. He had tried to get those with smaller crops to harvest by hand, but even they had someone with a binder cut their crop for them. Had he expressed "violent opposition to the Indians, I should only have achieved the result of making the smaller farmers so sullen, that they would have put in no crop at all, had they the prospect to cut it with a sickle, and the large farmers would have met me with contempt, and gone their own way, with a wide breach between us." MacDonald noted that the harvest of 1896, amounting to over 9,000 bushels of wheat, as well as 3,500 bushels of oats, "would have been impossible without implements."[135]

J.P. Wright, the Touchwood Hills agent, also admitted that the harvest in his agency was accomplished with the aid of labour-saving machinery. Gordon and Poor Man's bands each owned a self-binder, and it was useless, the agent claimed, to ask them to cut their grain with sickles and cradles, for they would not do it. Wright reminded Reed, as all the agents did, that the Indians were busy with haying at harvest time and the grain had to be cut with as little delay as possible.[136] Other agents in the North-West in 1896 claimed to have accomplished one-half or less of the harvest by hand methods before they were obliged to save the balance of the crop with machinery.[137] Reed remained adamant, demanding that the peasant policy be rigorously pursued.[138] Although he admitted that machinery might be necessary if Indians had large crops, he nonetheless expected that a strong effort be made to carry out the policy for all others.

INDIAN PROTESTS TO PEASANT FARMING AND OTHER RESTRICTIONS

The agents' reports reveal some glimpses of how Indian farmers reacted to the peasant farming policy. As noted, many became angry and discouraged, while some refused to work and gave up farming altogether. The outlets for Indian protest during the 1890s were few. Grievances related to instructors and agents generally went no further. Inspectors were not allowed to hold audiences with the Indians. The published reports of agents and inspectors were to divulge only that "which it was desired the public should believe."[139] Visiting officials, journalists, or other observers were taken to a few select agencies. When the governor general planned a visit to the West in 1895, Reed arranged to have him visit only the most advanced reserves, such as Crooked Lakes.[140] The August visit was to be hastily diverted elsewhere, however, if the crops failed on the reserves.

An 1893 petition from the headmen of the Pasquah and Muscowpetung bands, addressed to the House of Commons, succeeded in gaining a little attention from officials in Ottawa. The Indians resented the restrictions on their freedom and the interference of the agent in all their affairs. They were angry that they were not allowed to take their grain to the mill without the permission of the instructor; as a result, families did not have an adequate supply of flour on hand. They claimed that rations were not sufficient to support the old people unable to work. They protested the permit system. "Whenever we have a chance to sell anything and make some money the Agent or Instructor steps in between us and the party who wants to buy, and says we have no power to sell: if this is to continue how will we be able to make a living and support ourselves? We are not even allowed to sell cattle that we raise ourselves." The petitioners wished to purchase a binder, noting that taking off the grain with a cradle was too slow, but "the Commissioner objected to us buying a Binder as he said it would make the young men lazy." The Indians claimed that "when we ask the Agent for farm implements he sends us to the Commissioner, and he in turn sends us back to the Agent. This has completely discouraged us, as our old implements are worn out," and "many of the fields we used to farm are now all grown over with grass."[141]

The petition received no action; the allegations were dismissed and the document filed away and forgotten. Hayter Reed denied the legitimacy of and refuted the charges and grievances. In a memo dealing with the petition, Reed stated that Treaty Four did not promise support for old people unable to work. Friends and relatives were expected to care for the needy according to their ability. He explained that Indians were required to have permission to take their grain to the mill to prevent them from gristing what they should retain for seed or for flour later on. Reed vigorously defended his department. The permit system, he argued, was a necessity. Without it, "Indians would be defrauded, and would part with hay while their cattle was left to starve – grain and roots which they require for sustenance, etc. etc., squander the proceeds, and then come on the Government for support. Our object is to make them acquire the limit of stock to afford them an annual surplus to dispose of, meanwhile when they have a steer or other animal which can not be profitably kept longer they are allowed to sell. If left to their own discretion there would not be a head of stock left."[142]

In the tradition of department officials, agent J.B. Lash placed the blame for the petition on the sinister motives of one man, which discredited all the grievances. Interpreter Thomas Stevenson was in "comfortable" circumstances, with a few cattle, horses, and implements, but was bitter, according to Lash, because his application for rations had been refused. Stevenson had been trying to make the Indians dissatisfied and had been urging them to "send a Petition to Ottawa," hoping that by doing so Lash would be removed from his position. The Indians, Lash believed, simply wanted more rations and more cash for whatever they did.[143]

The 1893 petition from the Pasquah and Muscowpetung Indians was dismissed, but in the 1890s a protest such as theirs was not an isolated incident. Discontent over the peasant policy, permit system, and other restrictions was widespread. In 1893 the Dakota of the Oak River reserve in southwestern Manitoba began a protest over the same issues, particularly the permit system, and they succeeded in receiving wider attention.[144] The Oak River Dakota, pronounced by Inspector T.P. Wadsworth in 1891 to be "in the van of Indian farmers in this country," had 540 acres under cultivation, 350 head of livestock, and a number of implements, mowers and rakes, binders, and a threshing machine.[145] All had been accomplished without the aid of a resident farm instructor and without benefit of the original home farm program. A farm instructor was stationed on the reserve in 1891, however, and he began to carry out department policy with respect to labour-saving machinery. The permit system was also strictly implemented so that control of the proceeds of the grain crop was taken out of the hands of the farmers. Instructor Scott was to see that no grain left the reserve without a permit. The department professed particular concern that certain individuals owed money to implement dealers. Three who were singled out as heavily in debt owed $214, $147, and $119 to Massey Harris.[146] Here and on other reserves, the permit system became a means of paying off debts over the heads of the Indians. Grain buyers, when presented with a permit, were asked to pay a sum to the implement dealers, a sum to the instructor, and any balance to the Indians. From his fund, the instructor was to pay certain bills, such as those for threshing rentals.

Residents of Oak River found the presence of the instructor and his regulations an unnecessary encumbrance on their freedom after years of handling their own financial affairs. Three Dakota visited

Ottawa in 1893 to explain their grievances, and petitions and letters were sent to department officials. Their main objection was that the permit system discouraged their interest in farming, as they did not know what they got in return for their crops. They protested that they could not sell their grain without a permit, and they resented the fact that the farm instructor kept some of the proceeds.[147] The Dakota received the standard response from the department; they were told they had no grounds for complaint and that they should obey their instructor, who had their best interests in view. As usual, "outsiders" were blamed for fomenting discontent.[148] Department officials variously blamed the missionary at Oak River, another man believed to be scheming for the position of instructor on the reserve, and a Dakota from a neighbouring reserve who was associated with the Presbyterian church.

The Dakota continued the protest, however, by defying regulations and marketing their grain without permits. The department then took action against the grain buyers at Oak Lake, who were fined for buying grain from Indians without permits. The buyers were enraged at this action and at the entire permit system, which they felt turned them into collection agencies for Massey Harris.[149] The grain buyers were convinced that the government was working in the interests of the implement dealers. The fact that the presiding magistrate at the grain buyers' convictions was the agent for Massey Harris at nearby Griswold did little to allay their suspicions. At least one grain dealer threatened to instruct his agents not to buy wheat from Indians, with or without permits, as the best means of protecting the interests of his company.[150]

The Oak River residents succeeded in attracting the attention and sympathy of the Virden *Chronicler*, which demanded an investigation into the grievances of the Indians and the grain buyers about the permit system. The citizens of Oak Lake, Griswold, and Oak River were reported to be "greatly incensed" over the actions of department officials. It was felt that the matter might assume serious proportions, "and we do not want another rebellion." The permit system, it was claimed, had become a source of annoyance and injury to the Indians, as they farmed their own land, worked hard all summer, yet through the "obnoxious order are not allowed the full benefit of the fruit of their labour. They are thus placed at a disadvantage in competition with their white and more highly civilized neighbors." The *Chronicler* considered that the way in which permits were issued was very irregular and peculiar. Some of them read: "Pay Indian $2.00, pay John Jones $3.00, and pay the Massey Harris Co. balance of proceeds on sale of grain." In this way, parties who purchased from Indians were turned into collection bureaus, the article continued. In light of the recent convictions and fines, grain buyers had almost concluded not to purchase any more grain from Indians except at low rates: "An Indian's wheat is just as good as a white man's but dealers claim that by purchasing it, [they] are making themselves liable for prosecution." The item concluded: "White civilized men often find it annoying to have to submit to obnoxious regulations and Orders-in-Council and how much more so do the untutored children of the plains, who but a few short years ago, roamed at will over the prairies, knowing no master but their own sweet fancy."[151]

The Dakota continued to protest the permit system in 1894 with a letter and a petition, and they also asked that the farm instructor be removed. Officials were eventually persuaded to hold an investigation into their complaints. Citizens of Griswold were interviewed first. All declared that the permit system was decidedly in the interests of the Indians, and all spoke in favour of the farm instructor. At two days of meetings held on the Oak River reserve, the residents were divided into two factions. The largest group of twenty-five supported the protest. A group of ten, led by Chief Pat, advocated compliance with the rules and regulations of the department. The complainants stated that they no longer cared whether they raised large crops because they never knew what they got in return for them. They admitted to selling their wheat without permits contrary to the rules of the department. One farmer defiantly stated that he relied on his own opinion when to sell and that he would sooner give his grain away for pig feed than be governed by the permit system. Supporters of the department claimed that the others spoke nonsense and that without the agent, instructor, and the regulations there would be alcohol and crime on the reserve. They did not approve of the petitions, letters, and the visit to Ottawa, as they knew all complaints should go through the agent.[152]

On the basis of the inquiry, Wadsworth concluded that all evidence was in favour of the permit system and the farm instructor. He believed the Dakota were attributing their distressed condition to their farm instructor and the permit system, when their debt burden and series of poor crops were at the root of the problem. Once again, outside agitators were seen to be behind the protest. An outsider, in Wadsworth's opinion, gave the Dakota the idea they had "the right to dictate to the Department." Wadsworth also believed that the Dakota were lazy and that this was at the heart of the matter. Indians would rather "trust to luck" than work if they could get out of it.[153]

The agent was instructed to read to the Oak River residents a letter from Hayter Reed informing them that the permit system was in their best interests. If the department did not control their business affairs, they would only deteriorate. Reed wanted the Dakota to know that the purchase of machinery on credit had adversely affected white settlers to the extent that laws were being considered to control sales on credit by implement dealers. Reed expressed strong disapproval of the protestors, for trying to find fault with their instructor and for refusing obedience to lawful instruction. He asked the agitators to emulate the example set by Chief Pat, whose conduct the department approved of.[154]

The protest led by the Dakota was the most successful of those in the 1890s, but it led to no reconsideration or revamping of the permit system. Yet the 1893 Pasquah and Muscowpetung petition and the Dakota protest marked the beginning of a lengthy tradition of western Indian protest against this system. The consistent point of the protest was that the permit system curbed enthusiasm for farming among reserve residents. Along with severalty and peasant farming, it further precluded Indians from commercial farming, as they could not buy, sell, or transact business. Indian farmers had no control over the marketing aspects of their economic strategies. An eventual consequence of the permit system was that grain and stock buyers hesitated to do business with Indians.

Indians farther east, where the permit system was in place earlier, began to protest well before the 1890s. In 1883 Indians at Long Sault of northwestern Ontario objected to restrictions forbidding them to dispose of surplus corn, potatoes, fish, and hay. In one example, a chief had ten sacks of potatoes, which he could have sold but which were eventually all frozen and lost. His son had offered to sell seventy bushels of potatoes to a lumbering camp, but no one would purchase them because of the penalty he would incur. One chief maintained that "those restrictions have a tendency to discourage them from cultivating more land than is required to produce enough food for themselves and families." Another stated that "they were told to cultivate the soil, and forbidden to sell the products of the same, consequently their young men would not engage in farming."[155]

EFFECTS OF THE RESTRICTIVE POLICY

The department's "kindly supervision" over the sale of the Indians' produce, seen as a regulation necessary for their welfare, raised resentment and led to a sense of despondency and defeat. Western Canadian Indian authors claim that the permit system, along with other regulations, created a listless and discouraged people. "Robbed of pride, independence and initiative, many willing and honest workers had been destroyed by the 'loaded gun' in the permit system meant to protect them. They usually assumed an outward attitude of indifference but underneath it they felt very deeply a sense of failure and the waste of their life."[156]

In his book *Voices of the Plains Cree*, Edward Ahenakew portrayed a fictional character Old Keyam, who tried to fit himself to the new ways in his youth and met with success. Suddenly he slackened all effort and ceased to work or to care. (*Keyam*, a Cree word with many shades of meaning, has been interpreted as "I do not care" or "The hell with it.") Old Keyam described how every man on the reserve had to go begging for a permit every time he wanted to sell even a load of hay.

This may be "kindly supervision", but it is most wretchedly humbling to many a worthy fellow to have to go, with assumed indifference to ask or beg for a permit to sell one load of hay that he has cut himself, on his own reserve, with his own horses and implements ... what kind of policy is it that aims at bringing a people to a point of self-respect, and then by the nature of its regulations destroys the very thing for which it works ... For myself, I think that I would rather starve than go to beg for such a trifling thing as a permit to sell one load of hay, while I am trying to make every hour of good weather count.[157]

Old Keyam resented the fact that Indians had to waste days in some cases, waiting to receive permits, while their families were short of food, or when they were in a hurry or busy. They might have driven miles from another reserve only to find the agent away. Several trips might have to be made before an Indian received a hearing. On some agencies, the permit system became a disciplinary device in the hands of the agent. An agent could refuse to grant a permit to an Indian he did not like, totally crippling his ability to buy necessary implements, seed, or stock.[158]

Resentment was particularly high over restrictions on the sale of cattle, which was also regulated by the permit system. It did not matter whether a man was destitute or owed money; he had no say about when or whether he could sell or slaughter. As Old Keyam explained, such restrictions meant that the Indian with cattle but no money could not plan in the same way as a white man. "He is told that the commissioner has said that no cattle are to be sold until the fall. It is useless to plan under this system, yet planning is what successful work requires. He does not get the chance to practise the adjusting of his work to his means."[159] Old Keyam knew Indians who would not invest in cattle when they had money, after they sold furs, for example, because once the animals were branded ID, that would be the end of any say they had in the matter.

Indian authors describe a pattern of an initial positive response to farming, attended with some success, that was eroded especially because of the weight of crippling regulations.[160] Joe Dion wrote in *My Tribe the Crees* that it was "small wonder that the best men in our ranks eventually got discouraged and simply gave up trying because even the most humble wage earner will resist a domineering employer when his direct supervision gets to be a hindrance rather than an asset."[161] Dion believed that because of the permit system and other regulations, the cattle business on his reserve died and many discontinued farming entirely. Even some of the most successful farmers like Louis O'Soup gave up farming. In 1898 he left the Cowessess reserve and transferred his band membership to Pine Creek in Manitoba where he made his living by hunting.[162]

Outsiders found conditions on prairie reserves disturbing. Missionary John McDougall often railed against the living conditions as well as the rigid regime that required a permit for all activities.

> He cannot visit a friend on a neighboring reserve without a permit. He cannot go to the nearest market town unless provided with a permit. In what was his own country and on his own land he cannot travel in peace without a permit. He cannot buy and sell without a permit. He may raise cattle but he cannot sell them unless the government official allows. He may cultivate the soil but he is not the owner of his own produce. He cannot sell firewood or hay from the land that is his by Divine and citizen right, and thus reap the result of his own industry unless subject to the caprice or whim of one who often becomes an autocrat. Said an Indian to me a few days since "I raise cattle, they are not mine, my wood I cannot sell – my own hay I cannot do what I would with – I cannot even do as I like with the fish I may catch.[163]

In 1899 a resident of Prince Albert, William Miller Sr, wrote to the minister of the interior that in passing through the Duck Lake and Carlton reserves, he noted "no less than five fields [which can] be seen from the trail now without a bushel of grain sown in them ... that previously used to be an example to the settlers around."[164] Reports that Indians were utterly destitute were common in the 1890s. A teacher on Thunderchild's reserve near Battleford wrote in

1893 that the people there were obliged to eat leaves to keep them from hunger.[165] That same year Rev. Leonard Dawson, a Church of England missionary in the Touchwood Hills, stated in several newspaper interviews that "I consider that the Indians at Touchwood are being half-starved. I have carefully calculated what they receive, and their rations will feed them three days out of the seven." The annual reports of the department and the Indian exhibit at the World's Fair in Chicago that year reminded Rev. Dawson "of the drawing classes at School just before show or inspection day, at the end of a term. They do not convey a fair idea of the general state of the Indian, and are only a fancy picture of the situation."[166]

Hayter Reed devoted a great deal of energy to the creation of this "fancy picture." He organized his department's contribution to Canada's exhibit at the Chicago World's Fair, which received much attention from the press. As noted in the Ottawa *Journal* on 29 April 1893, "There is nothing of which [Canada] has more reason to feel satisfied than the samples of her redskin wards and their little ones, and their products ... The exhibit will be one of the most valuable from the standpoint of our common humanity that the entire World's Fair can furnish." Part of the display was placed on view in the reading room of the House of Commons before shipment to Chicago. It consisted of large frames of photos of Indians at work in their fields, stacking hay, harvesting, and threshing, and of their houses and barns. On 9 March the *Journal* stated that "the advance made in the arts and civilization is truly wonderful and is due to the policy of the governments towards the Indians, and the efficiency and faithfulness of the agents and missionaries in carrying it out." The exhibit in Chicago was much grander, consisting of Indian children from Manitoba and the North-West working at their trades and household duties, while alongside them were displayed trophies and curios from the "warpath" days. No part of the Canadian exhibit had more visitors than this section.[167] On 19 September the correspondent for the Montreal *Gazette* congratulated Hayter Reed for having "portrayed to all visitors the splendid treatment and the intelligent supervision and provision of the Canadian Government for these wards of the country ... it is an 'object' lesson indeed for other nations." Reed also arranged a magnificent display of people, including himself, in Indian costume for Lady Aberdeen's fancy dress ball at Rideau Hall in February 1896.[168]

As noted those who had the opportunity to view actual conditions on reserves seldom found much to boast about regarding Canada's treatment of Indians. Official pronouncements of the Department of Indian Affairs emphasized that Indian interests were paramount and that such measures as the peasant policy and the permit system were undertaken out of concern for their welfare and development. In this period and well into the twentieth century, however, the Indians' interests were consistently sacrificed to those of the new settlers, and there was little concern to develop independent Indian production. White settlers proved loathe to see the Indians establish any enterprise that might compete with or draw business away from them. Organized groups were able to influence the course of Indian policy by petitioning and lobbying their Members of Parliament. Agents on the spot and visiting officials were pressured from neighbouring whites. The Indians' interests were easily sacrificed, as they had no vote and no economic power. The pattern continued into the twentieth century when effective pressure was mounted to have the Indians surrender reserve land suitable for agriculture.

This pattern was all too common in the British colonial world of the late nineteenth century. In Kenya, for example, the colonial administration assumed that the most effective way to exploit the country's vast resources was to establish a viable community of immigrant white farmers.[169] The economic interests of the indigenous population were thus not advanced, and African agriculture was systematically suppressed. Roads and railways bypassed African reserves, denying access to markets. Heavy taxation prevented the accumulation of capital necessary for efficient agriculture, ensuring instead a steady flow of cheap labour. Africans in Kenya were forbidden to grow coffee, the most lucrative cash crop.

In South Africa, an African "peasantry" emerged, responded positively to the new colonial market economy in the nineteenth century, and began to account for a large share of agricultural exports.[170] These farmers responded vigorously and effectively to new market conditions. They experimented with new crops, adopted new tools, and entered agricultural production on a commercial basis. But this stage was short-lived. The price for competing too successfully with white farmers was a barrage of legislative measures designed to inhibit African farming, while white agriculture was aided by a massive program of grants and subsidies. By the 1880s peasant production began to decline, and once fertile agricultural communities became pockets of rural poverty. In southern Zimbabwe (then Rhodesia) measures were taken to ensure that African farmers were not in a position to compete with immigrant European farmers, who benefited from special tax measures and favourable marketing arrangements. Their African counterparts meanwhile had limited land, training, and access to credit. Policies were designed to maintain the different standards of living of each group. As one com-

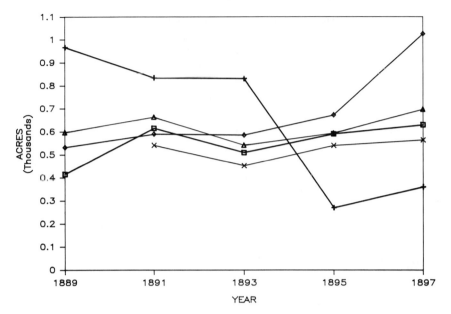

Figure 3. Acres under cultivation, selected Indian agencies, 1889–97: □ = Onion Lake; + = Battleford; ◊ = Duck Lake; △ = Crooked Lakes; x = Carlton
Sources: Canada, House of Commons, Sessional Papers, vol. 23, no. 12 (1889), 180–91; vol. 25, no. 14 (1891), 254–73; vol. 27, no. 14 (1893), 312–31; vol. 24, no. 10 (1895), 372–411; vol. 32, no. 14 (1897), 436–51.

mentator has noted, "The whole system of economic and social control was geared to protecting European incomes and maintaining high levels of living among the European minority at the expense of the African majority."[171]

Similarly, in western Canada, measures like the permit system, severalty, and peasant farming combined to undermine and atrophy agricultural development on reserves. Not surprisingly, reserve farming made litle progress during the 1890s. See figures 3 and 4. On some reserves the acreage increased moderately, while on others it stayed at about the same or even decreased. The administration acted, not to promote the agriculture of the indigenous population, but to provide an optimum environment for the immigrant settler. Comparisons between the situation in colonial Africa and that in western Canada, however, remain dubious, as the Africans were always in the majority. Yet in the 1880s and 1890s the West was sparsely settled by non-Indians, and a similar anxiety to see an immigrant farming class established was evident. After 1885 immigration to the West was at a virtual standstill and the drought years of the 1880s did little to attract settlers. Consideration was not

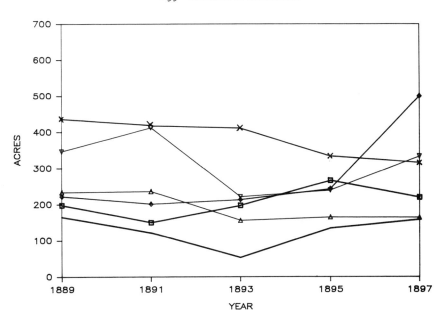

Figure 4. Acres under cultivation, selected Indian agencies, 1889–97; □ = Moose Mountain; — = Fort Pelly; ◊ = Assiniboine; △ = File Hills; x = Muscowpetung; ▽ = Touchwood Hills
Sources: Canada, House of Commons, *Sessional Papers*, vol. 23, no. 12 (1889), 180–91; vol. 25, no. 14 (1891), 254–73; vol. 27, no. 14 (1893), 312–31; vol. 24, no. 10 (1895), 372–411; vol. 32, no. 14 (1897), 436–51.

given to the possibility of enhancing Indian production as a means of creating an export sector, although it was grumbled in the Regina *Leader* of 10 October 1892 that it would be preferable to make farmers of Indians and have them settle on empty lands than to bring in "Russians and Jews." Instead, new settlers were to be attracted, and policies were determined by the need to maintain the viability of this community.

In the United States, government policy of the 1880s led to a marked decline in Indian farming.[172] Before general allotment was enacted in 1887, reservation agriculture had grown steadily but was followed by stagnation and regression. American Indian policy, though distinct from the Canadian in many ways, was similarly shaped by non-Indian economic interests.

The motivations behind the severalty and peasant farming policies had very little to do with the encouragement of agriculture on reserves. Hayter Reed's central concern was to erode further the Indians' land base until eventually reserves were abolished altogether. Severalty was a short-cut policy through which Reed hoped to accelerate the process of Indian enfranchisement, which meant the end of reserves. Severalty would confine the Indians within circumscribed boundaries, and their "surplus" land could be defined and sold. The veneration of private property, self-sufficiency, and individual initiative gave severalty its veneer of humanitarianism and allowed many to believe that what was being done was in the best interests of the Indian. The convenient doctrine that the Indians must be taught to farm was once again drawn upon to justify divesting the Indians of their land. The Indians saw through the rhetoric and attempted to oppose severalty. They realized that what was at stake was their land.

The peasant farming policy served to justify severalty. It would demonstrate that Indians could indeed subsist on small plots of land without modern methods or equipment. To encourage or enhance farming under western conditions was clearly not at the basis of this policy. The agents reported that the program was not feasible, given the geographic and climatic conditions of the prairies. It was evident that the simple farming life of the individualistic, self-sufficient yeoman would not have a significant part in the future of the West. Farmers were having to adopt the costly technology, large acreages, and dry-land techniques that western conditions demanded, or be left behind permanently. Yet, as with earlier programs, officials and politicians could readily fall back on a host of widely accepted myths about the Indians' supposed cultural unsuitability for farming to account for "failure" or tardy progress.

CHAPTER SEVEN

Without a Leg to Stand On: Undermining Reserve Agriculture

The Laurier Liberals were fortunate to win the election of 23 June 1896 just at the dawn of a new age of prosperity in Canada. Conditions favourable to the National Policy of industrialization, east-west railway traffic, and western settlement had at long last come into being. The end of a drought cycle ushered in a period of greater rainfall on the prairies. In the wheat boom of the first decade of the new century, the hard spring wheat of the West became the leading export staple of the Canadian economy. As the frontier of free homestead land closed in the United States, the Canadian prairies became the site of the last great land rush in North American history. Land values on the prairies rose dramatically and interest in the Indian lands of western Canada increased. Indian farmers of the West, however, had little place in this new age of prosperity. By the turn of the century agriculture did not form the basis of a stable reserve economy. After that date, that likelihood faded even further as the new administrators of Indian Affairs promoted land surrenders, which further limited the agricultural capacity of reserves. As in the 1870s Indians were encouraged to sell their land as a means of acquiring the necessities to begin a life of agriculture.

The central aim of Indian administration under the Liberals was to keep expenses at an absolute minimum, to centralize operations in Ottawa, and to see that patronage was extended to Liberals rather than Conservatives.[1] Clifford Sifton, minister of the interior and superintendent general of Indian affairs, immediately began overhauling Indian administration in the interests of efficiency and economy by slashing budgets, dismissing personnel, and reducing salaries. Farm instructors, for example, who had earned up to $600 a year had their salaries reduced to a range of between $300 and

$480, and many were dismissed entirely, which indicated that reserve agriculture was not a priority of the new government.[2]

One of Sifton's first actions was to place the Departments of the Interior and Indian Affairs under a single deputy minister. Deputies A.M. Burgess of the Interior and Hayter Reed were dismissed, a move that was not then customary practice on the part of an incoming minister.[3] There was controversy about Reed's expenditure as a public official at Battleford in 1881. This controversy was used in part as justification for his dismissal. In a letter to Sifton in 1897, Reed blamed the charges against him on "certain clerks" within his own department, who "as soon as a change of government occurred, caballed against me, employed their leisure time, of which some have too much, in intriguing newspaper attacks, and, at any rate, in one instance, hunted the fyles in an effort to find something calculated to throw discredit on me."[4] But Reed's career in the civil service abruptly ended. He was given the humiliating choice of a lower position or superannuaton. Reed chose the latter and from 1 July 1897 was placed upon the retired list at the age of only forty-eight. "My services," Reed later bemoaned, "were dispensed with much against my consent, while I was in the prime of life and in good health of mind and body."[5] Reed appealed to Laurier, who replied that he could not interfere in the organization of the department and that his minister must exercise his own judgment. Laurier counselled Reed that "if you were to take the advice of a friend, I would think that you would serve your interest by quietly acquiescing."[6] In 1905 Reed found employment as manager-in-chief of the Canadian Pacific Railway's hotel department.

Many of the new faces appointed to posts in Indian Affairs were, like Sifton, residents of the West, but they were not by virtue of this more knowledgeable about or tolerant of Indians. Some viewed Indians merely as obstacles to western development, and some believed that programs aimed at "educating and elevating" them were foolhardy.[7] James A. Smart, a political friend of Sifton, was placed in charge of the Departments of Indian Affairs and the Interior. Smart, former mayor of Brandon and a hardware merchant, who was also involved in real estate, insurance, and the loans business, knew nothing about Indians.[8] The amalgamation of the two departments under one head tended to reinforce the view of Indians only in the context of western development, although in 1902 Indian Affairs was once again given its own deputy superintendent general when Frank Pedley, a Toronto lawyer, was appointed. Other new men in the department had "little direct contact with Indians, and most were relatively unsympathetic, if not 'hardline' in their attitudes."⁹

THE FILE HILLS COLONY

The encouragement of agriculture on reserves was not completely ignored under the Liberal administration. It was during the Laurier years that the File Hills Colony won even international recognition. The colony was a showpiece of Indian farming, the department's model farm to which visiting dignitaries, officials, journalists, and just the curious were taken. It was photographed and written about often. By 1914 there were 33 farmers in the colony of 134 people, and 2,000 acres of wheat and oats were under cultivation. Each farmer was equipped with up-to-date implements and owned in common two steam threshing outfits.¹⁰ The colonists lived in comfortable whitewashed homes furnished with pictures, clocks, sewing machines, and rugs. Some had splendid homes and barns that surpassed those of their white neighbours in the district. There was a Roman Catholic and a Presbyterian church in the colony, each constructed and maintained by its congregation. There was also a cottage hospital, built by the department.

The colonists, all carefully selected graduates of industrial and residential schools, were under the constant supervision of the agent and farm instructors and were governed by rigid rules and regulations. Women, for example, were not allowed to visit frequently with one another, as they were to be attending to their duties in the home. The use of Indian languages was strictly forbidden.¹¹ Church personnel and employees of the File Hills Presbyterian Boarding School also helped oversee the activities of the colonists. Sermons imparted correct values and attitudes, such as industry, self-discipline, and punctuality. Leisure time was controlled as well. Traditional, popular recreations or ceremonies, even fiddle dances, were prohibited, in place of brass bands, sewing circles, and lecture groups. The colony had a fine brass band, which entertained in the schoolhouses and town halls of the surrounding settlements. (Two of the musicians were "natural comedians," who "never failed to bring down the house.")¹² In the winter literary evenings were held and a farmers' institute sponsored visiting lecturers. Baseball was the acceptable summer recreation as was the annual File Hills agricultural exhibition, which did not afford the opportunity for drinking, gambling, and wearing traditional attire that other fairs offered.

In the effort to control and monitor all aspects of life on the colony,

File Hills was similar to settlements advocated by individuals and charitable organizations as a means of improving and reforming the needy, the urban working class, and a variety of groups such as criminals and veterans.[13] The Salvation Army, for example, promoted farm colonies to uplift thieves, drunkards, and other "lost souls" of the city and make them industrious, honest, pious, and thrifty citizens. In "social settlements" such as two in Gary, Indiana, in the early twentieth century, Europeans, Mexicans, and Afro-Americans from the U.S. South were weaned away from their old culture and indoctrinated with American customs and values.[14] The program included home visits, health clinics, classes in cooking and sewing, and religious services.

William Morris Graham, File Hills agent since 1897, founded the File Hills Colony in 1901.[15] In that year the File Hills and Muscowpetung agencies had been amalgamated and Graham had been placed in charge. Before that time Hayter Reed had endorsed the idea of setting up a farm colony for former pupils rather than allowing them to return to the reserve, a dangerous, "retrograde" step. In his day no steps had been taken to establish such a settlement.[16] An effort was made instead to administer an outing system under which girls and boys were placed in neighbouring farm homes to work as domestics or hired hands but were still supervised by their school principal. This program of supervised out-service was allowed to lapse, however, under the Liberal government, as it was expected that Indian children would return to their reserves upon graduation.[17] In 1905 Indian Commissioner David Laird wrote that he "discouraged the employment of our ex-pupils in cities and towns where they are exposed to intoxicating liquor and other temptations than on reserves." Male graduates were to farm on the reserves and female graduates were to be "suitable helpmates to prevent retrogression."[18]

Much ink was spilled over the problem of "retrogression" in the years around the turn of the century. More children graduated from schools, but once they returned to their reserves, the results became less and less encouraging. Educators and department officials were concerned that rather than acting as the "leaven" of civilization on reserves, the former pupils "reverted" to Indian habits and went "back to the blanket." Some attributed the difficulties to the chasm created between student and parent because of the long period of separation. The returning student was laughed at because of his un-Indian ways and was "suspended between heaven and earth." Most authorities, however believed that their progress was retarded, not by the chasm between parents and children, but by the "proximity to, and influence of, family connections of the old type who oppose submission to the new order of things," combined with a lack of the means to begin farming.[19] In 1901 Father J. Hugonard of the Qu'Appelle school wrote that as few graduates had the "means to start for themselves, their progress is uncertain after leaving the routine and discipline of the school, and [it] depends very much on their environment whether they marry and settle down, or have to live with their parents who, if pagan, too often exercise a detrimental influence over them."[20]

The Department of Indian Affairs gave assistance to select former pupils who showed an inclination to establish themselves as farmers on the reserves. Aid in the way of oxen, wagons, harness, seed, and materials for building a home was loaned, the value to be repaid within a certain number of years, usually four. Girls were given a small sum with which to purchase "useful articles" such as sewing machines or furniture. Indian agents drew up lists of former pupils and recommended some as clean, industrious, and worthy of assistance but described others simply as "no good."[21] There was disappointment, however, with many who were given assistance. The authorities generally agreed with Rev. W. McWhinney of the Crowstand Boarding School, who believed that the problem lay with proximity to the older "lodge" Indians. "It is not pleasant," he wrote, "to see our best and most hopeful boys shipwrecked by these derelicts."[22]

The separation of the "lodge" Indians from the school Indians was the method pursued at the File Hills Colony, and one that extended the process begun in the institutions. In its structured activity, discipline, and daily supervision, the colony was also very much like the schools. "Hardly a day passes," Graham wrote in 1911, "that some officer of the department does not visit them, and if there has been success, it has been the result of this close and constant supervision."[23]

The colony was distinct from school life in that participation was voluntary. Colonists had to agree to join and they were free to withdraw, as some indeed did. Nor could they simply be ousted from the colony if Graham found their behaviour unsuitable. There is evidence that while colonists were pleased to accept the economic opportunities offered by the settlement, they did not intend to give up their cultural heritage. They were expected to assist Graham to "further the interests of the Department" in return for their admission, but they did not always yield to his authority.[24] Indian dances, feasts, and funerals continued to take place, although in secret.[25] In 1910 Joseph Ironquill, a well-established farmer, headed a movement to "start dancing on the colony." In 1911 Ironquill also led the Peepeekisis band's opposition to Graham's desire to admit fifty new graduates to the colony, although Graham eventually acquired the necessary consent of the band. There was little Graham could do to remove those, like Ironquill, who opposed his authority, but he wrote to his superior that "a serious mistake was made the day this man was admitted to the Colony, and if there is any way by which he could be removed it would mean a great deal for the future harmony and progress of the Colony."[26]

In his official reports, however, Graham boasted about the accomplishments of Ironquill and other colony farmers. Ironquill's fields were a "magnificent site"; his buildings, "splendid."[27] He had an enormous forty by twenty-eight foot barn on a cement foundation with the name of his farmstead, Lakeview Farm, lettered on the front of it. He shipped grain by the carload and in 1914 had ten head of heavy horses, twenty head of cattle, as well as pigs and poultry. Ironquill managed his home by employing a white man and his wife year round, paying them five hundred dollars. He had his clothes made to order and used printed stationery for his business correspondence. In 1917–18 he attended the Manitoba Agricultural College in Winnipeg to make a special study of traction engines and their management. He became an expert with motor engines and did all his own repairs.[28]

Fred Dieter, the first boy to be admitted to the colony, also had a large house and barn, two granaries, and a full complement of machinery. He employed a white man as a farm labourer and paid him thirty dollars a month. For many consecutive years Dieter won a bronze shield, donated by Gov. Gen. Earl Grey on his first visit to the colony, which went to the farmer with the highest yield from a field of wheat. His was the first bride in the colony, Maybelle Coté, a granddaughter of Chief Gabriel Coté and a former pupil of the Regina Industrial School. Graham complimented Mrs Dieter highly as "a bright woman and competent housekeeper who kept her children neat and tidy."[29] He considered the hired man lucky to be employed in such a comfortable home.

Among other names continually cited as the most prosperous of the colony farmers were John R. Thomas, Ben Stonechild, Frank Dumont, John Bellegarde, and Mark Ward. They were described as hard workers who were willing to be guided and take advice and who caused no trouble. Their wives were praised for their abilities to keep clean homes, milk cows, make butter, and beautify the grounds of their homes. That there were some less sterling examples was only alluded to. In 1910 Graham wrote, "Of course there have been failures, some few doing little better than those Indians who have never been at school, but those who belong to that class are few, I am glad to say, and the proportion of those who have not done well is no greater than it would be among so many white settlers under similar conditions."[30] Between 1901 and 1911, three deserted the colony.

Graham tirelessly promoted the success of the colony he had founded. In 1907 he boasted that the colony was a "success," the results "phenomenal." "No white community," he wrote, "has made such a showing as these young people have. The style of farming here is not surpassed in any of the farming districts in the country."[31] The success of the colony enhanced Graham's reputation and played a role in his promotion from agent to inspector to commissioner for the prairie provinces, but his ultimate goal, the position of deputy superintendent general, eluded him.[32] All the while he directed the colony, however, Graham used every means at his disposal to see that "surplus" land on prairie reserves was surrendered, which militated directly against agricultural prosperity on reserves. Yet the colony at File Hills demonstrated to all that the goal of Graham's department was to make a farmer out of the Indian. Dignitaries were toured through the colony rather than through any other reserve. Frederick H. Abbott, secretary of the American Board of Indian Commissioners, toured the colony in 1914 as part of his eight-week study of the methods and policies of Indian administration in Canada. His publication, which was highly complimentary of the "simplicity, comprehensiveness, elasticity and efficiency" of Canadian Indian policy, presented the File Hills Colony as the best illustration of this system.[33] Despite Graham's claim that "if the same methods were adopted in other parts of the territories in twenty-five years the Indian population could be converted into thrifty and industrious people," no effort was made to duplicate the methods that proved so successful at File Hills.[34] As a showpiece for the public, and a means of acquiring promotion for Graham, the colony accomplished its objective.

According to Edward Ahenakew's Old Keyam, the colony was looked on with some suspicion and scepticism by other prairie Indians. Old Keyam too was concerned about the aimlessness and apathy apparent among former pupils, who were in his view robbed of initiative because they were accustomed to constant supervision, to acting under orders rather than making up their own minds. The File Hills colony, which perpetuated this rigid regime, was not the answer.

I've read about the colony at File Hills, made up of graduates from boarding school. They are said to be doing well. I have boasted about them myself when I had nothing better to do. But they are under the guidance of an official who has more authority than most, and he is an able man whose authority these young people accept in the way to which they become accustomed in boarding school ... I do not think that if he were asked to do the same thing again, that he would be willing. That colony is a tribute to his own ability and to his strong desire to improve the Indian, but I do not believe that it is a natural development.[35]

THE PUSH FOR LAND SURRENDER

While the File Hills Colony may have left the public impression that reserve farmers were prosperous, the major preoccupation of Indian Affairs administrators was to induce Indians to surrender substantial portions of their reserves, a policy which ran counter to efforts to create a stable agricultural economy on reserves. Under the Laurier government, the Indian Act was amended to facilitate that surrender. A 1906 amendment allowed the government to distribute in cash up to 50 per cent of the purchase price of the land, from a former ceiling of 10 per cent.[36] The reasoning behind the department's policy on land surrenders was explained in 1908.

So long as no particular harm nor inconvenience accrued from the Indians' holding vacant lands out of proportion to their requirements, and no profitable disposition thereof was possible, the department firmly opposed any attempt to induce them to divest themselves of any part of their reserves. Conditions, however, have changed, and it is now recognized that where Indians are holding tracts of farming or timber lands beyond their possible requirements and by so doing seriously impeding the growth of settlement, and there is such a demand as to ensure profitable sale, the product of which can be invested for the benefit of the Indians and relieve *pro tanto* the country of the burden of their maintenance, it is in the best interest of all concerned to encourage such sales.[37]

Not all department officials were in favour of an unrestrained, comprehensive program of reserve land surrender. Indian Commissioner David Laird often opposed specific surrenders on the grounds that the residents required the timber, hay, or farm land they were being asked to give up.[38] Laird believed in general, however, that reserve lands were "much in excess" of what the Indians could profitably use, "even when their maximum working power was reached."[39] Sifton himself was reluctant at least publicly to give in to pressure to surrender Indian land and insisted that the government's role was to act as trustee for the Indians.[40] His attitude did not prevent his civil servants, such as Smart and Pedley, from speculating in Indian lands, even while acting as the supposed representative of the Indians.[41]

Others in Indian administration, such as Frank Oliver, appointed superintendent general of Indian affairs in 1905, favoured the wholesale alienation of reserve land. Oliver even originally hoped reserve land could be thrown open for settlement without the consent of the Indians.[42] During his term of office, bands across the North-West were pressured to surrender, and hundreds of thousands of acres were alienated.[43] It was Oliver who introduced the 1906 amendment to the Indian Act that permitted the distribution of 50 per cent of the purchase price, a measure he predicted would accelerate the surrender process. In 1911 two amendments introduced by Oliver gave the department even greater powers of coercion. The most controversial was section 49a, known as the Oliver Act, which permitted the removal of Indians from any reserve next to a town of eight thousand or more inhabitants.[44]

Oliver had a low estimate of the potential of Indians; he believed they would never be "civilized" and would never profitably use their land. Therefore it was useless to try to make farmers out of Indians.[45] Their presence in areas of settlement, he was convinced, retarded the progress of a district. The Edmonton *Bulletin*, Oliver's newspaper, campaigned from the 1880s for the removal of Indians from areas of settlement. In 1901, for example, the *Bulletin* welcomed the surrender of the Passpasschase reserve.

The lesson of this reserve may very well be applied to the case of others similarly situated. The Indians make no practical use of the reserves which they hold. Where the land is good and well situated for market white men can turn it to much better account than the Indians do. A township in a good hunting country and near a fishing lake is more valuable to the Indians than a township of fine agricultural land near a railway station. It is a loss to the country to have such lands lying idle in the hands of the Indians when white men want to use them and are willing to pay for them. It is a loss to the Indian to compel him to remain in uncongenial surroundings to which he cannot adapt himself when he has the opportunity to remove to congenial surroundings, and by the sale of the land ensure himself a comfortable annuity.[46]

These sentiments received widespread support from farmers, townspeople, merchants, railroad executives, newspapermen, and speculators. All those with a stake in the expansion of agriculture were interested in reducing the size of Indian landholdings. Reserves were viewed as barriers to prosperity because it appeared the residents made no practical use of their land. It was widely believed that Indians held land out of proportion to the number of occupants. Large tracts of "idle," "unused," "excess," or "surplus" land were seen as retarding influences on the economic development of a district, especially when these tracts were first-class agricultural lands and were situated close to railways.

Letters from all over the country and the United States flooded in to the department, asking whether it was true that Indian reserves were to be thrown open for settlement and just how this land might be acquired.[47] Some requests were as simple as that of two residents of Mowbray, Manitoba, in 1908: "Dear Sir I hear that you are throwing indian [sic] reserves Yours Truly."[48] Toronto lawyers wrote on behalf of anonymous clients who wished to acquire a western Indian reserve. Parties in Seattle, Washington, wanted reserve land near the Touchwood Hills and requested information that would allow them to be there "just in time when, the first [reserve] is opened."[49] A resident of Grangeville, Idaho, wanted to know whether Indian land was for sale in Canada and whether this land had been cleared by Indian agents as it was in his country.[50]

In certain circles it was reasoned that land sales were in the best interests of the Indians, as reserves prevented assimilation into the mainstream of Canadian society.[51] Whatever arguments were expedient, no matter how contradictory, were used to advance the cause. In the case of some surrenders, such as that of portions of the Coté reserve for the Kamsack townsite, it was argued that the Indians should be close to an active, prosperous railway town with a well-established market, since they had to learn to make their living in the same way as other settlers.[52] In other circumstances, however, as in the case of the Roseau River reserve in Manitoba, it was claimed that Indians should occupy isolated territory where they would not be tempted to drift into the settlements.[53] There was also some public support for the notion that Indians should not occupy large tracts of land but be concentrated for their own benefit. As the Anglican bishop of Saskatchewan remarked in 1907, it "is time the Reserves were re-arranged and the Indians more concentrated. At present it takes a whole army of farm instructors and school teachers for a few hundred Indians."[54]

As had been argued earlier by Sir John A. Macdonald, surrender was in the best interests of the Indians because funds could be created from the sale of land. These funds could alleviate distress on the reserves and further relieve the country of the burden of supporting Indians. An incentive held out to the Indians was that if they disposed of their excess property, they would be able to obtain the means to become farmers. They were assured that, with the money from land surrenders, they could buy the machinery and horses required to start farming. It was proposed to the Coté Indians, for example, that the money be used to outfit young men willing and able to farm.[55] The cost of each outfit would eventually be repaid to the band and would provide a perpetual source of farm outfits. Ten years after the surrender, a new agent to the Coté band urged that a further surrender of land was required as the only way "to get these men in good shape again."[56] The surrender of more land would place the Indians further from the bad influence of the town, it was reasoned, and they would be able to work together communally at farming tasks.

Indian resistance to surrender was generally pronounced and adamant to begin with but was broken down through a variety of tactics. There were factions; bands were rarely unanimous in a decision to surrender. Much discontent was deflected by the lure of immediate cash payment, by the prospect of paying off debts, raising the standard of living, aiding the aged and infirm, and acquiring the means with which to farm.[57] In some cases not just one but a number of votes were taken until the desired results were achieved.

In the Qu'Appelle district of Treaty Four, many thousands of acres of reserve land were surrendered. Most negotiations were handled by W.M. Graham, who was enthusiastic in his pursuit of reserve land surrender. Graham was certain that reserve agriculture would never expand greatly and for that reason Indians could well afford to surrender extensive tracts.[58] Graham obtained large surrenders from the Pasquah and Muscowpetung bands in 1906 and 1909, and he eventually succeeded in securing surrenders of parts of the Crooked Lakes reserves, a goal long sought by local non-natives.

Pressure for the surrender of portions of the Crooked Lakes reserves, which, as previously noted, began in 1886, continued throughout the 1890s. Agent MacDonald's consistent response to such pressure was that the land coveted by the settlers, the southern boundary near the Canadian Pacific Railway line, contained the best hay land for the bands and that no amount of cash could adequately recompense them for the loss of this land.[59] Pressure intensified after 1896 with a new government in power and a new agent at the Crooked Lakes. In the Indian Affairs file dealing with the surrender is a sheet of stationery with the letterhead Rideau Club, Ottawa, and dated 25 February 1899, on which an anonymous cipher calculated the amount of land each Crooked Lake chief was "entitled" to.⁶⁰ It was reckoned that Ochapowace, for example, was entitled to twenty-four square miles. Twenty-eight square miles of the reserve could be sold, which would still leave the residents with sixty-four square miles. The statistician was likely R.S. Lake, Member of the Legislative Assembly for the North-West Territories, who approached Sifton in 1899 about the surrender of a three-mile strip along the southern boundary of the Crooked Lakes reserves.

Lake's figures were investigated by surveyor A.W. Ponton, who found them correct according to the census of 1898, the population of the bands having greatly decreased since the reserves were first set aside. Ponton recommended that Lake's suggestion be adopted, as he believed that the Indians were not benefited by the land, that it was altogether unoccupied, and that "while it remains tied up, settlement of the large agricultural district lying south of the railway is prevented owing to the lack of market towns between Whitewood and Grenfell."⁶¹ MacDonald's replacement at the Crooked Lakes, agent J.P. Wright, felt the surrender unwise for the same reasons as his predecessor did. If his experiment with the cultivation of brome grass as a substitute for hay was successful, however, he believed the Indians might agree to surrender, since they would no longer have to haul hay from the south.⁶²

In 1902 the residents of Broadview, Whitewood, and surrounding district submitted a petition with two hundred signatures, requesting the sale of a three-mile strip along the southern boundary of the Crooked Lakes reserves to "actual settlers."⁶³ The petitioners claimed that the reserves severely retarded the development of their towns, that the Indians occupied land in excess of their requirements, and that the three-mile strip was not being used – no one resided, hunted, or farmed there. The department's reply was that an effort would be made to procure the consent of the Indians to a surrender.⁶⁴

Commissioner Laird discussed the question of surrender with residents of Crooked Lakes in the spring of 1902. He found the Indians "strongly opposed to surrendering any portion of their reserves." Many clearly remembered that Laird had been present at the signing of Treaty Four almost thirty years earlier. Chief Kahkewistahaw, over ninety years old, remembered Laird well. "When we made the treaty at Qu'Appelle you told me to choose out land for myself and now you come to speak to me here. We were told to take this land and we are going to keep it. Did I not tell you a long time ago that you would come some time, that you would come and ask me to sell you this land back again, but I told you at that time. No." Others also considered the reserve as land set aside under the terms of solemn treaties, to be handed down inviolate and in trust. A member of Ochapowace's band remembered that at Qu'Appelle Laird had "advised our chief and all of us to take up land and bring up our people on the land. When our chief died he left us instructions to look after the reserve ... we cannot consent to part with any of it." One spokesman stated that "the quantity you have asked us for is the only decent farming land on my reserve and I don't think any of my partners will agree to the sale of any of it."[65] Another informed the Indian commissioner that his reserve was small enough. Laird admitted that the surrender of the southern portion of the reserves would mean the loss of their best land.

Pressure for surrender did not ease, however. In June 1906 Graham returned from a meeting at Crooked Lakes convinced that if he had had the papers and cash handy, he could have secured a surrender.[66] According to Graham, the residents were at the time interested because they had heard that Pasquah's band had received a substantial cash payment for surrendering land. In January 1907 Graham obtained the surrender of 53,985 acres from the Cowessess and Kahkewistahaw bands. A number of meetings had been required before a majority signed the documents. Graham described those in opposition as "non-progressive," while those in favour were "very intelligent." Reserve residents that had land in active cultivation on the surrendered portion were paid five dollars an acre but were not compensated for certain other improvements. Alex Gaddie, for example, received no compensation for a hay slough he had drained over three years, although he had dug out big rocks and made the land very valuable. If compensation had been given to this man, according to Graham, then every Indian would have a claim "because they all ploughed land at one time or another and piled stones which would mean that they improved the land." But the people of Broadview were "delighted." "As you are aware," Graham wrote to Laird, "this land lying idle has been a great drawback to these towns and they have been trying for years to bring about a surrender."[67] Large tracts of reserve land went to distant buyers in the eastern provinces, Chicago, and Mason City, Iowa.[68]

IN THE CAUSE OF THE WAR

There were other means, aside from land surrenders, through which reserve land was eroded as the twentieth century proceeded. The greater production campaign, launched in 1918, was designed to increase food production for the war effort by intensively cultivating the largest possible area of "unused" reserve land on the prairie and by investing the Indian bands' "idle funds" in the scheme.[69] In the early years of World War 1, Indians were merely encouraged to contribute their share to the preservation of food supplies by reducing their home consumption of flour, bacon, and beef, and by voluntarily increasing their agricultural products and earnings from other industries. They were also urged to help the white farmers with their harvest because of the scarcity of labour. Such help would assist the "Empire" and was the "next best thing to enlisting."[70] The 1918 program was more comprehensive, and much of the voluntary nature of earlier initiatives was eliminated. In that year W.M. Graham was appointed commissioner for greater production for the prairie provinces and three hundred thousand dollars was advanced from the War Appropriation to the Department of Indian Affairs for machinery, implements, seed, and livestock, the amount to be refunded from the sales of produce as they accrued.[71]

A 1918 amendment to the Indian Act allowed the superintendent general to lease uncultivated reserve lands for this patriotic purpose without a surrender, or the consent, of the band members.[72] Reserve residents greatly resented the measure; in some cases the Indians hastened to fence their land so that it could not be considered unused and leasing would be prevented.[73] The rationale for the policy was that Indians were reluctant or unwilling to cultivate or otherwise productively use their land. Arthur Meighen, superintendent general of Indian affairs from 1917 to 1920, explained the amendment this way. "The Indian Reserves of Western Canada embrace very large areas far in excess of what they are utilizing now for productive purposes ... We would only be too glad to have the Indian use this land if he would; production by him would be just as valuable as production by anybody else. But he will not cultivate this land, and we want to cultivate it; that is all. We shall not use it any longer than he shows a disinclination to cultivate the land himself."[74] When asked in the House how reserve residents would fare if some of their best lands were expropriated for the scheme, Meighen replied, "I do not think we need waste any time in sympathy for the Indian, for I am pretty sure his interests will be looked after by the Commissioner." A further amendment allowed the department to spend band funds for public works to "improve productivity," without the consent of the Indians.[75]

Under the greater production scheme, individual Indians were encouraged to increase their crop production, reserve land was leased to non-Indians for cultivation or grazing, and on some reserves, such as Cowessess and Muscowpetung, "greater production farms" were established. These farms were managed by the department agents, using Indian labour. The project, however, was plagued by problems of mismanagement and the financial returns were not impressive. The experiment was soon phased out.[76]

Graham had never intended that the greater production farms should outlive the war. In April 1919 he informed Meighen that he did not believe the operation of these farms was properly within the scope of the department and recommended that "we should withdraw from the business of grain-growing, independently of the Indians." Graham urged that the "unused" land, machinery, and buildings be turned over to the Soldier Settlement Board and "thus the results of our efforts could be conserved for the benefit of the country."[77] Presumably to allow Indians the use of this equipment and their own land was not seen as in the interests of the country.

Graham also believed the system of leasing reserve land should be discontinued and instead the land surrendered. Although it was officially argued that leasing was undesirable because it allowed Indians to sit by and derive an "unearned" income from the work of others, in private Graham saw leasing as a "serious hindrance" to Indians' surrendering their land, as they would be inclined to retain land from which they derived an income. Graham felt it was essential that "we should break up the reserves which are much too large for the small number of Indians scattered over them." If they were broken up, he argued, the Indians could be "segregated" and brought closer together. Concentration would simplify and increase the efficiency of administration on reserves: agents would not be obliged to travel long distances and so could devote all their attention to their work, keep farm instructors under close surveillance, and "generally avail themselves of all opportunities for improvement that would result from concentration." The Battleford and Carlton agencies were Graham's most obvious examples of reserves too large for their populations. As always, the loss of more land, and the further concentration of the Indians, were presented as in their best interests. The residents of the Battleford and Carlton agencies could be moved with "the utmost advantage to themselves and us by locating them in the best possible situation." The need of such action in Graham's view was "so imperative in the interest of the Indians" that should they be unwilling to comply, the department should be provided with "comprehensive legislation whereby they might be compelled to do so."[78]

After the war, the Department of Indian Affairs worked closely with the Soldier Settlement Board. Almost all unsold surrendered Indian land was turned over to the board, and Indians were induced to surrender further reserve land, sixty thousand acres in Saskatchewan alone, because of the terms of the Soldier Settlement Act. That act empowered the Soldier Settlement Board to acquire for veterans by means of "compulsory purchase" any agricultural land in areas where "lands remain underdeveloped, and agriculture is being retarded."[79] The department resolved to seek further surrenders of reserve land for settlement by non-Indian veterans.[80] Under the threat of expropriation, many Indian bands surrendered their "underdeveloped" land.

In the summer of 1919, Graham launched a concerted campaign to procure Indian reserve land for the Soldier Settlement Board. He went on a tour of inspection of reserves to decide which would be ideal for soldier settlement. There were only a few he found unsuitable. One was the Birdtail reserve in Manitoba. Residents there had "scarcely enough land for their own use," Graham decided, and he refused to bow to public pressure for surrender, which was in this case considerable.[81] The Birtle Returned Soldiers Association had sent to Arthur Meighen a petition requesting that the reserve be made available for settlement.[82] The veterans there, all of whom had been occupied in farming before they had enlisted, found on their return that no land was available in the district. Therefore they would be forced to leave, it was claimed, if the reserve was not opened for soldier settlement.

Graham did not give in to public pressure in the case of the Birdtail reserve, but he successfully secured large tracts of reserve land elsewhere. In 1919 he finally succeeded in securing the surrender of southern sections of the Ochapowace reserve, 18,240 acres. The Indians of this reserve had consistently resisted surrender, even in 1907 when they had been offered nearly three times as much money as the residents of neighbouring reserves had.[83]

Indian veterans were not treated in the same way as other returning soldiers. Land was not purchased for them under the Soldier Settlement Act. Instead a new addition to the Indian Act in 1919 empowered the superintendent general to grant location tickets for reserve land to Indian veterans, without the necessity of acquiring band council assent.[84] In this way the amount of reserve land held in common was further eroded.

Compulsory enfranchisement, which was enacted in 1920, modified two years later, but reenacted in 1933, also eroded reserve land. Enfranchised Indians received title to a share of reserve land, further dwindling the amount of land under band control. The goal of Indian Affairs administrators remained the abolishment of reserves. As Duncan Campbell Scott, deputy superintendent general, succinctly stated in 1920: "I want to get rid of the Indian problem. I do not think as a matter of fact, that this country ought to continuously protect a class of people who are able to stand alone. Our object is to continue until there is not a single Indian in Canada that has not been absorbed into the body politic and there is no Indian question, and no Indian Department."[85]

THE OBSOLESCENCE OF EQUIPMENT

Following the days of Hayter Reed, the ban on labour-saving machinery was not officially enforced, but was unofficially so. When the Red Pheasant band wished to buy a tractor-plowing outfit in 1902, for example, Inspector W.J. Chisholm replied that the purchase should not be encouraged. The agent would be burdened with collecting debts, and "if one is purchased it will be no time until every reserve will be after one or more."[86] The Indians' equipment, such as their threshing machinery, became further and further out of date and out of commission and was rarely replaced. The son of a man who had spent forty-eight years as a farm instructor on an Alberta reserve remembered the situation in the early decades of this century.

My father being a farm instructor was interested in machinery but the first grain separator, threshing separator, that I saw, didn't even have an elevator to elevate the grain into the granary. You caught the grain at the bottom of a pipe in a sack and you carried it from that separator to the granary ... they were fifty years behind the times in their machinery. The first binder that I saw operate was not a binder that tied the sheaves together, it simply shuffled out the sheaves like a swather, shuffled out the grain. And the women, the Indian women, would tie a bit of grain together like a rope and make a sheaf and stook. My father had an awful time trying to get the Indian agent to buy even one mower for twenty-seven farmers. You can imagine how much hay was harvested with one mower.[87]

The department's reluctance to replace, repair, or lend threshing machinery to reserve farmers became marked after a 1911 Saskatchewan Supreme Court decision.[88] In the fall of 1910 threshing operations were being conducted on a windy day on the Pasquah reserve with a machine owned and operated by the department when the stacks and the separator caught fire. The fire rapidly spread to the stubble, swept to the edge of the reserve, jumped the railway grade, and destroyed the grain, haystacks, wood, and fence posts of a neighbouring farmer named Carter. Carter successfully sued Indian agent Horatio Nichol for $625 in damages, which would have amounted to over half the agent's yearly salary. Nichol was not present on the Pasquah reserve that day, but Judge J. Lamont found him nonetheless guilty of a breach of duty imposed on him by law, as the agent was shown to have been aware that the operation of the machine was dangerous. The engine was too small to run the separator, which added to the danger of fire, and certain statutory regulations, such as attaching buckets of water to the outfit, were not observed. Nichol fully appreciated the danger of operating the machine with the light engine and had applied to the department for a heavier one. Reserve farmers provided evidence damaging to Nichol's defence. Antoine Cyr, whose grain was being threshed, told the engineer earlier in the day that it was a dangerous day for threshing and that he was afraid of fire.

A resident of the Ochapowace reserve remembered that around 1912 the Indian agent refused to thresh for the band members and would not lend them a thresher.[89] Agent Nichol complained in 1913 that an operable threshing outfit was not to be had in his agency and outlined the many reasons it was impossible for the Indians to buy one themselves. To expect to pay for such an outfit from threshing returns would be "suicidal." Nor would the department allow the Indians to pay for one out of capital funds derived from land already surrendered. The only solution Nichol could see was to surrender more land in order to raise funds. All this, the agent wrote, combined with complete crop failures in 1911 and 1912, "has a very discouraging effect upon those farming."[90]

By 1915 the department no longer allowed the cost of farming operations to be charged against the interest account accruing from land surrenders, which was held in trust by the department. It did agree to a short-term loan to be repaid from the sale of the crops harvested. If the crops did not cover expenses, "farming may be considered a failure and it would be unwise to continue it."[91] This statement must have come as a cruel surprise to Indians in favour of surrender, who had been promised the means to establish themselves in farming. The reasoning of the department was that interest funds were the property of the band as a whole; they could not be used for the advantage of those who farmed because the grain raised was not the property of the whole band. For these reasons the want of threshing machinery in particular became a chronic problem throughout the prairie reserves. By 1922, for example, the Battleford agency was greatly handicapped for the want of proper threshing outfits.[92] Sweet Grass' was out of date and Poundmaker's entirely out of commission.

Indian farmers, who had lost the opportunity to participate in commercial agriculture in the 1890s by not being allowed to raise and dispose of a surplus and invest in higher yielding methods of production, did not regain any ground in the early years of the twentieth century. They fell further behind and became increasingly isolated. They fell behind in technology as well as training, as they did not participate in either the formal or informal agricultural education programs of the wider farming community. Few Indian farmers attended the new agricultural colleges in the prairie provinces, and the training programs and extension services of farm organizations did not extend to Indians. Indian attendance at fairs and exhibitions was discouraged by the department. Reserve residents were not active in farm organizations or farm politics. W.M. Graham, for example, did not approve of Indian participation in wheat pools.[93]

CONTINUING PROTESTS

At no time, however, did Indians adopt a policy of passive submission, disinterest, or apathy. The tradition of protest continued. In 1917 Indians of the Qu'Appelle agency sent to J.D. McLean, secretary of Indian affairs, a petition objecting to the permit system.[94] The response of officials varied little over the years. The writer of any petition or letter was dismissed as a "troublesome Indian," in this case, one who was "not in his own mind." It was "easy," Graham wrote, "to get Indians to sign anything, no matter what the letter might contain."[95]

The growing literacy of Indians made such a situation increasingly implausible and was the cause of some distress to department officials. Agent M. Millar of Crooked Lakes wrote in 1911 that some of the young people read newspapers regularly and were aware of debates in Parliament over issues such as the controversial surrender of the St Peter's reserve, legislation banning the potlach, and Indian participation in parades in Alberta. "Unfortunately," Millar noted, "their knowledge of affairs and power to correctly discriminate is so limited that they fail to catch the correct conclusion."[96] When a western paper reported in 1910 that an act had been passed granting the Indians the same privileges as the white man, Indians of the Qu'Appelle agency soon asked the agent what procedures they should follow to obtain homesteads.[97] (No such amendment had been made to the Indian Act to allow treaty Indians to take up homesteads.)

In January 1911 a well-organized deputation of nine representatives of Treaty Four reserves visited Ottawa.[98] One of the main organizers was Louis O'Soup, who had returned to the Cowessess reserve in 1908. A series of meetings to plan the deputation had begun in June 1910 on the Cowessess reserve. Discussion focused on the treaty promises that had not been carried out and on disaffection with the school system in which there was "too much work for the children and not enough book learning."[99] Planning was thorough and many details were decided, such as how money would be raised to fund the delegation and how the families of the delegates were to be provisioned while they were away.

The meetings in Ottawa between the delegates, Frank Pedley, and Frank Oliver lasted eight days. Alex Gaddie acted as interpreter. The opening comments of the Indians centred on general dissatisfaction with a treaty that did not allow them to make a living. "I was very young when the Treaty was made," said O'Soup, "but I was with the crowd that he [Alexander Morris] made the bargain with. When I heard what was said I thought to myself 'Oh, we will make a living by the promises that are made to us.'" A number of issues were raised, including the education of children, the control of resources on reserves, the removal of chiefs and headmen, and the ban on sacred ceremonies. They objected to the application of game laws to Indians as a violation of treaty rights. Concern about the opportunities for former pupils was voiced. "For many years," O'Soup stated, "we have put our children to school and there is not one yet that has enough education to make a living." If they want to farm, "they go to their parents for a start and their parents have nothing to give them, and the young men is [sic] reported as lazy. But he has nothing to scratch the ground with, and cannot farm." Delegate Joe Coté added that the Indians had surrendered their land in order to "get the worth of it in implements for the young men to use at their work." It was on the question of the disposal of funds from land surrenders that the delegates were most adamant. Oliver was obliged to go through the accounts with them and to provide written statements of the amount of land that had been sold, the price, the amount of money already collected, and the amount that had been spent.[100]

One demand that O'Soup brought to the meeting was that he be provided with an artificial limb. He had lost his lower right leg in a railway accident. "All the Indians," he said, "wished him to come home with a leg on which he will be able to walk about." To department officials such a request seemed to trivialize and personalize the deputation, but O'Soup's point was that Indians were not receiving the medical assistance promised and that even though his band had surrendered land, he did not have the means to obtain an artificial limb. O'Soup was authorized to purchase a peg leg in Winnipeg.[101]

Upon their return to Saskatchewan, the Indians were far from completely satisfied with the statements provided in Ottawa. In March 1911 the Cowessess band members made further inquiries, which they communicated through their lawyer, H.W. MacDonald of Broadview. They argued, for example, that the department should not be debiting a 10 per cent "management fund" for taking care of their money. They also objected to the debit of their medical fees, which, they had understood, were to be provided free of charge under the terms of the treaty.[102] MacDonald was curtly informed that the department did not "give explanations to Indians except through their Agents."[103] In studying the information furnished him by Ottawa officials, however, agent Millar was "at a loss to understand them," as he found a number of discrepancies. The statement the Indians brought from Ottawa differed "widely" from the "corrected" version he was given. Millar could conclude only that Ottawa officials were wrong to give written documents to Indians.[104] By the end of August the Indians, through their lawyer, complained that their agent had not given them the information they had requested, and they asked that the documents be forwarded. It is not clear how this particular dispute was resolved, but by the winter of 1912 the Qu'Appelle Indians were once again holding meetings. One of their main goals at this time was to have "an Indian institution established where they can receive the higher education, so that they may become Indian Agents, clerks, and professional men."[105]

The tradition of protest continued, but, as before, little attention was paid. The 1911 delegates, for example, were dismissed as "a few misguided malcontents."[106] The reserves remained pockets of rural poverty. Twentieth-century visitors to reserves in some cases found Indians living in the midst of fine farmland that was not cultivated at all, was leased to non-natives, or worked with obsolete methods and technology.[107] Indians appeared to be clinging stubbornly to the past and to be impervious to "progressive" influences. It was concluded that Indians lacked industry and were not natural farmers. Their "failure" to farm was seen as the result of personal weakness: they were "shiftless" and did not like physical drudgery. Because of inherent and unalterable differences between white and Indian, it was believed, the Indian would never succeed at farming.

Indians and agriculture remained incompatible in the mind of the non-native. Even Inspector Wadsworth, who saw Indians farming daily, wrote to Reed in 1891 that "one is constantly surprised when viewing their work, and those in the act of performing it." When they were dressed in "civilized" attire, one was "apt to forget they are Indians," but when they were not, "one is constantly excited by the incongruous fact of seeing wild Indians performing deftly the work of civilization."[108] Agent Ostrander of the Crooked Lakes reserves expressed similar sentiments to anthropologist D.G. Mandelbaum over forty years later. Ostrander told him that the "ordinary white loses interest in the Indian if he knows that the Indian has spent 10 hours on a binder instead of 10 hours jumping up and down behind a fence and blowing a whistle [dancing]. There the Indian ceases to be an Indian and becomes a farmer. When he puts on beads and feathers instead of overalls, he immediately is a highly romantic figure."[109]

Indians and agriculture were irreconcilable. These observations, which differed little from the perceptions of Victorian Canadians and which have been reflected in histories written until very recently, obscure or overlook the Indians' positive response to agriculture in earlier years. Equally obscured and forgotten has been the role of Canadian government policy in restricting and undermining reserve agriculture.

Appendix One

OFFICIALS OF THE DEPARTMENT
OF INDIAN AFFAIRS

Superintendents General of Indian Affairs
- John A. Macdonald   1878–1883 (and 1887)
- Edgar Dewdney   1888–1892
- T.M. Daly   1892–1896
- Hugh J. Macdonald   1896
- Clifford Sifton   1896–1905
- Frank Oliver   1905–1911
- R. Rogers   1911–1912
- W.J. Roche   1912–1917
- Arthur Meighen   1917–1920

Deputy Superintendents General of Indian Affairs
- Lawrence Vankoughnet   1874–1893
- Hayter Reed   1893–1897
- James A. Smart   1897–1902
- Frank Pedley   1902–1913
- Duncan Campbell Scott   1913–1932

Indian Commissioners
- Edgar Dewdney   1879–1888
- Hayter Reed   1888–1893
- Amédée Forget   1893–1897
- David Laird   1897–1909

Appendix Two

AGRICULTURAL STATISTICS

Table 1
Reserve Agriculture, 1884

Reserves	Pop.	Families farming	Families not farming	Acres cultivated	Oxen
Gordon	229	22	22	115	5
Muscowequan	269	16	29	60	7
Poor Man	160	25	2	79	7
Day Star	97	13	9	67	7
Pasquah	273	33	39	189	28
Muscowpetung	182	23	21	68	13
Ochapowace	363	18	51	74	8
Kahkewistahaw	248	12	37	55	8
Cowessess	285	16	54	86	18
Sakimay	138			17	6
Little Black Bear	141	13	16	47	6
Star Blanket	111	10	12	31	4
Okanese	82	9	12	41	6
Peepeekisis	142	15	19	55	2

Source: Canada, House of Commons, *Sessional Papers*, vol. 18, no. 3 (1884), 192–205.

Table 2
Reserve Agriculture, 1890

Reserves	Pop., approx.	Acres broken	Acres under crop, 1890	Acres under crop, 1889	Acres fenced	Hay cut, tons	Wheat Acres sown	Wheat Yield, bu.	Oats Acres sown	Oats Yield, bu.	Barley Acres sown	Barley Yield, bu.	Rye Acres sown	Rye Yield, bu.	Roots Acres sown	Roots Yield, bu.	Garden, acres sown	Livestock under loan Horses	Livestock under loan Oxen	Livestock privately held Horses	Livestock privately held Oxen
File Hills Agency																					
Little Black Bear	80		68	60	70	100	50	250					12		4	500	2	12	30		
Star Blanket	47		31	31	35	100	20	75					6		4	500	2	8	10		
Okanese	59	10	1	2	65	150											1	16	14		
Peepeekisis	77	10	126	141	75	100	80	2,000	20	800			12	250	12	2,000	2	17	15		
Total	263	20	226	234	245	450	150	2,325	20	800			30	250	20	3,000	7	53	69		
Crooked Lakes Agency																					
Ochapowace	146	250	128	128	240	260	95	1,100	2	32			10	58	18	1,384	2	31	25		4
Kahkewistahaw	124	280	118	105	380	180	87	1,335			4	30	12	48	10	870	5	27	24		
Cowessess	150	580	224	207	740	160	170	2,335	23	625			12	130	13	1,230	5	25	43		4
Sakimay	192	210	99	134	600	150	85	1,142					4	50	6	591	3	23	50		
Total	612	1,320	569	574	1,960	750	437	5,932	25	657	4	30	38	286	37	4,075	15	106	142		8
Muscowpetung Agency																					
Piapot	216	315	126	136	320	450	91	1,330			9	20			22	1,956		43	105		
Muscowpetung	104	122	63	94	97	337	52	541							7	311		29	32		
Pasquah	124	157	96	124	200	300	77	1,580	2	102	6	87			9	926		39	70		
Total	444	594	285	354	617	1,087	220	3,451	2	102	15	107			38	3,193		111	207		
Touchwood Hills Agency (1889 returns, 1890 not available)																					
Muscowequan	160	20	96	72	100	250	70	175	8						17	120	2	17	15	1	
Gordon	159	69	132	94	160	350	101	300	7	4					19	150	5	21	22		5
Day Star	81	43	24	46		160	12	20							11	42	5	14	15		
Poor Man	117	93	85	65	93	150	70	160	4						10	45	3	15	20		
Total	517	225	337	277	353	910	253	655	19						57	357	15	67	72		6

Sources: Canada, House of Commons, *Sessional Papers*, vol. 24, no. 18 (1890), 250–79; for Touchwood Hills, ibid., vol. 23, no. 12 (1889), 182–9.

Table 3
Reserve Agriculture, 1897

Agencies	Pop.	Acres cult.*	Acres fenced	Wheat Acres sown	Wheat Yield, bu.	Oats Acres sown	Oats Yield, bu.	Barley Acres sown	Barley Yield, bu.	Roots Acres sown	Roots Yield, bu.
Touchwood Hills	850	333	2,429	86	358	111	1,436	31	144	39	4,879
Moscowpetung	715	315	700	231	4,955	24	833	8	70	49	7,012
File Hills	280	165	165	–	–	70	1,300	22	380	27	1,995
Crooked Lakes	636	697	1,280	491	9,032	139	2,983	–	–	65	4,864

Implements

	Ploughs	Harrows	Seed drills	Mowers	Reapers	Thresh. mach.	Wagons
Touchwood Hills	64	21	–	4	1	–	17
Moscowpetung	80	44	2	27	4	4	67
File Hills	45	18	2	17	1	2	22
Crooked Lakes	93	42	11	27	11	3	49

Livestock

	Work oxen	Steers	Milk cows	Young stock
Touchwood Hills	57	206	230	312
Moscowpetung	97	124	110	159
File Hills	45	142	212	145
Crooked Lakes	96	102	195	187

* Includes made pasturage.
Source: Canada, House of Commons, Sessional Papers, vol. 32, no. 14 (1897), 436–51.

Table 4
Indian Reserve Land Losses

Reserves	Original area (acres)	Per capita acreage, 1900	Area, 1928 (acres)
Muscowpetung Agency			
Pasquah	38,496	258	22,141
Muscowpetung	38,080	401	20,123
Piapot	34,560	203	16,755
Crooked Lakes Agency			
Kahkewistahaw	46,720	412	13,404
Cowessess	49,920	300	29,083
Ochapowace	52,864	482	34,624
Touchwood Hills Agency			
Muscowequan	24,256	153	16,423
Poor Man	27,200	238	18,934
File Hills Agency			
Little Black Bear	27,760	425	17,055

Source: Raby, "Indian Land Surrenders," 39.

Notes

ABBREVIATIONS

CHC Canada, House of Commons
CMS Church Missionary Society
CPRC Canadian Plains Research Centre
DSG Deputy Superintendent General of Indian Affairs
GAI Glenbow–Alberta Institute
McM McCord Museum, McGill University
NA   National Archives
PAM Provincial Archives of Manitoba

INTRODUCTION

1 Hawkes, *Story of Saskatchewan*, 80.
2 Philip Mason, *Patterns of Dominance*, 13.
3 Stanley, *Birth of Western Canada*, vii.
4 Ibid., 196, 197.
5 Ibid., 198, 217.
6 Ibid., 214.
7 Ibid., 236.
8 Ibid., 218.
9 Ibid., 238–9.
10 See, for example, John N. Jennings, "North West Mounted Police," 277–9; Looy, "Indian Agent," chap. 6.
11 Samek, *Blackfoot*, 57, 183.
12 Ibid., 57, 69.
13 Ibid., 57.
14 See, for example, James R. Gibson, *Farming the Frontier*, 186.
15 Hughes, *American Indian Ecology*, 67.

16 McLuhan, *Touch the Earth*, 56.
17 See, for example, Vecsey and Venables, eds., *American Indian Environments*, 26.
18 James R. Gibson, *Farming the Frontier*, 186.
19 Hughes, *American Indian Ecology*, 106.
20 Ibid.
21 Hanks, *Tribe under Trust*, 18.
22 Ibid., 177.
23 Ibid., 177, 34.
24 Hawthorn, ed., *Contemporary Indians*, 160.
25 Ibid., 57.
26 Palmer and Parsons, eds., *Roots of Rural Poverty*, 4.
27 Bundy, *Rise and Fall*, 2.
28 George Reid Andrews, "Black and White Workers," 506–7.
29 Bundy, *Rise and Fall*, 3.
30 Cell, *Highest Stage*, 201.
31 Yudelman, *Africans on the Land*, 92–3.
32 See Palmer and Parsons, eds., *Roots of Rural Poverty*; Bundy, *Rise and Fall*.
33 Holzkamm and Waisberg, "Our Land."
34 Dyck, "Opportunity Lost." See also idem, "Administration of Federal Indian Aid." Dyck pointed out that many bands made sustained efforts to farm.
35 Kennedy, *Islands of White*, 160–1.
36 Friesen, "Magnificent Gifts," 41–51.
37 Milloy, "Early Indian Acts," 60.

CHAPTER ONE

1 McM, Reed Papers, "Address on the Aims of the Government in Its Dealings with the Indians," n.d., 24, 19–20.
2 Frederick Turner, *Beyond Geography*, 31–47.
3 Gen. 1:28.
4 Houghton, *Victorian Frame of Mind*, 27–53.
5 McDougall, *Western Trails*, 18.
6 McDougall, *Saddle*, 261–2.
7 McDougall, *Forest*, 76.
8 Young, *On the Indian Trail*, 50–1.
9 See, for example, Young, *By Canoe*, 63.
10 Ferrier, *Indian Education*, 2.
11 McDougall, *Red River Rebellion*, 112.
12 Trant, "Treatment," 511.
13 Ryerson, *Hudson's Bay*, 150.

14 West, *Substance*, 117.
15 Trant, "Treatment," 510.
16 Butler, *Great Lone Land*, 317–18.
17 See, for example, Young, *By Canoe*, 65.
18 Ferrier, *Indian Education*, 27–8.
19 Dippie, *Vanishing American*, 102–4.
20 Maclean, *Indians*, 278.
21 Jones, "There is Some Power."
22 Ibid., 96, 99.
23 Regehr, "Religious Attitudes to the Land," 14.
24 Young, "Indian Problem," 468.
25 Surtees, "Indian Reserve Policy," 89.
26 Quoted in ibid., 89.
27 Trant, "Treatment," 512.
28 Maclean, *Savage Folk*, 540.
29 McDougall, *Red River Rebellion*, 33–4.
30 Maclean, *Savage Folk*, 543.
31 McDougall, *Western Trails*, 46.
32 Fowke, *National Policy*, 26–45.
33 Taylor, "Canada's Northwest Indian Policy," 14–15.
34 This section on Canada's early Indian policy is based on the following: Stanley, "Indian Background," 14–31; Surtees, *Canadian Indian Policy*, 111–25; idem, "Indian Reserve Policy"; Tobias, "Protection"; and Upton, "Canadian Indian Policy," 51–61.
35 Surtees, "Indian Reserve Policy," 89–90.
36 Hodgetts, *Pioneer Public Service*, 206.
37 Surtees, "Indian Reserve Policy," 58.
38 Ibid., 90–2.
39 Hodgetts, *Pioneer Public Service*, 209.
40 Surtees, "Indian Reserve Policy," 93.
41 Ibid., 94.
42 Tobias, "Protection," 42.
43 Ibid., 48.
44 Hodgetts, *Pioneer Public Service*, 215–19.
45 Ray, *Indians in the Fur Trade*, 75.
46 GAI, Fraser Papers, "Plains Cree," 5.
47 Butler, *Great Lone Land*, 199.
48 Moodie and Ray, "Buffalo Migrations," 46.
49 Ibid.
50 Milloy, "Plains Cree," 84.
51 Ewers, *Horse in Blackfoot Culture*, 40.
52 Mandelbaum, *Plains Cree*, 110.
53 Kehoe, *North American Indians*, 300.

54 Kaye and Moodie, "'Psoralea' Food Resources," 332.
55 Arthur, "Bison Pounds," 80.
56 Denig, *Five Indian Tribes*, 118.
57 Mandelbaum, *Plains Cree*, 71.
58 Ibid., 105.
59 Ibid., 107.
60 The Hudson's Bay Company recognized and subsidized individuals as chiefs. The company sought "good reliable" Indians who had a history of paying their debts and were peacemakers rather than warriors. These chiefs, however, may not necessarily have been recognized by their bands as leaders. See Cowie, *Company of Adventurers*, 335.
61 Mandelbaum, *Plains Cree*, 110.
62 *Proceedings of the Plains Cree Conference*, 20.
63 Mandelbaum, *Plains Cree*, 107.
64 Cowie, *Company of Adventurers*, 279.
65 Denig, *Five Indian Tribes*, 133.
66 Cowie, *Company of Adventurers*, 225.
67 Mandelbaum, *Plains Cree*, 15–16.
68 Ray, *Indians in the Fur Trade*, 12.
69 Ibid., 51–71.
70 Milloy, "Plains Cree," 28–30.
71 Ibid., 45.
72 Ray, *Indians in the Fur Trade*, 59.
73 Milloy, "Plains Cree," 37.
74 See Robin Fisher, *Contact and Conflict*; Francis and Morantz, *Partners in Furs*; Ray, *Indians in the Fur Trade*.
75 Ray and Freeman, *"Give Us Good Measure."*
76 Ray, *Indians in the Fur Trade*, 72–9.
77 Ibid., 102.
78 Milloy, "Plains Cree," 84, 90.
79 Manitoba Department of Cultural Affairs and Historical Resources, *Introducing Manitoba Prehistory*, 110–1.
80 Milloy, "Plains Cree," 127.
81 Ray, *Indians in the Fur Trade*, 147.
82 A.S. Morton, ed., *Journal of Duncan McGillivray*, 47.
83 Mandelbaum, *Plains Cree*, 267–88.
84 See, for example, Stanley, *Birth of Western Canada*.
85 Milloy, "Plains Cree."
86 Ibid., 104.
87 Ibid., 127ff.
88 McDougall, *Wa-pee Moos-tooch*, 75.
89 Milloy, "Plains Cree," 202.
90 Ray, *Indians in the Fur Trade*, 224.

91 Cowie, *Company of Adventurers*, 307; Milloy, "Plains Cree," 253.
92 Milloy, "Plains Cree," 259, 260, 262.
93 Ibid., 241.
94 Tobias, "Canada's Subjugation," 523.
95 CHC, *Sessional Papers*, vol. 10, no. 11 (1876), xxxiv.
96 Kempton, "Maize," 20.
97 Wessel, "Agriculture, Indians," 14.
98 Driver, *Indians*, 38.
99 Weatherwax, "Origin of the Maize Plant," 17.
100 Driver, *Indians*, 53-4.
101 Moodie, "Agriculture and the Fur Trade," 277.
102 Meyer, *The Village Indians*, 63-4; see also Gilbert L. Wilson, *Buffalo Bird Woman's Garden*.
103 Manitoba Culture, Heritage, and Recreation, Historic Resources Branch, *Prehistory of the Lockport Site*, 11.
104 "1985 Excavations at Lockport Site," 2.
105 Syms, "History of a Refuse Pit," 306-15.
106 Helgason, *First Albertans*, 109-13.
107 Moodie and Kaye, "Indian Agriculture in the Fur Trade North West," 172.
108 Moodie and Kaye, "Northern Limit of Indian Agriculture," 513.
109 Ibid., 519.
110 Tanner, *Narrative*, 117.
111 Quoted in Roe, "Early Agriculture," 109.
112 CHC, *Sessional Papers*, vol. 9, no. 9 (1875), xxxi.
113 Hind, *Narrative*, 121.
114 Payne, "Fairford."
115 CHC, *Sessional Papers*, vol. 9, no. 9 (1875), 38.
116 Ibid., vol. 16, no. 5 (1882), 154.
117 Elias, "First American Refugees," 23.
118 Quoted in Ray, *Indians in the Fur Trade*, 219.
119 CHC, *Sessional Papers*, vol. 9, no. 9 (1875), 32.
120 Cowie, *Company of Adventurers*, 174.
121 See, for example, Ray, *Indians in the Fur Trade*, 219.
122 Coutts, "Role of Agriculture."
123 Hind, *Narrative*, 223.
124 W.L. Morton, "Agriculture in the Red River," 79, 80.
125 Thomas, "Agriculture," 36.
126 Sarah Carter, "Souris-Mouth Posts."
127 Atwood, ed., *In Rupert's Land*, 85.
128 In Cowie's ten years in the West these plagues occurred almost annually. See Cowie, *Company of Adventurers*, 336.
129 Atwood, ed., *In Rupert's Land*, 86.

130 Denig, *Five Indian Tribes*, 109. The research of F.V. Hayden, published in 1862, confirmed the existence of a Cree band known as the Magpies. See Swanton, *Indian Tribes of North America*, 554.
131 Denig, *Five Indian Tribes*, 109.
132 Personal interview with Father G. Laviolette, St Boniface, Manitoba, 27 July 1983.
133 Denig, *Five Indian Tribes*, 105.
134 NA, RG 10, vol. 3622, file 4945, Rev. Joseph Reader to Lt.-Gov. Morris, 17 May 1875.
135 Spry, ed., *Palliser Expedition*, 125n, 136, 432.
136 Goosen, "Indians of the Fort Ellice Region," 17.
137 Tyler, "Paskwāw," 674–5.
138 NA, RG 10, vol. 3578, file 505, J.C. Nelson to Edgar Dewdney, 6 November 1883.
139 Ibid.
140 Ibid., vol. 3642, file 7581, Angus McKay's Report on Treaty Four for 1876; ibid., vol. 3625, file 5489, W. Christie's Report on Treaty Four for 1875.
141 NA, RG 10, vol. 3642, file 7581, McKay's Report, 1876.
142 Ibid., vol. 3625, file 5489, Christie's Report, 1875.
143 Ray, *Indians in the Fur Trade*, 220–1, 224.
144 Mandelbaum, *Plains Cree*, 11.
145 GAI, Fraser Papers, 7.
146 Mandelbaum, *Plains Cree*, 9–10.
147 CPRC, Mandelbaum Field Notes, Qu'Appelle Agency 4, 3.
148 NA, RG 10, vol 3642, file 7581, McKay's Report, 1876, 32.
149 Cowie, *Company of Adventurers*, 239, 326.
150 CPRC, Mandelbaum Field Notes, Touchwood Agency 2, 2.
151 Cowie, *Company of Adventurers*, 239, 414.
152 GAI, Fraser Papers, 28.
153 Cowie, *Company of Adventurers*, 338.
154 CPRC, Mandelbaum Field Notes, Touchwood Agency 1, 2.
155 NA, RG 10, vol. 3642, file 7581, McKay's Report, 1876, 31.
156 CPRC, Mandelbaum Field Notes, Touchwood Agency 2, 3.
157 GAI, Fraser Papers, 24.
158 Sanderson, *Indian Tales*, 6–7.
159 NA, RG 10, vol 3632, file 6379, M.G. Dickieson to the minister of the interior, 7 October 1876; and vol. 3672, file 10,853, pt. 1, Dickieson to L. Vankoughnet, 26 February 1879.
160 Ibid., vol. 3642, file 7581, McKay's Report, 1876, 37.
161 CPRC, Mandelbaum Field Notes, File Hills Agency 1, 4.
162 NA, RG 10, vol. 3642, file 7581, McKay's Report, 1876, 37.

163 Cowie, *Company of Adventurers*, 278.
164 Sanderson, *Indian Tales*, 3.
165 McKenzie, *Men of the HBC*, 125.
166 GAI, Fraser Papers, 21.
167 NA, RG 10, vol. 3642, file 7581, McKay's Report, 1876, 39.
168 GAI, Fraser Papers, 19.
169 Cowie, *Company of Adventurers*, 385.
170 Tyler, "Paskwāw," 674–5.
171 GAI, Fraser Papers, 18.
172 Cowie, *Company of Adventurers*, 389.
173 CPRC, Mandelbaum Field Notes, File Hills Agency 3, 2.
174 GAI, Fraser Papers, 22.
175 NA, RG 10, vol. 3642, file 7581, McKay's Report, 1876, 37.
176 Ibid., 34.
177 GAI, Fraser Papers, 20.
178 PAM, CMS Records, Charles Pratt Journal, no. 161, 1872, Rev. Joseph Reader's Annual Reports for 1874, no. 324, 1876, no. 488.

CHAPTER TWO

1 Stanley, *Birth of Western Canada*, 196–7.
2 Leighton, "Vankoughnet."
3 Ibid., 106.
4 Cell, *British Colonial Administration*, xi.
5 Goldring, "First Contingent," 10.
6 John N. Jennings, "North West Mounted Police."
7 NA, RG 10, vol. 3609, file 3229.
8 Gwyn, *Private Capital*, 127.
9 NA, RG 10, vol. 3609, file 3229, A.R. Selwyn to E.H. Meredith, 21 April 1874.
10 Ibid., Meredith's Memorandum on Indian Policy in the North-West Territories, "The Food Question," n.d.
11 Ibid., letter of C.N. Bell, 23 March 1874.
12 PAM, John Christian Schultz Papers, box 17, no. 7809, "The Indian Question," extract from the Official Report of the Senate Debates, Thursday, 16 April 1885. Dr McInnes read Schultz's speech, originally delivered in the House of Commons, March 1873.
13 Tobias, "Canada's Subjugation," 520–1.
14 Taylor, "Meaning of Treaties Six and Seven," 15.
15 Morris, *Treaties*, 169.
16 Ibid., 169–71.
17 NA, RG 10, vol. 3609, file 3229, letter of C.N. Bell, 23 March 1874.

18 Ibid.
19 NA, David Laird Letterbooks, copy of a protest of Indians against the survey, Fort Ellice, 11 October 1873, addressed to Lt.-Gov. Morris, 53.
20 Ibid., memorandum of a conversation between "Kamooses," a Cree Indian of the Qu'Appelle, and Lt.-Gov. Morris, 18 May 1874, 44.
21 Quoted in Morris, *Treaties*, 170–1.
22 Taylor, "Meaning of Treaties Six and Seven," 15.
23 Hunt, "Notes on the Qu'Appelle Treaty," 179. M.G. Dickieson, clerk in the Department of the Interior, noted that "The 'Big(?) Governor' one of the most powerful chiefs of the Plains Cree was not present. He has probably the largest band of any chief on the Plains." NA, RG 10, vol. 3613, file 4013, Dickieson to Meredith, 19 November 1874.
24 Morris, *Treaties*, 82.
25 Ibid., 331.
26 Ibid., 332–3.
27 Ibid., 354–5.
28 NA, RG 10, vol. 3622, file 5007, Department of the Interior memorandum, 7 July 1875.
29 PAM, William Joseph Christie Papers, introd. to "Finding Aid."
30 Looy, "Dickieson."
31 NA, RG 10, vol. 3622, file 5007, instructions to Christie from the minister of the interior, 16 July 1875.
32 Ibid., memorandum, Col J.S. Dennis, surveyor general, 15 July 1875.
33 Hind, *Narrative*.
34 Quoted in Tyman, *By Section*, 37.
35 Ibid., 35.
36 NA, RG 15, Records of the Department of the Interior, vol. 237, file 8015, Christie to Dennis, 12 April 1877.
37 Morris, *Treaties*, 96, 215.
38 NA, RG 10, vol. 3625, file 5489, Christie to David Laird, 7 October 1875.
39 Ibid., vol. 3632, file 6418, W.L. Wagner to Laird, January 1876, 13.
40 Ibid., 15–16.
41 Ibid., vol. 3642, file 7581, McKay's Report, 1876, 30.
42 Sarah Carter, "Angus McKay."
43 NA, RG 10, vol. 3642, file 7581, McKay's Report, 1876, 33.
44 Ibid., 31–2.
45 Ibid., 36.
46 Ibid., vol. 3622, file 5007, telegram, Morris to Laird, 10 July 1875.
47 Ibid., Laird to Morris, 12 July 1875.
48 Morris, *Treaties*, 217.
49 NA, RG 10, vol. 3622, file 5007, superintendent general of Indian affairs to Christie, 24 July 1875.

50 Ibid., Christie to Laird, 16 July 1875.
51 Ibid.
52 Ibid., vol. 3632, file 6418, Wagner to Laird, January 1876, p. 10.
53 Ibid., file 6379, instructions to McKay from the Department of the Interior, 26 April 1876.
54 Ibid., McKay to Meredith, 20 June 1876.
55 Ibid., vol. 3642, file 7581, McKay's Report, 1876, 52. The implements issued were twelve scythes and snaithes (the curved shaft or handle of a scythe), ten axes, twelve spades, a crosscut saw, a pit saw, a grindstone, a whipple tree (or whiffletree, single tree), twelve scythe stones, five augers, and twelve files.
56 Gordon's band received fifty bushels of seed potatoes, a chest of tools, a plough, two harrows, forty-four hoes, twenty-four scythes and snaithes, twenty-four axes, five handsaws, a crosscut saw, a pit saw, eighteen spades, a grindstone, two pair of chain traces, two whipple trees, a crossbar, twelve scythe stones, five augers, and fourteen files.
57 NA, RG 10, vol. 3632, file 6379, McKay to Meredith, 18 August 1876.
58 Ibid., vol. 3642, file 7581, McKay's Report, 1876, 1–2.
59 Ibid., vol. 3648, file 8162-2, confidential memorandum, Vankoughnet to J.A. Macdonald, 8 May 1879.
60 Ibid., file 8162-1, newspaper clipping, n.d., "A Link Broken." See also Cole, *Exile in the Wilderness*. According to Cole, all the sons of Archibald McDonald changed the spelling of their family name to MacDonald in the 1850s.
61 Looy, "Dickieson," 104.
62 Chalmers, *Laird*.
63 Looy, "Dickieson," 104.
64 NA, RG 10, vol. 3672, file 10,853, pt. 1, Dickieson to Vankoughnet, 26 February 1879.
65 Ibid., vol 3654, file 8904, Agent A. MacDonald's Report for 1877, 28 December 1887.
66 Ibid.
67 Ibid., Laird to David Mills, 31 December 1877, 4.
68 Chalmers, *Laird*, 8, 134.
69 NA, RG 10, vol. 3609, file 3229, Dickieson to Laird, 7 January 1875.
70 Ibid., vol. 3649, file 8187, extract from a description of the Moose Mountain reserve.
71 Ibid., vol. 3654, file 8904, Mills to Laird, 22 May 1878.
72 Ibid., fragment of a letter, Laird to Mills, n.d. (1878).
73 Ibid., and vol. 3672, file 10,853, pt. 1, Dickieson to Meredith, 2 April 1878.

74 Ibid., vol. 3654, file 8904, Mills to Laird, 22 May 1878, 1, 3.
75 Ibid., fragment of a letter, Laird to Mills, 4.
76 Ibid., Mills to Laird, 22 May 1878, 6.
77 Ibid., vol. 3665, file 10,094, Laird to Mills, 11 November 1878.
78 CHC, *Sessional Papers*, vol. 12, no. 7 (1878), 56.
79 Ibid.
80 NA, RG 10, vol. 3672, file 10,853, pt. 1, Dickieson to Vankoughnet, 26 February 1879.
81 CHC, *Sessional Papers*, vol. 12, no. 7 (1878), 64.
82 PAM, CMS Records, no. 913, Charles Pratt Journal, March 1878.
83 Stanley, *Birth of Western Canada*, 225.
84 McKenzie, *Men of the HBC*, 62–3.
85 Hildebrandt, "P.G. Laurie," *Prairie Forum*, 166.
86 *Saskatchewan Herald* (Battleford), 26 April 1879.
87 Hildebrandt, "P.G. Laurie" (MA thesis), 111.
88 *Saskatchewan Herald*, 17 November 1879.
89 Aitkens, *Harvest of Grief*.
90 Tobias, "Treaty Rights," 241–52.
91 NA, RG 10, vol. 3622, file 5007, Christie to Meredith, 9 September 1875.
92 Ibid., Maclean to Christie, 29 July 1875.
93 Ibid., vol. 3625, file 5489, Christie to Laird, 7 October 1875.
94 Morris, *Treaties*, 86.
95 NA, RG 10, vol. 3625, file 5489, Christie to Laird, 7 October 1875.
96 Morris, *Treaties*, 79.
97 NA, RG 10, vol. 3637, file 7088, Inspector J.M. Walsh's Report on the Payment of Annuities, 12 September 1876.
98 CHC, *Sessional Papers*, vol. 10, no. 11 (1876), xxxvii.
99 NA, RG 10, vol. 3656, file 9092, MacDonald's Report on Annuity Payments in Treaty Four, 20 October 1877.
100 Ibid., vol. 3664, MacDonald to the deputy minister of the interior, 6 June 1878.
101 Morris, *Treaties*, 122.
102 NA, RG 10, vol. 3656, file 9092, MacDonald's Report, 20 October 1877.
103 Ibid., vol. 3665, file 10,094, interpreter to Joseph Cauchon, 1 June 1878.
104 Ibid.
105 Ibid.
106 Looy, "Dickieson," 110–1.
107 NA, RG 10, vol. 3665, file 10,094, Laird to the minister of the interior, 11 November 1878.
108 Ibid., vol. 3672, file 10,853, pt. 1, extract of a letter, Dickieson to Robert Sinclair, 16 November 1878.

CHAPTER THREE

1 NA, RG 10, vol. 3665, file 10,094, Mills to Laird, 29 July 1878.
2 Ibid., Laird to Macdonald, 11 November 1878.
3 Ibid.
4 Ibid., vol. 3672, file 10,853, Macdonald to Vankoughnet, November 1878.
5 Ibid., Dickieson to Vankoughnet, 26 February 1879.
6 Ibid., vol. 3665, file 10,094, Christie to Vankoughnet, 31 March 1879.
7 CHC, *Sessional Papers*, vol. 12, no. 7 (1878), 5–7.
8 Larmour, "Dewdney," 13.
9 Looy, "Dickieson," 113.
10 NA, RG 10, vol. 3635, file 6567, Dennis to Dewdney, 30 May 1879.
11 Dalal-Clayton, *Black's Agricultural Dictionary*, 33.
12 *Facts*, 22.
13 NA, RG 10, vol. 3695, file 14,748, Vankoughnet to T.P. Wadsworth, July 1879.
14 Ibid.
15 Ibid., vol. 3648, file 8162-2, memorandum, 28 June 1879.
16 CHC, *Sessional Papers*, vol. 13, no. 4 (1879), 100.
17 Ibid., vol. 14, no. 14 (1880), 2.
18 Ibid., vol. 13, no. 4 (1879), 100.
19 1880 *Commons Debates*, 2: 1941 (Macdonald).
20 NA, RG 10, vol. 3695, file 14,763, Dennis to Edmund Hooper, 1 May 1879.
21 Ibid., T. Farrow to Dennis, 22 July 1879.
22 Ibid., Vankoughnet to Macdonald, 3 November 1879.
23 1886 *Commons Debates*, 1: 719 (M.C. Cameron).
24 1880 *Commons Debates*, 2: 1944 (Macdonald).
25 NA, RG 10, vol. 3682, file 12,516, personnel file, James Scott.
26 Ibid., Scott to Dennis, 21 August 1879, and vol. 3699, file 16,431, Scott to Dennis, 1 October 1879.
27 Ibid., vol. 3706, file 18,745, Wadsworth to Vankoughnet, 10 February 1880.
28 CHC, *Sessional Papers*, vol. 13, no. 4 (1879), 99.
29 NA, RG 10, vol. 3699, file 16,431, Scott to Dennis, 1 October 1879.
30 GAI, Allan MacDonald Papers, Scott to MacDonald, 1 November 1889.
31 Ibid., 26 January 1880.
32 Ibid., 31 March 1881.
33 CHC, *Sessional Papers*, vol. 13, no. 4 (1879), 100, 101.
34 NA, RG 10, vol. 3682, file 12,516, Vankoughnet to Scott, 17 September 1879.

35 Ibid., vol. 3706, file 18,745, Wadsworth to Vankoughnet, 10 February 1880.
36 Ibid., vol. 3687, file 13,698, Frank L. Hunt to Macdonald, 28 May 1879.
37 Hunt, "Notes on the Qu'Appelle Treaty."
38 NA, RG 10, vol. 3687, file 13,698, Hunt to Dewdney, 16 March 1880.
39 Ibid., vol. 3706, file 18,847, W.L. Orde to Dewdney, 14 January 1880, and vol. 3701, file 17,309, Dewdney to Vankoughnet, 17 April 1880.
40 Ibid., vol. 3701, file 17,309, Dewdney to Vankoughnet, 17 April 1880.
41 Ibid., vol. 3728, file 25,940, R.W. Gowan to C.T. Galt, 3 May 1880.
42 Ibid., vol. 3714, file 21,229, Galt to Vankoughnet, 22 May 1880.
43 Ibid., vol. 3701, file 17,309, L.F. Masson to Macdonald, 27 November 1879.
44 Ibid., Dewdney to Vankoughnet, 17 April 1880.
45 Ibid., Wadsworth to Vankoughnet, 30 September 1881.
46 Ibid., vol. 3739, file 28,416, J. Ouimet to Macdonald, 7 April 1881.
47 1880 *Commons Debates*, 2: 1942 (Mills).
48 Ibid., 1942–3 (Joseph Royal).
49 Ibid., 1691 (Mills).
50 Ibid., 1692 (Edward Blake).
51 Ibid., 1694–5 (Schultz).
52 Ibid., 1943.
53 Ibid., 1684 (Macdonald).
54 Ibid., 1693.
55 Ibid., 1944.
56 Ibid., 1693.
57 W.L. Morton, *Manitoba*, 164–5.
58 Ibid., 164.
59 NA, RG 10, vol. 3706, file 18,745, Wadsworth's instructions, 18 January 1879.
60 W.L. Morton, *Manitoba*, 164.
61 1885 *Commons Debates*, 2: 3316 (W. Paterson).
62 CHC, *Sessional Papers*, vol. 15, no. 6 (1881), 78.
63 Spector, "Field Agriculture," 114, 117.
64 NA, RG 10, vol. 3706, file 18,745, Wadsworth's instructions, 17 January 1879.
65 CHC, *Sessional Papers*, vol. 15, no. 6 (1881), x, xxv, xxix.
66 Ibid., vol. 17, no. 4 (1883), 73.
67 Allan R. Turner, "Pioneer Farming," 49.
68 Jefferson, *Fifty Years*, 36.
69 NA, RG 10, vol. 3665, file 10,094, Vankoughnet to Macdonald, 17 January 1879.
70 Larmour, "Dewdney," 18.

71 PAM, CMS Records, no. 913, Charles Pratt Journal, 1878.
72 CHC, *Sessional Papers*, vol. 18, no. 3 (1884), 66.
73 Ibid., vol. 15, no. 6 (1881), xvli.
74 Ibid., 41, xxxiv.
75 Ibid., vol. 16, no. 5 (1882), 50, 208.
76 Ibid., 50.
77 Kaye, "'The Settlers' Grand Difficulty,'" 8.
78 W.L. Morton, *Manitoba*, 165.
79 CHC, *Sessional Papers*, vol. 15, no. 6 (1881), xiii.
80 Ibid., vol. 17, no. 4 (1883), 75.
81 Ibid., 121.
82 Ibid., vol. 15, no. 6 (1881), xiii, and vol. 17, no. 3 (1883), 121.
83 Ibid., vol. 16, no. 5 (1882), 174.
84 McKenzie, *Men of the HBC*, 52.
85 W.L. Morton, *Manitoba*, 182; Thomas, "Agriculture," 41–2.
86 CHC, *Sessional Papers*, vol. 15, no. 6 (1881), x, xiii.
87 Ibid., vol. 16, no. 5 (1882), 195.
88 Ibid., vol. 17, no. 4 (1883), 102, 122.
89 NA, RG 10, vol. 3706, file 18,745, Wadsworth to Vankoughnet, 10 February 1880.
90 Ibid., vol. 3720, file 23,325, Dewdney to Vankoughnet, 28 August 1880.
91 Ibid., vol. 3706, file 18,745, Wadsworth to Vankoughnet, 10 Feburary 1880.
92 CHC, *Sessional Papers*, vol. 15, no. 6 (1881), xiv, xxx.
93 Ibid., vol. 16, no. 5 (1882), 50.
94 Ibid., vol. 14, no. 14 (1880), 91, 99, 97.
95 NA, RG 10, vol. 3668, file 10,644, Reed to Dewdney, 28 December 1883.
96 CHC, *Sessional Papers*, vol. 16, no. 5 (1882), 208.
97 NA, RG 10, vol. 3705, file 18,260, Reed to Vankoughnet, 31 January 1885.
98 CHC, *Sessional Papers*, vol. 14, no. 14 (1880), 91.
99 Ibid., vol. 17, no. 4 (1883), 121.
100 Ibid., vol. 14, no. 14 (1880), 101, 105, 106, and vol. 15, no. 6 (1881), xi, xiii, xxiv, and vol. 16, no. 5 (1882), 52.
101 Ibid., vol. 15, no. 6 (1881), 75.
102 Ibid., xviii.
103 NA, RG 10, vol. 3733, file 26,743, Dewdney to Reed, 25 February 1881.
104 1881 *Commons Debates*, 2: 1351 (Macdonald).
105 NA, RG 10, vol. 3686, file 13,057, John Tomkins to Dewdney, 20 January 1881.
106 Ibid., vol. 3687, file 13,611, James Johnston to Dewdney, 24 February 1881.

107 Ibid., vol. 3682, file 12,516, Scott to Dewdney, 21 January 1881.
108 1881 *Commons Debates*, 2: 1350 (Mills).
109 Ibid.
110 1884 *Commons Debates*, 2: 1610 (Mills).
111 Ibid., 1108.
112 Ibid., 1103 (James Fleming).
113 Ibid., 1105 (Philipe Casgrain).
114 1881 *Commons Debates*, 2: 1351 (Macdonald).
115 1884 *Common Debates*, 2: 1450 (Macdonald).
116 Ibid., 1107.
117 NA, Sir John A. Macdonald Papers, vol. 149, memorandum, Vankoughnet to Macdonald, 31 January 1884.
118 1884 *Commons Debates*, 1: 59 (Cameron).
119 CHC, *Sessional Papers*, vol. 16, no. 5 (1882), xi.
120 NA, RG 10, vol. 3664, file 9,834, Vankoughnet to Macdonald, 13 November 1884.
121 NA, Edgar Dewdney Papers, reel M-2816, Vankoughnet to Dewdney, 5 December 1884.
122 CHC, *Sessional Papers*, vol. 16, no. 5 (1882), 190.
123 Ibid., vol. 13, no. 4 (1879), 107.
124 Ibid., vol. 17, no. 4 (1883), 192–3.
125 Ibid., vol. 15, no. 6 (1881), 121.
126 NA, RG 10, vol. 3668, file 10,644, Reed to Dewdney, 28 December 1883.
127 CHC, *Sessional Papers*, vol. 17, no. 4 (1883), 120.
128 Ibid., vol. 16, no. 5 (1882), 204.
129 Ibid., vol. 15, no. 6 (1881), 133.
130 Ibid., vol. 17, no. 4 (1883), 120.
131 NA, RG 10, vol. 3703, file 17,728, J.C. Nelson to Dewdney, 31 December 1884.
132 CHC, *Sessional Papers*, vol. 15, no. 6 (1881), 121.
133 Ibid., vol. 17, no. 4 (1883), 71.
134 Ibid., vol. 15, no. 6 (1881), 134.
135 Ibid., vol. 17, no. 4 (1883), 71.
136 Tyler, "Kiwisānce," 477.
137 NA, RG 10, vol. 3757, file 31,397, Edwin Allen to Dwedney, 5 July 1881.
138 McKenzie, *Men of the HBC*, 70.
139 CHC, *Sessional Papers*, vol. 14, no. 14 (1880), 105.
140 Ibid., vol. 15, no. 6 (1881), 44–5.
141 Tobias, "Canada's Subjugation," 529–31.
142 The site of the J.J. English home farm later became the Horace A. Greeley ranch, and is commemorated by a plaque on the road from Maple Creek to the Cypress Hills Provincial Park.

143 McKenzie, *Men of the HBC*, 70.
144 CHC, *Sessional Papers*, vol. 15, no. 6 (1881), 47.
145 NA, RG 10, vol. 3744, file 29,506-2, MacDonald to E.T. Galt, 20 June 1882.
146 Tyler, "Kiwisānce," 477.
147 CHC, *Sessional Papers*, vol. 18, no. 3 (1884), 138.
148 Cowie, *Company of Adventurers*, 214.
149 McKenzie, *Men of the HBC*, 82.
150 CHC, *Sessional Papers*, vol. 17, no. 4 (1883), 71.
151 Ibid., vol. 14, no. 14 (1880), 115.
152 NA, RG 10, vol. 3703, file 17,728, Nelson to Dewdney, 31 December 1884.
153 CHC, *Sessional Papers*, vol. 17, no. 4 (1883), 72.
154 NA, RG 10, vol. 3768, file 33,642, Qu'Appelle Chiefs' Address.
155 Ibid.
156 CHC, *Sessional Papers*, vol. 17, no. 4 (1883), 117–18.
157 NA, RG 10, vol. 3673, file 10,986, clipping from the *Bulletin* (Edmonton), 7 January 1883.
158 Ibid., vol. 3732, file 26,638, MacDonald to Dewdney, 7 January 1881.
159 NA, Edgar Dewdney Papers, reel M-2816, translation, Red Pheasant to Dewdney, 31 August 1881.
160 CHC, *Sessional Papers*, vol. 16, no. 5 (1882), 195.
161 NA, RG 10, vol. 3673, file 10,986, clipping from the *Bulletin*, 7 January 1883.
162 1884 *Commons Debates*, 2: 1107 (Macdonald).
163 NA, RG 10, vol. 3697, file 15,423.
164 Ibid., Reed to Vankoughnet, 25 January 1885.
165 Ibid.
166 Ibid., vol. 3666, file 10,181, Dewdney to Vankoughnet, 10 December 1883.
167 Ibid., vol. 3670, file 10,772, Peter Hourie to MacDonald, 28 December 1883.
168 Ibid., Hourie to Dewdney, 29 December 1883.
169 Ibid., vol. 3755, file 30,961, Reed to Dewdney, 13 June 1881.
170 Ibid., vol. 3666, file 10,181, Reed to Vankoughnet, 27 February 1884.
171 Isabel Andrews, "Yellow Calf."
172 NA, RG 10, vol. 3666, file 10,181, Hilton Keith to Dewdney, 19 February 1884.
173 Ibid., Report of Inspector Richard Burton Deane, 28 February 1884.
174 Fraser, *British Welfare State*, 119.
175 NA, RG 10, vol. 3666, file 10,181, Reed to Vankoughnet, 27 February 1884.
176 Hildebrandt, "Fort Battleford."
177 NA, RG 10, vol. 3744, file 29,506-2, MacDonald to Reed, 18 July 1882.

178 Ibid., J. McIlree to Dewdney, 27 June 1882.
179 Ibid., MacDonald to Galt, 29 July 1882.
180 Tobias, "Canada's Subjugation," 531.
181 NA, RG 10, vol. 3655, file 9,026, Sam Macdonald to Dewdney, 13 September 1883.
182 Ibid., vol. 3745, file 29,506-4, Dr O.C. Edwards to MacDonald, 13 May 1884.
183 Ibid., vol. 3686, file 13,168, MacDonald to Dewdney, 15 May 1884.
184 Ibid., Reed to Vankoughnet, 15 May 1884; NA, Reed Papers, vol. 21, small letterbook, no. 49, Reed to Vankoughnet, 1 April 1884.
185 Quoted in Beal and Macleod, *Prairie Fire*, 89.
186 NA, RG 10, vol. 3686, file 13,168, MacDonald to Dewdney, 15 May 1885.
187 Ibid., Reed to Vankoughnet, 15 May 1884.
188 Ibid., vol. 3579, file 619, pt. 1, MacDonald to Reed, 9 June 1884.
189 Ibid., MacDonald to Dewdney, 8 July 1884.
190 Ibid., vol. 3687, file 13,642, John Nichol to Dewdney, 5 May 1884.
191 Hildebrandt, *Battle of Batoche*, 7–20; idem, "North-West Rebellion."
192 Stonechild, "Indian View of 1885," 159.
193 Ibid., vol. 3710, file 19,550-3, memorandum, Reed to Dewdney, 20 July 1885.
194 McKenzie, *Men of the HBC*, 127.
195 NA, RG 10, vol. 3709, file 19,550-1, MacDonald to Dewdney, 8 April 1885.
196 Ibid., telegram, Qu'Appelle chiefs to Macdonald, n.d., 1885.
197 Ibid., file 19,550-2, Chief Piapot to Macdonald, 30 April 1885.
198 Ibid., vol. 3710, file 19,500-3, MacDonald to Dewdney, 5 June 1885.
199 Lalonde, "North-West Rebellion," 96–7.
200 NA, RG 10, vol. 3709, file 19,550-2, MacDonald to Dewdney, 26 April 1885.
201 Ibid., 6 May 1885.
202 Ibid., vol. 3710, file 19,550-3, MacDonald to Dewdney, 29 May 1885.
203 McKenzie, *Men of the HBC*, 130.

CHAPTER FOUR

1 1886 *Commons Debates*, 1: 718–30 (Cameron).
2 Ibid.
3 Young, "Indian Problem," 469.
4 Lupul, "Bobtail Land Surrender," 29.
5 Maclean, *Indians*, 267.
6 CHC, *Sessional Papers*, vol. 19, no. 6 (1885), xi.
7 Ibid., 141.

8 1886 *Commons Debates*, 2: 1761 (Macdonald).
9 Ibid., 1762.
10 *The Facts*, 3–7.
11 Ibid., 4, 13.
12 See, for example, *Free Press* (Manitoba), 4 January 1889; *The Empire* (Toronto), 16 January 1889; *Vidette* (Qu'Appelle), 19 December 1889; *Mail* (Toronto), 2 December 1889; *The Week* (Toronto), 13 February 1892.
13 See, for example, the *Leader* (Regina), 3 October 1888, 21 May 1889, 14 October 1890; *Saskatchewan Herald*, 26 July 1884, 5 March 1890; *Free Press*, 8 February 1889, 3 December 1889, 1 May 1890.
14 *Free Press*, 1 January 1891.
15 *The Empire*, 8 December 1890.
16 *Mail*, 20 April 1891.
17 *Vidette*, 3 March 1892.
18 *Globe* (Toronto), 22 October 1892.
19 *Leader*, 21 May 1889.
20 *Free Press*, 3 December 1889.
21 *Citizen* (Ottawa), 13 November 1890.
22 Lupul, "Bobtail Land Surrender," 29.
23 *Free Press*, 4 January 1889.
24 *Vidette*, 19 December 1889.
25 NA, RG 10, vol. 3665, file 10,080, Dewdney to Vankoughnet, 28 May 1885.
26 Ibid., vol. 3752, file 30,421, Reed to Vankoughnet, 2 August 1886.
27 Ibid.
28 Ibid., Vankoughnet to Dewdney, 14 August 1886.
29 1886 *Commons Debates*, 1: 720 (Cameron).
30 NA, RG 10, vol. 3755, file 31,061, Dewdney to Vankoughnet, 19 February 1886.
31 Canada, *Senate Journals*, 1887, vol. II, app. 1, Select Committee on the Existing Natural Food Products of the North-West Territories, 24, 23.
32 Ibid., 34, 48.
33 Ibid., 5.
34 McM, Reed Papers, Reed to Laurier, 9 February 1900, and Audet's biographical notes.
35 NA, RG 15, vol. 245, file 23,563, pt. 1.
36 Ibid., Hayter Reed, "Canadian and United States Immigration," May 1880.
37 McM, Reed Papers, Audet's biographical notes.
38 NA, RG 10, DSG Letterbooks, vol. 21, large letterbook, Reed to T.M. Daly, April 1893, no. 470–1.
39 Beal and Macleod, *Prairie Fire*, 79.

40 McM, Reed Papers, "Address," 33.
41 Ibid., 4, 65.
42 NA, RG 10, vol. 3755, file 30,961, Reed to Dewdney, 13 June 1881.
43 Jefferson, *Fifty Years*, 126.
44 "Harry Loucks," in *Voice of the People*, 129.
45 Quoted in Beal and Macleod, *Prairie Fire*, 331.
46 NA, RG 10, vol. 3710, file 19,550-3, Reed, "Memorandum Relative to Future Management of Indians," 14 August 1885.
47 Ibid.
48 Ibid., 20 July 1885.
49 CHC, *Sessional Papers*, vol. 23, no. 12 (1889), 165.
50 McM, Reed Papers, "Address," 30.
51 CHC, *Sessional Papers*, vol. 23, no. 12 (1889), 165.
52 Ibid., 166.
53 McM, Reed Papers, "Address," 29.
54 CHC, *Sessional Papers*, vol. 20, no. 6 (1886), 108-9.
55 Ibid., vol. 22, no. 16 (1888), 125.
56 McM, Reed Papers, "Address," 27.
57 CHC, *Sessional Papers*, vol. 23, no. 12 (1889), 161.
58 Ibid., vol. 19, no. 6 (1885), 98.
59 Ibid., vol. 16, no. 5 (1882), 50.
60 NA, RG 10, vol. 3760, file 32,025-10, McGibbon's Report on the Touchwood Agency, 1886.
61 Ibid., vol. 3795, file 46,769, Report of E.C. Stewart, File Hills, 3 January 1889.
62 CHC, *Sessional Papers*, vol. 23, no. 12 (1889), 166.
63 NA, RG 10, vol. 3911, file 111,404, Reed to Vankoughnet, 5 March 1891.
64 Tobias, "Indian Reserves," 94.
65 Quoted in Bennett, "Passes for Indians," 1, 2.
66 NA, RG 10, vol. 3584, file 1,130, notice, 6 May 1885.
67 Bennett, "Passes for Indians," 2.
68 Morris, *Treaties*, 353.
69 John N. Jennings, "North West Mounted Police," 289-90.
70 *Settlers and Rebels* (1883), 16.
71 Bennett, "Passes for Indians," 3.
72 NA, RG 10, 3710, file 19,550-3, Reed, "Memorandum Relative to Future Management of Indians," 20 July 1885, and "Memorandum Relative to Future Management of Indians," 14 August 1885.
73 Ibid., Dewdney, marginal notes.
74 Quoted in John N. Jennings, "North West Mounted Police," 291.
75 Bennett, "Passes for Indians," 4.
76 CHC, *Sessional Papers*, vol. 21, no. 15 (1887), 73.

77 Bennett, "Passes for Indians," 4.
78 John N. Jennings, "North West Mounted Police," 281.
79 *Law and Order* (1886), 45.
80 *Saskatchewan Herald*, 8 March 1886.
81 *Law and Order* (1887), 87; Donkin, *Trooper*, 241.
82 *The New West* (1889), 76.
83 Steele, *Forty Years*, 258.
84 John N. Jennings, "North West Mounted Police," 295–6.
85 Donkin, *Trooper*, 241.
86 *The New West* (1888), 68.
87 Quoted in John N. Jennings, "North West Mounted Police," 298.
88 *The New West* (1888), 68.
89 Quoted in Bennett, "Passes for Indians," 4.
90 *The Herald* (Calgary), 15 January 1890.
91 Macleod, *Law Enforcement*, 146.
92 Quoted in ibid.
93 Quoted in John N. Jennings, "North West Mounted Police," 299.
94 Macleod, *Law Enforcement*, 146.
95 Maclean, *Indians*, 26.
96 Maclean, *Savage Folk*, 18.
97 The population of the North-West in 1885 was as follows:

	Whites	Métis	Indians	Total
Assiniboia	16,574	1,017	4,492	22,083
Saskatchewan	4,486*		6,260	10,746
Alberta	4,878	1,237	9,418	15,533
Total	25,938	2,254*	20,170	48,362

* The Saskatchewan figure includes whites and Métis.
Source: Waite, *Arduous Destiny*, 149.

98 Lalonde, "North-West Rebellion," 97.
99 John N. Jennings, "North West Mounted Police," 315.
100 NA, RG 10, vol. 3710, file 19,550-3, memorandum, Reed to Dewdney, 20 July 1885.
101 Bennett, "Passes for Indians," 5.
102 *The Herald*, 15 January 1890.
103 *The Gazette* (Fort Macleod), 24 March 1893; *The Herald*, 14 June 1893.
104 *The Herald*, 14 June 1893.
105 Bennett, "Passes for Indians," 7.
106 Tobias, "Protection," 48.
107 Isabel Andrews, "Crooked Lakes Reserves," 112.
108 *Historical Development of the Indian Act*, 93.
109 CHC, *Sessional Papers*, vol. 25, no. 14 (1891), xvii.

110 1884 *Commons Debates*, 2: 1063 (Macdonald).
111 Sluman and Goodwill, *Tootoosis*, 127.
112 *Settlers and Rebels* (1882) 39, (1883), 49.
113 Quoted in Isabel Andrews, "Crooked Lakes Reserves," 108.

CHAPTER FIVE

1 Dick, "Abernethy District," 245.
2 Warkentin, "Western Canada in 1886," 44.
3 Dick, "Farm-Making Costs," 196.
4 Allan R. Turner, "Pioneer Farming," 46–7.
5 Warkentin, "Western Canada in 1886," 46.
6 See Rasporich, "Utopian Ideals," 37–62.
7 Morgan, "Bell Farm," 45–63.
8 Friesen, *Canadian Prairies*, 222.
9 Strange, *Prairie Agriculture*, 26.
10 A.S. Morton, *Prairie Settlement*, 87–8.
11 Ibid., 84.
12 Dick, "Factors affecting Prairie Settlement," 12, 20.
13 A.S. Morton, *Prairie Settlement*, 83.
14 *Historical Development of the Indian Act*, 68.
15 NA, RG 10, vol. 3739, file 28,571, Dewdney to Vankoughnet, 15 April 1886.
16 Bryce, *Holiday Rambles*, 52.
17 CHC, *Sessional Papers*, vol. 20, no. 6 (1886), lvi.
18 NA, RG 10, vol. 3761, file 32,182, MacDonald to Dewdney, 8 August 1886; CHC, *Sessional Papers*, vol. 21, no. 15 (1887), 80.
19 NA, RG 10, vol. 3686, file 13,168, MacDonald to Dewdney, 25 June 1884.
20 Ibid., vol. 3687, file 13,642, John Nichol to Dewdney, 30 May 1884.
21 CHC, *Sessional Papers*, vol. 24, no. 18 (1890), 120.
22 NA, RG 10, vol. 3812, file 55,895, W.E. Jones to Reed, 18 September 1890.
23 CHC, *Sessional Papers*, vol. 21, no. 15 (1887), 82.
24 NA, RG 10, vol. 3795, file 46,759, H.L. Reynolds to Indian commissioner, 6 June 1888.
25 Ibid., vol. 3761, file 32,182, MacDonald to Indian commissioner, 6 March 1888.
26 Isabel Andrews, "Crooked Lakes Reserves," 127–8.
27 Saskatchewan Archives Board, William Gibson Papers, *The Ayrshire Post*, December 1889.
28 CHC, *Sessional Papers*, vol. 21, no. 15 (1887), 80; NA, RG 10, vol. 3761, file 32,182, MacDonald to Dewdney, 5 March 1887.

29 Dick, "Abernethy District," 137.
30 NA, RG 10, vol. 3806, file 52,332, Reed to Vankoughnet, 27 October 1888.
31 Ibid., vol. 3761, file 32,182, MacDonald to Indian commissioner, 10 January 1888.
32 CHC, *Sessional Papers*, vol. 23, no. 12 (1889), 281.
33 Ibid., vol. 22, no. 16 (1888), lx.
34 Ibid, vol. 27, no. 14 (1893), 77.
35 NA, Reed Papers, file W. McGirr, McGirr to Reed, 8 May 1889; CHC, *Sessional Papers*, vol. 19, no. 6 (1885), 141.
36 NA, RG 10, vol. 3761, file 32,182, MacDonald to Indian commissioner, April 1888.
37 Ibid., vol. 3845, file 73,406-9, Wadsworth's Report on the Muscowpetung Agency, 8 April 1891.
38 Ibid., file 73,406-5, Wadsworth's Report on the Crooked Lakes Agency, 19 December 1890.
39 Ibid., file 73,406-8, Wadsworth's Report on the File Hills Agency, 7 March 1891.
40 Saskatchewan Archives Board, Mitchell-Stobart Store Correspondence, file 21, Memorandum of Agreement, November 1891; NA, Reed Papers, vol. 14, Hillyard Mitchell to Dewdney, 14 May 1891, and Mitchell to Reed, 4 June 1891.
41 NA, Reed Papers, vol. 14, 14 May 1891.
42 Ibid., vol. 13, MacDonald to Reed, 23 February 1890.
43 CHC, *Sessional Papers*, vol. 25, no. 14 (1891), 198.
44 NA, RG 10, DSG Letterbooks, no. 964, Vankoughnet to Dewdney, 11 January 1890.
45 Ibid., no. 965.
46 CHC, *Sessional Papers*, vol. 25, no. 14 (1891), 62-3.
47 NA, RG 10, vol. 3761, file 32,182, MacDonald to Reed, 12 June 1889.
48 Ibid., vol. 3728, file 25,550, Inspector L. Herchmer's Report for 1885.
49 Ibid., vol. 3795, file 46,759, Reynolds to Reed, 30 June 1889.
50 Ibid., vol. 3845, file 73,406-5, Wadsworth's Report on the Crooked Lakes Agency, 19 December 1890.
51 Ibid.
52 NA, Reed Papers, vol. 15, no. 1678, Wadsworth to Reed, 21 November 1895.
53 Ibid., vol. 13, G.H. Harpur to Reed, 20 February 1891.
54 Ibid., vol. 15, no. 1676, Wadsworth to Reed, 4 October 1895.
55 NA, RG 10, vol. 3795, file 46,759, Reynolds to Reed, 30 April 1890.
56 Spector, "Field Agriculture," 118-19.
57 Ibid.; Regehr, *Remembering Saskatchewan*, 34.
58 Spector, "Field Agriculture," 119.

59 NA, RG 10, vol. 3761, file 32,182, MacDonald to Dewdney, 8 August 1886.
60 CHC, *Sessional Papers*, vol. 21, no. 15 (1887), 190.
61 Spector, "Field Agriculture," 224.
62 NA, RG 10, vol. 3760, file 32,025-10, McGibbon's Report on the Touchwood Agency, 8 November 1886.
63 Ibid., Hilton Keith to Dewdney, 26 November 1886.
64 Ibid., vol. 3761, file 32,182, MacDonald to Reed, 2 August 1889.
65 Spector, "Field Agriculture," 115.
66 NA, RG 10, vol. 3761, file 32,182, MacDonald to Dewdney, 8 August 1886.
67 Ibid., 18 May 1889.
68 A.S. Morton, *Prairie Settlement*, 71–2.
69 NA, Reed Papers, vol. 12, no. 446, Dewdney to Reed, 23 March 1892.
70 NA, RG 10, vol. 3761, file 32,248, J.B. Lash to Indian commissioner, 9 May 1888.
71 A.S. Morton, *Prairie Settlement*, 89.
72 Warkentin, "Western Canada in 1886," 47.
73 Betke, "Pioneers and Police," 25–9.
74 CHC, *Sessional Papers*, vol. 21, no. 15 (1887), 79.
75 NA, RG 10, vol. 3761, file 32,182, MacDonald to Indian commissioner, 7 June 1888, and vol. 3795, file 46,759, Reynolds to Reed, 31 May 1890.
76 CHC, *Sessional Papers*, vol. 22, no. 16 (1888), lxix, and vol. 23, no. 12 (1889), 144.
77 Ibid., vol. 20, no. 6 (1886), v.
78 Ibid., vol. 23, no. 12 (1889), 144.
79 NA, RG 10, vol. 3761, file 32,182, MacDonald to Indian commissioner, 7 June 1888.
80 Bryce, *Holiday Rambles*, 56.
81 University of Saskatchewan Archives, A.S. Morton Manuscript Collection, Indian Head and Qu'Appelle Agricultural Society Minutes, 28 October 1886.
82 Ibid., Minutes of 1886–96.
83 CHC, *Sessional Papers*, vol. 22, no. 16 (1888), 67.
84 *Leader*, 14 October 1890.
85 CHC, *Sessional Papers*, vol. 25, no. 14 (1891), 195.
86 *Leader*, 11 October 1887.
87 Jones, *Midways, Judges*, 3.
88 Dion, *My Tribe*, 114.
89 Ibid., 115.
90 NA, RG 10, vol. 3761, file 32,182, MacDonald to Dewdney, 8 August 1886.

91 Gibson, "Homestead Venture," 108.
92 NA, RG 10, vol. 3845, file 73,406-7, Wadsworth to Reed, 17 February 1891.
93 Ibid., vol. 3859, file 82,250-6, Wadsworth to Reed, 9 November 1891.
94 Brass, "Miracle of Butter," *Leader Post* (Regina), 28 June 1960.
95 Gowanlock and Delaney, *Two Months*, 103.
96 Brass, *I Walk in Two Worlds*, 37.
97 NA, RG 10, vol. 3765, file 32,784, P.J. Williams to Reed, 31 December 1889.
98 Ibid., vol. 3845, file 73,406-8, Wadsworth to Reed, 7 March 1891.
99 Ibid., file 73,406-7, Wadsworth to Reed, 17 February 1891.
100 Ibid., file 73,406-9, Wadsworth to Reed, 8 April 1891.
101 Ibid.
102 Prentice et al., *Canadian Women*, 117–18.
103 NA, RG 10, vol. 3845, file 73,406-9, Wadsworth to Reed, 8 April 1891.
104 Pamela Margaret White, "Restructuring the Domestic Sphere."
105 Cran, *Woman in Canada*, 106.
106 NA, RG 10, vol. 3859, file 82,250-6, Wadsworth to Reed, 9 November 1891.
107 Ahenakew, *Voices*, 112.
108 NA, RG 10, vol. 3760, file 32,025-9, McGibbon's Report on the Muscowpetung Agency, 27 October 1886.
109 Ibid., vol. 3761, file 32,263, Williams' Report on the File Hills Agency, 31 July 1886.
110 Ibid., vol. 3766, file 32,985, D. McIntosh to Lash, August 1886.
111 Ibid., vol. 3753, file 30,664, Keith to Dewdney, 31 May 1886.
112 Ibid., vol. 3760, file 32,025-9, McGibbon's Report on the Muscowpetung Agency, 27 October 1886.
113 Ibid., vol. 3761, file 32,263, Williams' Report on the File Hills Agency, 31 July 1886.
114 CHC, *Sessional Papers*, vol. 23, no. 12 (1889), 59.
115 NA, RG 10, vol. 3761, file 32,182, MacDonald to Indian commissioner, 6 August 1888.
116 Ibid., 18 May 1889.
117 Ibid., 27 July 1889.
118 Ibid., vol. 3795, file 46,759, Reynolds to Reed, 30 November 1889.
119 Ibid., 31 July 1889.
120 Ibid., vol. 3761, file 32,182, MacDonald to Reed, 10 July 1890.
121 Ibid., vol. 3795, file 46,759, J.P. Wright to Reed, 3 October 1890.
122 Ibid., vol. 3761, file 32,248, Lash to Reed, 14 November 1889.
123 Ibid., vol. 3795, file 46,759, Reynolds to Reed, October 1889.
124 Ibid., 28 February 1890.
125 Raby, "Prairie Fires," 84.

126 Qu'Appelle Historical Society, *Qu'Appelle: Footprints to Progress*, 106.
127 Raby, "Prairie Fires," 89.
128 NA, RG 10, vol. 3761, file 32,248, Lash to Reed, 11 November 1889.
129 Ibid., vol. 3795, file 46,759, Reynolds to Reed, 31 December 1889.
130 Ibid., vol. 3835, file 65,911, Nelson to Dewdney, 31 November 1889.
131 Ibid., vol. 3795, file 46,759, Reynolds to Reed, 31 August 1889.
132 Ibid., vol. 3596, file 1,322, Lash to Indian commissioner, 6 August 1888.
133 Ibid., Lyndwoode Periera to Vankoughnet, 27 January 1890.
134 Ibid., Lash to Vankoughnet, February 1890.
135 Ibid., vol. 3732, file 26,623, A.M. Burgess to Vankoughnet, 4 March 1886.
136 Ibid., MacDonald to Dewdney, March 1886.
137 Ibid., Vankoughnet to Burgess, 7 April 1886.
138 Ibid., MacDonald to Vankoughnet, 10 March 1890.
139 *Saskatchewan Herald*, 25 December 1889.
140 Ibid., 24 September 1890.
141 NA, RG 10, vol. 3782, file 40,316, Williams to Reed, 24 September 1890.
142 Ibid., E. Brokowski to Reed, 22 November 1889.
143 *Saskatchewan Herald*, 17 September 1890.
144 Ibid., 24 September 1890.
145 Ibid., 13 October 1888.
146 CHC, *Sessional Papers*, vol. 22, no. 16 (1888), 127.
147 *Saskatchewan Herald*, 27 February 1889.
148 1888 *Commons Debates*, 2: 1610.
149 *Saskatchewan Herald*, 13 October 1888.
150 NA, RG 15, vol. 245, file 23,563, pt. 1.
151 NA, RG 10, vol. 3806, file 52,332, Reed to Vankoughnet, 27 October 1888.
152 NA, Reed Papers, vol. 21, large letterbook file, no. 19, Reed to Williams, March 1889.
153 Ibid., no. 21, Reed to Forget, 8 March 1889.
154 *Bulletin*, 17 January 1881.
155 NA, RG 10, vol. 3761, file 32,182, MacDonald to Dewdney, 11 May 1889.
156 Ibid., vol. 3781, file 40,166, C. Marshallsay to Dewdney, 4 June 1887.
157 Ibid., MacDonald to Dewdney, 5 June 1887.
158 Ibid., vol. 3797, file 47,659, W. Anderson to Macdonald, 4 June 1888.
159 Ibid., vol. 3761, file 32,182, MacDonald to Dewdney, 11 May 1887.
160 CHC, *Sessional Papers*, vol. 20, no. 6 (1886), 152.
161 NA, RG 10, vol. 3812, file 55,895, W.E. Jones to Reed, 18 September 1890.

162 CHC, *Sessional Papers*, vol. 25, no. 14 (1891), 59.
163 NA, RG 10, vol. 3795, file 46,759, Reynolds to Indian commissioner, 31 March 1888.
164 Hudson's Bay Company Archives, Fort Qu'Appelle Report on Districts 1–13, sec. b, class 334/e, 2 May 1888.
165 Ibid., 10 May 1889.
166 CHC, *Sessional Papers*, vol. 21, no. 15 (1887), 78, 172.
167 Qu'Appelle Historical Society, *Qu'Appelle: Footprints to Progress*, 101.

CHAPTER SIX

1 CHC, *Sessional Papers*, vol. 22, no. 16 (1888), 28.
2 Milloy, "Early Indian Acts," 58.
3 Ibid., 57.
4 Tobias, "Protection," 45.
5 Milloy, "Early Indian Acts," 59.
6 Ibid., 62.
7 Tobias, "Protection," 44.
8 Ibid., 47.
9 CHC, *Sessional Papers*, vol. 23, no. 12 (1889), x.
10 *Historical Development of the Indian Act*, 77.
11 Tobias, "Protection," 45.
12 CHC, *Sessional Papers*, vol. 12, no. 7 (1878), 6.
13 Ibid., 65.
14 Tyler, "Tax-eating Proposition," 114.
15 NA, RG 10, vol. 3774, file 37,060, Dewdney to superintendent general, 9 February 1887.
16 Ibid., vol. 3806, file 52,332, Reed to superintendent general, 27 October 1888.
17 Ibid.
18 CHC, *Sessional Papers*, vol. 24, no. 18 (1890), xxviii.
19 Ibid., vol. 23, no. 12 (1889), lx.
20 Ibid., vol. 24, no. 18 (1890), xxvii.
21 Ibid., vol. 23, no. 12 (1889), 165–6.
22 Ibid., x, 166.
23 Ibid., vol. 24, no. 18 (1890), 136.
24 Ibid., vol. 23, no. 12 (1889), x, lx.
25 NA, RG 10, DSG Letterbooks, Vankoughnet to Dewdney, November 1889.
26 CHC, *Sessional Papers*, vol. 23, no. 12 (1889), lx.
27 Dippie, *Vanishing American*, 160.
28 Priest, *Uncle Sam's Stepchildren*, 126.
29 Mardock, *Reformers*, 213.

30 Dippie, *Vanishing American*, 162.
31 Ibid., 163.
32 Priest, *Uncle Sam's Stepchildren*, 232.
33 Dippie, *Vanishing American*, 163.
34 Priest, *Uncle Sam's Stepchildren*, 217.
35 Dippie, *Vanishing American*, 190.
36 Milner, *With Good Intentions*, 197.
37 Samek, *Blackfoot*, 139.
38 Tyler, "Tax-eating Proposition," 114.
39 Ibid.
40 Morris, *Treaties*, 332.
41 Tyler, "Tax-eating Proposition," 151-4.
42 NA, Reed Papers, vol. 21, large letterbook file, no. 94, Reed to Vankoughnet, November 1889.
43 Ibid., no. 200, Reed to Reynolds, 2 May 1890.
44 Ibid., vol. 15, no. 1598, Vankoughnet to Reed, 13 November 1889.
45 CHC, *Sessional Papers*, vol. 23, no. 12 (1889), 166.
46 Ibid., 302; NA, RG 10, vol. 3811, file 55,152-1, Reed to Indian agents, 19 November 1889.
47 Venne, *Indian Acts and Amendments*, 110.
48 NA, RG 10, vol. 3811, file 55,152-1, Reed to Vankoughnet, 3 July 1889, and Reed to Indian agents, 19 November 1889.
49 CHC, *Sessional Papers*, vol. 23, no. 12 (1889), 302.
50 Ibid., vol. 26, no. 14 (1892), 222.
51 NA, RG 10, vol. 3811, file 55,152-1, Reed to Indian agents, 19 November 1889.
52 Venne, *Indian Acts and Amendments*, 110.
53 NA, RG 10, DSG Letterbooks, vol. 1114, p. 107, Reed to Indian agent, Battleford, 24 November 1893.
54 NA, RG 10, vol. 3806, file 52,332, Vankoughnet to Reed, n.d., 1888.
55 Ibid., vol. 3811, file 55,152-1, Reed to Vankoughnet, 30 July 1891.
56 Ibid., John R. Hall to Vankoughnet, 1 December 1891.
57 Ibid., Reed to Vankoughnet, 14 June 1890.
58 Ibid., memorandum, 25 June 1890.
59 Ibid., vol. 3854, file 79,422, Reed to Nelson, n.d., 1891.
60 Ibid., vol. 3835, file 65,911, Nelson to Dewdney, 31 November 1889.
61 Ibid., vol. 3579, file 619, pt. 2, Nelson to Reed, 8 July 1889.
62 Ibid., Reed to MacDonald, 10 July 1889.
63 Ibid., MacDonald to Reed, 15 July 1889.
64 CHC, *Sessional Papers*, vol. 23, no. 12 (1889), 304.
65 Ibid., vol. 24, no. 18 (1890), 136.
66 Ibid., 147, 136.
67 NA, Reed Papers, vol. 12, no. 421, Dewdney to Reed, 16 July 1891.

68 NA, RG 10, vol. 3959, file 141,977-4 and 141,977-7.
69 Ibid., vol. 3651, file 82, pt. 4, J.A. Sutherland to J. McKenna, 14 June 1904.
70 CHC, *Sessional Papers*, vol. 23, no. 12 (1889), 162.
71 Ibid., vol. 25, no. 14 (1891), 193.
72 Ibid.
73 McM, Reed Papers, "Address," 28.
74 CHC, *Sessional Papers*, vol. 26, no. 14 (1892), 48.
75 NA, RG 10, vol. 3964, file 148,285, Reed to Amédée Forget, 24 August 1896.
76 NA, Reed Papers, vol. 13, no. 869, Alex McGibbon to Reed, 16 March 1891.
77 NA, RG 10, vol. 3793, file 46,062, Reed to Dewdney, 11 April 1888.
78 Ibid., vol. 3746, file 29,690-3, Reed to superintendent general, 30 September 1886.
79 Ibid., vol. 3964, file 148,285, Reed to Forget, 24 August 1896.
80 Ibid., vol. 3908, file 107,243, Reed to agent Markle, March 1895; CHC, *Sessional Papers*, vol. 25, no. 14 (1891), xvii.
81 *Historical Development of the Indian Act*, 64–9.
82 CHC, *Sessional Papers*, vol. 25, no. 14 (1891), xviii.
83 Ibid., vol. 23, no. 12 (1889), 162.
84 Ibid., vol. 25, no. 14 (1891), 196.
85 GAI, Battleford Indian Agency Correspondence, box 19, vol. 33, 23 December 1889, 16–17.
86 Ibid., Reed to Forget, April 1895.
87 Dippie, *Vanishing American*, 164–71.
88 NA, RG 10, vol. 3964, file 148,285, Reed to Forget, 24 August 1896.
89 McM, Reed Papers, "Address," 28.
90 CHC, *Sessional Papers*, vol. 23, no. 12 (1889), 162.
91 NA, RG 10, vol. 3964, file 148,285, Reed to Forget, 24 August 1896.
92 CHC, *Sessional Papers*, vol. 23, no. 12 (1889), 162.
93 Loehr, "Self-sufficiency," 37; Danhof, *Change in Agriculture*, 15.
94 Danhof, *Change in Agriculture*, 18.
95 Dewey, "Rehabilitation of the Peasant," 32–47.
96 Jay, *Joseph Chamberlain*, 99.
97 Seaton, "Idylls of Agriculture."
98 Fowke, *National Policy*, 12.
99 Fowke, *Canadian Agricultural Policy*, 3.
100 Fowke, *National Policy*, 12–13.
101 Sarah Carter, "Materials History," 274.
102 Loehr, "Self-sufficiency," 41.
103 Ibid.
104 Danhof, *Change in Agriculture*, 78–9.

105 GAI, Battleford Indian Agency Correspondence, box 19, vol. 33, 1 November 1889.
106 Ibid., Hobbema Agency Correspondence, file 4.
107 NA, RG 10, DSG Letterbooks, vol. 1115, p. 220, Reed to Forget, 12 June 1894.
108 Ibid.
109 NA, Reed Papers, vol. 14, Reed to T.M. Daly, 10 March 1893.
110 NA, RG 10, vol. 3964, file 148,285, de Cases to Reed, 19 November 1896.
111 Ibid.
112 Ibid., W.S. Grant to Reed, 1 October 1896.
113 Ibid., W.E. Jones to Reed, 1 November 1896.
114 NA, Reed Papers, vol. 13, no. 869, McGibbon to Reed, 16 March 1891.
115 NA, RG 10, vol. 3843, file 72,695-1, McGibbon's Report, 2 October 1890.
116 NA, Reed Papers, vol. 14, no. 989, R.S. McKenzie to Reed, 16 December 1890.
117 NA, RG 10, vol. 3964, file 148,285.
118 Ibid., Grant to Reed, 1 October 1896.
119 Ibid., J.J. Campbell to Reed, 8 October 1896.
120 Ibid., Grant to Reed, 1 October 1896.
121 Ibid., vol. 3812, file 55,895, W.E. Jones to Reed.
122 Ibid., vol. 3964, file 148,285, Grant to Reed, 1 October 1896.
123 NA, Reed Papers, vol. 13, no. 869, McGibbon to Reed, 16 March 1891.
124 Ibid., vol. 14, no. 989, McKenzie to Reed, 16 December 1890.
125 Scott, "Some Features of Indian Administration," 95.
126 NA, Reed Papers, vol. 14, no. 1206, Reed to McGibbon, 7 November 1891.
127 NA, RG 10, vol. 3964, file 14,285, Reed to Forget, 24 August 1896.
128 Ibid., DSG Letterbooks, vol. 1115, p. 220, Reed to Forget, 12 June 1894.
129 NA, Reed Papers, vol. 14, Reed to Daly, 10 March 1893.
130 NA, RG 10, vol. 3964, file 14,285, Campbell to Reed, 8 October 1896.
131 NA, Reed Papers, vol. 14, no. 1206, Reed to McGibbon, 7 November 1891.
132 Ibid., Reed to Daly, 10 March 1893.
133 NA, RG 10, DSG Letterbooks, vol. 115, p. 382, Memorandum Relative to Mr Agent Finlayson.
134 NA, RG 10, vol. 3964, file 148,285, Forget to Reed, 20 August 1896.
135 Ibid., MacDonald to Reed, 16 February 1897.
136 Ibid., J.P. Wright to Reed, 16 February 1897.

137 Ibid., Grant to Reed, 1 October 1896; Jones to Reed, 1 November 1896; de Cases to Reed, 19 November 1896.
138 Ibid., Reed to Forget, 25 February 1897.
139 Ibid., DSG Letterbooks, vol. 1115, Reed to J. Wilson, 3 August 1894.
140 Ibid., vol. 1117, p. 319, Reed to Forget, 20 July 1895.
141 NA, Reed Papers, vol. 13, no. 960, McGirr to Reed, 8 March 1893.
142 Ibid., vol. 14, no. 1353, Reed to Daly, 13 March 1893.
143 NA, RG 10, vol. 3900, file 99,907, J.B. Lash to Reed, 14 March 1893.
144 See Sarah Carter, "Agriculture and Agitation," 2-9.
145 NA, RG 10, vol. 3859, file 82,250-2, Wadsworth's Report on the Birtle Agency, 1890.
146 Ibid., vol. 3908, file 107,243, agent Markle to Reed, 25 November 1893.
147 Ibid., Wadsworth to Forget, 2 November 1893.
148 Ibid., Markle to Reed, 25 November 1893.
149 Ibid., William Chambers to F.W. Thompson, 4 January 1894.
150 Ibid., Thompson to Forget, 8 January 1894.
151 Ibid., *Chronicler* (Virden), 11 January 1894.
152 Ibid., Wadsworth to Forget, appendix, 26 December 1894.
153 Ibid., Wadsworth to Forget, 26 December 1894.
154 Ibid., Reed to Markle, March 1895.
155 CHC, *Sessional Papers*, vol. 17, no. 4 (1883), 130, 133.
156 Sluman and Goodwill, *Tootoosis*, 127. See also Dion, *My Tribe*, 132.
157 Ahenakew, *Voices*, 13, 148.
158 Sluman and Goodwill, *Tootoosis*, 127.
159 Ahenakew, *Voices*, 149.
160 Dion, *My Tribe*, 145; Sluman and Goodwill, *Tootoosis*, 127.
161 Dion, *My Tribe*, 145.
162 NA, RG 10, vol. 4053, file 379-203-1.
163 GAI, John McDougall Papers, "The Future of the Indians," n.d. (1902).
164 Ibid., vol. 3993, file 187,812, William Miller to the minister of the interior, 21 July 1899.
165 NA, Reed Papers, D.D. Macdonald to J.A. Macdonald, 22 August 1893.
166 *Leader*, 6 July 1893; *Mail*, 11 July 1893.
167 *Gazette* (Montreal), 19 September 1893.
168 Gwyn, *Private Capital*, 288.
169 Wolff, *Economics of Colonialism*; Brett, *Colonialism and Underdevelopment*.
170 Bundy, *Rise and Fall*.
171 Yudelman, *Africans on the Land*, 49-50, 51.
172 Carlson, *Indians, Bureaucrats and Land*.

CHAPTER SEVEN

1 Hall, "Clifford Sifton," 129.
2 Ibid., 132.
3 Ibid., 129; idem, *Clifford Sifton*, 1: 127.
4 NA, Sifton Papers, series 2, p. 20,363, 25 January 1897.
5 NA, Reed Papers, no. 42225, Reed to Wilfrid Laurier, 9 February 1900.
6 McM, Reed Papers, Laurier to Reed, 24 February 1897.
7 Tyler, "Tax-eating Proposition," 158n.
8 Tyler and Wright Research Consultants, "Alienation," 21; Hall, "Clifford Sifton," 130.
9 Hall, "Clifford Sifton," 130.
10 CHC, *Sessional Papers*, vol. 50, no. 27 (1914), 229.
11 Brass, *I Walk in Two Worlds*, 11.
12 W.W. Gibson, "Indians at Work."
13 Spence, *Salvation Army*, 2–7.
14 Mohl and Betten, "Paternalism and Pluralism."
15 William Morris Graham, born in Ottawa, Ontario, in 1867, was first employed by the Department of Indian Affairs in 1885 as a clerk in the Moose Mountain agency. He later joined the staff of the commissioner's office in Regina and in 1897 was appointed File Hills Indian agent. Titley, *Narrow Vision*, 186ff.; idem, "W.M. Graham," 25–41.
16 CHC, *Sessional Papers*, vol. 23, no. 12 (1889), 169.
17 Pamela Margaret White, "Restructuring the Domestic Sphere," 188.
18 Quoted in ibid., 189.
19 CHC, *Sessional Papers*, vol. 45, no. 27 (1911), 336, 347.
20 Ibid., vol. 36, no. 27 (1901), 368.
21 GAI, Blood Indian Agency Correspondence, file 97, Indian agent to J.D. McLean, 31 March 1914.
22 NA, RG 10, vol. 4072, file 431,636, Rev. W. McWhinney to McLean, 26 February 1913.
23 CHC, *Sessional Papers*, vol. 45, no. 27 (1911), 520.
24 NA, RG 10, vol. 7768, file 27,111-2, W.M. Graham to McLean, 17 June 1911.
25 Brass, *I Walk in Two Worlds*, 13.
26 NA, RG 10, vol. 7768, file 27,111-2, Graham to McLean, 17 June 1911.
27 CHC, *Sessional Papers*, vol. 50, no. 27 (1914), 229.
28 *Free Press*, March 1918, clipping contained in NA, RG 10, vol. 7768, file 27,111-2.
29 CHC, *Sessional Papers*, vol. 42, no. 27 (1907), 157.
30 Ibid., vol. 45, no. 27 (1910), 418.
31 Ibid., vol. 42, no. 27 (1907), 156.
32 Titley, *Narrow Vision*, chap. 10.

33 Abbott, *Administration*, 51.
34 CHC, *Sessional Papers*, vol. 42, no. 27 (1907), 156.
35 Ahenakew, *Voices*, 133, 131.
36 Tobias, "Protection", 49.
37 Quoted in *Historical Development of the Indian Act*, 107.
38 Lupul, "Bobtail Land Surrender," 31.
39 *Historical Development of the Indian Act*, 108.
40 Hall, "Clifford Sifton," 142.
41 Tyler and Wright Research Consultants, "Alienation," 40–74.
42 Hall, "Clifford Sifton," 142.
43 Tyler, "Tax-eating Proposition," 159.
44 Titley, *Narrow Vision*, 21, 95.
45 Ibid., 158n.
46 Quoted in Tyler, "Tax-eating Proposition," 2.
47 NA, RG 10, vol. 4007, file 241,354.
48 Ibid., M.G. Jackson and Peter Parker to Department of Indian Affairs, March 1908.
49 Ibid., Michael Anderson to secretary, Department of Indian Affairs, 8 June 1907.
50 Ibid., J.B. Dougherty to minister of the interior, September 1909.
51 Tobias, "Protection," 48–9.
52 Raby, "Indian Land Surrenders," 40.
53 Hall, "Clifford Sifton," 143.
54 Saskatchewan Archives Board, Campbell Innes Papers, 5, Rev. J.A. Mackay Papers, box 5, Indian Schools, 1907–8.
55 NA, RG 10, vol. 3560, file 81, pt. 8, J. Carruthers to Laird, 25 January 1904.
56 Raby, "Indian Land Surrenders," 42.
57 Ibid., 42–6.
58 Ibid., 41.
59 NA, RG 10, vol. 3732, file 26,623, MacDonald to Dewdney, 10 March 1891.
60 Ibid., Rideau Club, Ottawa, note, 25 February 1899.
61 Ibid., A.W. Ponton to J. McKenna, 17 February 1899.
62 Ibid., Laird to superintendent general, 22 April 1899.
63 Ibid., Petition from the Residents of Broadview and Whitewood, 1902.
64 Ibid., J.D. McLean to Rev. J.G. Stephens, 2 April 1902.
65 Ibid., Laird to McLean, 6 May 1902.
66 Ibid., Graham to Frank Oliver, 19 June 1906.
67 Ibid., Graham to McLean, 18 February 1907.
68 Ibid., vol. 4007, file 241,354.
69 Titley, *Narrow Vision*, 40.
70 NA, RG 10, vol. 1392, D.C. Scott to T.E. Donnelly, 26 July 1917.

71 Ibid., certified copy of a report of the Committee of the Privy Council, 16 February 1912.
72 *Historical Development of the Indian Act*, 113.
73 Sluman and Goodwill, *Tootoosis*, 121.
74 Quoted in *Historical Development of the Indian Act*, 112–13.
75 Quoted in Titley, *Narrow Vision*, 41.
76 Ibid., 42.
77 NA, RG 10, vol. 4069, file 427,063, memorandum to Arthur Meighen from Graham, 3 April 1919.
78 Ibid.
79 Lupul, "Bobtail Land Surrender," 36.
80 Titley, *Narrow Vision*, 46.
81 NA, RG 10, vol. 7533, file 26,106, Graham to Scott, 26 August 1919.
82 Ibid., petition to Meighen from Birtle Returned Soldiers Association, 24 June 1919.
83 Ibid., vol. 3732, file 26,623, Graham to McLean, 18 February 1907.
84 *Historical Development of the Indian Act*, 114.
85 Quoted in ibid., 115.
86 GAI, Battleford Agency Correspondence, box 5, file 24, W.J. Chisholm to Indian agent, 22 May 1902.
87 GAI, Hart Cantelon interview.
88 Carter v. Nichol, 1911, 4, Sask. L.R. 382, see Slattery and Charlton, *Canadian Native Law Cases*, v. 4.
89 Saskatchewan Archives Board, Joe Kapoese interview 1, 4.
90 NA, RG 10, vol. 1993, H. Nichol to McLean, 20 September 1913.
91 Ibid., vol. 7596, file 10,116-11, pt. 1, McLean to H.A. Gunn, 17 May 1915.
92 GAI, Battleford Agency Correspondence, box 1, file 2, S.L. McDonald to Graham, 6 October 1922.
93 NA, RG 10, vol. 4093, file 600,003, Graham to secretary, Department of Indian Affairs, 12 September 1923.
94 Ibid., vol. 1392, petition to J.D. McLean, 26 June 1917.
95 Ibid., Graham to McLean, 3 July 1917.
96 Ibid., vol. 4053, file 379,203-1, M. Millar to McLean, 10 January 1911.
97 Ibid., vol. 1392, Nichol to McLean, 27 January 1910.
98 Ibid., vol. 4053, file 379,203-1.
99 Ibid., statement of Joe Larat, 15 December 1910.
100 Ibid., transcript of meetings, January 1911.
101 Ibid.
102 Ibid., H.W. MacDonald to McLean, 16 March 1911.
103 Ibid., McLean to MacDonald, 22 March 1911.
104 Ibid., Millar to McLean, 14 June 1911.
105 Ibid., vol. 1392, Nichol to McLean, 28 February 1912.

106 CHC, *Sessional Papers*, vol. 46, no. 27 (1911), 138.
107 Hawthorn, ed., *Contemporary Indians*, 57–8, 159–60.
108 NA, RG 10, vol. 3859, file 82,250-5, Wadsworth to Reed, 20 October 1891.
109 CPRC, Mandelbaum's Field Notes, Round Lake 1, 3.

Bibliography

ARCHIVAL SOURCES

Canadian Plains Research Centre
   David Mandelbaum Field Notes
Glenbow–Alberta Institute. Archives
   Hart Cantelon Interview
   Edgar Dewdney Papers
   William A. Fraser Papers
   Allan MacDonald Papers
   John McDougall Papers
Hudson's Bay Company Archives
   Fort Qu'Appelle Report on Districts 1–13
McCord Museum. McGill University
   Hayter Reed Papers
National Archives of Canada
   Department of Indian Affairs Records
      Black Series Headquarters Files
      Deputy Superintendent Letterbooks
      Indian Affairs Scrapbook
   Department of the Interior Records
   Edgar Dewdney Papers
   David Laird Letterbooks
   Sir John A. Macdonald Papers
   Hayter Reed Papers
   Clifford Sifton Papers
Public Archives of Manitoba
   William Joseph Christie Papers
   Church Missionary Society Journals and Correspondence
   John Christian Schultz Papers

Saskatchewan Archives Board
  William Gibson Papers
  Indian History Film Project Interviews
  Campbell Innes Papers
  Mitchell-Stobart Store Correspondence
  Pioneer Questionnaires
University of Saskatchewan Archives
  A.S. Morton Collection

GOVERNMENT PUBLICATIONS

Canada. Parliament. House of Commons. *Debates*.
Canada. *Senate Journals*. 1887. Vol. II, App. 1.
Canada. Parliament. House of Commons. *Sessional Papers*.

NEWSPAPERS

Battleford *Saskatchewan Herald*
Calgary *Herald*
Carlisle, Pennsylvania *The Red Man*
Edmonton *Bulletin*
Fort Macleod *Gazette*
Manitoba *Free Press*
Montreal *Gazette*
Moosomin *Courier*
Ottawa *Citizen*
Ottawa *Journal*
Qu'Appelle *Vidette*
Regina *Leader*
Toronto *The Empire*
Toronto *Mail*
Toronto *The Week*

PRIMARY SOURCES: BOOKS AND ARTICLES

Abbott, Frederick H. *The Administration of Indian Affairs in Canada*. Washington: n.p., 1915.

Atwood, Mae, ed. *In Rupert's Land: Memoirs of Walter Traill*. Toronto: McClelland and Stewart Ltd, 1970.

Bryce, George. *Holiday Rambles between Winnipeg and Victoria*. Winnipeg: n.p., 1888.

Butler, William Francis. *The Great Lone Land*. 1872. Reprint. Edmonton: Hurtig Publishers, 1968.

Cowie, Isaac. *The Company of Adventurers: A Narrative of Seven Years in the Service of the Hudson's Bay Company during 1867–74 on the Great Buffalo Plains*. Toronto: William Briggs, 1913.

Cran, G. *A Woman in Canada*. London: John Milne, 1910.

Denig, Edwin T. *Five Indian Tribes of the Upper Missouri: Sioux, Arickaras, Assiniboines, Crees, Crows*. Norman: University of Oklahoma Press, 1973.

Donkin, John George. *Trooper in the Far North-West: Recollections of Life in the North-West Mounted Police, Canada, 1884–1888*. 1889. Reprint. Saskatoon: Western Producer Prairie Books, 1987.

"The Edwin J. Brooks Letters." *Saskatchewan History* 10, no. 3 (1957); 11, no. 2 (1958).

The Facts respecting Indian Administration in the North-West. Ottawa: Department of Indian Affairs, 1886.

Ferrier, Thompson. *Indian Education in the North West*. [Canada]: n.p., n.d.

Gibson, W.W. "Indians at Work for the War." *East and West: A Paper for Young Canadians*. Toronto, 14 April 1917.

Gibson, William. "Homestead Venture, 1883–1892, An Ayrshire Man's Letters Home." *Saskatchewan History* 14, no. 3 (1961); 15, no. 1 (1962).

Gowanlock, Theresa, and Theresa Delaney. *Two Months in the Camp of Big Bear: The Life and Adventures of Theresa Gowanlock and Theresa Delaney*. Toronto: Parkdale, 1885.

Hind, H.Y. *Narrative of the Canadian Red River Exploring Expedition of 1857 and of the Assiniboine and Saskatchewan Exploring Expedition of 1858*. 1860. Reprint. New York: Greenwood Press, 1969.

Hunt, F.L. "Notes on the Qu'Appelle Treaty." *The Canadian Monthly and National Review* 9, no. 3 (1876).

Impey, Frederic. *Three Acres and A Cow: Successful Small Holdings and Peasant Proprietors*. London: Swan Sonnenschein, Le Bas and Lowrey, 1885.

Jefferson, Robert. *Fifty Years on the Saskatchewan*. Battleford: Canadian North-West Historical Society Publications, 1929.

Law and Order: Being the Official Reports to Parliament of the Activities of the Royal North-West Mounted Police Force from 1886–1887. 1886–87. Reprint. Toronto: Coles Publishing Co., 1973.

McDougall, John. *Forest, Lake and Prairie: Twenty Years of Frontier Life in Western Canada, 1842–62*. Toronto: William Briggs, 1895.

– *In the Days of the Red River Rebellion: Life and Adventure in the Far West of Canada, 1868–72*. Toronto: William Briggs, 1903.

– *On Western Trails in the Early Seventies: Frontier Pioneer Life in the Canadian Northwest*. Toronto: William Briggs, 1911.

– *Saddle, Sled and Snowshoe: Pioneering on the Saskatchewan in the Sixties*. Toronto: William Briggs, 1896.

– *Wa-pee Moos-tooch or White Buffalo, the Hero of a Hundred Battles: A Tale of Life in Canada's Great West during the Early Years of the Last Century*. Calgary: The Herald Job Printing Co., 1908.

McKenzie, N.M.W.J. *The Men of the Hudson's Bay Company*. Fort William: Times-Journal Presses, 1921.
Maclean, John. *Canadian Savage Folk: The Native Tribes of Canada*. Toronto: William Briggs, 1896.
– *The Indians of Canada: Their Manners and Customs*. Toronto: William Briggs, 1889.
Morris, Alexander. *The Treaties of Canada with the Indians of Manitoba and the North-West Territories*. 1880. Reprint. Toronto: Coles Publishing Co., 1971.
Morton, A.S., ed. *The Journal of Duncan McGillivray of the North West Company*. Toronto: The Macmillan Co., 1929.
The New West: Being the Official Reports to Parliament of the Activities of the Royal North-West Mounted Police Force from 1888–1889. 1888–89. Reprint. Toronto: Coles Publishing Co., 1973.
Ryerson, John. *Hudson's Bay: Or A Missionary Tour in the Territory of the Hon. Hudson's Bay Company*. Toronto: G.R. Sanderson, 1855.
Scott, D.C. "Some Features of Indian Administration in Canada." Lake Mohonk Conference Proceedings. Sixth session, 1916.
Settlers and Rebels: Being the Official Reports to Parliament of the Activities of the Royal North-West Mounted Police Force from 1882–1885. 1882–85. Reprint. Toronto: Coles Publishing Co., 1973.
Skinner, Alanson. "Plains Cree Tales." *Journal of American Folk-Lore* 24 (1916): 341–67.
Steele, Sir S.B. *Forty Years in Canada*. Winnipeg: Russell Lang and Co., 1915.
Tanner, John. *A Narrative of the Captivity and Adventures of John Tanner during Thirty Years Residence among the Indians in the Interior of North America*. Edited by Edwin James. 1830. Reprint. Minneapolis: Ross and Haines Inc., 1956.
Trant, William. "The Treatment of the Canadian Indians." *Westminster Review* 144 (1895): 506–27.
West, John. *The Substance of a Journal during a Residence at the Red River Colony, British North America, and Frequent Excursions among the North West American Indians, in the Years 1820, 1821, 1822, 1823*. London: L.B. Seeley and Son, 1824.
Young, E.R. *By Canoe and Dog Train among the Cree and Saulteaux Indians*. Toronto: William Briggs, 1890.
– "The Indian Problem." *Canadian Methodist Magazine and Review* (June 1885): 465–9.
– *On the Indian Trail: Stories of Missionary Work among the Cree and Saulteaux Indians*. New York: Young People's Missionary Movement, 1897.

SECONDARY SOURCES

Ahenakew, Edward. *Voices of the Plains Cree*. Toronto: McClelland and Stewart Ltd, 1973.

Aitkins, Annette. *Harvest of Grief: Grasshopper Plagues and Public Assistance in Minnesota, 1873–78*. St Paul: Minnesota Historical Society Press, 1984.

Andrews, George Reid. "Black and White Workers: Sao Paulo, Brazil, 1888–1928." *Hispanic American Historical Review* 68, no. 3 (1988): 491–524.

Andrews, Isabel. "The Crooked Lakes Reserves: A Study of Indian Policy in Practice from the Qu'Appelle Treaty to 1900." MA thesis, University of Saskatchewan, 1972.

– "Indian Protest against Starvation: The Yellow Calf Incident of 1884." *Saskatchewan History* 28, no. 2 (1975): 41–51.

Arthur, George. "Bison Pounds." In *Proceedings of the Plains Cree Conference*. Regina: Canadian Plains Research Centre, 1979.

Axtell, James. *The European and the Indian: Essays in the Ethnohistory of Colonial North America*. Toronto: Oxford University Press, 1981.

Barron, F. Laurie, and James B. Waldram, eds. *1885 and After: Native Society in Transition*. Regina: Canadian Plains Research Centre, 1986.

Bartlett, Richard. "Indian Reserves on the Prairies." *Canadian Native Law Reporter* 3 (1980): 3–53.

Beal, Bob, and Rod Macleod. *Prairie Fire: The 1885 North-West Rebellion*. Edmonton: Hurtig Publishers, 1984.

Beeton, Beverly. "Teach Them to Till the Soil: An Experiment with Indian Farms, 1850–1862." *American Indian Quarterly* (1977–78): 299–320.

Bennett, B. "Study of Passes for Indians to Leave Their Reserves." Ottawa: Treaties and Historical Research Centre, 1974.

Berkhofer, Robert J., Jr. *The White Man's Indian: Images of the American Indian from Columbus to the Present*. New York: Alfred A. Knopf, 1978.

Betke, Carl. "Pioneers and Police on the Prairies, 1885–1914." In *Historical Papers, 1980*, 9–32. Canadian Historical Association.

Bocking, D.H., ed. *Pages from the Past: Essays on Saskatchewan History*. Saskatoon: Western Producer Prairie Books, 1979.

Booth, William. *In Darkest England and the Way Out*. London, 1890.

Brass, Eleanor. "The File Hills Ex-Pupil Colony." *Saskatchewan History* 6, no. 2 (1953): 66–9.

– *I Walk in Two Worlds*. Calgary: Glenbow Museum, 1987.

– "Miracle of Butter." *Leader Post* (Regina), 28 June 1960.

Brett, E.A. *Colonialism and Underdevelopment in East Africa: The Politics of Economic Change, 1919–1939*. London: Heinemann, 1973.

Bundy, Colin. *The Rise and Fall of the South African Peasantry*. Berkeley and Los Angeles: University of California Press, 1979.

Carlson, Leonard A. *Indians, Bureaucrats and Land: The Dawes Act and the Decline of Indian Farming*. Westport, Conn.: Greenwood Press, 1981.

Carter, R.C. "Canadian Bar Association Committee on Native Justice: The Position of Canada's Aboriginal Peoples within the Legal and Justice Systems. An Opening Statement." 1988.

Carter, Sarah. "Agriculture and Agitation on the Oak River Dakota Reserve, 1875–1895." *Manitoba History* 6 (1983): 2–9.
- "Angus McKay." *Dictionary of Canadian Biography* 12, 640–1.
- "The Genesis and Anatomy of Government Policy and Indian Reserve Agriculture on Four Agencies in Treaty Four, 1874–1896." PH D diss., University of Manitoba, 1987.
- "A Materials History of the Motherwell Home." In *Motherwell Historic Park*. History and Archaeology, no. 66. Ottawa: Parks Canada, 1983.
- "The Souris-Mouth Posts, 1793–1832." Manitoba Historic Resources Branch, 1980.
Cell, John W. *British Colonial Administration in the Mid-Nineteenth Century: The Policy-Making Process*. New Haven: Yale University Press, 1970.
- *The Highest Stage of White Supremacy: The Origins of Segregation in South Africa and the American South*. Cambridge: Cambridge University Press, 1982.
Chalmers, John W. *Laird of the West*. Calgary: Detselig Enterprises Ltd, 1981.
Cherwinski, W.J.C. "Wooden Horses and Rubber Cows: Training British Agricultural Labour for the Canadian Prairies, 1890–1930." In *Historical Papers, 1980*, 133–54. Canadian Historical Association.
Clifton, James A. *The Prairie People: Continuity and Change in Potawatomi Indian Culture, 1665–1965*. Lawrence: Regents Press of Kansas, 1977.
Cole, Jean M. *Exile in the Wilderness: The Biography of Chief Factor Archibald McDonald, 1800–1853*. Don Mills, Ont.: Burns and MacEachern Ltd, 1979.
Coutts, Robert. "The Role of Agriculture in an English Speaking Halfbreed Economy: The Case of St. Andrew's, Red River." *Native Studies Review* 4, nos. 1 and 2 (1988): 67–94.
Cuthand, Stan. "The Native Peoples of the Prairie Provinces in the 1920's and 1930's." In *One Century Later: Western Canadian Reserve Indians since Treaty Seven*, edited by Ian A.L. Getty and Donald B. Smith, 31–42. Vancouver: University of British Columbia Press, 1978.
Dalal-Clayton, D.B. *Black's Agricultural Dictionary*. London: Adams and Charles Black, 1981.
Danhof, Clarence H. *Change in Agriculture: The Northern United States, 1820–1870*. Cambridge: Harvard University Press, 1969.
Dempsey, Hugh A. "One Hundred Years of Treaty Seven." In *One Century Later: Western Canadian Reserve Indians since Treaty Seven*, edited by Ian A.L. Getty and Donald B. Smith, 20–30. Vancouver: University of British Columbia Press, 1978.
Dewey, Clive J. "The Rehabilitation of the Peasant Proprietor in Nineteenth-Century Economic Thought." *History of Political Economy* 6, no. 1 (1974): 17–47.
Dick, Lyle. "Estimates of Farm-Making Costs in Saskatchewan, 1882–1914." *Prairie Forum* 6, no. 2 (1981): 183–201.

- "Factors affecting Prairie Settlement: A Case Study of Abernethy in the 1880's." In *Historical Papers, 1985*. Canadian Historical Association.
- "A Social and Economic History of the Abernethy District, Saskatchewan, 1880–1920." Parks Canada, Prairie Region, 1982. Typescript.

Dion, Joe. *My Tribe the Crees*. Calgary: Glenbow–Alberta Institute, 1979.

Dippie, Brian W. *The Vanishing American: White Attitudes to U.S. Indian Policy*. Middletown, Conn.: Wesleyan University Press, 1982.

Driver, Harold E. *Indians of North America*. Chicago: University of Chicago Press, 1961.

Dyck, Noel, "The Administration of Federal Indian Aid in the North West Territories, 1879–1885." MA thesis, University of Saskatchewan, 1970.

- "An Opportunity Lost: The Initiative of the Reserve Agricultural Programme in the Prairie West." In *1885 and After: Native Society in Transition*, edited by F. Laurie Barron and James B. Waldram, 121–37. Regina: Canadian Plains Research Centre, 1986.

Elias, Peter Douglas. *The Dakota of the Canadian Northwest: Lessons for Survival*. Winnipeg: University of Manitoba Press, 1988.

- "The First American Refugees." *Ontario Indian* 5, no. 4 (1982).

Ewers, John. *The Horse in Blackfoot Indian Culture*. Smithsonian Institution, Bureau of American Ethnology Bulletin no. 159. Washington, DC, 1955.

Fisher, A.D. "The Cree of Canada: Some Ecological and Evolutionary Considerations." *Western Canadian Journal of Anthropology* 1, no. 1 (1969).

- "Introducing 'Our Betrayed Wards,' by R.N. Wilson." *Western Canadian Journal of Anthropology* 4, no. 1 (1974): 21–59.

Fisher, Robin. *Contact and Conflict: Indian-European Relations in British Columbia, 1774–1890*. Vancouver: University of British Columbia Press, 1977.

Fitz-Gibbon, Mary, ed. *The Diaries of Edmund Montague Morris: Western Journeys, 1907–1910*. Toronto: Royal Ontario Museum, 1985.

Fowke, Vernon C. *Canadian Agricultural Policy: The Historical Pattern*. Toronto: University of Toronto Press, 1946.

- *The National Policy and the Wheat Economy*. Toronto: University of Toronto Press, 1957.

Francis, Daniel, and Toby Morantz. *Partners in Furs: A History of the Fur Trade in Eastern James Bay, 1600–1870*. Kingston and Montreal: McGill-Queen's University Press, 1983.

Fraser, Derek. *The Evolution of the British Welfare State: A History of Social Policy since the Industrial Revolution*. New York: Barnes and Noble, 1973.

Friesen, G. *The Canadian Prairies: A History*. Toronto: University of Toronto Press, 1984.

Friesen, J. "Magnificent Gifts: The Treaties of Canada with the Indians of the Northwest, 1869–76." *Transactions of the Royal Society of Canada*, series 5, vol. 1 (1986): 41–51.

Garrioch, A.L. *The Correction Line*. Winnipeg: Stovel Co. Ltd, 1933.

Getty, Ian A.L., and Antoine S. Lussier, eds. *As Long as the Sun Shines and Water Flows: A Reader in Canadian Native Studies*. Vancouver: University of British Columbia Press, 1983.
Getty, Ian A.L., and Donald B. Smith, eds. *One Century Later: Western Canadian Reserve Indians since Treaty Seven*. Vancouver: University of British Columbia Press, 1978.
Gibson, James R. *Farming the Frontier: The Agricultural Opening of the Oregon Country, 1786–1846*. Vancouver: University of British Columbia Press, 1985.
Gill, Sam D. *Mother Earth: An American Story*. Chicago: University of Chicago Press, 1987.
Goldring, Philip. "The First Contingent: The North-West Mounted Police, 1873–74." *Occasional Papers in Archaeology and History*, no. 21. Ottawa: National Historic Parks and Sites Branch, 1979.
Goosen, N. Jaye. "Indians of the Fort Ellice Region." Manitoba Historic Resources Branch, 1976.
Grigg, David. *The Harsh Lands: A Study in Agricultural Development*. London: Macmillan and Co., 1970.
Gwyn, Sandra. *The Private Capital: Ambition and Love in the Age of Macdonald and Laurier*. Toronto: McClelland and Stewart Ltd, 1984.
Hall, D.J. *Clifford Sifton*. Vol. 1, *The Young Napoleon, 1861–1900*. Vancouver: University of British Columbia Press, 1981.
– "Clifford Sifton and Canadian Indian Administration, 1896–1905." *Prairie Forum* 2, no. 2 (1977): 127–51.
Hanks, Lucien M., Jr, and Jane Richardson Hanks. *Tribe under Trust: A Study of the Blackfoot Reserve in Alberta*. Toronto: University of Toronto Press, 1950.
Hawkes, John. *The Story of Saskatchewan and Its People*. 3 vols. Regina: S.J. Clarke Publishing Co., 1924.
Hawthorn, H.B., ed. *A Survey of Contemporary Indians of Canada: Economic, Political, Educational Needs and Policies*. Ottawa: Indian Affairs Branch, 1966.
Helgason, Gail. *The First Albertans*. Edmonton: Lone Pine Publishing, 1987.
Hildebrandt, W.H. *The Battle of Batoche: British Small Warfare and the Entrenched Métis*. Ottawa: National Historic Parks and Sites Branch, 1985.
– "Fort Battleford: A Cultural History." Environment Canada, Parks, 1988. Typescript.
– "North-West Rebellion." *Canadian Encyclopedia* 2: 1270.
– "P.G. Laurie: The Aspirations of a Western Enthusiast." *Prairie Forum* 8, no. 2 (1983): 157–78.
– "P.G. Laurie: The Aspirations of a Western Enthusiast." MA thesis, University of Saskatchewan, 1978.
The Historical Development of the Indian Act. Ottawa: Indian and Northern Affairs, 1978.

Hodgetts, J.E. *Pioneer Public Service: An Administrative History of the United Canadas, 1841–67*. Toronto: University of Toronto Press, 1955.
Holzkamm, Tim E., and Leo G. Waisberg. "'Our Land Here Is Not as on the Plain': The Development and Decline of Ojibway Agriculture in Northwestern Ontario, 1805–1915." Paper presented to the American Society for Ethnohistory. November 1989.
Horn, Michiel, and Ronald Sabourin, eds. *Studies in Canadian Social History*. Toronto: McClelland and Stewart Ltd, 1974.
Houghton, Walter E. *The Victorian Frame of Mind, 1830–1870*. New Haven: Yale University Press, 1973.
Hoxie, Frederick E. *A Final Promise: The Campaign to Assimilate the Indians, 1880–1920*. 1984. Reprint. Cambridge: Cambridge University Press, 1989.
Hughes, J. Donald. *American Indian Ecology*. El Paso: Texas Western Press, 1983.
Ingels, Ernest B. "The Custom Threshermen in Western Canada, 1890–1925." In *Building beyond the Homestead*, edited by David C. Jones and Ian MacPherson, 135–60. Calgary: University of Calgary Press, 1985.
Jay, Richard. *Joseph Chamberlain: A Political Study*. Oxford: Clarendon Press, 1981.
Jenness, Diamond. *The Indians of Canada*. Ottawa: National Museum of Canada, 1932.
Jennings, Francis. *The Invasion of America: Indians, Colonialism and the Cant of Conquest*. New York: W.W. Norton and Co., 1975.
Jennings, John N. "The North West Mounted Police and Indian Policy, 1873–1896." PH D diss., University of Toronto, 1979.
Jones, David C. *Midways, Judges and Smooth-Tongued Fakirs: The Illustrated History of Country Fairs in the Prairie West*. Saskatoon: Western Producer Prairie Books, 1983.
– "There Is Some Power about the Land: The Western Agrarian Press and Country Life Ideology."*Journal of Canadian Studies* 7, no. 3 (1982): 96–108.
Jones, David C., and Ian MacPherson, eds. *Building beyond the Homestead*. Calgary: University of Calgary Press, 1985.
Judd, Carol, and Arthur J. Ray, eds. *Old Trails and New Directions: Papers of the Third North American Fur Trade Conference*. Toronto: University of Toronto Press, 1980.
Kaye, Barry. "'The Settlers' Grand Difficulty': Haying in the Economy of the Red River Settlement." *Prairie Forum* 9, no. 1 (1984): 1–12.
Kaye, Barry, and D.W. Moodie. "The 'Psoralea' Food Resources of the Northern Plains." *Plains Anthropologist* 23, no. 82, pt. 1 (1978): 329–36.
Kehoe, Alice B. *Hunters of the Buried Years: The Prehistory of the Prairie Provinces*. Regina: School Aids and Text Book Publishing Co. Ltd, n.d.
– *North American Indians: A Comprehensive Account*. Englewood Cliffs, NJ: Prentice-Hall Inc., 1981.

Kempton, James H. "Maize as a Measure of Indian Skill." In *Symposium on Prehistoric Agriculture*. University of New Mexico Bulletin. Millwood: Kraus Reprint Co., 1977.

Kennedy, Dan. *Recollections of an Assiniboine Chief*. Toronto: McClelland and Stewart Ltd, 1972.

Kennedy, Dane. *Islands of White: Settler Society and Culture in Kenya and Southern Rhodesia, 1890–1939*. Durham, NC: Duke University Press, 1987.

Kennedy, Jacqueline Judith. "Qu'Appelle Industrial School: White 'Rites' for the Indians of the Old North-West." MA thesis, Carleton University, 1970.

Klassen, Henry C., ed. *The Canadian West: Social Change and Economic Development*. Calgary: Comprint Publishing Co., 1977.

Knight, Rolf. *Indians at Work: An Informal History of Native Indian Labour in British Columbia, 1858–1930*. Vancouver: New Star Books, 1978.

Kubicek, Robert V. *The Administration of Imperialism: Joseph Chamberlain at the Colonial Office*. Durham, NC: Duke University Press, 1969.

Lalonde, André N. "The North-West Rebellion and Its Effects on Settlers and Settlement in the Canadian West." *Saskatchewan History* 27, no. 3 (1974): 95–102.

Larmour, Jean. "Edgar Dewdney: Indian Commissioner in the Transition Period of Indian Settlement, 1879–1884." *Saskatchewan History* 33, no. 1 (1981): 13–24.

LaRoque, Emma. *Defeathering the Indian*. Agincourt, Ont.: The Book Society of Canada Ltd, 1975.

Lee, David. "Foremost Man, and His Band." *Saskatchewan History* 36, no. 3 (1983): 94–101.

Leighton, J.D. "The Development of Federal Indian Policy in Canada, 1840–1890." PH D diss., University of Western Ontario, 1975.

– "A Victorian Civil Servant at Work: Lawrence Vankoughnet and the Canadian Indian Department, 1874–1893." In *As Long as the Sun Shines and Water Flows*, edited by Ian A.L. Getty and Antoine S. Lussier, 104–19. Vancouver: University of British Columbia Press, 1983.

Loehr, Rodney C. "Self-sufficiency on the Farm." *Agricultural History* 26, no. 2 (1952): 37–41.

Looy, A.J. "The Indian Agent and His Role in the Administration of the North-West Superintendency." PH D diss., Queen's University, 1977.

– "Saskatchewan's First Indian Agent, M.G. Dickieson." *Saskatchewan History* 32, no. 3 (1979): 104–15.

Lupul, David. "The Bobtail Land Surrender." *Alberta History* 26, no. 1 (1978): 29–39.

Mckay, Raoul J. "A History of Indian Treaty Number Four and Government Policies in Its Implementation, 1874–1905." MA thesis, University of Manitoba, 1973.

McKillop, A.B., ed. *Contexts of Canada's Past*. Carleton Library, no. 123. Toronto, 1980.
Macleod, R.C. *The North West Mounted Police and Law Enforcement, 1873–1905*. Toronto: University of Toronto Press, 1976.
McLuhan, T.C. *Touch the Earth: A Self-Portrait of Indian Existence*. New York: Pocket Books, 1972.
Mandelbaum, David G. *The Plains Cree: An Ethnographic, Historical and Comparative Study*. Regina: Canadian Plains Research Centre, 1979.
Manitoba Culture, Heritage, and Recreation, Historic Resources Branch. *The Prehistory of the Lockport Site*. Winnipeg, 1985.
Manitoba Department of Cultural Affairs and Historical Resources. *Introducing Manitoba Prehistory*. Papers in Manitoba Archaeology Popular Series, no. 4. Winnipeg, 1983.
Mardock, R.W. *The Reformers and the American Indian*. Columbia, MO: University of Missouri Press, 1969.
Mason, Carol I. "Prehistoric Maple Sugaring: A Sticky Subject." *North American Anthropologist* 7, no. 4 (1986): 305–9.
Mason, Philip. *Patterns of Dominance*. Toronto: Oxford University Press, 1970.
Meyer, Roy W. *The Village Indians of the Upper Missouri: The Mandans, Hidatsas and Arikaras*. Lincoln: University of Nebraska Press, 1977.
Miller, J.R. "The Irony of Residential Schooling." *Canadian Journal of Native Education* 14, no. 2 (1987): 3–14.
Miller, Robert I. "The Indian Reserve System in Manitoba, 1870–1900." Master of Development Studies of the Institute of Social Studies. The Hague, 1981.
Milloy, John S. "The Early Indian Acts: Developmental Strategy and Constitutional Change." In *As Long as the Sun Shines and Water Flows*, edited by Ian A.L. Getty and Antoine S. Lussier, 56–64. Vancouver: University of British Columbia Press, 1983.
– "The Plains Cree: A Preliminary Trade and Military Chronology, 1670–1870." MA thesis, Carleton University, 1972.
– *The Plains Cree: Trade, Diplomacy and War, 1790 to 1870*. Winnipeg: University of Manitoba Press, 1988.
Milner, Clyde A., II. *With Good Intentions: Quaker Work among the Pawnees, Otos, and Omahas in the 1870's*. Lincoln: University of Nebraska Press, 1982.
Mohl, Raymond A., and Neil Betten, "Paternalism and Pluralism: Immigrants and Social Welfare in Gary, Indiana, 1906–1940." *American Studies* 15, no. 1 (1974): 5–30.
Moodie, D.W. "Agriculture and the Fur Trade." In *Old Trails and New Directions: Papers of the Third North American Fur Trade Conference*, edited by Carol Judd and Arthur J. Ray. Toronto: University of Toronto Press, 1980.

Moodie, D.W., and Barry Kaye. "Indian Agriculture in the Fur Trade Northwest." *Prairie Forum* 11, no. 2 (1986).
– "The Northern Limit of Indian Agriculture in North America." *The Geographical Review* 59, no. 4 (1969): 513–29.
Moodie, D.W., and Arthur J. Ray. "Buffalo Migrations in the Canadian Plains." *Plains Anthropologist* 21, no. 71 (1976): 45–51.
Morgan, E.C. "The Bell Farm." In *Pages from the Past: Essays on Saskatchewan History*, edited by D.H. Bocking. Saskatoon: Western Producer Prairie Books, 1979.
Morton, A.S. *History of Prairie Settlement*. Canadian Frontiers of Settlement Series. Toronto: Macmillan, 1938.
Morton, W.L. "Agriculture in the Red River Community." In *Contexts of Canada's Past*, edited by A.B. McKillop. Carleton Library, no. 123. Toronto, 1980.
– *Manitoba: A History*. Toronto: University of Toronto Press, 1970.
Muise, D.A., ed. *Approaches to Native History in Canada*. National Museum of Man, Mercury Series, History Division Paper no. 25. Ottawa, 1977.
"1985 Excavations at Lockport Site." *Manitoba Culture and Heritage* 3, no. 3 (1985).
Palmer, Robin, and Neil Parsons, eds. *The Roots of Rural Poverty in Central and Southern Africa*. Berkeley and Los Angeles: University of California Press, 1977.
Payne, Michael. "A History of Fairford Mission." Manitoba Historic Resources Branch, 1981.
Pearce, Roy Harvey. *Savagism and Civilization: A Study of the Indian and the American Mind*. Baltimore: Johns Hopkins Press, 1965.
Pennington, William D. "Government Agricultural Policy on the Kiowa Reservation, 1869–1901." *Indian Historian* 11, no. 1 (1978): 11–15.
– "Government Policy and Indian Farming on the Cheyenne and Arapaho Reservations, 1869–1880." *Chronicles of Oklahoma* 57 (1979): 171–89.
Pettipas, Katherine Ann. "Severing the Ties That Bind: The Canadian Indian Act and the Repression of Indigenous Religious Systems in the Prairie Region, 1896–1951." PH D diss., University of Manitoba, 1989.
Prentice, Alison, et al. *Canadian Women: A History*. Toronto: Harcourt Brace Jovanovich, 1988.
Price, Richard, ed. *The Spirit of the Alberta Indian Treaties*. Toronto: Butterworth and Co., 1979.
Priest, Loring B. *Uncle Sam's Stepchildren: The Reformation of United States Indian Policy, 1865–1887*. New York: Octagon Books, 1969.
Prince Albert Historical Society. *The Voice of the People: Reminiscences of Prince Albert Settlement's Early Citizens*. Prince Albert, 1985.
Proceedings of the Plains Cree Conference. Regina: Canadian Plains Research Centre, 1979.

Purich, Don. *Our Land: Native Rights in Canada.* Toronto: James Lorimer and Co., 1986.
Qu'Appelle Historical Society. *Qu'Appelle: Footprints to Progress: A History of Qu'Appelle and District.* 1980.
Raby, Stewart. "Indian Land Surrenders in Southern Saskatchewan." *The Canadian Geographer* 17, no. 1 (1973): 36–52.
– "Prairie Fires in the North-West." *Saskatchewan History* 19, no. 3 (1966): 81–99.
Rasporich, A.W. "Utopian Ideals and Community Settlements in Western Canada, 1880–1914." In *The Canadian West: Social Change and Economic Development,* edited by Henry C. Klassen. Calgary: Comprint Publishing Co., 1977.
Ray, Arthur J. *Indians in the Fur Trade: Their Role as Hunters, Trappers and Middlemen in the Lands Southwest of Hudson Bay, 1660–1870.* Toronto: University of Toronto Press, 1974.
– "The Northern Great Plains: Pantry of the Northwestern Fur Trade, 1774–1885." *Prairie Forum* 9, no. 2 (1984): 263–80.
Ray, Arthur J., and Donald Freeman. *"Give Us Good Measure": An Economic Analysis of Relations between the Indians and the Hudson's Bay Company before 1763.* Toronto: University of Toronto Press, 1978.
Regehr, T.D. "The Land God Gave to His Children: An Examination of Religious Attitudes to the Land in Western Canada." Paper prepared for the Western Development Museum, Saskatoon, 1978.
– *Remembering Saskatchewan: A History of Rural Saskatchewan.* Saskatoon: University of Saskatchewan, 1979.
Ricciardelli, Alex F. "The Adoption of White Agriculture by the Oneida Indians." *Ethnohistory* 10, no. 4 (1963).
Richards, J.H., and K.I. Fung. *Atlas of Saskatchewan.* Saskatoon: Modern Press, 1969.
Robinson, Ronald, and John Gallagher. *Africa and the Victorians: The Official Mind of Imperialism.* London: The Macmillan Press Ltd, 1978.
Roe, F.G. "Early Agriculture in Western Canada in Relation to Climatic Stability." *Agricultural History* 26, no. 3 (1952): 104–23.
Rogers, E.S., and Flora Tobobondung. "Parry Island Farmers: A Period of Change in the Way of Life of the Algonkians of Southern Ontario." In *Contributions to Canadian Ethnology, 1975,* edited by David Brez Carlisle. National Museum of Man, Mercury Series, no. 31. Ottawa, 1975.
Russell, Bill. "The White Man's Paper Burden: Aspects of Record Keeping in the Department of Indian Affairs, 1860–1914." *Archivaria* 19 (1984–85): 50–72.
Sahlins, Marshall. *Stone Age Economics.* New York: Aldine Publishing Co., 1972.
Samek, Hana. *The Blackfoot Confederacy, 1880–1920: A Comparative Study of*

Canadian and U.S. Indian Policy. Albuquerque: University of New Mexico Press, 1987.

Sanderson, James F. *Indian Tales of the Canadian Prairies*. Calgary: Historical Society of Alberta, 1965.

Seaton, Beverly. "Idylls of Agriculture: Or, Nineteenth-Century Success Stories of Farming and Gardening." *Agricultural History* 1 (1981): 21–30.

Slattery, Brian, and Linda Charlton. *Canadian Native Law Cases* 4 (1911–1930). Saskatoon: University of Saskatchewan Native Law Centre, 1986.

Sluman, Norma, and Jean Goodwill. *John Tootoosis: A Biography of a Cree Leader*. Ottawa: Golden Dog Press, 1982.

Snow, John. *These Mountains are Our Sacred Places*. Toronto: Samuel Stevens, 1977.

Spector, David. "Field Agriculture on the Canadian Prairies, 1870–1940." In *Agriculture on the Prairies, 1870–1940*. Ottawa: National Historic Parks and Sites Branch, 1983.

Spence, Clark C. *The Salvation Army Farm Colonies*. Tucson, 1985.

Sprague, D.N., and J.L. Finlay. *The Structure of Canadian History*. Scarborough, Ont.: Prentice-Hall Canada Inc., 1984.

Spry, Irene. *The Papers of the Palliser Expedition, 1857–1860*. Toronto: The Champlain Society, 1968.

– "The Tragedy of the Loss of the Commons in Western Canada." In *As Long as the Sun Shines and Water Flows*, edited by Ian A.L. Getty and Antoine S. Lussier, 203–28. Vancouver: University of British Columbia Press, 1983.

– "The Transition from a Nomadic to a Settled Economy in Western Canada, 1856–96." *Transactions of the Royal Society of Canada*, series 4, vol. 6 (1968): 187–201.

Stahl, Robert John. "Farming among the Kiowa, Comanche, Kiowa Apache, and Wichita." PH D diss., University of Oklahoma, 1978.

Stanley, G.F.G. *The Birth of Western Canada: A History of the Riel Rebellions*. 1936. Reprint. Toronto: University of Toronto Press, 1975.

– "The Indian Background to Canadian History." *Canadian Historical Association Report*. 1952.

Stonechild, A. Blair. "The Indian View of the 1885 Uprising." In *1885 and After: Native Society in Transition*, edited by F. Laurie Barron and James B. Waldram, 157–70. Regina: Canadian Plains Research Centre, 1986.

– "The Uprising of 1885: Its Impact on Federal Indian Relations in Western Canada." *Saskatchewan Indian Federated College Journal* 2, no. 2 (1986): 81–96.

Strange, H.G.L. *A Short History of Prairie Agriculture*. Winnipeg: Searle Grain Co. Ltd, 1954.

Street, Brian V. *The Savage in Literature: Representations of "Primitive" Society in English Fiction, 1858–1920*. London: Routledge and Kegan Paul, 1975.

Surtees, Robert J. *Canadian Indian Policy: A Critical Bibliography*. Bloomington: Indiana University Press, 1982.
- "The Development of an Indian Reserve Policy in Canada." *Ontario History* 61 (1969): 87–98.
Swanton, John R. *The Indian Tribes of North America*. Smithsonian Institution, Bureau of American Ethnology Bulletin no. 145. Washington, DC, 1953.
Syms, E. Leigh. "History of a Refuse Pit: Interpreting Plains Camp Activities at a Microcosmic Level." *Plains Anthropologist* 19 (1974): 306–15.
Taylor, John L. "Canada's Northwest Indian Policy in the 1870's: Traditional Premises and Necessary Innovations." In *The Spirit of the Alberta Indian Treaties*, edited by Richard Price. Toronto: Butterworth and Co., 1979.
- "The Development of an Indian Policy for the Canadian North West, 1864–79." PH D diss., Queen's University, 1975.
- "Two Views on the Meaning of Treaties Six and Seven." In *The Spirit of the Alberta Indian Treaties*, edited by Richard Price. Toronto: Butterworth and Co., 1979.
Thomas, L.H. "A History of Agriculture on the Prairies to 1914." *Prairie Forum* 1, no. 1 (1976): 31–45.
Thompson, John Herd. *The Harvests of War: The Prairie West, 1914–1918*. Toronto: McClelland and Stewart Ltd, 1978.
Titley, E. Brian. *A Narrow Vision: Duncan Campbell Scott and the Administration of Indian Affairs in Canada*. Vancouver: University of British Columbia Press, 1986.
- "W.M. Graham: Indian Agent Extraordinaire." *Prairie Forum* 8, no. 1 (1983): 25–41.
Tobias, John L. "Canada's Subjugation of the Plains Cree, 1879–1885." *Canadian Historical Review* 64, no. 4 (1983): 519–48.
- "Indian Reserves in Western Canada: Indian Homelands or Devices for Assimilation." In *Approaches to Native History in Canada*, edited by D.A. Muise, 89–103. National Museum of Man, Mercury Series, History Division Paper no. 25. Ottawa, 1977.
- "The Origins of the Treaty Rights Movement in Saskatchewan." In *1885 and After: Native Society in Transition*, edited by F. Laurie Barron and James B. Waldram, 241–52. Regina: Canadian Plains Research Centre, 1986.
- "Protection, Civilization, Assimilation: An Outline History of Canada's Indian Policy." In *As Long as the Sun Shines and Water Flows: A Reader in Canadian Native Studies*, edited by Ian A.L. Getty and Antoine S. Lussier, 13–30. Vancouver: University of British Columbia Press, 1983.
Turner, Allan R. "Pioneer Farming Experiences." *Saskatchewan History* 8, no. 2 (1955).
Turner, Frederick. *Beyond Geography: The Western Spirit against the Wilderness*. New York: Viking Press, 1980.

Tyler, Kenneth J. "Kiwisānce." *Dictionary of Canadian Biography* 11: 477–8.
- "Paskwāw." *Dictionary of Canadian Biography* 11: 675–6.
- "A Tax-eating Proposition: The History of the Passpasschase Indian Reserve." MA thesis, University of Alberta, 1979.

Tyler and Wright Research Consultants Ltd. "The Alienation of Indian Reserve Lands during the Administration of Sir Wilfrid Laurier, 1896–1911." No. 4, "St Peter's Reserve." Prepared for the Manitoba Indian Brotherhood, 1978.

Tyman, John L. *By Section, Township and Range: Studies in Prairie Settlement.* Brandon: Assiniboine Historical Society, 1972.

Upton, Leslie F.S. "The Origins of Canadian Indian Policy." *Journal of Canadian Studies* 8 (1973): 51–61.

Vecsey, Christopher, and Robert W. Venables, eds. *American Indian Environments: Ecological Issues in Native American History.* Syracuse, NY: Syracuse University Press, 1980.

Venne, Sharon Helen. *Indian Acts and Amendments, 1868–1975: An Indexed Collection.* Saskatoon: University of Saskatchewan Native Law Centre, 1981.

Voget, Fred. "A Six Nations' Diary, 1891–1894." *Ethnohistory* 16 (1969): 345–60.

Waiser, W.A. *The Field Naturalist: John Macoun, The Geographical Survey, and Natural Science.* Toronto: University of Toronto Press, 1989.

Waite, P.B. *Canada, 1874–1896: Arduous Destiny.* Toronto: McClelland and Stewart Ltd, 1971.

Warkentin, John H. "Western Canada in 1886." In *Studies in Canadian Social History*, edited by Michiel Horn and Ronald Sabourin. Toronto: McClelland and Stewart Ltd, 1974.

Watetch, Abel. *Payepot and His People.* Saskatoon: Modern Press, 1959.

Weatherwax, Paul. "The Origin of the Maize Plant and Maize Agriculture in Ancient America." In *Symposium on Prehistoric Agriculture*, 1936. Reprint. Millwood: Kraus Reprint Co., 1977.

Wessell, Thomas R. "Agriculture, Indians and American History." *Agricultural History* 50, no. 1 (1976): 9–20.

- "Agriculture on the Reservations: The Case of the Blackfeet, 1885–1935." *Journal of the West* 23, no. 4 (1979): 17–24.

- "Phantom Experiment Station: Government Agriculture on the Zuni Reservation." *Agricultural History* 61, no. 4 (1987): 1–12.

White, Pamela Margaret. "Restructuring the Domestic Sphere – Prairie Indian Women on Reserves: Image, Ideology and State Policy, 1880–1930." PH D diss., McGill University, 1987.

White, Richard. *The Roots of Dependency: Subsistence, Environment and Social Change among the Choctaws, Pawnees and Navajos.* Lincoln: University of Nebraska Press, 1983.

Wilden, Anthony. *The Imaginary Canadian*. Vancouver: Pulp Press, 1980.
Wilson, Gilbert L. *Buffalo Bird Woman's Garden*. St Paul: Minnesota Historical Society, 1987.
Wilson, Monica, and Leonard Thompson, eds. *The Oxford History of South Africa*. Vol. 2, *South Africa, 1870–1966*. Oxford: Clarendon Press, 1971.
Wishart, David. "Agriculture at the Trading Posts on the Upper Missouri prior to 1843." *Agricultural History* 47, no. 1 (1973): 57–62.
Wolff, Richard D. *The Economics of Colonialism: Britain and Kenya, 1870–1930*. New Haven and London: Yale University Press, 1974.
Wood, David L. "American Indian Farmland and the Great War." *Agricultural History* 55, no. 3 (1981): 249–65.
Yudelman, Montague. *Africans on the Land: Economic Problems of African Agricultural Development in Southern, Central and East Africa, with Special Reference to Southern Rhodesia*. Cambridge: Harvard University Press, 1964.

Index

Abbott, Frederick H., 243
Aberdeen, Lady, 232
Abernethy, 161, 170
Africa, agriculture in, 9, 10, 11, 233–4
Agriculture, Indian: pre-contact, 6, 37–9; pre-treaty, 11, 39–41, 43, 48, 61
Ahenakew, Edward, 180, 230, 243
Ahkingkahpempatoot, 113
Ahtakakoop (Upstream Cree), 71
Archibald, Adams, 55
Arikara, 38
Asham, Charles, 127
Assiniboine Indians, 25, 29, 31–2, 48, 111, 122, 135, 219

Baie St Paul, 41
Balcarres, 161
Batoche, 126–7, 129, 150
Battleford, 67, 68, 71, 87, 140, 142, 145, 197; farm instructors at, 91, 92; Reed as agent at, 101, 120, 141, 238; Indian farmers in district of, 135, 151, 152, 196, 221, 231, 254; agency at, 165, 251; residents of,

object to Indian competition, 186–9
Bear, Jacob, 113
Beardy reserve, 175
Beaver Hills, 183–4
Belcourt, Father G.A., 40
Bell, Charles N., 53
Bell, Robert, 139–40
Bell, Major William R., Farm, 160–1, 165, 170
Bellegarde, John, 242
Belly River, battle of, 46
Big Bear, 36, 126, 163, 202
Big Sand Hills, 45
Bird Tail Creek, 106
Birdtail reserve, 252
Birtle, 148, 252
Blackfoot, 5, 7, 32, 34, 35, 36, 80, 151
Blacksmiths, 74, 81, 168
Blake, Edward, 93
Blood, 80, 131, 153
Booth, William, 215
Brandon House, 35, 41, 39, 42
Brass, Eleanor, 178
Brazil, labour market in, 9
Broadview, 114, 127–8, 167, 185, 191, 216, 248, 249, 257
Brokowski, E., 187
Buffalo, 4, 5, 16; hunted by pounds, 18, 28–9; habits of, 27–8; grow-

ing scarcity of, 35–6, 52, 69, 80
Bulletin (Edmonton), 117, 245
Bundy, Colin, 10
Burgess, A.M., 238
Butler, William, 26

Cadis, Charles Daunais De, 91–2
Cameron, Malcolm, 130–3, 137, 138
Campbell, J.J., 220
Canadian Pacific Railway, 59, 127, 185, 186, 238, 247; and employment of Indians, 101; settlement along line of, 159, 216; and fireguards, 183
Cannington Manor, 160
Carlson, Leonard A., 11
Carlton (Indian agency), 118–19, 219, 221, 251
Casgrain, Philipe, 105
Cauchon, Joseph, 76–7
Cell, John, 51
Chacachase, 47, 61, 62, 113, 163
Chicago World's Fair, 232
Chisholm, W.J., 253
Christie, William Joseph, 55–6, 58, 60, 61, 63, 64, 66, 73–4, 80
Chronicler (Virden), 227–8

Citizen (Ottawa), 135, 198
Cluny site, 39
Cochran, Archdeacon, 40
Coldwater, 24
Corn, 34, 37, 38, 41, 42
Coté, Gabriel, Chief, 44, 242
Coté, Joe, 256
Coté, Maybelle, 242
Coté reserve, 183, 246, 247
Courier (Moosomin), 198
Cowessess, Chief, 48, 61, 113, 123
Cowessess reserve, 98, 111, 113–14, 172, 174, 205, 208, 209, 231, 249, 250, 255–7
Craig incident, 122
Credit, 164–5, 211–12, 229
Cree, Plains, 12, 25; annual cycle, 26–8; band organization and leadership, 29–30, 47; and Hudson's Bay Company, 31; movements of, 31–3; allied with Assiniboine, 31–2; effect of horse on, 34–5; war with Blackfoot, 36, 46; acquainted with agriculture, 38–43; Downstream People, 45; Upstream People, 45, 48; Calling River People, 45, 47, 48; Rabbit Skin People, 45, 47; Touchwood Hills People, 45, 46; Young Dogs, 45, 46, 48
Cree, Woodland, 46, 69, 80, 139–40
Crooked Lakes, 45, 106, 250; bands that settled in, 47, 48; survey of reserves in, 62, 112–14; Yellow Calf protest in, 120–2; and 1885 resistance, 126, 127; agriculture on reserves in, 135, 163–91 passim;
administration of, 149–50; subdivision in severalty in, 202, 205, 207; "peasant" policy in, 221, 223–4, 225; land surrenders in, 247–9; 1911 delegation from, 255–7
Crow Indians, 35, 46
Cypress Hills, 5, 26, 36, 45, 47, 48, 60, 71, 74, 82, 113, 122–3, 254; home farms in, 111–12
Cyr, Antoine, 254

Dakota, 12, 25, 40, 52, 76, 82, 126; protest of Oak River, 226–9
Dawes Severalty Act, 11, 198–200
Dawson, Rev. Leonard, 232
Day Star, Chief, 46, 61, 62, 110, 115, 123
Day Star reserve, 62, 67, 110, 128, 178, 181
Deane, Richard Burton, 121, 153
Delorme, Andrew, 174
Denig, Edwin T., 42–3
Dennis, John Stoughton, 58–9, 85
Department of Indian Affairs: created, 50; attitude toward Indians, 51, 71, 101–2, 118–19, 124, 133–4, 211, 249, 255–7; home farm program of, 79–158; criticisms of, 130–1, 134, 136; defence of, 132–3, 134–5; concerned with public image, 137, 175, 232–3; policy of, after 1885, 141–58; severalty policy of, 193–209; "peasant" farming policy of, 209–29; land surrender policy of, 237, 244–9; assists former pupils, 241; and Soldier Settlement
Board, 251–2; loan policy of, 254
Department of the Interior, 25, 50, 73, 142, 159, 204
Dewdney, Edgar, 89, 124, 128, 130, 144, 162, 167, 171, 173; appointed Indian commissioner, 81–3; and home farm program, 90–2, 94, 97, 99, 100, 101, 116; on Indian participation in 1885 resistance, 132; and severalty policy, 147, 195, 196, 197, 198, 201, 202, 209, 218; and pass system, 150, 151, 153; and permit system, 157
Dick, Lyle, 161
Dickieson, M.G., 58, 67, 68–70, 78, 80, 81
Dieter, Fred, 242
Dion, Joe, 176, 231
Dippie, Brian, 199
Dodd, Henry, 135
Donkin, John G., 152
Donnelly, farm instructor, 91
Drought, 99, 161, 170, 172, 181–2, 184
Dualism theory, 8–10
Duck Lake, 103, 106, 126–7, 152, 154, 167, 211, 231
Dumont, Frank, 242
Dyck, Noel, 12

East London Artisan's Colony, 160
Edwards, O.C., 123
Enfranchisement, 194–5, 236
English, J.J., 111–12
Esterhazy, 160
Experimental Farm, Central, 172, 173

The Facts respecting Indian Administration in the North-West, 133, 134
Fairford, 40

Fairs, agricultural, Indian participation in, 135, 137, 174–6, 255
Fall ploughing, 171–2
Farm instructors, 7, 144, 149, 151, 162–3, 237–8; required by Plains Indians, 68–9, 79–81; appointed under home farm program, 84–92, 95–7, 102–3; criticisms of, 104–5, 109; dismissals of, 108
Farm instructresses, 178–9
Farrow, Thomas, 85
Fernandes, Florestan, 9
Fertile belt, 59, 61
File Hills, 45, 59, 125, 205, 240; bands that settled in, 48, 49; survey of reserves in, 114–15; and 1885 resistance, 126, 127–9; 1880s agriculture in, 161–91 passim; plan to dissolve agency of, 202
File Hills Colony, 239–44
Fishing Lake, 44, 109
Fleming, James, 105
Foremost Man, 36
Forget, Amédée, 139–40, 218, 223
Fort Alexander, 40
Fort Calgary, 82, 156
Fort Carlton, 41, 80
Fort Edmonton, 41, 46, 55, 60, 62, 117, 131, 219
Fort Ellice, 35, 42, 43, 44, 55, 66, 80, 82, 86, 114
Fort Macleod, 71, 82, 91, 152, 153, 157, 187
Fort Pelly, 42, 66, 80, 82, 86, 106
Fort Pitt, 80, 90
Fort Qu'Appelle, 35, 42, 64, 65, 71, 73, 74, 80, 86, 109, 110, 111, 113, 115, 126, 127, 166, 167, 192, 216
Fort Union, 42
Fort Walsh, 5, 71, 82, 111–12

Fowke, Vernon, 215
Fox, Chief, 47, 48, 90
Free Press (Manitoba), 136
Frog Lake, 126, 154, 162

Gaddie, Alex, 113–14, 174, 223, 249, 256
Gainsborough Creek, 39
Gambler, Chief, 56
Gambler reserve, 162
Gazette (Fort Macleod), 187
Gazette (Montreal), 232
Gordon, George, Chief, 46, 60, 65, 128
Gordon reserve, 61, 67, 88, 110, 128, 183, 224
Gowan, R.W., 91
Gowanlock, Theresa, 178
Gradual Civilization Act, 24–5, 194
Graham, William Morris, 240, 241–3, 247–9, 250–2, 255
Grand Rapids, 40
Grant, W.S., 219, 221
Grasshoppers, 42–3, 72
Greater production campaign, 249–51
Grenfell, 191, 248
Grey, Earl, 242
Grist mills, 73, 96, 99, 112, 117, 165, 222; subsidized by Department of Indian Affairs, 166–8
Griswold, 227–8

Halpin, Henry, 162
Hanks, L.M., and J.R., 7
Harmon, D.W., 40
Harvesting: with hand implements, 98, 219–24; with self-binding reaper, 160, 164, 211, 219, 221, 223, 224, 225
Hawthorn, H.B., 8
Hay and hay-making: with mechanical mowers and rakes, 97–8, 163–4; scarcity of, 161, 183; destruction of, by fire, 184; sale of, 185–6;

increase in competition for, 185–90; with scythes, 219, 222
Heenan, Thomas, 86
Herald (Calgary), 153
Herchmer, Lawrence, 148, 154
Herchmer, W.M., 121
Hidatsa, 38
Hind, H.Y., 41, 59
Hockley, S., 110
Holzkamm, Tim E., 11
Homestead policy, 20, 160
Horses, 7, 27, 34–5, 44, 49
Hourie, Peter, 120
Hudson's Bay Company, 55, 56, 58, 80, 192, 216; and Indians, 29, 31–2, 35, 40, 43, 46, 47, 48, 113–14; farms at posts of, 41–2; and farm instructors, 86, 87, 88, 90
Hugonard, Father J., 241
Hunt, Frank L., 90, 92, 110
Hunting: of buffalo, 27–9; as perceived by non-Indians, 17–18; of small game, 29, 191–2

Implements, agricultural: precontact, 37–8; promised in treaties, 57–8; distribution of, 63, 137–8; complaints about quality of, 88, 89, 95, 118–19; scarcity of, 100–1; given in return for "loyalty" in 1885, 129, 145; Department of Indian Affairs policy on, 147–8, 210–13; homemade, 210, 212, 221; disadvantages of hand, 219–24
Indian Act, 156–8, 162, 194–5, 201, 203, 211, 244, 245, 250, 252. *See also* Permit system
Indian agents, 67, 70, 149, 164, 218–24

Indian Head, 106, 122, 123, 135, 160, 166, 170, 216
Industrial schools, 107, 151
Ironquill, Joseph, 241–2
Irvine, A.G., 150–1

James Smith reserve, 8
Jennings, John, 155
John Smith reserve, 71, 221
Johnston, James, 103
Journal (Ottawa), 198, 232

Kahkewistahaw, Chief, 47–8, 61, 62, 116, 182, 208, 248
Kahkewistahaw reserve, 113, 164, 169, 189, 205, 249
Kakenawup, 47
Kamsack, 246
Kanocees, 46, 55, 56, 115
Keith, Hilton, 121, 163, 172
Kenya, 233
Key, Chief, 44
Kishikonse, 44
Kootenays, 32

Lacombe, Father, 197
Laird, David, 56, 58, 63, 66, 67, 68–71, 74, 76, 78, 79–80, 81, 195, 240, 244, 248–9
Lake of the Woods, 39
Lake, R.S., 248
Lake St Claire, 24
Lamont, Judge J., 254
Lash, J.B., 162, 185, 226
Last Mountain, 125
Laurie, P.G., 72, 141
Laurier, Sir Wilfrid, 237, 238
Leader (Regina), 135, 235
Leech Lake, 44, 48, 61, 189
Lestanc, Rev. Joseph, 87
Lethbridge, 153
Little Black Bear, Chief, 46, 48, 61, 116

Little Black Bear reserve, 100, 114, 164, 183
Little Bones, 44, 163, 189
Little Mountain, Chief, 36
Little Pine, Chief, 36
Little Pine reserve, 122
Livestock: at Hudson's Bay Company posts, 41; Indian ownership of, before treaties, 44–5, 48; issued under treaty, 57, 63–5, 130, 137; non-native view of Indian attitude toward, 63–4, 139, 213; shortages of, 65, 99, 101, 116–17; complaints about quality of, 96, 118; oxen as motive power, 96–7; and loan system, 97, 148–9, 169–70; as factor for success, 111; wintering of, 183; and permit system, 230–1
Lockport, 38
Long Sault, 229
Lorne, Marquis of, 115–16
Loud Voice, 47, 48, 56, 61, 62, 75, 112–13, 115, 116, 124
Louison, 113

MacDonald, Allan, 88, 109, 112, 124, 182, 248; appointed Treaty Four agent, 66–7; and Indian requests, 74–5, 116, 125, 163, 164–5, 168; assesses reserves, 111, 114, 122; moved to Crooked Lakes, 149, 162; and farming techniques, 171, 174; and competition for hay land, 186, 189, 190, 247; and subdivision in severalty, 207–8; and "peasant" farming policy, 223–4
Macdonald, Hugh John, 50

MacDonald, H.W., 257
Macdonald, Sir John A., 22, 50, 66, 79–80, 81, 117, 131–2, 190, 246; patronage appointments of, 85, 86, 91, 92; and home farm program, 93–4, 105–7; and pass system, 145, 150–1; on permit system, 157; and severalty policy, 195–6, 201
McDougall, John, 231
McGibbon, Alex, 148, 172, 174, 181, 190, 192, 211, 220, 221, 222
McKay Angus (farmer), 170
McKay, Angus (Indian agent), 62–6
McKay, James, 43, 66
McKenzie, N.M.W.J., 114, 126, 129
Maclean, John, 131
McLean, J.D., 255
McMillan, Malcolm, 135
Macoun, John, 59
McWhinney, Rev. W., 241
Magpie, Cree band, 42–3
Man Who Took the Coat, Chief, 48
Mandan, 33, 34, 38
Mandelbaum, D.G., 258
Maple Creek, 111–12, 123, 151, 162
Maple sugar, 29, 177
Markets for agricultural products: absence of, 100–1; concern over Indian competition for, 141, 185–90
Maskepetoon, 36
Masson, Louis F., 91
Meighen, Arthur, 250, 251, 252
Meredith, E.H., 52–3
"Messiah craze," 134
Methodists, Primitive, 160
Métis, 36, 41, 42, 46, 62, 126–7, 145, 154, 155, 188

Middleton, Maj.-Gen. Frederick, 126, 150
Mill, John Stuart, 214
Millar, M., 255, 257
Miller, William, Sr, 231
Milloy, John, 14
Mills, David, 69–70, 79, 92, 104–5
Minnesota uprising, 52
Mistawasis, 71, 221
Mitchell, Hillyard, 167
Moore, Arthur, 189
Moose Jaw, 159
Moose Mountain, 26, 35, 91, 126, 166, 208, 220
Moosomin reserve, 220
Moosomin (town), 160, 185, 216
Morley, 91
Morris, Alexander, 55, 56, 63, 64, 75, 256
Motherwell, W.R., 170
Muscowequan, Chief, 47
Muscowequan reserve, 61
Muscowpetung, Chief, 116, 127
Muscowpetung reserve, 48, 111, 125, 162, 163, 165, 166, 167, 181, 184, 185, 190–1, 202, 205, 208, 225–6, 240, 247, 250

Nanawanan, Chief, 40
Nasaagan, 113
National Policy, 22, 155, 237
Nelson, John C., 111, 114, 184, 203, 206–7, 208
Nepahpahness, 113–14, 174, 223
Netley Creek, 39, 40
New Finland, 160
New Sweden, 160
Newlove, G., 110
Nez Percé, 6
Nichol, Horatio, 253–4
North West Company, 33, 40
North-West Mounted Police, 5, 52, 74, 76, 127, 150–4, 163, 173, 188

North-West resistance, 12, 126–9, 145, 150, 152, 154
North-West Territories Council, 130, 140
Norway House, 40
Nut Lake, 109

Oak Lake, 227
Oak River reserve, 8, 12, 226–9
Ochapowace, Chief, 47, 208
Ochapowace reserve, 112–13, 169, 248, 252, 254
Ojibway. *See* Saulteaux, Plains
Okanese, Chief, 48, 56, 61
Okanese reserve, 114–15, 128, 184
Okemasis reserve, 175
Oldman River, battle of, 36
Oliver, Frank, 245, 256
One Arrow reserve, 126
Onion Lake, 176, 220
O'Soup, Louis, 48, 74–5, 113–14, 115, 116, 121–2, 127, 174, 207–8, 223, 231, 255–6
Ostrander, agent, 258
Ottawa Indians, 39, 40
Otter, Lt-Col William, 126
Oxen. *See* Livestock

Palliser, Capt. John, 43, 59
Parry Island, 11
Pasquah, Chief, 44, 48, 61, 63, 64, 65, 76–8, 79, 124, 127, 149
Pasquah reserve, 62–3, 82, 90, 98, 110–1, 124–5, 174, 175, 181, 183, 205, 208, 225–6, 247, 249, 253
Pass system, 145–6, 149–56
Passpasschase reserve, 204, 245
Patrick, Allan, 114

Patterson, James, 85–6
"Peasant" farming policy, 193, 209–10; rationale for, 209–18; and home-made implements, 210, 212, 221; enforcement of, 218–24; effects of, 229–36
Pedley, Frank, 238, 245, 256
Peepeekisis, Chief, 49, 116, 149
Peepeekisis reserve, 114
Peguis reserve, 8
Pelly agency, 103, 202
Permit system, 149, 156–8, 179, 188, 225, 226, 231, 257
Petewaywaykeesick, 113
Piapot, Chief, 36, 48, 56, 61, 112, 122–5, 127, 207–8
Piapot reserve, 8, 137, 152, 165, 205–8
Piegan, 100
Pine Creek, 231
Pipe Stem, Chief, 46
Pis cha kaw a kis, 42
Plains Indians: non-Indian attitudes toward, 3–23, 37, 49, 50, 71, 72, 73, 78, 93, 94, 101–2, 104, 105, 106, 134–6, 139–40, 143–4, 155–6, 157, 175, 180, 187, 189, 190, 197, 211–12, 213, 233, 245, 255, 257–8; attitudes of, toward agriculture, 12–14, 72–4; protests of, against government policy, 13, 73–8, 115–19, 152–3, 189, 194, 224–31, 255–8; health and lack of clothing of, 99, 120, 122–3, 190. *See also* Cree, Plains; Saulteaux, Plains
Pollock, John, 168
Ponton, A.W., 196, 248
Poor Man, Chief, 46, 55, 60, 63

Poor Man reserve, 62, 87, 224
Portage la Prairie, 39, 40, 60, 86
Poundmaker, Chief, 99, 116–17, 126
Poundmaker reserve, 144, 254
Prairie fire, 27, 183–4
Pratt, Charles, 43, 71, 124
Prince Albert, 106, 231
Provencher, J.A.N., 40

Quill Lake, 44

Rations, 5, 74–5, 90, 99–100, 120–2, 123, 147, 232; required on reserves in spring, 68, 69; "work for rations," 72, 82, 84, 88–9, 144; Indian objections to quality of, 89, 225
Reader, Rev. Joseph, 43
Ready Bow, 46, 48, 61, 62
Red Deer Lake, 125
Red Ochre Hill, battle of, 46, 48
Red Pheasant, Chief, 116
Red Pheasant reserve, 71, 253
Red River Settlement, 3, 41, 53
Red Sand Hills, 125
Reed, Hayter, 15, 136, 137–8, 165, 168, 235–6, 257; view of Indians, 101, 143–4; as assistant Indian commissioner, 109–10, 118–19; and Yellow Calf incident, 120–2; and Piapot protest, 124; background, 141–2; policy endorsed by, after 1885, 145–58; appointed Indian commissioner, 146; meets Battleford citizens, 187–90; and severalty policy, 193, 196–7, 201, 202; and "peasant" farming policy, 209–29; and Chicago World's Fair, 232; dismissal of, 238; and farm colonies, 240
Regina, 163
Reserves, Indian: origin in Upper Canada, 23–4; proposals about in the North-West, 53, 54; consultations with bands on, 58, 62; government view on locations of, 58–9; survey of, in Treaty Four, 60–3, 112–15; shortage of arable land on, 110; subdivision in severalty of, 147, 193–209; housing on, 179–80; surrender of land on, 185–7, 193, 200–2, 244–9; viewed by non-Indians as too large, 244, 246, 248, 250, 251; leasing of land on, 250–1; for non-Indian soldier settlement, 251–2
Riel, Louis, 115, 132, 150
Rogers, E.S., 11
Roseau River, 39, 40, 246
Round Lake, 112–13
Royal, Joseph, 92–3
Royal Proclamation (1763), 22–3

Saddle Lake, 91
St Andrew's, 41, 120
St Boniface, 86
St Laurent, 126
St Peter's, 40, 255
Sakimay, 47, 62, 98, 114, 163, 186, 205, 208
Salvation Army, 215, 240
Samek, H., 6
Sarcee, 80, 156
Sasalue, 113
Saskatchewan Herald (Battleford), 72, 104, 141, 188, 197
Saulteaux, Plains, 25, 29, 33, 39, 40, 43–5, 48, 54–5, 56, 113–14, 162
Saunders, William, 173
Schultz, John Christian, 53–4, 93, 139
Scott, Duncan Campbell, 222, 252–3
Scott, James, 86–9, 92, 103, 109
Seed grain: initial distribution of, 64–8; Red and White Fife, 98–9, 172; Ladoga, 173
Seed grain relief, 173
Seeding: by hand, 95, 161; with drills, 96
Sekaskootch reserve, 90
Selkirk Treaty (1817), 47
Selwyn, Alfred, 52–3
Senate Committee on the Existing Natural Food Products, 138–41
Setter, John, 112, 120
Severalty policy, 235–6; in the United Canadas, 194; Indians' protest about, 194, 205–9; rationale for, 196–7, 199; compared with the United States allotment policy, 198–201; on reserves in the North-West, 202–5
Sherrin, instructor, 90, 91, 92
Short Legs, 47
Sifton, Clifford, 237–9, 248
Simpson, W.M., 40
Sintaluta, 26
Sitting Bull, 82, 134
Smallpox, 36
Smart, James, 238, 245
Smohalla, 6
Snake Indians, 32
Soldier Settlement Board, 251–2
Sonnant, Le, 47
South Africa, 233–4
Sprevier, Joseph, 113
Stanley, G.F.G., 4–5
Stanley, Lord, 168
Star Blanket, Chief, 48, 61
Star Blanket reserve, 114, 184
Starvation in the North-West, 70, 71, 90, 116,

131, 134, 231–2; reports of, denied in the press, 72, and denied by Department of Indian Affairs, 124
Steele, Col S.B., 152, 153
Stevenson, Thomas, 226
Stewart, E.C., 178
Stonechild, Ben, 242
Stoney Indians, 43, 91
Summer-fallowing, 94, 170–1
Swan River, 36, 44, 67
Sweet Grass, Chief, 55
Sweet Grass reserve, 254

Tanner, John, 39
Tanner, Joseph, 162
Taylor, H., 91
Thingvalla, 160
Thomas, John R., 242
Threshing: by flail, 98; by machine, 98, 148, 165–6, 253–4
Thunderchild reserve, 231
Tobias, John, 12
Tomkins, John, 103
Touchwood Hills, 26, 32, 35, 59, 80, 202, 205, 246; agriculture of Magpie Cree band in, 42–3; bands that settled in, 45–7; reports of starvation in, 49, 71, 232; survey of reserves in 60–2; agriculture during 1870s in, 64, 67; and home farm policy, 82, 86–9, 96, 103, 108, 109, 110, 120, 123, 124; and 1885 resistance, 127–8; cattle on reserves in, 148; agriculture in, 163–91 passim; and "peasant" farming policy, 223, 224
Traill, Walter, 42
Treaties, 22–3, 24; strategies and goals of Indians, 3, 54–5; between the Plains Cree and Blackfoot, 36; Treaties One, Two, Three, and Five, 53, 54–6, 82; government view of, 74; Treaty Seven, 82, 98, 151, 197
Treaty Four, 90, 248; bands of, 46–9; negotiation of, 56–7; selection of reserves in, 57–63; initial distribution of promised goods, 63–8; adhesions to, 73–4
Treaty Six, 58, 63, 67, 68, 73, 74, 80, 82, 98, 108, 118–19, 150, 176, 205, 221; differences between Treaty Four and, 57, 60; agriculture in, compared with Treaty Four district, 71
Turtle Mountain, 35

United States Indian policy, 134, 197, 198–200, 235

Vagrancy Act, 151, 152
Vankoughnet, Lawrence, 116, 124, 145, 185; appointed deputy superintendent general, 50–1; on transfer of McKay, 66; and home farm policy, 81, 85, 91, 106–7; and financial retrenchment policy, 108, 144; on distribution of implements, 137–8; replaced, 142; and pass system, 150–1; on grist mills, 168; on surrender of hay lands, 186; and severalty policy, 195, 196, 202, 204
Vattel, Emmerich de, 20
Victoria (Pakan), 80
Vidette (Fort Qu'Appelle), 136
Virden, 159

Wadsworth, T.P., 82, 87, 90, 96, 99, 108, 109, 110, 113, 165–6, 167, 169, 179–80, 226, 228
Wagner, William, 58, 61–2, 64, 69
Walsh, James Morrow, 74, 123
Wapella, 160
War of 1812, 23
Ward, Mark, 242
Wheat pools, 255
White, F., 85
White Bear, 208
White Calf, 48
White Cap reserve, 126
Whitewood, 160, 166, 216, 248
Wild rice, 141
Williams, P.J., 90, 163, 181, 186
Wing, 46
Winnipeg, 86, 87, 91, 142
Wolseley, Col G., 67
Wolseley (town), 166
Women, Indian, 14, 138; as perceived by non-Indians, 17, 18–19, 180; traditional economic activities of, 28–9, 176–7; prostitution, 117, 154–5; acquire new skills, 178–9; and "peasant" farming policy, 211, 212; employed as domestics, 240; former pupil assistance for, 241; at the File Hills Colony, 239–42
Wood Mountain, 26, 48, 113
World War I, 249–52
Wounded Knee, 134
Wright, J.P., 224, 248

Yellow Calf, 114, 120–2, 124, 125, 163, 208
Yellow Quill, Chief (Assiniboia), 44, 115
Yellow Quill, Chief (Manitoba), 40
York Factory, 32
Young, Rev. E.R., 131

Zimbabwe, 233